D1237086

CONSULTING EDITOR

BENJAMIN A. WHISLER

HEAD, DEPARTMENT OF CIVIL ENGINEERING

PENNSYLVANIA STATE UNIVERSITY

Properties of

Engineering Materials

GLENN MURPHY

Anson Marston Distinguished Professor of Engineering

Head, Department of Theoretical and Applied Mechanics

IOWA STATE COLLEGE

Third Edition

1957 *International Textbook Company* · *Scranton*

Fourth Printing, March, 1964

Preface
to the Third Edition

Engineering design and development are increasingly dependent upon materials. Among the critical problems facing the designer in a number of areas of engineering development is that of selecting or developing materials that will withstand higher operating temperatures. At the present time, the limitations on the power that may be developed in jet engines are strictly limitations imposed by the temperatures at which the available materials may be used. New alloys are continually being studied in an attempt to increase operating temperatures.

As expanding applications are found for rockets and as the development of satellites takes form, attention is focused on the problem of selecting materials to withstand the high temperatures induced by the friction of the atmosphere. Even in high-speed aircraft the problem is recognized as significant.

The advent of nuclear reactors has opened up a new vista of materials. Not only have many new design problems involving materials been created, but a vast number of potential applications of materials is arising. The study of the influence of nuclear radiation on materials is in its infancy. It is known, of course, that the chemical nature of materials may be changed by radiation; controlled transmutation of elements is a reality. Some materials are weakened, others are strengthened and improved by exposure to radiation. It is entirely possible that irradiation will assume importance as a step in the processing of certain products.

One important key to the understanding of how materials will perform in various environments is that of the basic structure of the material. An increased knowledge of structure and its influence on properties together with a better understanding of the bonding forces between atoms, ions, and other structural units is now making possible the design of materials to develop specific characteristics. Much more remains to be learned before general techniques of design are available, but success has been achieved in special cases.

Thus, the study of materials must develop along analytical lines, and in the revision for this edition increased emphasis has been placed on the need for understanding the basic behavior of materials in various environments. However, because of the placement of most materials courses in engineering curricula the mathematical level of the text has not been altered. Because many engineering graduates are expected to have readily available, certain practical facts regarding materials, descriptions of processes and products have been retained and brought up to date. In these descriptions increased emphasis has been placed on the control of properties through the control of structure and composition.

A number of valuable suggestions have been received from users of the second edition and these are gratefully acknowledged. Special credit is due Frances Murphy for valuable assistance in the preparation of the revision.

GLENN MURPHY

Ames, Iowa
October, 1957

Preface
to the Second Edition

In the past half-decade many important advances have been made in the production of engineering materials. New materials have been developed to meet special needs, and the usefulness of many familiar materials has been reevaluated as new facts and principles have become evident.

Research in materials fostered by the war with its unusual demands and critical shortages has led to important findings, many of which are already being applied to peacetime activities. Certain aspects of metallurgy have undergone marked modifications, and the goal of being able to predict the mechanical properties of new alloys with the accuracy with which a chemist is able to predict the chemical properties of undiscovered elements appears to be one step nearer.

New methods of testing materials have been devised, and the significance of standardized existing tests is better understood. The application of materials has been extended, particularly into the high-temperature range. New and improved shaping and fabrication techniques have made possible important applications heretofore impossible.

Despite these advances and innovations, the objectives of a course in engineering materials remain unchanged. It is increasingly important that engineering students know something of the materials which are available and know how the characteristics of those materials are controlled in production. It is still of paramount importance that the principles governing the behavior of the materials in service be understood to the fullest extent of available knowledge. As a result, the general plan of the text has not been altered appreciably in revision. The attempt to give the student a comprehensive and well balanced perspective of the field of engineering materials has been maintained, and an effort has been made to lengthen the text as little as possible. Data on properties of metals, plastics, and other materials have been brought up to date; and nearly one hundred new problems have been added. The treatment of the control of properties has been consolidated into one chapter which deals with both physical and chemical techniques. The portion of the text dealing with metallurgy of ferrous materials has been revised to conform to the latest concepts.

Among the many new developments discussed are powder metallurgy, laminated products, cold treatment of metals, high-temperature alloys, silicones, and synthetic rubber.

The author wishes to acknowledge the many helpful comments which he has received from his colleagues and from teachers at other institutions. The New Jersey Zinc Company and Revere Copper and Brass, Inc., generously provided photographs and supplied specimens from which stress-strain diagrams were obtained. Credit is likewise due to the Drop Forging Association for the use of photographs. In addition, the author wishes to thank the many manufacturers who liberally supplied data concerning their products.

GLENN MURPHY

Ames, Iowa
December, 1946

Preface to the First Edition

This book, as its name implies, deals with the properties of engineering materials with special emphasis upon the specific properties which are of major importance to the student of engineering.

The book is an outgrowth of a series of mimeographed notes used by the author and his colleagues in presenting an elementary course in materials to undergraduate engineering students. In developing the course the author has endeavored to present the material in such a way that the emphasis is placed upon the basic principles underlying the behavior of all engineering materials under conditions of usage, rather than the traditional presentation in which the student is given the impression that he must memorize a vast number of totally unrelated facts.

The presentation involves (1) a study of what constitutes failure of a material or a structural member, the ways in which failure may be expected to occur, and what properties may be used to estimate the resistance of a material to failure; (2) a study of the important properties and the reasons for their importance to the engineer, including definitions, methods of measurement, and problems providing drill in the application of the general principles to specific engineering applications; and (3) a study of the principal materials used for engineering purposes, with the attention of the student directed toward the principles underlying the methods for altering the properties, rather than toward specific details of manufacturing processes which may be obsolete before the student graduates. Problems are included to provide further drill in the application of the principles. The text is designed for use in teaching engineering students rather than for use as a source book of general miscellaneous information concerning materials. For most effective use, the assignments must be shorter than in the traditional course, with time allotted for working problems.

The preparation of a book of this type necessarily involves the use of material from a number of different sources. Specific acknowledgements have been made in a number of places throughout the work. Use has been made of the references listed at the end of each chapter, and in particular the works of Professors J. B. Johnson, A. P. Mills, and H. F.

Moore.   Valuable suggestions have been made by a number of the author's former and present associates.   The author is especially grateful to Professor H. J. Gilkey, Professor W. M. Dunagan, and Mr. W. B. Stiles of Iowa State College and to Professor G. C. Ernst of the University of Maryland for their cooperation, criticism, and assistance.

A revision of one of the early editions of the mimeographed notes was used as a thesis for the degree, Civil Engineer, at the University of Colorado in the Department of Civil Engineering of which Professor C. L. Eckel is head.

The helpful cooperation of the Aluminum Company of America, the A. M. Byers Company, the Dow Chemical Company, and the Republic Steel Corporation in furnishing data and illustrations is deeply appreciated.

Special credit is due Frances Murphy for preparation of the drawings and for valuable assistance with the preparation of the manuscript.

GLENN MURPHY

Ames, Iowa
May, 1939

Contents

*Properties of
Engineering Materials*

1 Materials and the Engineer

1.1 Introduction

The activities of the engineer center about materials. The mining engineer who decides the manner in which the raw material is to be obtained and processed, the designing engineer who plans the product, the production or construction engineer who supervises its fabrication, the sales engineer who manages the marketing of the product—each must visualize his objective in terms of materials.

It is the engineer who bears responsibility for all of the operations involved in the transformation of commonplace raw materials into a Golden Gate Bridge, a streamlined train, a nuclear power plant, or a high-speed transport airplane. The engineer who can design and build such structures successfully and efficiently must have a clear, accurate understanding of materials—a knowledge of how materials will react when subjected to heat, wind, sun, loads, and all the other forces of destruction to which they are constantly subjected.

This knowledge of materials cannot be merely factual—cannot be obtained simply from a handbook. It must include an understanding of the basic laws governing the behavior of materials under various conditions of usage—an understanding which is so thorough that it becomes an integral part of the permanent intellectual equipment of the engineer.

The facts and principles which are known about materials today have been evolved through the observations and experiments—and the analytical skill—of many investigators. Experiments, hypotheses, and tests, continually modified and improved, have led to the formulation of a number of general principles.

However, there is still much to be learned about materials. There remain to be discovered other facts and principles, the acceptance of which will make possible the construction and efficient operation of many structures, machines, and other products which cannot now be built because of insufficient knowledge of materials.

Although advances in the technique of efficient utilization of materials are being made rapidly as needs arise, still much research of a basic character remains to be accomplished before materials can be used to their maximum efficiency. These discoveries will be made by the engineers and research workers of the future.

At the present time the field of metallurgy offers one of the greatest challenges. For example, industry would be revolutionized by the discovery of a principle or method by which the properties of an alloy could be predicted from the properties of its constituent elements. This discovery would make possible the production of metals which would meet specific needs more adequately, without all of the costly experimental procedure which is now necessary, and, more important, would indicate the ultimate limitation of what can be expected from alloys.

It is inevitable that new materials will be developed and used in engineering in the future. Economic pressure, dwindling sources of raw materials, the demands for new types of machines—these and other causes will force their development. The engineer who understands the significance of the fundamental properties of materials will be in the best position to develop new materals and utilize them to the maximum advantage.

1.2 Development of Use of Materials

Many of the common engineering materials, such as wood, stone, copper, bronze, and the clay products, have been known and utilized for centuries. The Pyramids and Sphinx in Egypt, ruins of enormous palaces in Assyria and Chaldea, and remains of many smaller structures and tools from these and other ancient civilizations are ample evidence of the ability of the early builders to use materials effectively, if not always efficiently.

Despite their apparently very limited knowledge of mechanics, the ancient builders achieved remarkable results. They proceeded with the only means at their disposal—a cut-and-try process of construction. From their successes and their failures they gradually developed arbitrary rules to guide them in future work, and what had been at first but crude and clumsy attempts at construction developed into an art. The successes of the art can still be viewed today; all evidences of its failures have long since vanished.

As the needs and desires of men increased, construction and other early manifestations of engineering were developed in many fields. Demand for more-adequate transportation facilities led to advances in the construction of ships, roads, and bridges. New needs and new materials for buildings resulted in the development of new styles of architecture. Such structures as the Parthenon, the Colosseum, the Appian Way, and the Roman aqueducts are testimony to the ingenuity of the builders of ancient Greece and Rome in meeting varied demands upon their skill.

Although the Greeks developed some of the most beautiful architectural styles in the world, they did not encourage investigation of the natural laws governing materials and structures.

With the advent of the Roman Empire, construction flourished. As the Romans sought to spread their civilization, increased demands were thrust upon builders, forcing the development of new methods of construction and the use of new materials. By the time of the height of the Empire, additional building materials, such as bronze, iron, lead, and cementing materials were in general use, but little systematic information had been acquired concerning their properties. Building was still an art rather than a science.

The decline of the Roman Empire resulted to a certain extent in decreased demands upon the builders, more noticeably in the field of transportation.

As the unity of the Roman Empire crumbled, the forces of state which had been pushing engineering construction for expansion of political influence were destroyed. The so-called Dark Ages began, but the desire of men to build continued. Engineering materials were used for the expression of religious activities, rather than as a means of extending the influence of state, giving rise to the construction of many magnificent cathedrals. The cathedrals of St. Sophia (Constantinople, sixth century), St. Mark (Venice, eleventh century), Notre Dame (Paris, twelfth century), and Rheims (thirteenth century), are enduring monuments to the zeal and patience of their builders, who worked under tremendous handicaps.

While many features of the styles of architecture which were evolved during the Middle Ages display the use of sound scientific principles, written records indicate that the excellence of construction was intuitive or the result of long practice. Building was not yet based on scientific analyses of the forces involved.

The beginnings of the modern approach to problems of construction were made about the end of the fifteenth century. Leonardo da Vinci, painter, architect, and inventor, laid the foundations for an age of reason by his critical study of natural phenomena. However, his ideas were rejected by his contemporaries.

It was not until the time of Galileo, a century later, that the first effective steps were taken in developing a science of construction from the art of building. Galileo introduced two new trends: (1) the attempt to discover by experimentation, and to explain scientifically, the laws governing the behavior of a structural member as it is loaded; (2) the attempt to test materials to determine the qualities which make them suitable for various uses. The importance of his approach was not fully appreciated by his contemporaries, but it constituted the foundation work for the scientific era.

With Sir Isaac Newton's discovery, near the end of the seventeenth century, of the laws governing the motion of bodies, the way was made clear for rapid development. By the end of the next hundred years building had ceased to be entirely an art and had become a science, although much still remained to be discovered.

At the present time the laws governing the behavior of such materials as metals, wood, stone, and concrete are fairly well understood, in the simpler structural members, but the laws governing the behavior of some other materials such as soil, sand, and rubber are still the object of many investigations.

The study of the action of a simple structural member, such as a tension member, beam, or column under load, is known as mechanics of materials. Mechanics of materials and properties of materials are the tools with which the engineer designs modern structures.

Concurrently with the development of mechanics, the development of commercial methods of reducing ores to useful metals has been playing a large part in making possible a more efficient use of engineering materials. As has been pointed out, the early builders used materials such as wood, stone, and clay, which required only shaping, without elaborate processing. Copper was the first metal to be used, as it was found in a nearly pure form and was easily worked. Gradually, bronze and iron came into use, largely through accidental discoveries. However, with the haphazard manufacturing processes then known, these metals were too costly for extensive use, and their quality was frequently uncertain.

Not until the development of the blast furnace, the Bessemer converter, and the open-hearth furnace as cheap methods of steel production, was extensive use of the ferrous metals possible. At the present time a very large share of the engineering activities in the world are directly dependent upon the steel industry.

Aluminum, also, was known for many years to have desirable properties, but it was far too expensive for commercial use—until the discovery, in 1886, of the electrolytic process for its reduction from the ore. In the last two decades there has been a spectacular growth of the aluminum industry. Now, other metals are receiving attention. Titanium, magnesium, and beryllium are examples of metals which have valuable properties and which give promise of becoming increasingly important as more-suitable methods of manufacture are developed.

While many of the earlier developments of manufacturing processes were the result of chance discovery, today the application of our increasing knowledge of chemistry and metallurgy plays a very important role. The field of solid state physics, in particular, is contributing to an increased understanding of the factors that control the characteristics of materials.

1.3   Requirements for Materials

The selection of the proper material for a new product rests in general with the engineer.   What is the best material to use for the wings of a supersonic airplane, a pressure unit used in the manufacture of liquid air, coolant tubes for a nuclear reactor, or an electric heating unit?   Such questions are continually raised, and much depends upon the correctness of the answer.   The engineer's professional reputation hinges upon his ability to find the answer with little delay, and upon his certainty that the answer is correct.   In some instances an improper selection of materials has involved a cost of thousands of dollars in replacement.

Finding the best answer to the problem of determining the most suitable material for a given usage is by no means a simple matter, for there are many factors to be considered.   Frequently there is no single answer, since several materials, each with its particular advantages and disadvantages, may be about equally suitable.   The engineer must then use his best judgment in making the final selection of the material to be used—a judgment based on his own experience and study, and that of other engineers and scientists.   This cumulative engineering judgment as applied to the problem of selection of materials, based in part upon observation and empirical generalizations developed from observations, and in part upon exact science, has led to the general conclusion that the material most suitable for a given use will be that material which most nearly supplies the *necessary durability,* with a *satisfactory appearance,* at the *lowest cost* in place. Several interrelated factors enter into the consideration of each of these elements, the nature of the factors depending upon the particular situation in which the material is to be used.

Durability.   If a material is to be satisfactory for a given use, it must be durable—that is, it must continue to function properly, resisting destruction from all causes during the useful life of the structure in which it is used. Many factors may lead to destruction, for forces are set up whenever any of the several forms of energy come into contact with a material.

Mechanical energy, chemical energy, electrical energy, heat, light, and radiation all tend to alter the characteristics of materials.   Sometimes alteration of characteristics has a beneficial effect; but when it occurs as a result of exposure to nature during service, it has an effect which is more often regarded as destructive from an engineering viewpoint.   To be durable, a material must resist all forms of destruction to such a degree that their combined effect will not render the structure unsafe or inefficient at any time during its prescribed lifetime.

Appearance.   The well-designed product, whether it be a structure, a machine part, a tool, or any other device, is in harmony with its environment.   Both its lines and the material of which it is composed will influence its final appearance.   For a machine part which is hidden from view appearance may not be vital, but for any exposed part the material employed should be chosen with due consideration to appearance as well as to durability.

For a material such as stone or concrete, the workability, or ease with which the material can be shaped, has an appreciable influence upon appearance.

Materials which do not present a pleasing appearance may often be painted or metalplated to improve their appearance as well as to provide a durable covering which will resist corrosion or decay.

TOTAL OVER ALL COST.

Economy.   Common sense advocates, and competition usually forces, the use of the cheapest material which will satisfy the considerations of durability and appearance.   The items included in the *initial cost* of the product will be dependent upon the quality, availability, and workability of the material, but the *total cost* should include such additional items as the cost of installation, maintenance, and repair, the interest on the investment, and, in the event that the product must be used longer than the anticipated life of the material, the cost of replacement.   Unless these additional items are considered, a material with a low initial cost may ultimately prove to be very uneconomical as compared with a more durable material of higher initial cost.

1.4   Use of Properties

As might be expected, because of the large number of complex items which are involved in the consideration of a material for a given use, the true measure of the suitability of the material may be obtained only from a study of its behavior in that particular use.   The product itself is the final authority on the subject.   However, actual service tests require years and, valuable as they may be, modern construction demands of the engineer answers which can be obtained in a short time, and answers which will assure a safe structure.

To provide such answers, the engineer must consider each cause of destruction, and evolve a dependable and ready means of isolating and evaluating that quality of the material which measures its resistance to destruction from each of the given causes.   Then, having for a given material a measure of its resistance to each of the destructive forces, he may, using his trained imagination, reproduce synthetically any condition of operation, and predict the behavior of the material in that environment. The perfection of this procedure is the ideal toward which materials engineers are working.   The ideal has not yet been reached, but progress is being made, and as laboratory findings are correlated with actual service results, more-reliable predictions of the behavior of materials in service can be made.

The suitability of a *new* material for a given use is predicted by comparing certain qualities of the proposed material with the same qualities of a material which has proved satisfactory in that use or in a laboratory test (which is, in effect, an accelerated or exaggerated service test). If the use itself is also new, a simulated service test in the laboratory may be used.

Since abstract *qualities* of a material cannot be compared, specific terms have been devised to describe more exactly the particular characteristics in question, and also to give a numerical indication of the extent of their presence. These definite descriptive measures of the qualities are called the *properties* of a material. For example, the term "strength," which is a quality, gives an indication of certain characteristics of a material, but is indefinite in meaning, whereas "ultimate compressive strength," which is a property, not only conveys the impression of a definite characteristic but also can be assigned a definite numerical value for a given material. The statement "This stick of wood is strong" is indefinite and therefore of little value to the engineer, whereas the statement "The wood in this stick has an ultimate compressive strength of 10,000 lb per sq in. parallel to the grain" is definite and gives the engineer an idea of how much load the wood will support safely under certain conditions.

Thus properties serve as the language by which the designer can express his needs for a material which will be resistant to loads, decay, chemical action, or other forces which his product must withstand. Properties also serve as a basis for comparing different materials, and for comparing the uniformity of different samples of one material.

1.5 Variation in Properties

No two pieces of any material have identical properties. The differences in properties of two samples of the same material may be due to factors entering into the manufacturing or formation processes, or may be due to changes occurring within the material subsequent to manufacture. For example, the variation in yield strength of 1000 specimens of a metal made under laboratory conditions, with every effort made to eliminate variations, is shown in Fig. 1.1. Along the x axis are plotted the strength ranges, and in the y direction are plotted the number of specimens having a strength in the indicated range. Although the variation in chemical composition was less than 0.1 per cent and the manufacturing conditions were almost identical for the different specimens, an appreciable variation in strength resulted from minor uncontrolled variables. For most mate-

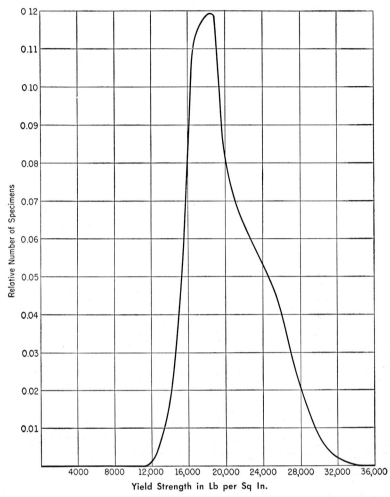

FIG. 1.1   Variation of yield strength among 1000 specimens of a metal.

rials the variation will be greater than that indicated in Fig. 1.1, above.

In order to attain reasonable uniformity in the properties of materials, careful control must be exercised in the selection of the raw materials, in every step of the manufacturing and fabrication process, and in the environment and treatment after completion of the product. Carefully as the manufacturing process may be carried out, a material may ultimately prove unsatisfactory because of its susceptibility to change of properties after fabrication. Aluminum, brass, bronze, concrete, timber, and many other materials are affected by age, changes in temperature and humidity, and other factors. For example, the ultimate compressive strength of the concrete in a bridge or pavement slab may be altered as much as 30 per cent by a change from a dry condition to a saturated condition such as might be caused by a heavy rain.

Not only may the properties of a piece of material vary from time to time, depending upon the environment, but the properties always vary from point to point within the piece, because of irregularities within the material itself. Nonuniformities are readily visible in some materials, such as granite, while others, such as a pure metal, appear at first examination to be perfectly uniform. Actually, no material is perfectly homogeneous.

If a piece of metal is carefully polished, immersed for a short time in an acid or other appropriate reagent, and then examined under a microscope, it will be seen to be composed of small particles or crystals. The metal, instead of being perfectly uniform, is built up of these small units of matter.

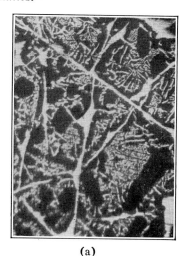 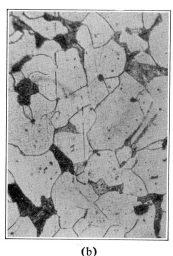

(a)   (b)

FIG. 1.2 Characteristic structure of two metals, × 500. (a) Typical bearing metal.
(b) Structural steel.

The photomicrographs of a bearing metal and structural steel shown in Fig. 1.2 readily illustrate that materials which appear to be perfectly homogeneous are in reality composed of an aggregate of grains or crystals of distinctly different materials. A piece of the material will therefore have different properties at different points within the piece. Even chemically pure metals are shown to be made up of an aggregate of crystals having different properties in different directions.

Other materials, as well as metals, are composed of small units. Timber consists of fibers and cells; many building stones are made up of small particles cemented together, and concrete consists of a heterogeneous mass of aggregates cemented together. The organization or arrangement of these small units, as well as the nature of the units themselves, has an appreciable effect upon the properties of a larger piece of the material. Since the arrangement of the different individual particles in a given piece of material seems to be a matter of chance, the numerical values of the properties obtained from tests on the piece will be only statistical averages.

A bar of steel, composed of many individual crystals, may be likened to a group of men, composed of many individuals. To say that the ultimate tensile strength of this bar of steel is 80,000 lb per sq in. is comparable to saying that the average age of death of the men in the group is 62 years. Just as individual men in the group will live to lesser or greater ages, depending upon their inherited characteristics and upon their environment, so individual crystals in the bar will have greater or lesser strengths, depending upon their inherent chemical characteristics and their placement with respect to other crystals in the bar. But just as the statistical age of death of a group of men is of use to the insurance companies, so the statistical strength of the bar of steel is of use to the engineer.

Thus, in order to use a material intelligently, the engineer must know the limits within which the statistical-average values of the properties may be expected to vary during the life of the structure, and what control, if any, he may have over those variations. In order to know these things, the engineer must understand not only what the properties represent, but also what factors in the manufacture and use of the materials will affect the properties.

The changes which take place in a material during its processing and in service are dependent upon the nature of the elementary physical and chemical units of which that material is composed, and the manner in which those elementary units are structurally combined.

1.6 Structure of Materials

The exact nature of the ultimate structure of material has been for many years the subject of intensive research and heated controversy. The answer is still unknown, although many enlightening hypotheses have been advanced to explain various physical and chemical phenomena. Although the engineer is concerned primarily with the determination of the properties of materials in finite quantities, and with the methods of altering the properties, detailed information concerning the structure of materials is becoming increasingly important in explaining some of the changes that occur in properties. Hence, the testing machine, in its many forms, which has been the principal tool used in the evaluation of properties is now being supplemented by the optical microscope and the electron microscope, and by X-ray and spectrographic equipment.

It is evident that the properties of a material are dependent upon the chemical composition of the material, and on the physical structure of the particles in the mass. Marble and limestone have essentially the same chemical composition ($CaCO_3$) but their physical properties are different because marble has been subjected to a higher temperature and greater pressure during the formation process, with the result that the particles are compacted more, resulting in a different structure. On the other hand, aluminum and copper have the same type of crystalline structure, but their properties are different because of a difference in chemical composition.

One of the convenient hypotheses for explaining some of the similarities and differences in the characteristics of metals is that of the arrangement of atoms in the individual crystals of the material. The most commonly accepted theory of the structure of materials is that all materials are composed of atoms consisting of a nucleus, with one or more positive charges of electricity, surrounded by electrons, each having one negative charge of electricity. The number of electrons associated with each atomic nucleus controls the chemical properties of the material, while the physical properties are fixed, not only by the nature, but also by the arrangement, of the individual atoms.

1.7 Space Lattice

An ideal crystal of a given material may be assumed to be composed of atoms arranged in a definite and regular geometrical pattern. This pattern is known as a space lattice and may be determined by X-ray studies. The atoms in iron at room temperature, for example, are arranged in what is called a body-centered cubic lattice. That is, the atoms are located as at the corners of a cube 2.87×10^{-8} cm on a side, with one atom in the center, as shown in Fig. 1.3a. This pattern repeats itself throughout a single crystal, as indicated in Fig. 1.3b. Two adjacent crystals in a bar of iron will have the same lattice formation, but their orientation—that is, the directions of the axes of the space lattice—will probably be different. Chromium, vanadium, molybdenum, and tungsten also have the body-centered cubic lattice.

Lead, aluminum, copper, iron (at high temperature), cobalt, nickel, silver, platinum, and gold crystallize in what is known as the face-centered cubic lattice—that is, with an atom at each corner of a cube, and an atom in the center of each face, as in Fig. 1.3c.

Zinc, magnesium, and beryllium are among the metals having a hexagonal space lattice containing 17 atoms in a unit cell. Tin crystallizes in a body-centered tetragonal system (forming a rectangular parallelepiped), while indium and manganese form a face-centered tetragonal system. There are fourteen basic lattice systems.

Each one of these space-lattice systems has been found to have certain planes of weakness—that is, certain planes along which the atoms may be more easily displaced with respect to one another—so the orientation of adjacent crystals in a mass has a direct influence upon the properties of the material in the mass.   If all of the crystals in a mass have the same orientation, the properties of the mass will be different than if the same crystals have their usual haphazard arrangement.   For example, single crystals of aluminum have been stretched to several times their original length without breaking, whereas a bar of aluminum will stretch only a fraction of its original length before it breaks.   A mass composed of large crystals has different properties than it would have if the crystals were smaller.   Because of the added mutual interference to slip along the planes of weakness, the mass of small crystals will have greater strength than the mass of large crystals of the same material, but cannot be stretched so much without breaking.

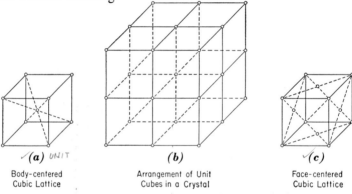

(a) UNIT   (b)   (c)

Body-centered | Arrangement of Unit | Face-centered
Cubic Lattice | Cubes in a Crystal | Cubic Lattice

FIG. 1.3   Patterns of atoms in typical space lattices.

By introducing certain reasonable assumptions regarding the laws of attraction and repulsion of atoms, it is possible to calculate the magnitude of the cohesive forces in metals.   The fact that these computed cohesive strengths are always considerably greater than the strengths obtained in tests on large specimens is attributed to the flaws and imperfections in the larger specimens.

Tests made upon metals indicate that the effective strength of a material varies inversely with the size of specimen being tested.   Tungsten wire about 0.001 in. in diameter has been found to be more than three times as strong in tension in proportion to its size as wire 0.080 in. in diameter.[1]   The ultimate tensile strength of very fine glass fibers has been found to be more than one hundred times the strength of the same glass in the form of rods. The fiber strength is about one-fourth of the potential strength of approximately 12,000,000 lb per sq in. computed on the basis of the lattice formation. Single crystals of highly purified iron in the form of whiskers less than one-thousandth of an inch square and up to two inches long develop an ultimate tensile strength of over one million pounds per square inch. The high strength is attributed to the freedom from impurities and the perfection of the crystal. Whiskers of tin have also been grown, and they too develop high tensile strengths.

While engineers and scientists may ultimately develop processes whereby a high percentage of the potential strength of materials may be developed, it is also possible that such ultrastrength materials may be found to have other properties which will make them less suitable for general usage than some of the materials now available. Meanwhile, engineering construction must continue, and for it to do so efficiently, the engineer must be familiar with the properties of the materials available. He must know how the behavior of the material in service will be affected by the size, shape, and chemical composition of the unit particles, and the way in which those unit particles are joined together; and he must know what factors in the manufacture, fabrication, and use of the material will influence the safety or efficiency of the structure for which he is responsible.

REFERENCES FOR FURTHER STUDY

BARRETT, C. S. *Structure of Metals,* 2d ed. New York: McGraw-Hill Book Company, Inc., 1952.

CLARK, G. L. *Applied X-rays,* 4th ed. New York: McGraw-Hill Book Company, Inc., 1955.

DUSHMAN, SAUL. "Cohesion and Atomic Structure," *Proceedings, American Society for Testing Materials,* Vol. 29 (1929), pp. 7–64.

MOORE, H. F. "The History of the Flexure Formula," *Journal of Engineering Education,* Vol. 21 (1930), p. 156.

SEELY, F. B. "The Statistical Element of Mechanics of Materials," *Mechanical Engineering,* Vol. 52 (1930), p. 839.

SEITZ, FREDERICK. *The Modern Theory of Solids.* New York: McGraw-Hill Book Company, Inc., 1940.

WESTERGAARD, H. M. "One Hundred Fifty Years Advance in Structural Analysis," *Proceedings of the American Society of Civil Engineers,* Vol. 52 (1928), p. 993.

2 Behavior of Materials under Load

2.1 Stress

If the eyebar in Fig. 2.1a is supported at the upper end and is loaded by a weight or other applied force (assumed to be 1000 lb) on the pin at the lower eye, an equal resisting force[1] must be developed at the upper eye in order that the bar may support the weight. The resisting force which must be developed on a horizontal plane at any section such as B may be determined by passing an imaginary plane through the bar at B and considering all of the forces acting on one portion of the bar. In Fig. 2.1b, which is called a "free-body diagram," are shown all of the forces acting on the portion of the bar below the plane at B. Each of the forces acting on that portion of the bar is indicated by an arrow, the arrow at the lower end representing the weight of 1000 lb. Obviously, if the lower portion of the bar is not going to move downward indefinitely under the action of the force on the pin, an upward force of 1000 lb must be developed at the top of the lower portion of the bar (at B). That force represents the resultant force which the upper portion of the bar exerts on the lower portion.

It is evident that the force will not be concentrated at one point, as suggested by the arrow, but will be distributed over the entire cross section of the bar. If the load on the bar is applied axially—that is, along the longitudinal axis of the member—and if the material in the bar is homogeneous, the force will be distributed approximately uniformly over the cross section, as indicated in Fig. 2.1c.

The intensity of the force (force per unit area) developed within the material is called the *unit stress,* or often simply the *stress*. The *average unit stress* on any plane in a homogeneous member subjected to an axial load may be evaluated by dividing the total force acting upon (or trans-

---

[1] The weight of the bar itself is assumed to be negligible in comparison with the 1000-lb force.

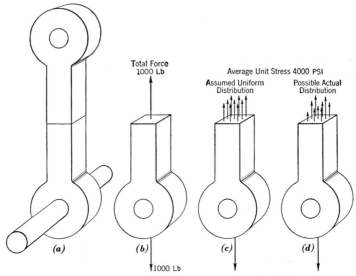

FIG. 2.1   Free-body diagram and stress distribution.

mitted across) that plane by the area of the plane section.   Expressed in equation form, the relation is

$$S = \frac{P}{A}$$ (2.1)

in which S = unit stress, P = total force, and A = area.

In engineering practice in the United States, P is usually expressed in pounds, and A in square inches, in which case the stress will be in pounds per square inch (lb per sq in. or psi).   In countries using the metric system, stress is usually expressed in kilograms per square centimeter, while in England the units are frequently tons per square inch.

If the eyebar in Fig. 2.1 is $\frac{1}{2}$ in. square in cross section, the average unit stress on a horizontal plane at B due to the 1000-lb load is

$$S = \frac{P}{A} = \frac{1000}{\left(\frac{1}{2}\right)\left(\frac{1}{2}\right)} = 4000 \text{ psi}$$

The *maximum unit stress* on a horizontal plane at B will exceed 4000 psi because the stress will not be uniformly distributed.   Actually, not all of the particles at the cut section will offer equal resistance to the force, and thus the true distribution of stress might be as shown in Fig. 2.1d. If the distribution of stress is not perfectly uniform, P/A gives only the average value of the unit stress on the plane, which is always less than the maximum intensity of the stress.   Irregularities, cracks, and other points of discontinuity all tend to cause stresses much greater than the average.

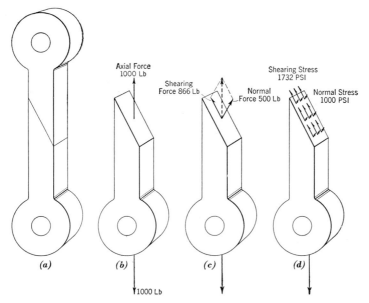

FIG. 2.2   Normal and tangential components of forces.

If the load is not axial, or if bending is present because of any other cause, the stress will not be uniformly distributed, even in an ideal material without flaws.   The average stress as determined from equation 2.1 may be only a small fraction of the maximum stress.   The increase in stress caused by the bending action may be determined from the flexure formula

$$S = \frac{Mc}{I} \tag{2.2}$$

in which S is the unit stress, M is the resultant moment of the forces producing bending, c is the distance from the centroidal axis to the point where the stress is desired, and I is the moment of inertia of the area with respect to the centroidal axis.   Equation 2.2 indicates that the stress due to bending varies with the distance from the centroidal axis of the section and is greatest at the outside.

Similarly, twisting or buckling tendencies will produce a nonuniform stress distribution throughout the member.   Details of methods for determining the stress distribution in such members as shafts, beams, and columns are presented in texts on mechanics of materials.

2.2 Normal and Tangential Stresses

The stress in the bar in Fig. 2.1 is called a normal stress because it acts normal (i.e., at right angles) to the plane.   Normal stress is designated as *tension* if it tends to stretch the member, and *compression* if it

(b) Brittle material in tension

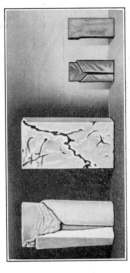

(d) Brittle materials in compression

(f) Brittle materials in torsion

(a) Ductile materials in tension

(c) Ductile material in compression

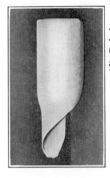

(e) Ductile material in torsion

Fig. 2.3   Types of failure.

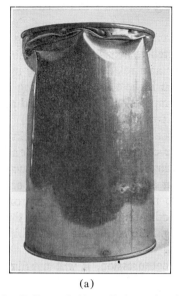

(a)   (b)

FIG. 2.4   Failure of thin-walled member by buckling.   (a) Loaded in compression.
(b) Loaded in torsion.

tends to shorten the member.   There may also be stresses parallel to the
plane, which tend to produce sliding of one portion of the member over
another portion.   These are called tangential or shearing stresses.   The
stress on the inclined plane indicated in Fig. 2.2a may be determined by
first drawing a free-body diagram of one portion of the bar, as shown in
Fig. 2.2b.   By means of the triangle law or the parallelogram law, the
1000-lb axial force on the inclined plane may be resolved into two components: a force normal to the plane, and a force parallel to the plane.
This is indicated in Fig. 2.2c.

The normal component of the force will produce tensile stresses on the
inclined plane, while the parallel component will produce shearing stresses.
If the plane makes an angle of 60 deg with the horizontal, for example,
the normal component of the 1000-lb force will be 500 lb and the tangential component will be 866 lb.   Since the area of the inclined section is
$\frac{1}{2}$ sq in., the average tensile stress on the inclined plane is 1000 psi, and
the average shearing stress is 1732 psi, both stresses being computed by
equation 2.1.

In a member subjected to axial tension or compression, the highest
average shearing stress theoretically occurs on a plane which makes an
angle of 45 deg with the axis of the member, and this stress has a magnitude of one-half the average normal stress on a plane perpendicular to the

axis.   Thus the highest average shearing unit stress in the bar of Fig. **2.1** is 2000 psi.

If the material is comparatively weak in shear, the shearing stresses which are built up in members subjected to tensile or compressive loads may cause the member to fail in shear at a relatively low load, by sliding along the plane or planes on which the highest average shearing stress is developed, rather than in tension or compression at a higher load as would be expected if the shearing stress were ignored.

Materials which are weaker in shear than in tension are known as *ductile materials,* while those which are comparatively weak in tension are called *brittle materials.*   Figure 2.3a illustrates failures of two ductile steel specimens which were subjected to an axial tensile load.   In each case the surface of the "cone-cup" fracture makes an angle of approximately 45 deg with the axis of the specimen, indicating the influence of the shearing stress.   The specimen shown in Fig. 2.3b is a brittle steel, which failed on the plane of maximum tensile stress.

If a ductile material is loaded in compression, it will usually fail by squeezing together in the direction of the load and spreading out laterally, as shown in Fig. 2.3c.   Since a brittle material is weaker in shear than in compression, a compressive specimen of a brittle material will often fail in shear by sliding on an inclined plane, as shown in Fig. 2.3d.   In the specimen on the left, which is plaster of Paris, and in the third specimen, which is wood, the shearing action at the top formed a wedge which later split the lower half of the specimen vertically.   The second specimen is concrete, and the one on the extreme right is wood, in which the shearing action took place on a single inclined plane.

If a cylindrical specimen is twisted—that is, loaded in *torsion*—the maximum shearing stress is developed on planes at right angles to the axis of the member, and the maximum tensile and compressive stresses are developed on planes inclined at an angle of 45 deg with the axis.   Therefore a ductile material loaded in torsion will fail on the plane of maximum shearing stress, as illustrated for structural steel in Fig. 2.3e, while a brittle material will fail in tension on an inclined plane, as shown in Fig. 2.3f.   The specimen on the left is plaster of Paris and that on the right is gray cast iron.   In each case the spiral fracture makes an angle of approximately 45 deg with the axis of the specimen.

A thin-walled member loaded in compression will often fail by buckling, as shown in Fig. 2.4a.   Thin-walled members loaded in torsion may fail also by compressive buckling, as shown in Fig. 2.4b.   In this case the spiral fold starts at an angle of about 45 deg with the axis of the specimen, since that is the direction of the maximum compressive stress.

The failures in Figs. 2.3 and 2.4 show the importance of considering all of the stresses which are developed in a member under load. The fact that a member is loaded in torsion does not necessarily mean that the critical stress will be the maximum shearing stress, for the member may fail in tension or compression instead of in shear. Tension, compression, and shear are present in practically every structural member.

2.3 Strain

Strain, also called *deformation,* is the change in the dimensions of a material. The bar in Fig. 2.1, for example, will stretch as the load is applied, and the amount which it lengthens is called the *total strain.* *Unit strain,* also called *unit deformation,* or simply *strain,* is the total change in length divided by the length over which that change occurs. Expressed in equation form, the relation is

$$\epsilon = \frac{e}{L} \tag{2.3}$$

where ϵ = strain;

  e = total elongation;

  L = length over which elongation occurs.

Both e and L are normally measured in inches, making ϵ a ratio or pure number without units. If the strain is not uniformly distributed along the member (as is usually the case), e/L will give the average unit strain. The magnitude of the strain developed in a material depends upon the material and usually upon the stress. If the bar of Fig. 2.1 were steel, the unit stress of 4000 psi would be accompanied by a unit strain of approximately 0.000133; that is, each inch of the bar would elongate about 0.000133 in. If the bar were a magnesium alloy, the unit strain would be about 0.000615 for the 4000-psi stress.

Stress and strain usually, but not always, accompany each other. Strain may be produced without stress, and stress may be produced without strain, by temperature changes and by certain types of loading. For example, if a bar is supported on rollers and then cooled, it will contract, producing strain without stress. If the same bar has its ends firmly clamped so that it cannot contract, and is then cooled, axial stress will be produced without axial strain. Strains, as well as stresses, are *tensile, compressive,* or *shearing.*

2.4 Stress-Strain Diagrams

Since the stresses and strains in a material, and the relationships between them, are indications of its behavior under load, most of the important mechanical properties which are useful to engineers may be obtained from a graph in which stresses are plotted against the coexistent strains.   Such a graph, called a stress-strain diagram, serves to present an approximate picture of what is taking place in a material as it is loaded.

A typical stress-strain diagram for a medium-strength concrete in compression is shown in Fig. 2.5.   The data for the curve were taken from measurements on a concrete cylinder 6 in. in diameter and 12 in. long, loaded axially in compression.   Each stress was calculated by dividing the load on the cylinder by its cross-sectional area, and the strains were calculated from measured shortenings over an 8-in. length in the center of the cylinder.   The diagram shows that stress and strain have a straight-line

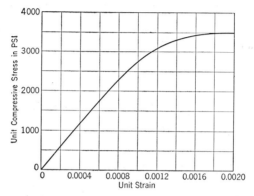

FIG. 2.5   Typical stress-strain diagram for concrete
in compression.

relationship up to about 2000 psi and that the specimen failed at a maximum stress of 3500 psi.   A similar diagram could have been plotted with total loads as ordinates, and total shortenings as abscissas, but it would give values usable only for that particular size of specimen.   The stress-strain diagram has the advantage of showing results for the material irrespective of the size of the specimen, so the results of tests upon specimens of different size may be compared directly on the same diagram.

The shape of the upper portion of the stress-strain diagram is dependent upon the rate at which the load or stress is applied, the strain tending to increase as the time increases.   Most stress-strain diagrams are based on a test of a few minutes' duration, and are directly comparable.   Identical materials tested under identical conditions will have identical stress-strain diagrams.

Stress-strain diagrams are very useful to the engineer in portraying graphically certain characteristics in the behavior of materials under stress. They are used in determining certain important properties of materials, and serve as a basis for comparing the characteristics of different materials.

2.5 Elastic Action

If the strain which accompanies a stress vanishes upon removal of the stress, *elastic* action is said to occur.   However, if a residual strain remains after the stress is removed, the action is said to be *inelastic* or *plastic*. Most engineering materials are nearly elastic at low stresses and are inelastic at higher stresses.   However, probably no material would be found to be absolutely elastic in any range of stress if a sufficiently sensitive device were used to measure the strains.

If a material is loaded part way to failure, and readings of load and deformation are taken for both increasing and decreasing loads, the stress-strain diagram plotted from those readings will reveal whether or not the action was elastic.   If the unloading curve comes back to the original origin, elastic action is indicated regardless of the shape of the diagram.

Figure 2.6a is a typical stress-strain diagram for a material which is considered to be elastic, and shows the usual condition of the loading and unloading curves coinciding.   Figure 2.6b illustrates nonelastic action, and Fig. 2.6c illustrates a possible type of elastic action which is typical of some grades of rubber.   When inelastic action occurs, the permanent or residual unit strain in the material after the load is removed is called the *permanent set*.

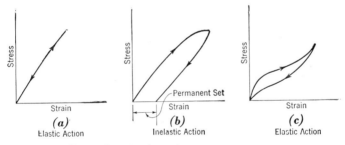

(a)
Elastic Action

(b)
Inelastic Action

(c)
Elastic Action

Fig. 2.6   Elastic and inelastic behavior.

2.6 Elastic Limit

The elastic limit of a material is the highest unit stress to which the material may be subjected without permanent set remaining upon removal of the stress.   The exact elastic limit of a material cannot be determined. Its apparent value will depend upon the sensitivity of the measuring instruments used, and the length of time the load is applied.   Usually a load of only a few minutes' duration is implied.

2.7 Hooke's Law

Hooke's law states that stress and strain are proportional.   It is based on observation and is approximately true for many materials at low stresses, but in general it is not true at higher stresses. The range of stress over which Hooke's law applies is evident on the stress-strain diagram as the range of stress within which the diagram is a straight line.

2.8 Inelastic Action

Three different types of inelastic action have been observed: *slip, creep,* and *fracture.* The term fracture is used to denote rupture, or complete separation of the material into two or more parts.

From the engineering standpoint the distinction between slip and creep may be made on the basis of whether or not the inelastic action continues indefinitely under constant stress. If the inelastic strain takes place within a few minutes after the stress is applied and if no increase in strain occurs with time while the stress remains, the action is called slip. However, if the strain continues to increase so long as the stress is applied, creep is said to occur.

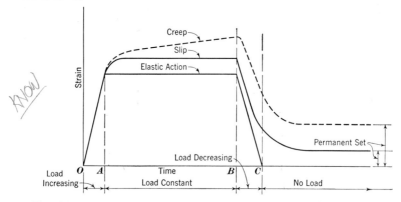

FIG. 2.7   Strain-time diagrams indicating elastic and inelastic behavior.

To determine whether slip or creep will occur in a given material under given conditions, a specimen is loaded and the deformation is noted at intervals. For example, to determine the characteristics of the material in tension, a vertical rod of the material is held at the top and weights are attached at the lower end to produce the desired stress. The elongation of the rod is measured at intervals, and the values are converted to unit strains. Values of unit strain are plotted against time, as indicated in Fig. 2.7. The time from *O* to *A* represents the interval during which the load is being increased uniformly to the predetermined test value. The load remains constant during the time interval from *A* to *B,* and it is then slowly removed, becoming zero at *C.*

Three distinct types of action are indicated in Fig. 2.7. In all three the strain increases uniformly while the stress is being increased. As soon as loading is stopped, however, there is a marked difference in behavior.

The lower curve indicates typical elastic action; in this case the strain remains constant during the interval in which the stress is constant, and becomes zero when the stress becomes zero.   In the case of the middle curve, which is indicative of slip, the strain increases for a short time after the stress becomes constant and then remains constant for the duration of the loading period.   After the load is removed, there remains a permanent set, which is approximately equal to the additional deformation under stress.   In the case of the top curve, which is indicative of creep, the *strain continues to increase under constant stress,* resulting in a larger permanent set upon removal of the load.   The strain-time curve for the interval of constant stress is not necessarily a straight line as shown in Fig. 2.7.   For some materials, particularly at low stresses, the curve tends to level off; for other materials, especially at high stresses, the strain tends to increase more rapidly and fracture results.

The fundamental distinction between creep and slip is in the time rate of deformation under constant stress.   If this rate becomes zero shortly after the maximum stress is applied, the phenomenon is called slip; if it does not become zero, the phenomenon is called creep.   Creep is the more dangerous of the two actions, as it may ultimately cause failure of a member supporting a permanent load even though a short-time test (in which creep does not have time to occur) indicates the material to be perfectly safe.

Although the exact physical nature of the action taking place in the material as it undergoes inelastic deformation is not completely understood, microscopic examination seems to indicate that slip occurs by the sliding of adjacent layers of particles within the material until sufficient frictional resistance is built up or until mutual interference of particles stops the movement.   The movements take place along certain definitely oriented planes of weakness in the space lattice.   The intersections of these planes with a polished surface of the material appear as lines, known as "slip lines," within individual crystals (see Fig. 3.6).

Lead specimens in which creep has occurred indicate that the distortion is a result of relative rotation of the crystals accompanied by some slip within individual crystals.[1]   The amount of slip may be so small or so well distributed that no slip lines are visible in a microscopic examination. Thus the total deformation includes initial slip followed by long-time creep. The flow at the crystal boundaries which accompanies the rotation of the crystals may be similar to the flow of a viscous liquid.

Figure 2.8 gives an approximate indication of the comparative distortions occurring in a crystal subjected to stress and evidencing elastic action, slip, and creep.

[1] H. F. Moore, B. B. Betty, and C. W. Dollins, *Investigation of Creep and Fracture of Lead and Lead Alloys for Cable Sheathing,* University of Illinois Engineering Experiment Station Bulletin 306 (1938).

For most materials there is a limiting stress below which *slip* is not appreciable.   The limiting stress below which no slip would occur is, of course, the elastic limit.

Whether or not there is for each material a limiting stress below which *creep* will not occur has not yet been definitely determined, although it is known that the rate of creep increases with an increase in stress.   Temperature also has an effect upon creep.   All metals will creep at elevated temperatures or temperatures approaching their melting points.   Some of the metals with low melting points, such as lead, tin, and their alloys, will creep at ordinary temperatures.

The inelastic action depicted in Fig. 2.7 is for conditions under which the material is subjected to a constant stress, with the strain increasing. Practical conditions arise in which the stress may vary but the strain remain constant, one example being a bolted connection.   As the nut is tightened the bolt is stretched, producing both stress and strain.   If the material is elastic and it is assumed that there are no other applied forces, the stress and strain remain constant until the nut is loosened.   If inelastic action occurs in the bolt and the nut is not adjusted, the stress in the bolt will

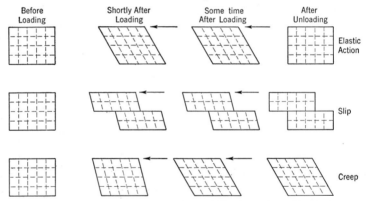

FIG. 2.8   Diagrammatic representation of elastic action, slip, and creep.

decrease.   In the inelastic action corresponding to slip there will be a decrease in stress over an initial time interval, and then the stress will remain constant.   However, if the action corresponds to creep, the stress in the bolt will continue to decrease.   The general phenomenon of decrease in stress under constant strain is known as *relaxation*.

2.9   Stress-Strain-Time Relationships

Both stress-strain diagrams and strain-time diagrams are of prime importance in depicting the characteristics of a material.   In the stress-strain diagram and strain-time diagrams for a material under different stresses, the engineer has most of the information necessary to learn how the material will perform under load.   Among other things, he must also know how the diagrams will be altered by all outside influences on the material during its life before he can make any reliable predictions regarding the behavior of the material in service.

The stress-strain diagram and strain-time diagrams may be combined into a three-dimensional diagram in which the performance of the material will be indicated as a space curve.   For example, if readings of stress,

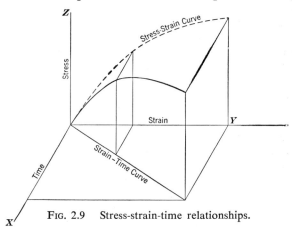

FIG. 2.9   Stress-strain-time relationships.

strain, and time are taken simultaneously at intervals during the testing of a specimen, and the reading of time is plotted in the X direction, the corresponding strain is plotted in the Y direction, and the corresponding stress is plotted in the Z direction, a space curve will be obtained.   The projection of this curve on the YZ plane will give the conventional stress-strain diagram, as indicated in Fig. 2.9, and the projection of the curve on the XY plane will give the strain-time diagram for the test.   If a number of such space curves are obtained for the same material, based on different rates of loading used during the test, they will form a surface which will aid in describing the behavior of the material under stress.

PROBLEMS

2.1 Indicate on a sketch the kinds of stress which may be acting on the indicated plane in each of the following members under their usual loading conditions: (a) overhead transmission line, plane perpendicular to axis; (b) connecting rod in an automobile on compression stroke, plane inclined to axis; (c) crankshaft of an automobile, plane perpendicular to axis; (d) floor beam in a building, vertical plane; (e) chimney in wind, horizontal plane; (f) steam pipe, diametral plane parallel to length of pipe.

2.2 A vertical post 8 in. square and 3 ft long carries a vertical axial load of 32,000 lb.   Determine the average unit stress on a plane normal to the axis.

2.3 For the same post (prob. 2.2), determine the stresses on a plane which makes an angle of 45 deg with one pair of the 8-in. sides and which is normal to the other pair.

2.4 What is the average shearing unit stress on a plane normal to the axis of a ¾-in. rivet which transmits a load of 2000 lb from one plate to another?

2.5 What is the highest axial load that may be placed on a 2-in. round bar if the average tensile stress is not to exceed 18,000 psi?

2.6 A cast-iron column has an external diameter of 12 in. and an internal diameter of 8 in. What maximum axial load may be placed on the column if the average compressive stress is not to exceed 4000 psi?

2.7 Determine the total force which will produce an average shearing unit stress of 8000 psi on a plane normal to the axis of a rivet ¾ in. in diameter.

2.8 Determine the maximum load carried by the concrete cylinder used to obtain the stress-strain diagram in Fig. 2.5.

2.9 The side rod of a certain locomotive has a 3-in. by 1¼-in. rectangular cross section and is 22 in. long. Determine the maximum permissible axial force to which the rod may be subjected if the compressive stress is not to exceed 10,000 psi.

2.10 Determine the normal and tangential unit stresses on a plane which is perpendicular to the 3-in. by 22-in. sides of the side rod in problem 2.9 and which makes an angle of 30 deg with the other two sides if the maximum compressive stress in the rod is 10,000 psi.

2.11 Determine the axial force required to develop a tensile stress of 16,000 psi on a plane that makes an angle of 60 deg with the axis of a ½-in. by ¾-in. bar.

2.12 Determine the shearing stress developed on the inclined plane of the bar in problem 2.11 when the tensile stress on the plane is 16,000 psi.

2.13 The maximum shearing load which a ⅛-in. duralumin rivet is permitted to transfer from one 0.040-in. duralumin sheet to another is 368 lb, according to ANC-5 specifications. Determine the maximum shearing unit stress in the rivet.

2.14 According to aircraft specifications an alloy-steel tube with an outside diameter of ¾ in. and a wall thickness of 0.028 in. will carry a maximum axial tensile load of 6030 lb. Determine the maximum tensile and shearing unit stresses produced by that load, and indicate the planes on which they occur.

2.15 The 1-in. diameter rod shown in the accompanying diagram is subjected to an axial pull of 11,500 lb. Determine (a) the maximum tensile unit stress in the rod, (b) the average shearing unit stress between the shank and the head of the rod, and (c) the average unit stress which the washer produces on the wall.

2.16 The propeller shaft of a certain airplane has an internal diameter of 2.40 in. and an external diameter of 3.00 in. If the propeller develops a total pull of 2500 lb, determine the average tensile unit stress on a plane normal to the axis of the shaft.

2.17 A steel tube with an external diameter of 2.00 in. is to be subjected to an axial tensile load of 16,000 lb. Determine the minimum wall thickness which the tube must have if the maximum tensile stress is not to exceed 18,000 psi and the maximum shearing stress is not to exceed 8000 psi.

2.18 A foundation wall is 12 in. thick and carries a uniform load along the top. If the maximum compressive stress is not to exceed 400 psi, neglecting bending, what is the maximum load in pounds per linear foot the wall may carry?

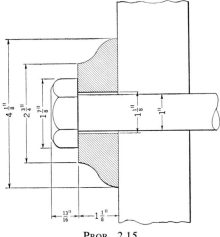

PROB. 2.15

2.19 What diameter of rod is required to carry an axial tensile load of 100,000 lb if the maximum tensile stress in the rod is not to exceed 18,000 psi and the maximum shearing stress is not to exceed 12,000 psi?

2.20 How much will a post 4 ft long shorten if the unit strain is 0.0005?

2.21 Compute the maximum tensile unit stress in a 1½-in. by ½-in. eyebar which is subjected to a total axial pull of 9000 lb. What is the unit strain if it stretches 0.096 in. in a length of 20 ft?

2.22 From the following data taken during a tensile test of a brass rod 1.000 in. in diameter, plot the stress-strain diagram. Within what range of stress does Hooke's law apply?

Load (lb)	Elong. in 10 In. (in.)	Load (lb)	Elong. in 10 In. (in.)
0	0	11,000	0.020
1710	0.002	12,580	0.030
3420	0.004	13,710	0.040
5130	0.006	14,750	0.050
6840	0.008	16,730	0.075
8550	0.010	18,180	0.100
9040	0.012	19,600	0.150
10,190	0.016	20,000	0.200

2.23 From the following data taken during a tensile test of a bronze rod 0.750 in. in diameter, plot the stress-strain diagram. The rod was not tested to failure.

Load (lb)	Elong. in 5 In. (in.)	Load (lb)	Elong. in 5 In. (in.)
0	0	4200	0.0030
1410	0.0005	4640	0.0035
2030	0.0010	4900	0.0040
2670	0.0015	5390	0.0050
3450	0.0020	6580	0.0100
3930	0.0025	6760	0.0150

2.24 In a tensile test of a 1.000-in. by 0.250-in. strip of celluloid, the following data were obtained. Plot the stress-strain diagram.

Load (lb)	Elong. in 6 In. (in.)	Load (lb)	Elong. in 6 In. (in.)
0	0	1000	0.081
200	0.013	1150	0.104
400	0.030	1250	0.147
600	0.048	1250	0.180 (failure)
800	0.064		

2.25 Sketch a stress-strain diagram for a hypothetical material which is elastic but to which Hooke's law does not apply, and sketch a diagram for an inelastic material which does obey Hooke's law.

2.26 A $1\frac{3}{8}$-in. diameter nylon cable for towing gliders is 350 ft long. Determine the total stretch in the cable when the unit strain is 0.21.

2.27 How much did the 8-in. gage length of the concrete cylinder of Fig. 2.5 change under a load of 60,000 lb?

2.28 A cable 1 in. in diameter is used for the hoist in a vertical mine shaft. A unit stress of 12,000 psi will produce a unit strain of 0.001 in the cable, and Hooke's law applies up to a stress of 50,000 psi. Determine the stretch in a 500-ft length of the cable resulting from a load of 6 tons on the hoist.

2.29 How much will an 8-in. length of a $\frac{3}{4}$-in. round wrought-iron bar stretch under a tensile load of (a) 9000 lb and (b) 18,000 lb? (See Fig. 8.8.)

2.30 Same data as problem 2.29, for a mild steel bar. (See Fig. 3.6.)

2.31 Same data as problem 2.29, for a copper bar. (See Fig. 9.1.)

2.32 Same data as problem 2.29, for an annealed nickel bar. (See Fig. 9.14.)

2.33 Determine the change in length which occurs in one year in a 3-in. portion of a rod in which creep is occurring at the rate of 0.00012 in. per in. per hr.

2.34 Determine the axial load required to produce the same change in length of a 2-in. square aluminum bar as would be produced by a 100 F change in temperature.

2.35 What is the greatest tensile load that may be placed on a 2-in. square steel bar if it is not to elongate more than 0.20 in. in a length of 20 ft? (See Fig. 3.6.)

2.36 The coefficient of thermal expansion of structural steel is 0.0000062 per deg F. (a) How much will a structural steel rod 2 in. in diameter shorten in a length of 10 ft when subjected to a temperature drop of 60 F? (b) How much axial force must be applied to each end of the rod to prevent it from shortening with the temperature change? (Assume that a stress of 30,000 psi on an unrestrained bar causes a strain of 0.001, and that the steel obeys Hooke's law up to 30,000 psi.)

2.37 What total force must be applied at the ends of a 2-in. square bronze rod to keep it from changing in length under a temperature drop of 40 F? A stress of 15,000 psi on an unrestrained bar causes a strain of 0.001, the material obeys Hooke's law up to a stress of 18,000 psi, and the coefficient of thermal expansion is 0.000030 per deg F.

2.38 A 1-in. by $\frac{1}{2}$-in. aluminum rod, for which the ratio of unit stress to unit strain is 10,000,000 psi up to a stress of 25,000 psi, and for which the coefficient of thermal expansion is 0.000025 per deg F, hangs in a vertical position, being held at the upper end.   A 10,000-lb load is then suspended from the lower end of the rod, after which the temperature drops 60 F.   What is the total change in length of a 10-in. section of the bar?

REFERENCES FOR FURTHER STUDY

BOYD, JAMES E., and SAMUEL B. FOLK.   *Strength of Materials,* 5th ed.   New York: McGraw-Hill Book Company, Inc., 1950.

LAURSON, P. G., and W. J. Cox.   *Mechanics of Materials,* 3d ed.   New York: John Wiley & Sons, Inc., 1954.

MURPHY, GLENN.   *Mechanics of Materials.*   New York: The Ronald Press Company, 1948.

POORMAN, ALFRED P.   *Strength of Materials,* 4th ed.   New York: McGraw-Hill Book Company, Inc., 1945.

SEELY, F. B.   *Resistance of Materials,* 4th ed.   New York: John Wiley & Sons, Inc., 1956.

TIMOSHENKO, S., and GLEASON H. MACCULLOUGH.   *Elements of Strength of Materials,* 3d ed.   New York: D. Van Nostrand Company, Inc., 1949.

3 Failure of Materials

3.1 Definition of Failure

A product or a material is said to have failed when it ceases to function properly in the use for which it was intended. A shaft bent slightly out of line may have failed just as definitely as though it were broken in two. In general, failure occurs when the distortion or rate of distortion of the material becomes excessive for the intended use of the material. The excessive distortion is usually manifested by slip, creep, or fracture of the material.

The failure of a member does not necessarily imply that the material in the member is damaged, for a structural member may fail because of excessive *elastic deformation*. For example, a lathe tool may deflect sufficiently within its elastic range of action to be useless for its intended purpose even though the material is uninjured.

3.2 Causes of Failure

The excessive deformation, or distortion, that is associated with failure of a member may be general, over an appreciable volume of the member, or it may be highly localized, involving a relatively small number of crystals, fibers, or atoms.

One cause of failure is the loads or physical forces which the member is required to withstand. Loading may cause an appreciable volume of material, involving millions of atoms, to be displaced. Splitting, buckling, crushing, tearing, spalling, cracking, and abrading are examples of the types of failure that may result from physical forces.

A second type of failure results when the valence electrons of the atoms of a material are transferred or exchanged with atoms of other elements, as manifested by chemical interaction between the material and a disintegrating or corroding foreign material. The rusting of steel and corroding of brass are examples of failure owing to chemical forces.

A third type of failure may result from nuclear interactions, as when a material is bombarded with neutrons, alpha particles, or other radiation. Changes in the nuclei may cause modifications of the individual atoms, which can result in spectacular failure of the mass of the material.

Other types of attack, such as those from termites, marine borers, erosion, or rot, may be wholly physical or wholly chemical or a combination of the two.

Failure resulting from load is probably the most common type of failure and will be considered in some detail in this chapter from the standpoint of the different types of physical loadings and their over-all effects on materials.

3.3   Types of Loading

The magnitude of load that a member of a given material will support without failure depends upon what is considered to constitute failure, upon the material, and upon the way in which the load is applied. There are three basic types of loading, differentiated by the length of time involved in the loading and the number of times that the load is applied. Each type affects the material somewhat differently.

The three basic types of loading are *static loading, dynamic loading,* and *repeated loading,* and each may be subdivided into additional classifications. In general, a given member is subjected to all three types of loading, but in most cases one type will predominate.

Static loading. Static loading, also called steady loading, is loading which is constant in magnitude, or which changes so slowly that the inertia of the member has no influence on the stress distribution. Static loading may be subdivided into two subgroups, continuous and slowly applied loading. However, the effect of the two on a material is the same.

——*Continuous loading.* If a load remains on a member for a long period of time, the member is said to be subjected to continuous loading. The weight of the member itself is the most common source of continuous loading. A cable of an overhead transmission line, for example, is subjected to continuous loading due to its own weight. A culvert at the bottom of an earth fill is an example of a member subjected to a continuous load which is not entirely its own weight. Continuous loading is present in many different structural members, in addition to other types of loading. Since the loading is applied for a long period of time, it offers the most favorable conditions for the development of creep. The load to which a member is subjected because of its own weight and the weight of other permanent parts of the structure that it must support is called the dead load on the member.

——*Slowly applied loading.* A slowly applied load is one which gradually builds up to its maximum value without any shock or vibration. The period of loading may be several hours or it may be but a few seconds; the important consideration is that there is no appreciable shock or vibration.

The stresses due to the slowly applied load increase as the load increases, and remain constant when the load remains constant.

As an example, an automobile running smoothly over a bridge represents a slowly applied loading on the bridge piers.

Dynamic loading. A load applied in such a manner that it sets up shock or vibration in the member is called a dynamic load or an impact load. It differs from a slowly applied load in that it sets up stresses which are greater, momentarily at least, than the stresses which would be produced by a steady load of the same magnitude. The momentary stresses may be sufficient to cause failure.

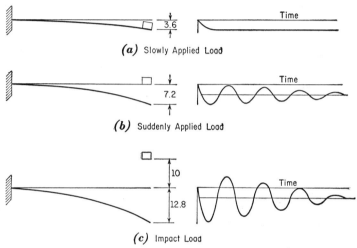

FIG. 3.1   Deflections produced by different methods of loading.

Dynamic loading also may be classified under two headings: suddenly applied loading and impact loading. The distinction between the two is based on whether or not the weight, load, or other factor causing the loading has an initial velocity at the beginning of the loading cycle. If it has initial velocity so that contact is made with a shock, it is called impact loading.

Suddenly applied loading. A weight that is slowly lowered onto the end of a diving board, which may be regarded as a cantilever beam, will cause a gradual increase in deflection until the beam supports the entire weight—provided that failure does not occur. For example, a 100-lb weight slowly lowered onto the end of a board 12 in. wide, 2 in. thick, and 10 ft long will cause a maximum bending stress of about 1500 psi and, if the board is oak, will result in a deflection of about 3.6 in. at the end, as indicated in Fig. 3.1a. This represents the condition of a slowly applied load.

If the 100-lb weight is lowered until it is in contact with the end of the beam and the rope is then cut suddenly, the beam will deflect to a maximum of 7.2 in. at the end, spring back almost to its unloaded position, again deflect, and continue to vibrate for some time until it finally reaches equilibrium in a position identical with that attained under the slowly applied load. This loading condition, illustrated in Fig. 3.1b, constitutes suddenly applied loading.

Suddenly applied loading results in deflections, strains, and stresses greater than those developed under the same load slowly applied, provided that the material is not overstressed by the suddenly applied load. It is obvious that a load of a given magnitude may be safe when slowly applied and can cause failure if applied suddenly.

The magnitude of the static or slowly applied load required to produce the same stress as the suddenly applied load is called the *equivalent static load,* and the ratio of the equivalent static load to the applied load is called the *load factor.* For the illustration in Fig. 3.1b the equivalent static load is 200 lb and the load factor is 2.

Suddenly applied loads are also produced in moving parts whenever a change in the magnitude or direction of the velocity occurs. For example, the stresses in the spokes and the rim of a rotating wheel as it is rapidly accelerated or braked are much larger than the corresponding stresses when the wheel is at rest. High suddenly applied loads are developed in airplane parts during maneuvers. For an airplane pulling out of a dive rapidly in still air, a load factor of 10 or more may be developed for the wings; that is, in order to prevent collapse, the wings may be required to support a load 10 times the weight of the airplane.

Impact loading. If the item causing the load on the member has a velocity relative to the member at the instant of contact, the member is said to sustain impact loading. The effect of a given weight is greater under conditions of impact than when applied suddenly. For example, if the 100-lb weight in Fig. 3.1c is dropped 10 in. onto the end of the board, it will result in a maximum deflection at the end of the board of about 12.8 in. If the stresses are not too high, the board will vibrate and finally come to equilibrium in the same position as it would under a static load of 100 lb.

For the condition shown in Fig. 3.1c the equivalent static load is 356 lb and the load factor is 3.56. The load factor increases as the distance through which the weight is dropped increases.

As a result of the impact load, a strain wave passes through the material. The wave originates at the point of impact and passes through the material with the speed of sound. The strain waves will reflect from any surface within the material and may superimpose, causing high instantaneous values of strain. The damage resulting from these instantaneous high values is not well understood, but there is evidence that a material may withstand momentarily, without damage, stresses that would cause failure under static loading. However, the effects of these stresses are not to be discounted.

One feature of impact strain is that the amplitude of the strain wave as it starts from the point of impact is equal to the relative velocity between the two bodies involved in the impact, divided by the velocity of sound in the material. Hence a light object traveling at a high velocity may inflict more damage than a heavy object moving more slowly at the instant of impact.

Under certain conditions the load factor or the equivalent static load may be obtained by direct computation; in other cases experimental evaluation is advantageous. If the dynamic loading is produced by a weight being dropped on a member, the computation of the load factor is based on the assumption that the total energy of the falling weight (total work done by the weight in falling) is absorbed by the member, or structure, upon which the weight falls.[1] The dynamic load for this condition is often called an *energy load* and is evaluated as the total number of inch-pounds of energy transmitted from the weight to the member. Load factors are also evaluated experimentally by measuring the strains developed in the material by the dynamic load.

In many situations, as when a heavy weight is dropped on a concrete floor, the effect of the dynamic load is localized, and the stresses produced cannot be determined accurately. In cutting materials with a chisel, use is made of the highly localized effect of the dynamic load produced by the blow of the hammer.

The resistance of materials to dynamic loading is much more difficult to evaluate than their resistance to static loading, particularly when the effect is localized.

Repeated loading. If a load is applied to a member a very large number of times, the member is said to be subjected to a condition of repeated loading. Repeated loading is of great importance because it may cause failure of a material at a stress which would be perfectly safe if the load were applied only once. It may be even more dangerous than creep in that it produces sudden failure without warning, whereas impending fracture due to creep may be evidenced by excessive deformation before breakage actually occurs. Repeated loading may be classified as either periodic loading or random loading.

---

[1] The assumption is usually conservative because the supports of the member will normally absorb some of the energy.

Periodic loading. ~~In periodic loading the stress-time, strain-time, or deflection-time diagrams form a pattern repeated at regular intervals of time.~~ In periodic loading the stresses may vary periodically (1) from a maximum value in tension to a maximum value in compression, (2) between a maximum value and zero, or (3) between a maximum value and some reduced value other than zero. Repeated stresses may be induced by either static loading or dynamic loading.

A piston rod of a steam engine is an example of a member subjected to periodic reversed repeated loading. The rod is alternately in compression and tension. A connecting rod in an automobile engine is another example of a member subjected to repeated loading. The stress varies from a small value in tension to a maximum value in compression. A pneumatic chisel or the hammer of a pile driver is subjected to repeated dynamic loading.

The axle of a railroad car is an example of a structural member subjected to periodic reversed bending or to repeated flexural loading. The fiber stress at a given point will have its maximum value in tension at some instant. When the axle has turned through 90 deg, the stress on that section will become zero. An additional 90 deg will bring the stress on the section to its maximum value in compression; and another half-revolution of the axle will bring the section back to the original position with the maximum tensile stress. Thus, for every revolution of the wheel the stress goes through a cycle, varying from a maximum value in tension to a maximum value in compression. The several elements in the track over which the car travels are likewise subjected to repeated loading as successive wheel loads travel over them.

Random repeated loading. Under some circumstances a member will be subjected to loads of different magnitude with no systematic pattern of loading. The floor system of a highway bridge is one example. With cars and trucks of different weights passing over the bridge at various speeds and at irregular time intervals, fluctuating stresses are developed which vary in magnitude from one loading to another. The spars of an airplane wing are subjected to random repeated loading as a result of the variation in gusts to which the airplane is subjected in flight.

Repeated loading, whether periodic or random, may lead to failure at comparatively low nominal stresses because under the action of this repeated loading or alternating stress, any crack, however small, is opened and closed slightly during each cycle. Since higher stresses exist at the base of the crack than would be present if the crack were not there, the crack will gradually extend across the member, causing failure. As the crack extends, it usually follows an irregular path, giving the fracture a crystalline appearance; this phenomenon gave rise to the explanation that the fracture was caused by the "crystallization" of the metal. However, it is well established that this idea of crystallization is erroneous. Examination shows that every metal has a crystalline structure initially, and experiments indicate that repeated loading does not cause the metal to crystallize.

The presence of cracks initially is not necessary to start this *progressive fracture* under repeated loading, but irregularities of the material, such as slag inclusions, scratches, or pitting that may result from corrosive action on the surface, supply starting points for progressive fracture.

High working stresses increase the rapidity of failure and reduce the effective life of a member. Experiments with ferrous metals have shown that there is a definite stress below which progressive fracture seems not to occur, regardless of the number of times the stress is applied and removed. This stress gives a measure of the resistance of the material to failure by repeated loading, and is called the *endurance limit*.

The term "fatigue failure" has been widely used to designate fracture from repeated applications of load. Any so-called "fatigue failure" is actually a failure by progressive fracture which spreads from some starting nucleus with the successive applications of the load.

3.4 Resistance to Failure

The resistance of a material to failure under load is called its *strength*. Since failure may occur by slip, creep, or fracture of the material under static loading, dynamic loading, or repeated loading, the term strength is indefinite unless it refers to one of the specific combinations of type of loading and type of failure.

TABLE 3.1

PROPERTIES MEASURING RESISTANCE TO FAILURE BY LOADING

Type of Failure	Type of Loading		
	Static	Dynamic	Repeated
Fracture	Ultimate strength (lb per sq in.)	Modulus of toughness (in.-lb per cu in.)	Endurance limit (lb per sq in.)
Slip	Elastic strength (lb per sq in.)	Modulus of resilience (in.-lb per cu in.)	....
Creep	Creep limit (lb per sq in.)	....	....

In general, materials do not offer equal resistance to tension, compression, and shear, so the term strength is not completely defined until it designates the kind of stress as well as the type of loading and the method of failure. The names which have been assigned to the properties which indicate the resistance of a material under the various conditions of failure are given in Table 3.1. The kind of stress must also be indicated, as, for example, *ultimate tensile strength* or *modulus of resilience in shear*.   The units in which these properties are commonly expressed in engineering use in the United States are indicated below each of the properties.   In England, strengths are commonly expressed in tons per square inch or, in the case of dynamic loading, in inch-tons per cubic inch.

FAILURE BY FRACTURE

3.5 Fracture

Fracture denotes destruction of cohesion, separation of adjacent particles, and loss of continuity of the material.   In general, the product will break into two or more parts, as illustrated in Fig. 2.3.   Fracture may occur suddenly without warning if the material is brittle; more slowly, after a large amount of inelastic deformation, if the material is ductile; or suddenly from a progressive crack which has worked its way through the material, in either a ductile or brittle material.   Obviously, a material can carry no additional load after it has fractured.   Articles like ropes, cables, wires, and chains are designed primarily to avoid failure by fracture.   In the design of parts such as turbine blades and railroad-car axles, which are subjected to many repetitions of stress, particular attention must be given to the possibility of progressive failure resulting in fracture, even though the intensity of stress may not be abnormally high.

3.6 Fracture under Static Load.   Ultimate Strength

The property which measures the resistance of a material to fracture under a steady load is called the *ultimate strength*.   It is defined as the maximum unit stress which the material will develop before fracture occurs. The ultimate strength of a material is normally evaluated by placing a suitable specimen in a testing machine, or a device that will stretch, compress, twist, bend, or shear the specimen as desired.   As the specimen is deformed, the resistance which it develops is indicated by the testing machine, usually as a load.   The maximum resistance is noted and converted to a unit stress.   In a tensile test, for example, the ultimate strength is equal to the maximum load divided by the original cross-sectional area.

When loaded in tension, some ductile materials, such as structural steel, exhibit considerable localized reduction in cross-sectional area after the maximum load has been reached, and immediately before failure.   For example, the diameter of the steel bar for which the stress-strain diagram is shown in Fig. 3.2 was 0.500 in. before loading, and after failure the diameter at the reduced section was 0.322 in.   If the loading is done in a testing machine, this reduction of area decreases the load-carrying capacity of the specimen being tested, even though the unit stress at the critical section is increasing with the continued application of strain by the testing machine.   The result is that the indicated load on the specimen decreases before fracture occurs.   Under such circumstances the ultimate strength is taken as the *maximum* load developed by the specimen divided by the *original* cross-sectional area.   ~~The load at failure divided by the area is called the *rupture strength*.~~   If the original cross-sectional area is used, the rupture strength will be less than the ultimate strength; but if the final area is used, the rupture strength will be greater than the ultimate strength.

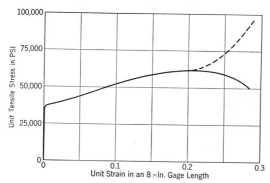

FIG. 3.2   Stress-strain diagram for mild steel in tension.

A typical fracture was illustrated in Fig. 2.3a, and Fig. 3.2 shows a typical stress-strain diagram for a rod of mild (or structural) steel in tension.   The portion of the curve from the origin to about 35,000 psi is a straight line, which apparently coincides with the vertical axis because of the scale selected for the unit strain.   The stress-strain diagram for that portion of the stress range is shown as the lower curve in Fig. 3.7.

In Fig. 3.2 the full line represents the stress based on the original area, while the dotted line represents the stress based on the actual areas.   The ultimate strength is the highest unit stress based on the original area, or 61,000 psi.   Based on the original area, the rupture stress is 50,000 psi; while, based on the final area, it is 98,000 psi.   However, the ultimate strength is of more use to the engineer than the rupture strength, since the ultimate represents the maximum load-carrying capacity of the material. Brittle materials usually fracture without appreciable change in area when the ultimate strength of the material is reached, making the rupture strength and the ultimate strength equal.

The shape of the curve between the ultimate strength and the rupture strength is dependent on the rate of strain and on the gage length over which the strains are measured.   Since the unit strain in ductile materials beyond the ultimate strength is not uniformly distributed along the gage length, but is concentrated at the section of impending rupture, a stress-strain diagram for mild steel based on a 2-in. gage length might indicate a strain of 0.45, and a diagram based on a 1-in. gage length might indicate a strain of 0.60, at the rupture strength.

The ultimate strength in tension or compression is obtained by simply dividing the maximum load by the cross-sectional area. The maximum static axial load which a given member will carry without fracture may be computed directly from the ultimate strength of the material and the cross-sectional area of the member; or, if the load is known, the required area may be determined.

ILLUSTRATIVE PROBLEM. Determine the minimum diameter of annealed copper wire required to suspend a static load of 200 lb without breaking.

Solution. Since the wire is required to support a static load without fracture, the significant property is the ultimate tensile strength. The Properties Index at the back of this book shows that the stress-strain diagram for copper is given in Fig. 9.1. From the curve for annealed copper, the ultimate strength (maximum ordinate) is 37,000 psi. The required area is

$$a = \frac{P}{S} = \frac{200}{37,000} = 0.0054 \text{ in.}^2$$

and the diameter is

$$d = 2\sqrt{0.0054/\pi} = 0.084 \text{ in.}$$

If the specimen is subjected to bending or to torsion, the maximum stress is not equal to the load divided by the area, nor can it be computed directly from the load and the dimensions of the specimen. In order to provide a suitable means for comparing the load-carrying capacity of torsional and flexural members, the property *modulus of rupture* has been introduced. It is defined as the maximum stress in the member at the highest load, computed from the ordinary beam formula, $S = Mc/I$, or from the torsion formula, $S = Tc/J$. Since these formulas are not valid above the range of stress for which Hooke's law is valid, the modulus of rupture is not an exact "ultimate strength" in bending or in torsion, but it does provide a basis for comparing the maximum resistances of members subjected to bending or torsion.

3.7 Fracture under Dynamic Load. Modulus of Toughness

The general term toughness denotes the capacity of a material for resisting fracture under dynamic loading. The specific property term *modulus of toughness* is defined as the maximum amount of energy which a unit volume of the material will absorb without fracture. The modulus of toughness is normally evaluated in inch-pounds per cubic inch, and may be approximated as the area under the entire stress-strain diagram for axial loading. This may be shown by noting that the area under the stress-strain diagram is equal to the average stress multiplied by the maximum unit strain. For the condition of axial loading the average unit stress is equal to the average load divided by the cross-sectional area of the member, and the unit strain is equal to the total axial deformation divided by the length.   Hence,

$$U_t = \frac{P_{\text{avg}} e_{\text{max}}}{AL} \qquad (3.1)$$

However, the average force P_{avg} multiplied by the total distance e through which it moves is the work done on the member, and AL is the volume of the member.   Therefore U_t, the area under the stress-strain diagram, represents the maximum amount of work, or energy, per unit volume which the material will absorb.

The modulus of toughness of the steel in Fig. 3.2 is

$$U_t = 55{,}000(0.29) = 16{,}000 \text{ in.-lb per cu in.}$$

That is, an average of 16,000 in.-lb of work was required to stress each cubic inch of the 8-in. gage length of the bar to failure.   For a bar having a diameter of $\frac{1}{2}$ in., a total of $16{,}000(0.196)(8) = 25{,}100$ in.-lb of work would be absorbed within an 8-in. gage length before fracture.   That is equivalent to the work done by a 1000-lb weight dropping through 25.1 in.

The evaluation of the dynamic load required to fracture a given specimen by equating the energy of the dynamic load to the modulus of toughness multiplied by the volume is only approximate, since the manner of application of the load, the means by which the member is held or supported, and other factors have an important effect upon the distribution of the energy throughout the bar at the instant of fracture.   As was mentioned in the discussion of dynamic loading, the effect of a shock is often concentrated, causing localized failure even though the average stress for the entire member may be low.   The length of the piece is also important. Because of the additional elongation at the section of rupture in a ductile material, the modulus of toughness of a material computed on the basis of a 1-in. gage length might be appreciably greater than the modulus computed on the basis of an 8-in. gage length.   However, the modulus of toughness is useful as an index for comparing the resistances of different materials to dynamic loads.

If the stress-strain diagram is not available, the modulus of toughness of the material may be obtained approximately by multiplying the average of the yield point or other measure of the elastic strength (sec. 3.10) and the ultimate strength by the unit strain at failure.   This procedure is equivalent to saying that the stress-strain diagram has the same area as a rectangle whose base is equal to the unit strain at failure, and whose altitude is the average of the yield point and ultimate strength.   Applying this method to the data of Fig. 3.2 gives, for the modulus of toughness,

$\frac{1}{2}(37,000 + 61,000)(0.29) = 14,200$ in.-lb per cu in., which is 11 per cent less than the true area. If the stress-strain diagram is a parabola, as is approximately the case for some grades of cast iron and concrete, the modulus of toughness is equal to two-thirds the ultimate strength times the unit strain at rupture.

It is evident that the capacity of a member for resisting a dynamic load applied axially is increased by increasing the length of the member, because the volume is increased directly with the length. However, the capacity for carrying a static load is not increased with an increase in length, because that capacity is dependent on the area. In fact, a long rod may actually have less resistance to failure under a static load than would a short rod of the same cross section because of the possibility of buckling or of introducing a weak section with the increase in length.

ILLUSTRATIVE PROBLEM. Determine approximately how much axial load an 8-in. length of annealed copper wire 0.084 in. in diameter will carry without breaking if the load is dropped 4 in. before its weight comes on the wire.

Solution. Since fracture under a dynamic load is being considered, the significant property is the modulus of toughness. This modulus, which is the area under the stress-strain diagram, may be found approximately by multiplying the average stress by the maximum strain. From the stress-strain diagram for annealed copper given in Fig. 9.1,

$$U_t = 30,000(0.34) = 10,200 \text{ in.-lb per cu in.}$$

The volume of the wire is

$$V = 8(0.084)^2 0.7854 = 0.0432 \text{ in.}^3$$

The total energy absorbed in the 8-in. length of the wire will then be

$$W = U_t V = 10,200(0.0432) = 440 \text{ in.-lb}$$

In other words, an energy load of 440 in.-lb will break the wire. Since a 110-lb weight will produce 440 in.-lb of energy in dropping 4 in., a 110-lb weight will be sufficient to break the wire, if all of the energy of the falling weight is absorbed by the 8-in. length of wire.

The illustrative problem given in section 3.6 indicates that the same wire will support a load of 200 lb if it is applied slowly.

The toughness of many materials may be altered by stressing them above about 60 per cent of the ultimate strength, as discussed in section 3.12. Since the effect of the prestressing is usually a lowering of the toughness, the amount of energy which a machine or structural part will absorb without failure cannot be counted upon to be equal to the toughness of a new specimen of the same material because of the possibility that the part has been accidentally overstressed in service.

The amount of energy required to break a specimen may be measured in other ways. In one type of impact machine a standard weight is dropped upon a specimen of the material from successively increasing heights until the specimen fails. The energy may be calculated as the product of the weight and height of drop which produced fracture.

The Charpy and the Izod impact testing machines, which are standard machines for metals, utilize the energy from the swing of a heavy pendulum. A standard specimen in the form of a small notched beam is fastened at the bottom of the arc described by the pendulum. The pendulum is released from a known height, and either a toughness index or the energy required to break the specimen may be determined as a function of the difference between the initial height and the height to which the pendulum rises on the other side, after breaking the specimen.

These tests may be expected to provide a qualitative indication of the toughness of the material. Numerical results obtained from the tests are relative, since the energy is not distributed uniformly throughout the specimen and may be more localized for specimens of some materials than for similar specimens of other materials. In fact, the notched-beam tests are usually regarded as giving an indication of the "notch sensitivity" of the material or its resistance to weakening by notches, cracks, or scratches.

As was noted in section 3.3, a dynamic load may be reduced to an equivalent static load for design purposes by multiplying the magnitude of the weight involved in the dynamic load by a load factor. Then the ultimate strength becomes the criterion of failure.

3.8 Fracture under Repeated Load. Endurance Limit

Fracture as a result of repeated loading is a common occurrence. The simple act of breaking a wire by bending it back and forth a few times utilizes the tendency of materials to fail as a result of repeated loading. The tragic explosive decompression of the Comet airliner is an example of failure progressing very rapidly from a small crack developed by repeated loading as a result of changes in external air pressure.

That property which serves as a measure of the resistance of a material to failure under repeated stress is called the *endurance limit.* It is defined as the maximum reversed unit stress to which the material may be subjected many millions of times without failing. As normally used, the term endurance limit implies a complete reversal of stress—that is, a stress alternating between equal values in tension and compression, or from shear in one direction to an equal value of shear in the opposite direction.

The endurance limit cannot yet be determined by a single short-time test, as can the ultimate strength or proportional limit of a material. The standard method for evaluating the endurance limit for a given material necessitates the testing to failure, or to millions of repetitions without failure, many similar specimens of the material subjected to different intensities of stress. Efforts to evolve other shorter or simpler tests to evaluate endurance limits give some indication that change in electrical resistance under stress may bear a significant relationship to the endurance limit of some materials.

One form of the setup for determining the endurance limit in reversed bending is indicated in Fig. 3.3. The specimen is a circular beam, turned down to a smaller diameter in the central portion. It is supported near the ends, and carries a weight so located that the highest stress will be produced in the reduced section of the beam. Tensile stresses are developed on the lower half of the beam, and compressive stresses on the upper half. As the specimen is rotated by the motor, the magnitude of the longitudinal stress on any fiber will vary through a complete cycle—from maximum tension to maximum compression during each complete revolution.

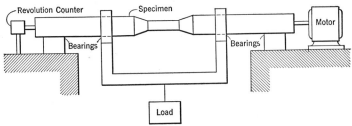

FIG. 3.3   Rotating beam machine for determining endurance limit in reversed bending.

The setup is arranged so that the motor will stop when the specimen breaks, the revolution counter thus recording the number of reversals of stress required to cause failure. As a single specimen will indicate only whether the applied stress was greater or less than the endurance limit, many specimens must be used, making the procedure expensive and time-consuming.

If the unit stress in each specimen is plotted to a natural scale against the number of cycles required to cause failure plotted to a logarithmic scale, a graph known as an S-N (stress-cycle) diagram will be obtained. Figure 3.4 shows typical S-N diagrams for a few common metals, each plotted point representing the results of a test on one specimen. The endurance limit may be found from the S-N diagram as the unit stress at which the curve becomes horizontal. Figure 3.4 indicates the endurance limit for structural steel in completely reversed bending to be 28,000 psi—somewhat lower than the elastic strength (sec. 3.10). That is, the resistance of a structural steel to fracture under repeated loading is less than its resistance to slip under steady loading. Most of the ferrous metals have rather well-defined endurance limits. The endurance limit for aluminum alloys and other metals which do not have a well-defined break in the S-N curve is usually taken arbitrarily as the maximum stress to which the material may be subjected 500,000,000 times without fracture.

Numerous tests have indicated that the endurance limit for most metals is approximately the same regardless of whether the stress is produced by bending or by axial loading, as long as the upper and lower limits of stress variation are the same in the two cases. Scratches, and surface irregularities due to pitting and corrosion, have a marked effect in reducing the endurance limit of a metal, because the irregularities serve as ideal starting points for cracks which will extend across the member.

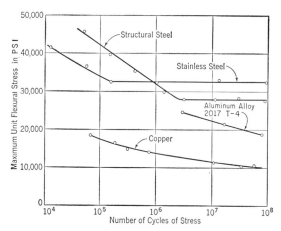

FIG. 3.4   Typical S-N diagrams.

A loading condition is frequently encountered where the stress varies from one value in tension to a different value in compression, or where the stress fluctuates between two different values in tension or two different values in compression. Under such conditions, the stress may be considered to be the sum of a steady stress and a completely reversed stress. For example, a member subjected to a stress which varies from 14,000 psi in tension to 30,000 psi in tension may be considered to be subjected to a steady tensile stress of 22,000 psi, plus a completely reversed repeated stress of 8000 psi.

The effect of the steady stress in reducing the magnitude of completely reversed bending stress to which the material may be subjected safely may be determined from a diagram of the type shown in Fig. 3.5. Results from a series of tests using different combinations of steady and reversed stresses are plotted with maximum safe reversed repeated stresses as ordinates and the corresponding steady stresses as abscissas.

As approximations to the plotted points, the three lines shown in Fig. 3.5 correspond to the following three theories as to what constitutes the limiting combinations of steady stress and repeated stress.

1. The Goodman theory is based on the assumption that a line should be drawn from the endurance limit on the vertical axis to the ultimate strength on the horizontal axis.

2. The Gerber theory is based on the assumption that a parabola should be so drawn as to have its vertex on the vertical axis at the value of the endurance limit and to pass through the ultimate strength plotted on the horizontal axis.

3. The Soderberg theory, or straight-line theory, is based on the assumption that a straight line should be drawn from the endurance limit to the elastic strength.

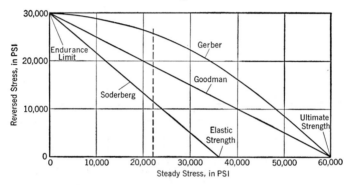

FIG. 3.5   Assumed limiting combinations of steady stress and reversed stress.

After the approximate curve or theory has been determined for a material, the maximum safe reversed repeated stress which may be superimposed upon a steady stress may be taken as the ordinate to the curve at an abscissa corresponding to the magnitude of the steady stress.

For example, if a material had the values indicated in Fig. 3.5 and was subjected to a steady stress of 22,000 psi, the Goodman theory would permit a reversed stress of 19,000 psi to be superimposed, the Gerber theory would permit a reversed stress of 26,000 psi, and the Soderberg theory would permit a reversed stress of 12,000 psi. That is, according to the Soderberg theory the limits of the fluctuating stress are 10,000 and 34,000 psi, even though the stress could vary from −30,000 psi to 30,000 psi without failure occurring.

One form of the electrical test mentioned earlier (the Ikeda test) makes use of the fact that the electrical resistance of a material is altered by the formation of cracks which develop under repeated loading.[2] The specimen may be placed in the machine represented in Fig. 3.3, and its resistance may be measured. A load is applied, the specimen is subjected to a

[2] Moore and Konzo, University of Illinois Engineering Experiment Station Bulletin 205.

few thousand cycles of stress, and the resistance is again measured. Then the load is increased, and the same steps are repeated. This is continued until a substantial increase in resistance is noted. The unit stresses are then plotted against resistance. In tests which have been performed, the unit stress at the point where the curve changes its characteristic shape has given values comparable with the endurance limit.

FAILURE BY SLIP

3.9 Slip

If, under constant stress, the time rate of inelastic deformation decreases and becomes zero within a short time after the stress has been applied, the inelastic action is called *slip*. The term slip is used because microscopic examination of the material reveals definite slip planes, also called glide

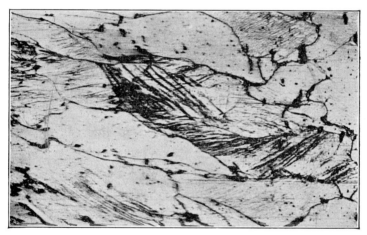

FIG. 3.6   Slip lines in ductile metal.

planes, along which part of the material slides with respect to the adjacent material. Sometimes the slip lines may be seen on the outside of a specimen, without the aid of a microscope. Figure 3.6 illustrates the nature of these slip planes as they appeared in a specimen of a ductile metal magnified about 500 times. The action seems to take place along definite planes of weakness within individual crystals, rather than between crystals, as is discussed in Chapter 6.

The inelastic action resulting from slip may or may not be harmful to a structural member or machine part, depending on the use to which the part is put. In members like gears or axles, excessive slip would make the part as unfit for further use as though it had actually fractured. In other parts, such as wire fencing or railroad-car couplers, a relatively large amount of slip is not objectionable, as it will not interfere with the safe or proper functioning of the member. Obviously, no single maximum allowable value of slip can be set for all conditions, but each class of service will demand a certain tolerance of dimension. For general use of steel in tension, a maximum permissible set of 0.002 has been suggested by the American Society for Testing Materials.[3]   Other tentative values from the same source are indicated in Table 3.2 in the following section.

3.10   Slip under Static Load.   Elastic Strength

The *elastic strength* of a material denotes its resistance to failure by slip, and is defined as the highest unit stress to which a material may be subjected without failure by slip.   Since there may be different criteria of exactly what constitutes failure by slip, several slightly different properties have been suggested as indexes of the elastic strength.   Five of the most important are the *elastic limit,* the *proportional limit, Johnson's apparent elastic limit,* the *yield point,* and the *yield strength.*

Elastic limit.   The elastic limit is the highest unit stress to which a material may be subjected without a permanent deformation remaining upon complete removal of the stress.   An accurate determination of the elastic limit would indicate the stress at which slip starts.   However, slip probably starts in some part of the specimen at a very low stress, and the resulting permanent deformation is too small to be indicated on the usual type of extensometer used to measure strain.   Consequently, the stress at which permanent set is first observed will depend on the sensitivity of the measuring device.   Also, the determination involves the time-consuming process of making a number of successive loadings and unloadings with gradually increasing stress until permanent deformation is observed.   This method of determining the elastic strength is seldom used.

Proportional limit.   The proportional limit is the highest unit stress at which strain is proportional to the accompanying stress.   It may be obtained readily as the unit stress at the upper end of the straight-line portion of the stress-strain diagram.   The proportional limit of the material in Fig. 3.7 is 32,000 psi.   This method of determining the elastic strength has the advantage that the value may be obtained from a stress-strain diagram for a single loading, and the value of the proportional limit is somewhat less dependent on the sensitivity of the measuring apparatus than is the value of the elastic limit.

For some materials, such as timber and concrete, accurate determination of the proportional limit is difficult, as the stress-strain diagram may show a slight curvature at low stresses and there may be no readily recognizable point of deviation from a straight line.   In many cases the straight

[3] ASTM Designation E 8.

line selected to represent the lower portion of the stress-strain diagram is a compromise among several lines, each of which appears to fit the plotted data about equally well, and each of which would give a different value for the proportional limit.

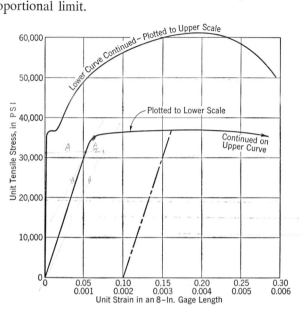

FIG. 3.7 Stress-strain diagram for mild steel in tension.

Johnson's apparent elastic limit. Johnson's apparent elastic limit is defined as the unit stress at which the slope of the stress-strain diagram is 50 per cent greater with respect to the axis of stress than the slope at the origin. In Fig. 3.7, Johnson's apparent elastic limit is 34,000 psi. This method for determining the elastic strength was suggested as a possible means of avoiding some of the difficulties involved in determining the proportional limit. A change in slope of the initial straight-line portion of the stress-strain diagram has much less effect upon Johnson's apparent elastic limit than upon the proportional limit.

Yield point. The yield point of a material is the unit stress (less than the ultimate strength) at which the specimen first exhibits an appreciable increase in strain with no increase in stress. The yield point may be determined from the stress-strain diagram as the unit stress at the point where the curve first becomes horizontal. However, a stress-strain diagram is not necessary for its determination. When the yield point is reached in a test of a material, the load-indicating mechanism stops, or shows a decrease in load, while the material deforms plastically without fracturing. The unit stress at which the load ceases to increase is the yield point. ~~The yield point is usually from six-tenths to seven-tenths of the ultimate strength for those materials which have a yield point, such as structural steel.~~ Most materials do not have a yield point; but, for those which do, it furnishes a very convenient basis for evaluating elastic strength, because it is the principal method of determining the elastic strength without the use of a stress-strain diagram. The yield point of the steel in Fig. 3.7 is 37,000 psi.

Yield strength. ~~Yield strength has been defined as the unit stress at which a material exhibits a specified limiting offset.~~ The limiting offset is expressed as a unit deformation, and its value is determined by the use to which the material is to be put. For uses where a very small amount of permanent set would be objectionable, the offset used in determining the yield strength should be correspondingly low. For general use, the percentages of offset given in Table 3.2 have been recommended tentatively. In reporting values of yield strength, the value of the limiting offset should be stated.

TABLE 3.2

RECOMMENDED OFFSETS FOR DETERMINING YIELD STRENGTH*

Material	Stress	Offset (%)	Corresponding Unit Deform.
Steel	Tension	0.20	0.0020
Wood	Compression, parallel to grain	0.05	0.0005
Gray cast iron	Tension	0.05	0.0005
Concrete	Compression	0.02	0.0002
Aluminum alloys	Tension	0.20	0.0020
Brass and bronze	Tension	0.35	0.0035

* Some of these offsets, and others not listed, may be found in ASTM Standards and Tentative Standards.

~~The yield strength may be determined from the stress-strain diagram by laying off the specified offset along the strain axis, and drawing through the point a line parallel to the straight-line portion of the diagram.~~ Then the unit stress at the intersection of this straight line and the stress-strain diagram is the yield strength.

Tests indicate that the offset is virtually equal to the permanent set which would remain if the material were loaded to the yield strength and then unloaded. In other words, the unloading stress-strain curve is generally a straight line parallel to the initial tangent. For the steel in Fig. 3.7 the yield strength corresponding to an offset of 0.2 per cent is 37,000 psi.

3.11 Slip under Dynamic Load. Modulus of Resilience

~~The resistance of a material to breakdown of elastic action under energy loads is called resilience.~~ The specific property used as a measure of resilience is the *modulus of resilience,* ~~defined as the maximum amount of energy per unit volume which may be stored in a material by stress and completely recovered when the stress is removed.~~ The property is of particular use in evaluating the resistance of the material to shock. Steel in springs often has a high modulus of resilience.

~~Under the condition of axial loading the modulus of resilience may be found as the area under the stress-strain diagram up to the elastic limit.~~ As it is difficult to determine the true elastic limit, the proportional limit is usually substituted, and the modulus of resilience may be evaluated as

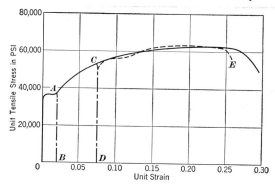

FIG. 3.8   Strain-hardening effect in structural steel.

the area under the stress-strain diagram up to the proportional limit. The modulus of resilience of the material in Fig. 3.7 is $\frac{1}{2}(32,000)(0.00107)$ = 17.1 in.-lb per cu in. This means that 17.1 in.-lb of energy can be stored in each cubic inch of the material without causing slip.

The *elastic strength* may also be used as a criterion of resistance to failure by slip under dynamic loading if the dynamic load is converted to an equivalent static load by multiplying its weight by the load factor.

3.12   Stresses above the Elastic Strength

Stresses below the proportional limit or elastic limit will have practically no effect upon the properties of most materials unless the stress is applied so many times that failure by repeated loading occurs. But, as was indicated in the discussion of toughness, stresses above about 60 per cent of the ultimate strength of many materials will affect some of the properties of those materials. While the amount of the effect will vary with different materials, the general behavior is the same for many of them and will be illustrated as observed in structural steel.

The heavy line in Fig. 3.8 indicates again the stress-strain diagram for a specimen of hot-rolled structural steel, such as is found in most structural shapes, as I beams, channels, and angles. If the material were stressed to

A and unloaded, the stress-strain diagram would return to the strain axis in practically a straight line *AB*, virtually parallel to the initial straight-line portion of the diagram which, with the scale used, is almost vertical.   If the stress were again applied, the stress-strain diagram would be similar to the original diagram.   If the material were stressed to *C* and then unloaded, the unloading curve would follow the line *CD*, also virtually parallel to the initial tangent.   However, if the stress were again applied, the yield point would be raised to *C*, the diagram following the dotted line *DCE*.

The effect of the single loading to *C* is to increase the elastic strength and the modulus of resilience and to decrease the modulus of toughness. The ultimate strength is practically unaltered, and the ultimate elongation is decreased materially.   This effect, known as *strain-hardening*, may be produced intentionally, by any of several forms of cold working used to increase the elastic strength and resistance to slip under dynamic loading, or it may be produced accidentally, resulting in an undesirable decrease of resistance to fracture under dynamic loading.

In bending a soft wire several times to break it, one utilizes the strain-hardening effect.   It is evident that the nearer the ultimate strength the stressing is carried, the more pronounced will be its effect.

FAILURE BY CREEP

3.13   Creep

If, under constant stress, the time rate of inelastic deformation does not become zero within a short time after the stress has been applied, the inelastic action is called *creep.*—Microscopic examination of metals which have undergone inelastic action by creep reveal not only definite planes of movement, such as are evident when slip has occurred, but also relative rotation of crystals as a result of plastic deformation at the crystal boundaries.   The action has been likened to the slow flow of a very viscous liquid, the internal deformation within the crystalline boundaries being well distributed throughout the crystal.   Professor H. F. Moore, B. B. Betty, and C. W. Dollins have reported that the relative rotation of crystals and the number of visible slip lines increase with the duration of the stress, but that no actual cracks develop until just before fracture.[4]

By the very nature of its action, creep is particularly prone to cause damage in structural parts subjected to constant stress over long periods of time.   The danger of creep is that it may produce, slowly but inevitably, sufficient deformation to cause failure even when the applied stress is much lower than that which would cause the more rapid and spectacular slip or

[4] *Investigations of Creep and Fracture of Lead and Lead Alloys for Cable Sheathing,* University of Illinois Engineering Experiment Station bulletins 272 and 306 (1938).

fracture.   Since the action of creep is similar to the flow of a viscous liquid, it will occur in all metals at temperatures near their melting points. In general, the tendency to creep increases as the temperature increases, even in ranges much below the melting point.

Some metals, such as lead and tin, and other materials, such as timber, will creep at ordinary temperatures.   Both the plastic elongation and the reduction of area in the vicinity of the fracture of ductile metals prior to failure in a tensile test are manifestations of creep.   Tests have not indicated clearly whether or not there is for each material a definite limiting temperature or stress below which creep will not occur.

Since inelastic action is one of the principal causes of failure of structural elements, a limiting value of allowable deformation is often specified for a given class of member.   Where failure by slip is being considered, the specified limiting permanent deformation automatically sets a limiting value of stress (the *yield strength*).   However, when failure by creep is being considered, the limiting deformation does not automatically set a limiting value of stress because the deformation might be attained either from a low stress acting for a comparatively long time or from a higher stress acting for a comparatively short time.   Therefore the element of time becomes important—the material must not deform more than the limiting amount during the life of the member.

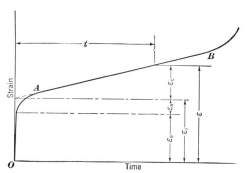

FIG. 3.9   Typical strain-time diagram for material
subject to creep.

Figure 3.9 shows a typical deformation-time diagram for a material which is subject to creep under a constant stress at a constant temperature. After the almost instantaneous elastic deformation ϵ_e has occurred, the curve continues to rise rapidly at first, and then gradually flattens out.   For a certain time, varying from a few minutes to several years (the period depends on the material, the stress, and the temperature), the curve is approximately a straight line.   Then the rate of deformation increases, and failure by fracture soon follows.   For the portion of the curve between

A and *B*, which is the interval of practical importance to the engineer, the total deformation ϵ at any time t after loading may be considered to be the sum of the initial deformation ϵ_i (elastic ϵ_e plus initial plastic ϵ_a) and the additional deformation ϵ_c due to creep.[5]   If the rate of creep is designated as v, the expression for the total deformation becomes

$$\epsilon = \epsilon_i + \epsilon_c = \epsilon_i + vt \qquad (3.2)$$

The rate of creep may be found as the slope of the straight-line portion of the deformation-time diagram.   Both the rate of creep and the initial deformation ϵ_i must be found experimentally for the particular material under the particular conditions of usage, as both are dependent on the temperature and the stress.

3.14 Creep Limit

The property which serves as a measure of the resistance of a material to failure by creep is called the *creep limit,* or *creep strength.*   It may be defined as the maximum unit stress to which the material may be subjected without having the inelastic deformation exceed a *specified amount* after a *specified time* at a *specified temperature.*

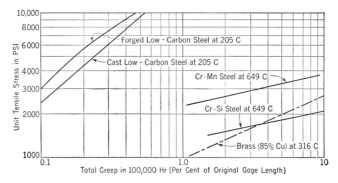

FIG. 3.10   Effect of stress on total creep.

The specific values of deformation, time, and temperature will be fixed by the conditions of usage of the material.   For example, in the discussion of failure by slip under static loading, a maximum allowable permanent set of 0.002 was suggested for determining the yield strength of steel for most machine parts.   To provide the same tolerance of permanent deformation under circumstances where creep might occur, a total creep of 0.002 during the life of the machine part would be set as the maximum allowable deformation.   The creep limit would be the maximum stress which could

---

[5] P. G. McVetty, "The Interpretation of Creep Tests," *Proceedings, American Society for Testing Materials,* Vol. 34 (1934), Part II, pp. 105-16.

be applied to the member without the total creep exceeding 0.002 at the end of the stated time. A total creep of 0.01 in 100,000 hr (11.4 years) has been suggested as a suitable upper limit for machine parts, while 0.01 in 10,000 hr has been used for lead cable sheathing.

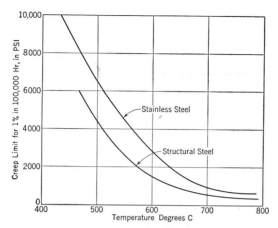

Fig. 3.11   Effect of temperature on creep limit.

To determine the creep limit of a material for a particular situation, several specimens of the material—each under a different stress—must be tested at the specific temperature, or results of tests under similar conditions must be available. If the deformation-time diagrams are plotted for each specimen, the initial creep and rate of creep may be determined as discussed in conjunction with Fig. 3.9. From these diagrams, the total creep at the end of the specified time interval may be evaluated for each of the stresses as $\epsilon - \epsilon_e$ or $\epsilon_a + \epsilon_c$.

If these values of total creep at the end of the time interval are plotted against the corresponding stresses, as in Fig. 3.10, the creep limit may be found from the curve through the points by determining the stress at which the actual total creep equals the specified maximum permissible total creep. For example, the creep limit of the brass in Fig. 3.10, based on a creep of 0.10 in 100,000 hr at 316 C, is 2500 psi.

As would be expected, the creep limit decreases as the temperature increases. Figure 3.11 indicates the variation in creep limit based on a deformation of 1 per cent in 100,000 hr for structural steel and a stainless steel.

As is evident from practical considerations, the evaluation of the creep limit must be accomplished in much less than 100,000 hr (or other anticipated life of the member). Hence the evaluation as outlined is based on the assumption that the rate of creep v, as determined in a short-time test, is constant over the entire life of the member. While the validity of this assumption seems to be reasonably well established for several materials, it is nevertheless an assumption which does not hold true automatically for all materials.

PROBLEMS

3.1 Name the type of loading to which each of the following members will be subjected in normal usage: (a) automobile bumper; (b) jaws of a stone crusher; (c) electrical transmission cable; (d) railroad car spring; (e) exterior wall of a building.

3.2 For what type of loading would each of the following products be designed? (a) Well casing; (b) turbine blades in jet engine; (c) watch spring; (d) automobile crankshaft; (e) guardrail of a bridge.

3.3 Name the type of loading to which each of the following members will be subjected in normal usage: (a) water main; (b) chimney; (c) piling for a pier; (d) automobile piston; (e) airplane propeller.

3.4 Name the principal type of loading for each of the following products: (a) diaphragm of aircraft altimeter; (b) impeller of centrifugal pump; (c) wheel of hand truck; (d) steamship hull; (e) railroad rail.

3.5 Calculate the load factor for the wings of a 10,000-lb airplane pulling out of a dive at 400 mph on a 2000-ft radius.

3.6 Evaluate the load factor for a weight w dropped from a height h onto the end of a cantilever beam. Assume that the proportional limit of the material is not exceeded.

3.7 A weight of 100 lb is dropped 4 in. onto the center of a steel beam $1\frac{1}{2}$ in. wide and 1 in. deep. The beam is simply supported on a 6-ft span. Determine the load factor, assuming that the beam absorbs one-half the total energy.

3.8 An airplane weighing 22,400 lb executes a turn in a horizontal plane (with the wings vertical) at a speed of 640 mph. Determine the equivalent static load for which the wings must be designed if the radius of the turn is to be 24,000 ft.

3.9 In general, is the load factor dependent on, or independent of, the magnitude of the weight? State one exception.

3.10 A unit for testing the resistance of individuals to blackout consists of a cage that revolves in a horizontal plane. If the distance from the cage to the center of rotation is 24 ft, at how many revolutions per minute must the unit be operated to develop a force of ten times the acceleration of gravity?

3.11 A steel rod $\frac{1}{2}$ in. in diameter with an effective length of 24 in. absorbs the energy due to a falling weight of 100 lb. The weight produces axial stress in the rod. From what distance must the weight be dropped to develop (a) a load factor of 2 and (b) a load factor of 4?

3.12 Name the properties that would be considered in measuring the resistance to failure of a material to be used for each of the following items: (a) floor beam; (b) piano wire; (c) tow rope; (d) watch spring; (e) cold chisel.

3.13 Name the properties used in measuring resistance to failure under stress that would be considered in selecting a material for each of the following uses: (a) spokes in a wheel; (b) band saw; (c) fishing pole; (d) pavement slab; (e) steam-shovel bucket.

3.14 Determine the diameter of rod required, of each of the following materials, to support a steady axial tensile load of 40,000 lb without fracture: (a) structural steel, Fig. 3.6; (b) gray cast iron, Fig. 8.5; (c) wrought iron, Fig. 8.8; (d) annealed copper, Fig. 9.1.

3.15 Determine the magnitude of the static axial tensile load which a 2-in. square rod of each of the following materials will support without failure by fracture: (a) cold-rolled aluminum, Fig. 9.2; (b) hot-rolled zinc, Fig. 9.9; (c) rolled nickel, Fig. 9.14; (d) malleable cast iron, Fig. 8.5.

3.16 (a) Which of the woods indicated in Fig. 10.6 would be the most suitable, on the basis of strength, for carrying a slowly applied axial compressive load of 40,000 lb without fracture?   (b) Determine the minimum cross-sectional area required.

3.17 How large an axial tensile load could a $\frac{1}{2}$-in. square bronze rod with 80 per cent copper (Fig. 9.18) be expected to carry without fracture?

3.18 Determine the diameter of a rod required, of each of the following materials, to absorb a dynamic load of 40,000 in.-lb without fracture.   Assume the effective length of each rod to be 8 in.   (a) Structural steel; (b) gray cast iron; (c) wrought iron; (d) annealed copper.

3.19 Determine the magnitude of the dynamic load that a $1\frac{1}{2}$-in. by $\frac{3}{4}$-in. by 8-in. rod of each of the following materials could absorb without fracture: (a) rolled annealed aluminum; (b) hot-rolled copper-zinc alloy No. 121; (c) wrought iron; (d) structural steel.

3.20 Assume that each of the materials in problem 3.19 is required to absorb without fracture the impact of a 300-lb weight dropped from a distance of 2 ft above the top of the material.   Determine the approximate required volume of each material.

3.21 How many cubic inches of structural steel would be required to absorb without fracture the kinetic energy in a 400-lb projectile traveling with a velocity of 2800 fps, if the energy of the dynamic load were absorbed uniformly and axially?

3.22 Determine the maximum axial load which may be dropped 4 in. onto the end of a structural-steel rod without fracturing it, if the rod is (a) $\frac{1}{2}$ in. in diameter with an effective length of 16 in. and (b) $\frac{1}{2}$ in. in diameter with an effective length of 16 in. but turned down to $\frac{1}{4}$-in. diameter for 8 in.

3.23 Approximately how large a block of soft rubber would be required to absorb the energy involved in stopping a 3000-lb automobile traveling at 30 mph if the average stress in the rubber is not to exceed 500 psi?

3.24 (a) Which of the woods indicated in Fig. 10.6 has the greatest modulus of toughness?   (b) How large a block of it would be required to avoid fracture under a dynamic load of 40,000 in.-lb if the length of the block is twice the least lateral dimension?

3.25 How large a dynamic load could a 6-in. by 6-in. by 12-in. block of the concrete of Fig. 2.5 be expected to absorb?

3.26 When placed in service, a structural-steel member failed by fracture under the action of an axial dynamic load.   It is proposed to replace the member with a 1.2 per cent carbon-steel part of the same dimensions.   (a) Would this substitution be satisfactory?   (b) Explain.

3.27 Compare the impact resistance of cold-rolled carbon steel in tension with that of hickory in compression.

3.28 Determine the length of time for which a shaft of the structural steel shown in Fig. 3.3 could be expected to serve when operated at 2000 rpm (a) if the maximum flexural stress is 20,000 psi, (b) if the maximum flexural stress is 30,000 psi, and (c) if the maximum flexural stress is 40,000 psi.

3.29 A shaft of stainless steel similar to that shown in Fig. 3.3 is subjected to a repeated flexural stress of 40,000 psi at 1800 rpm. (a) How long would it be expected to last? (b) How long would it last if the stress were reduced to 30,000 psi?

3.30 If a member composed of the stainless steel indicated in Fig. 3.3 has an elastic strength of 45,000 psi, how much steady load may be superimposed upon a completely reversed stress of 20,000 psi without causing failure?

3.31 A cold-rolled nickel shaft 2 in. in diameter is subjected to a reversed repeated stress of 20,000 psi. How large an axial tensile load could be added without danger of failure by progressive fracture? (Properties of nickel are given in Table 9.1 and Fig. 9.14.)

3.32 A cold-rolled aluminum shaft $1\frac{1}{2}$ in. in diameter carries a steady load of 20,000 lb. What would be the magnitude of the completely reversed stress that could be added without causing failure? (See Chapter 9 for properties of aluminum.)

3.33 Develop an expression for the magnitude of the maximum safe repeated stress S_r which may be superimposed upon a steady stress S_a for a material having an endurance limit S_e, a proportional limit S_p, and an ultimate strength S_u, according to the theories of (a) Goodman, (b) Gerber, and (c) Soderberg.

3.34 A structural-steel machine part is subjected to a push-pull load which fluctuates from 10,000 lb tension to 4000 lb compression. Determine the minimum cross-sectional area required for the machine part.

3.35 The load on a 2024-T4 aluminum-alloy connecting rod varies from 0 to 1500 lb. Determine the minimum cross-sectional area required for the rod.

3.36 Determine the diameter of rod of each of the following materials that would be required to support a static axial tensile load of 5 tons without failure by slip: (a) structural steel; (b) wrought iron; (c) annealed copper; (d) duralumin.

3.37 What maximum total static load would a 12-in. square member of the concrete in Fig. 2.5 support without danger of slip?

3.38 Determine the magnitude of static axial tensile load which a 1-in. by $1\frac{1}{2}$-in. bar of each of the following materials will support without danger of failure by slip: (a) cold-rolled aluminum; (b) hot-rolled zinc; (c) cold-rolled nickel; (d) malleable cast iron.

3.39 (a) Which of the woods indicated in Fig. 10.6 is the most resistant to failure by slip under steady load? (b) Determine the minimum cross-sectional area of a member which is to carry a load of 20 tons in axial compression.

3.40 Determine the yield strength of each of the following materials: (a) hickory in compression; (b) oak in compression; (c) duralumin in tension; (d) malleable cast iron in tension.

3.41 Determine the modulus of resilience of each of the following materials: (a) gray cast iron; (b) malleable cast iron; (c) wrought iron; (d) Monel metal.

3.42 Determine the energy load which a 2-in. by 2-in. by 8-in. specimen of each of the following materials could carry without failure by slip: (a) ash; (b) rolled brass (67 per cent Cu); (c) duralumin; (d) cold-rolled copper.

3.43 (a) Compare the static tensile loads which can be carried without slip by a 1-in. round mild-steel bar 1 ft long and a ¼-in. bar 20 ft long of the same material. (b) Compare the energy loads which they will carry without slip.

3.44 (a) Which will carry the greater static load without slip—hickory or cedar? (b) Which will carry the greater dynamic load without slip?

3.45 A 2-in. by 2-in. by 18-in. structural-steel rod is subjected to an axial dynamic load. If the rod absorbs 60 ft-lb of energy, how great a tensile stress is produced in the rod?

3.46 A certain structural-steel rod with an effective length of 10 in. is to be subjected to a dynamic load of 50 ft-lb. After the dynamic load is removed, it is to carry a slowly applied load of 80,000 lb. What must the diameter of the rod be if neither load is to produce slip?

3.47 Determine the maximum allowable static tensile load which can be left on a ¾-in. square steel rod at a temperature of 550 C.

3.48 Determine the maximum static tensile load which a 2-in. square stainless-steel rod may be expected to carry at 650 C.

3.49 A certain structural-steel member carries a static tensile load of 10,000 lb at 500 C. How much may the cross-sectional area of the member be reduced by substituting stainless steel?

3.50 A certain machine part made of structural steel carries a maximum static tensile load of 9000 lb at 550 C. If the temperature is increased to 650 C, what safe load will the member carry?

REFERENCES FOR FURTHER STUDY

AMERICAN SOCIETY FOR TESTING MATERIALS. *Standard Methods of Tension Testing of Metallic Materials,* Designation E 8.

BOYD, J. E., and SAMUEL B. FOLK. *Strength of Materials,* 5th ed. New York: McGraw-Hill Book Company, Inc., 1950.

DAVIS, R. E., and H. E. DAVIS. "Flow of Concrete Under Sustained Compressive Stress," *Proceedings, American Society for Testing Materials,* Vol. 30 (1930), Part II, p. 707.

GIBBONS, C. H. *Materials Testing Machines.* Instruments Publishing Company, 1935.

GOUGH, H. J. "Crystalline Structure in Relation to Failure of Metals—Especially Fatigue," *Proceedings, American Society for Testing Materials,* Vol. 33 (1933), Part II, p. 3.

LESSELLS, J. M. "Concerning the Yield Point in Tension," *Proceedings, American Society for Testing Materials,* Vol. 28 (1928), Part II, p. 387.

McVETTY, P. G. "Interpretation of Creep Test Data," *Proceedings, American Society for Testing Materials,* Vol. 43 (1943), p. 707.

MANN, H. C. "A Fundamental Study of the Design of Impact Test Specimens," *Proceedings, American Society for Testing Materials,* Vol. 37 (1937), Part II, p. 102.

————. "High-Velocity Tension-Impact Tests," *Proceedings, American Society for Testing Materials,* Vol. 36 (1936), Part II, p. 85.

————. "The Relation Between the Tension Static and Dynamic Tests," *Proceedings, American Society for Testing Materials,* Vol. 35 (1935), Part II, p. 323.

MOORE, H. F. *Materials of Engineering,* 5th ed. New York: McGraw-Hill Book Company, Inc., 1936.

————. "The Quest of Elasticity," *Civil Engineering* (1930), p. 171.

————, and M. B. MOORE. *Textbook of the Materials of Engineering,* 8th ed. New York: McGraw-Hill Book Company, Inc., 1953.

————, and J. B. KOMMERS. *The Fatigue of Metals.* New York: McGraw-Hill Book Company, Inc., 1928.

————, and OTHERS. *Creep and Fracture of Lead and Lead Alloys,* University of Illinois Engineering Experiment Station bulletins 243, 272, and 306.

NORTON, F. H. *Creep of Steel at High Temperatures.* New York: McGraw-Hill Book Company, Inc., 1929.

SAUVEUR, ALBERT. "The Torsion Test," *Proceedings, American Society for Testing Materials,* Vol. 38 (1938), Part II, p. 3.

SEELY, F. B. *Resistance of Materials,* 3d ed. New York: John Wiley & Sons, Inc., 1947.

"Symposium on Impact Testing," *Proceedings, American Society for Testing Materials,* Vol. 38 (1938), Part II, p. 21.

"Symposium on Significance of the Tension Test of Metals in Relation to Design," *Proceedings, American Society for Testing Materials,* Vol. 40 (1940), p. 501.

TAPSELL, H. J. *Creep of Metals.* London: Oxford University Press, 1931.

TEMPLIN, R. L. "The Determination and Significance of the Proportional Limit in the Testing of Materials," *Proceedings, American Society for Testing Materials,* Vol. 29 (1929), Part II, p. 523.

TIMOSHENKO, STEPHEN. *Strength of Materials,* Part II, *Advanced Theory and Problems,* 2d ed. New York: D. Van Nostrand Company, Inc., 1941.

GENERAL SOURCES

(1) *Proceedings, American Society for Testing Materials.* (2) Textbooks on strength of materials. (3) Trade publications on testing machines from Baldwin-Lima-Hamilton Corporation (Philadelphia), Tinius Olsen Testing Machine Company (Philadelphia), and Riehle Division of the American Machine and Metal Company (Moline, Illinois). (4) *Transactions of the American Society of Mechanical Engineers.*

4 Use of Properties in Design

4.1 Basis of Design

In general, the term design may be defined as the selection and arrangement of materials to satisfy a certain need. In engineering, this usually consists of two phases: (1) choosing the materials and planning the general, overall arrangement of the whole and (2) the detailing and dimensioning of the individual parts comprising the whole. For example, the designer of a bridge must first select the most suitable type of bridge—such as concrete arch, plate girder, or suspension—and determine the optimum overall arrangement of the members, and he must then detail each member so that it will serve its purpose to the best advantage. This second phase of the design—the detailing—is of equal importance, for all members in the bridge must function properly if the structure as a whole is to be satisfactory.

Discussion of the first phase of design is beyond the scope of this book, since that phase entails consideration of the social and economic need for a structure, its functions throughout its probable life, its environment, and many other factors, in addition to the materials involved. However, the second phase of design—the detailing—is within the scope of this text, since that phase entails a knowledge of the properties of the materials which are to be used in the individual parts of a structure.

Many qualities, such as appearance, stiffness, workability, and weight, usually enter into the detailing of the individual members and must be considered separately. One of the essential requirements is that the member be safe under all anticipated conditions of service. This means that the member must withstand all of the various loads and forces to which it will be subjected during the life of the structure and still function properly. Since the member is no more resistant to failure than the material of which it is composed, the material must be durable—it must resist disintegration, and it must have sufficient strength. To provide sufficient material, or material of sufficient strength to carry the load which will come upon that member, is one of the major responsibilities of the designer.

A step preliminary to the detailed designing of members is the determination of the total forces which must be carried by each individual member. Although even today this cannot always be done with accuracy, it was the first step which marked the advance of the modern engineer over the ancient builders, who apparently had no way of determining what total forces would bear upon their structures.

After the total forces acting on a member are known, or after reasonable values have been assumed, the engineer may compute the stresses in the member, and then compare the maximum stress with the strength of the proposed material or, more generally, with the allowable working stress. If the computed maximum stress is excessive, the size of the member must be altered, the shape of the member changed, or a more suitable material used.

4.2   Allowable Working Stress

The allowable working stress is the maximum *computed* unit stress which is permitted in a material. It is not a property of the material since its numerical value may be set by a building ordinance or other code of practice, by federal specifications, by the designing-office regulations, or by an engineer in charge of design.

The allowable working stress for a given material and use is always lower than the unit stress which would cause failure of the material under those conditions of use. For example, a tensile member in a steel bridge truss will in most cases fail (that is, cease to function properly) when the elastic strength of the material is exceeded. The American Society for Testing Materials (ASTM) specifies that steel for such a purpose must have a yield point (which is a measure of the elastic strength) of at least 33,000 psi, yet the allowable working stress in that same member would probably be set at 20,000 psi. This margin of stress is left because of (1) uncertainties concerning the *true properties* of the material, (2) the uncertainty of *future loadings,* and (3) the uncertainty of the *calculated maximum stresses.* The allowable working stress for a given member and material will depend upon the characteristics of the material and the amount and kind of damage which might result from failure.

The *true properties* of the material used in a structure may not be known for the following reasons:

1. The material which will actually be used in the structure is seldom tested for the particular property in question. For example, the ultimate tensile strength of a wire obviously cannot be determined if that piece of wire is to be used. The properties of the wire must be determined from another piece as similar as possible (no two pieces are identical). In some cases an approximate value of the

desired property may be obtained by correlation with another property determined in a nondestructive test. For example, the ultimate strengths of the ferrous metals are approximately 500 times their Brinell hardness numbers (sec. 5.10).

2. No engineering material is perfectly uniform. The nonuniformities of concrete, timber, and stone are readily apparent. The microscope may be needed to reveal the nonuniformities of other materials, such as metals, but they are present. Materials used in their natural state invariably contain defects, and no manufacturing process can completely eliminate flaws and imperfections from manufactured products. These irregularities may set up areas of high localized stress or weak spots from which unexpected failure may start, particularly under repeated stressing.

3. The properties of the material may become altered in service. Some of the metals, such as aluminum, brass, and bronze, undergo changes in properties for some time after being manufactured. Sometimes these changes may be predicted, but usually they are caused by unforeseen circumstances. Deterioration, such as rotting of wood, corrosion of metal, and spalling of concrete, may cause a change in properties and always reduces the effective size of the member. Accidental overloads during erection or service may cause stresses sufficiently high to alter the properties, as discussed in section 3.12.

There is also uncertainty in the *predicted loading* on the product at any future date because:

1. The magnitude of the expected routine loads is not known accurately in most cases. For example, the actual floor loads in a building cannot be predicted in advance. Therefore the structure is usually designed for a uniform floor load of 40, 50, or 100 lb per sq ft, the amount depending on the class of building. At best, the load on an airplane wing or tail surface can only be estimated. The amount of impact load to be absorbed by an automobile shock absorber when the car strikes an irregularity in the road is very difficult to evaluate.

2. The product may be called upon to carry larger loads than were anticipated at the time it was constructed. The designer of a railroad bridge cannot foresee the type of rolling stock which will be in use before the bridge is worn out. Hundreds of highway bridges in the United States became unsafe because they were designed to carry horse-and-buggy traffic. They were adequate at the time they were built, but were unsuitable for the heavy, high-speed motor trucks to which they were later subjected. Many

structures become obsolete long before the end of an otherwise useful life because of lack of judgment on the part of the engineer in providing for possible changes in loading requirements.

3. Unusual loading conditions may arise. The combination of a heavy snow or ice load on the roof of a building, a heavy wind load on one side, and a moving crowd of people on the inside has caused failure more than once. In the wake of every tornado, flood, or earthquake may be seen ample evidence of structural failure which might have been avoided. Automobile manufacturers try to simulate some of the more unusual loading conditions by subjecting their cars to spectacular tests on their proving grounds, and to endurance tests on the road or race track. Aircraft are subjected to extensive flight tests before certification or acceptance.

Because of the impossibility of knowing in most cases exactly what loads the product will be called upon to carry, the engineer should be generous in his estimate of probable loads. The cost of the additional material which will make a product safe is usually small in comparison with the inconvenience and expense of breakdown and replacement, not to mention the property damage and loss of life which may result in event of failure.

Even if the loads were accurately known, the *calculated stresses* in any member would be uncertain for the following reasons:

1. Assumptions regarding the behavior of the material may be in error. A number of approximations and assumptions are involved in all stress calculations. Conditions are idealized to simplify the mathematical operations in many types of analysis. For instance, when the unit stress in a member subjected to an axial tensile load is computed by dividing the load by the area, it is assumed that the material is both uniform and continuous; but neither of these assumptions is correct, as simple microscopic examination will reveal. This does not mean that such calculations are worthless, for they do serve a very useful purpose in giving average values which can be depended upon, as experience has shown. However, the type of stress calculations available for use will not give absolutely precise values of stress on any plane at any point in an actual material.

2. The calculation of stresses may be impracticable or impossible. The approximate stresses in the simple structural elements, such as beams, tension and compression members, columns, and circular shafts, may be readily calculated, but the mathematical determination of stresses in such members as noncircular shafts, gravity

arch dams, and other complex shapes is a tedious, if not impossible, task. New methods of stress calculation are being developed, and experimental methods have been devised for the determination of stresses, but there are still problems which have not been satisfactorily solved. In such cases, members must be designed on a cut-and-try basis.

4.3 Stress-Concentration Factor

The inaccuracy in the calculation of stresses by the simplest methods is often due to the concentration of stresses at certain points in a structural member or machine element. For example, a scratch, notch, groove, or hole, or an abrupt change in cross section, will result in localized stresses higher than those calculated by the ordinary formulas. ~~The stress-concentration factor is defined as the ratio of the actual stress existing on a given plane at a certain point to the stress as calculated by the ordinary methods without taking into account the possible causes of increased stress.~~

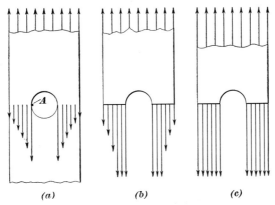

(a)   (b)   (c)

Fig. 4.1 Variation in stress near hole in tensile member.

For example, the stress-concentration factor for a small transverse hole in a member subjected to an axial tensile load is approximately equal to 3. That is, the stress at the edge of the hole is approximately three times the average stress on the cross section as determined by applying the ordinary formula $S = P/A$ and assuming that the hole was not there.

The material near the edge of the hole must carry more than its share of the load. In an ideal material the distribution of the tensile stress on a transverse plane through the center of the hole is as shown in Fig. 4.1a, provided that the stresses do not exceed the proportional limit. If the load is increased sufficiently to produce stresses above the proportional limit, the stress distribution will change. For example, if the material is

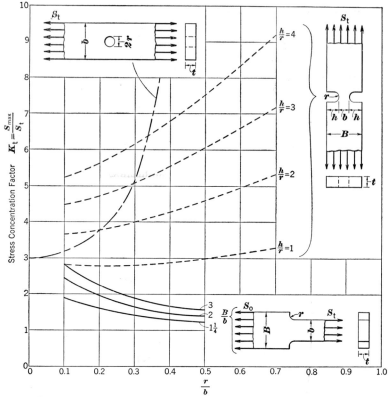

Fig. 4.2 Stress-concentration factors for axially loaded strips.

structural steel, an increasing load will cause an increased stress (and strain) at point A until the yield point is reached. Additional loads will produce additional strain at point A but will not increase the stress. However, additional stress must be developed on the transverse plane in order to balance the increased load. Hence the material adjacent to point A must develop increased stress, which will probably be above the yield point, and the stress distribution will be as indicated in Fig. 4.1b. If the material is sufficiently ductile, further increases in load or strain will produce a practically uniform stress distribution across the section, as indicated in Fig. 4.1c. In other words, the effect of the initial stress concentration is virtually nullified when yielding becomes general. However, if the material is brittle, the plastic redistribution of stress cannot occur and the stress concentration factor remains practically constant until the maximum stress reaches the ultimate strength of the material and failure occurs.

It is evident that the importance of the stress-concentration factor depends on the ability of the material to redistribute the stresses. This characteristic seems to be related to the ductility and grain size of the material. If the ductility is sufficiently great, the stress concentration factor may be disregarded under conditions of static loading; but if the material is brittle, the stress-concentration factor is highly significant.

Under conditions of dynamic loading or repeated loading, the stress concentration at discontinuities in a member must be taken into account for both ductile and brittle materials. Under the action of repeated loads a ductile material has the same characteristics as a brittle material, and a small crack which would be unimportant under a static load will produce a progressive failure if the load is repeated many times. A member containing a stress raiser will have a lower endurance limit than the same member without the stress raiser. The ratio of the two endurance limits is called the *endurance limit reduction factor*. In general, the endurance limit reduction factor for a given discontinuity is less than the stress-concentration factor for the same material, although it tends to approach the stress concentration factor if the material is brittle.

A dynamic load may be applied to a member so rapidly that there is not sufficient time for the completion of plastic flow necessary to distribute the stresses. A ductile material will then fail in the region of stress concentration in the same way as will a brittle material.

The stress-concentration factor should be used in design, except for ductile materials subjected only to static loading. In general, concentration of stress will occur at every change in cross section of the member. Values of stress-concentration factors for a few of the more common types of discontinuities are indicated in Fig. 4.2. It is apparent that the magnitude of the factor increases with the abruptness of the discontinuities.

In addition to the stress concentration which arises from *design features,* such as holes, threads, notches and re-entrant angles, other conditions that tend to act as stress raisers are caused by *accidental blemishes* arising from manufacturing processes, such as cracks, blowholes, slag inclusions, scratches, and tool marks. These blemishes are particularly undesirable, as one of them may serve as the starting point for a progressive fracture under repeated loading. A light scratch, scarcely visible to the unaided eye, may reduce the strength of a machine part to less than one-half of its potential value. Careful selection of materials, care in shaping operations, and careful inspection of the finished product are essential if fatigue failures are to be held at a minimum.

Stress concentration due to changes in cross section may be reduced by the proper use of fillets. In some cases, removal of material is more effective than adding material to reduce stress concentration. For example, threading a bolt beyond the section where the nut may be located reduces stress concentration materially, or drilling a hole at the end of a crack reduces the stress-concentration factor from a very large value to approximately 3.

While stress concentration is to be avoided as much as possible in most phases of design, it is also very useful. If it were not for stress concentration, most of the ordinary shaping operations, such as drilling, sawing, grinding, shearing, and punching, would be impossible.

4.4   Factor of Safety

The factor of safety is defined as the ratio of the strength of the material to the maximum calculated stress (or maximum amount of energy per unit volume) which will exist in the member. Since failure may occur in more than one way, a member may have more than one factor of safety. It may have a different factor of safety with respect to each combination of type of loading and type of failure that may occur.

For example, if a member is subjected to a static tensile stress of 18,000 psi the factor of safety with respect to failure by slip is the elastic strength divided by 18,000 psi; the factor of safety with respect to failure by creep is the creep limit divided by 18,000 psi; and the factor of safety with respect to failure by fracture is the ultimate strength divided by 18,000 psi. If the loading produced a repeated stress of 18,000 psi, the factor of safety with respect to fracture under the repeated loading would be the endurance limit divided by 18,000 psi. Similarly, the factor of safety with respect to failure by slip or fracture under dynamic loading would be found by dividing the modulus of resilience or the toughness by the maximum concentration of energy per cubic inch caused by the dynamic load.

ILLUSTRATIVE PROBLEM. A 2024-T4 aluminum-alloy tube is to be subjected to an axial tensile load of 8500 lb, which is applied with a load factor of 2.00. If the allowable working stress in tension is 20,000 psi, what are the factors of safety with respect to failure by slip and failure by fracture?

Solution. The first step is to determine the tensile stress in the tube. The working stress of 20,000 psi merely represents the maximum permissible stress; the actual tensile stress, upon which the factor of safety is based, depends on the actual size used. The minimum permissible cross-sectional area of the tube is

$$A = \frac{P}{S} = \frac{8500(2)}{20,000} = 0.850 \text{ in.}^2$$

A tubing list shows that the smallest tube which has an area of at least 0.85 in.^{2} is a tube with an outside diameter of 3.00 in. and a wall thickness of 0.095 in. Its area is 0.867 in.^{2} If this tube is used, the tensile stress will be

$$S = \frac{P}{A} = \frac{8500(2)}{0.867} = 19,600 \text{ psi}$$

Since the elastic strength of the material is 42,000 psi and the ultimate strength is 62,000 psi, the factor of safety with respect to failure by slip is

$$\text{F. S.} = \frac{42,000}{19,600} = 2.14$$

and the factor of safety with respect to failure by fracture is

$$\text{F. S.} = \frac{62,000}{19,600} = 3.16$$

In some fields, particularly aeronautical engineering, the term *margin of safety* is used. It is equivalent to the factor of safety minus 1. In the preceding illustrative problem, the margin of safety would be 1.14 if slip were the criterion of failure and would be 2.16 if fracture were the criterion.

Allowable working stresses are frequently set by dividing the strength of the material by an appropriate factor of safety. The minimum factor of safety to be permitted in a given product depends on the uniformity of the material, the possibility of its deterioration, the accuracy with which the predicted loads are known, the accuracy with which the stresses can be calculated from the loads, and the damage which would be done in the event of failure. Under some conditions a factor of safety of slightly over 1 might be acceptable; while under other circumstances a factor of safety of 20 would not be excessive. Values between 3 and 10 are common.

A more appropriate name for the factor of safety would be the *factor of ignorance,* since it is introduced to provide for all the uncertainties of design and material. A factor of safety of 3, for example, does *not* mean that the member will carry three times the design load without failure. It only means that the estimated strength of the material is about three times the stress computed on the basis of the designer's *best guess* of the probable future loading on the structure.

As engineers learn more about stress analysis, as methods of producing more-uniform materials are developed, and as more information is discovered about the behavior of materials, the allowance for the unknown factors may be decreased, and careful design will enable the engineer to utilize materials more efficiently and effectively. However, the uncertainty of loading will remain in most cases, necessitating a factor of safety greater than 1.

4.5 Biaxial and Triaxial Stress

In a structural member subjected to an axial stress, as tension for example, the factor of safety may be easily calculated if the load and the properties of the material are known. However, if the member is also subjected to a stress at right angles to the original axial stress, the calculation of the factor of safety is a more complicated procedure because of the presence of additional stress.

The block in Fig. 4.3a represents a small cube subjected to an axial compression. ~~If a stress is acting at right angles to the stress in the *x* direction, as in Fig. 4.3b, the stress situation is said to be biaxial. Biaxial stresses are developed in floor slabs, shafts, and boilers.~~

~~If stress is acting in each of the three coordinate directions, as indicated in Fig. 4.3c, the stress is said to be triaxial.~~ Triaxial stress would be developed in a block held beneath the surface of a liquid. It is also developed in thick-walled pressure vessels, and in heavy cannon barrels.

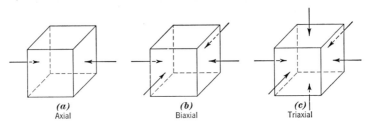

(a)
Axial   (b)
Biaxial   (c)
Triaxial

FIG. 4.3   States of stress.

The apparent properties of a material are affected by the state of stress to which it is subjected. For example, the material in the block in Fig. 4.3a might be found to have an ultimate compressive strength of 5000 psi. That same block could be subjected to triaxial stress, as in Fig. 4.3c, and the stress intensity could be increased to 10,000 psi without causing failure of the material, because the stress along each axis serves to reinforce the material against failure as a result of the other stresses. If the same block were subjected to compression along the *x* axis, as in Fig. 4.3a, and to tension along the *y* and *z* axes, failure might be produced long before the stress along any one of the axes reached 5000 psi. Where one axial stress is compression and the stress along a perpendicular axis is tension, each stress tends to intensify the effect of the other.

The properties of materials are normally expressed in terms of *axial stress*. Therefore it is important that the engineer who designs other than the simplest of structural units know something about the effects of biaxial and triaxial stress upon the safety of a structure for which he is responsible.

4.6 Theories of Failure

The attempts to predict the stresses which a material will withstand without failure when subjected to biaxial and triaxial stresses have led to the statement of several theories of failure.

Since the real cause of failure is not known, each of the theories of failure is based on a different assumption of the probable cause of failure. Each of the theories gives results which agree with actual tests under some combinations of stresses, and, in general, fails to give correct results under other combinations of stresses.   Of the many theories which have been proposed, five have found rather general use: the maximum normal stress theory, or Rankine's theory; the maximum strain theory, or St. Venant's theory; the maximum shearing stress theory, or Guest's theory; the maximum strain-energy theory; and the maximum distortion-energy theory, or the Hencky–von Mises theory.

Maximum-normal-stress theory (Rankine's theory).   The maximum-normal-stress theory is based on the assumption that a material will fail when the maximum normal unit stress on any plane in the material reaches a certain limiting value which is equal to the normal stress at failure under axial loading.   Naturally it yields satisfactory results, and is convenient to use, when the loading is axial, so it is the most commonly accepted theory. However, it does not yield satisfactory results with biaxial or triaxial stresses, as indicated in section 4.5.

Maximum-strain theory (St. Venant's theory).   The maximum-strain theory is based on the assumption that a material will fail when the unit strain reaches a maximum limiting value which is equal to the unit strain at failure under simple axial loading.

Maximum-shearing-stress theory (Guest's theory).   The maximum-shearing-stress theory is based on the assumption that a material will fail when the maximum shearing unit stress reaches a limiting value equal to the maximum unit shearing stress at failure under axial loading.

Maximum-strain-energy theory.   This theory is based on the assumption that a material will fail when the maximum-strain-energy per unit volume reaches a limiting value equal to the energy absorbed per unit volume at failure under axial loading.

Maximum-distortion-energy theory (Hencky–von Mises theory).   The maximum-distortion-energy theory expresses the condition of failure in equation form, as follows:

$$(S_u - S_v)^2 + (S_v - S_w)^2 + (S_w - S_u)^2 = 2S^2_m$$

in which S_u, S_v, and S_w are, respectively, the three maximum stresses (principal stresses) on three mutually perpendicular planes at the critical point, and S_m is the stress which an axially loaded specimen of the material will withstand at failure.

It will be noted that each of the terms in parentheses is twice one of the three maximum shearing stresses, and it can be shown that the sum of the three terms is equal to the strain energy stored in the material in shear when it is subjected to the principal stresses S_u, S_v, and S_w.   The theory has become known as the maximum-distortion-energy theory because the shearing stresses skew or distort a differential cube of the material.   It was originally developed by Hencky—and also by von Mises independently.

In many instances the differences between the results obtained from the various theories are not significant, being much less than the probable error involved in assuming the loads which the members will be called upon to carry. In situations where the loads are known accurately, and wherever appreciable differences do exist in the results obtained from the different theories, the member should be designed so that it will be safe under the assumptions of each of the theories.

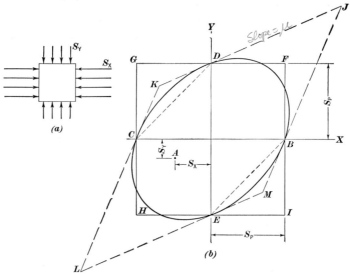

FIG. 4.4 Comparison of theories of failure.

A comparison of the different theories of failure for the condition of biaxial stress may be made on the basis indicated in Fig. 4.4. The device shown[1] may be extended to the condition of triaxial stress. Figure 4.4a indicates a small block subjected to stress in the x and y directions. If the intensity of stress in the x direction is plotted in the x direction on a graph, and the intensity of stress in the y direction is plotted in the y direction, from an arbitrary origin, any combination of stresses can be represented by a single point on the graph. If tension is considered positive and compression negative, the combination of stresses in Fig. 4.4a will give a point in the third quadrant, as indicated by point A in Fig. 4.4b.

If failure by slip under static load is being considered, the proportional limit may be taken as the criterion of failure. If, in Fig. 4.4a, S_y is zero

[1] B. P. Haigh, "The Strain-Energy Function and the Elastic Limit," *Engineering*, Vol. 109 (1920), p. 148; H. M. Westergaard, "The Resistance of Ductile Materials to Combined Stresses in Two or Three Directions Perpendicular to One Another," *Journal of the Franklin Institute* (1920); reprints of British Association for the Advancement of Science, 1919–23.

and S_x is increased in tension, failure will occur when S_x is equal to the proportional limit S_p. This condition will be represented by point B in Fig. 4.4b. Similarly, point C represents failure under an axial compressive load in the x direction, and points D and E represent, respectively, failures under axial tensile and compressive loads in the y direction.

Under the assumption of the maximum-stress theory, failure will occur whenever the stress in the x direction or the y direction exceeds S_p, regardless of the stress in the other direction. According to Fig. 4.4b, this means that failure will occur whenever the point representing the stress situation either has an abscissa which places it to the right of B or to the left of C, or has an ordinate which places it above D or below E. In other words, if the point falls outside the square $FGHI$ failure will be expected, and if the point falls within $FGHI$ the material will not fail. Actual test results from some ductile metals show the boundary between safe and unsafe stresses to have a shape something like the ellipse drawn in Fig. 4.4b. That ellipse indicates the maximum-stress theory to be unsafe where the stresses are of unlike sign (second and fourth quadrants) and to be conservative where the stresses are of like sign (first and third quadrants).

The limiting diagram for the maximum-strain theory may be shown to have a shape something like the figure $JKLM$ in Fig. 4.4b. The exact shape depends on the value of Poisson's ratio (sec. 5.3) for the material.

The maximum-shearing-stress theory gives the hexagon $BFDCHE$ for the criterion of safety. The curve for the test results indicates that the theory gives results on the safe side.

The maximum-strain-energy theory and the maximum-distortion-energy theory give ellipses similar in general form to the curve of test results. However, the maximum-strain-energy method is more difficult to apply than the others.

Although the validity of the curve of test results has not been established for all materials, the general indications are that the maximum-stress theory gives results on the safe side when a brittle material is involved, and that the maximum-distortion-energy theory gives the best results for a ductile material. However, the maximum-shearing-stress theory gives safe results under most conditions and is stipulated in many design codes.

PROBLEMS

4.1 A 2-in. square bar 12 ft long made of structural steel similar to the material shown in Fig. 3.6 is used as a balcony hanger to support a static tensile load of 80,000 lb. What is the factor of safety (a) with respect to failure by fracture and (b) with respect to failure by slip?

4.2 How many foot-pounds of energy load could the bar in problem **4.1** carry before it would (a) be permanently deformed and (b) pull in two?

4.3 A $\frac{1}{2}$-in. round stainless-steel bar used as a close-fitting machine part is subjected to a total axial tensile load of 400 lb. What is its factor of safety with respect to failure by creep at (a) 450 C and (b) 650 C?

4.4 An annealed aluminum bar (Fig. 9.2) $\frac{3}{4}$ in. by $1\frac{1}{2}$ in. in cross section is subjected to a slowly applied tensile load of 10,000 lb. What is the factor of safety with respect to failure by (a) slip and (b) rupture?

4.5 A member of cold-rolled nickel is subjected to a repeated stress of 10,000 psi. What is its factor of safety? (See Table 9.1.)

4.6 A structural-steel member $1\frac{1}{2}$ in. by 1 in. in cross section is subjected to an axial load which produces a stress of 30,000 psi. Determine the factor of safety with respect to failure by slip if the load is (a) static and (b) dynamic.

4.7 A structural-steel tie rod 1 in. in diameter is subjected to a static load which stretches it $\frac{1}{16}$ in. in a length of 10 ft. Determine the factor of safety with respect to failure by (a) slip and (b) fracture.

4.8 If the allowable single-shear load on a 2024-T4 aluminum-alloy rivet $\frac{1}{4}$ in. in diameter is 429 lb, what is the factor of safety with respect to failure by fracture?

4.9 A 2017-T4 aluminum-alloy tube with an outside diameter of 2 in. and a wall thickness of 0.065 in. carries an axial tensile load of 10,000 lb. Determine the factor of safety with respect to failure by slip.

4.10 A Douglas-fir beam 2 in. by 4 in. (actual dimensions $1\frac{5}{8}$ in. by $3\frac{5}{8}$ in.) is simply supported on an 8-ft span with the long dimension vertical. Determine the maximum uniform load which the beam will support with a factor of safety of 4 with respect to failure by slip.

4.11 A slowly applied axial tensile load acting on a structural-steel rod $\frac{3}{4}$ in. in diameter stores 13 ft-lb of energy in a 4-ft length. Determine the factor of safety with respect to failure by (a) slip and (b) fracture.

4.12 (a) Should the type of inspection of a machine part after fabrication have any influence on the maximum permissible working stress? (b) Explain.

4.13 A machine part is to support a slowly applied axial tensile load of 120,000 lb. (a) Determine the diameter required if a working stress of 18,000 psi is specified. (b) What is the factor of safety with respect to failure by fracture if the member is made of structural steel?

4.14 What diameter of structural-steel member would be required to absorb a dynamic load of 10,000 ft-lb in a length of 8 in. with a factor of safety of 2 with respect to failure by fracture?

4.15 A structural-steel member which is 2 in. in diameter and which has an effective length of 16 in. has a factor of safety of 2 with respect to failure by slip under dynamic load. What is its approximate factor of safety with respect to failure by fracture under the same dynamic load?

4.16 If a working stress of 600 psi in compression parallel to the grain is specified for air-dry Douglas fir under a static load, what is the approximate factor of safety? (See Fig. 10.5.)

4.17 To what maximum temperature may a $\frac{1}{2}$-in. square stainless-steel rod carrying a continuous load of 1000 lb be subjected if it is to have a factor of safety of 2 with respect of failure by creep?

4.18 A structural-steel plate $\frac{1}{2}$ in. thick and 8 in. wide has a $\frac{13}{16}$-in. hole drilled through the center. To what maximum static load may the plate be subjected in tension if any appreciable inelastic action would make it unfit for further use?

4.19 Determine the maximum load which may be applied to the member in the accompanying illustration if the maximum tensile stress is not to exceed 20,000 psi.

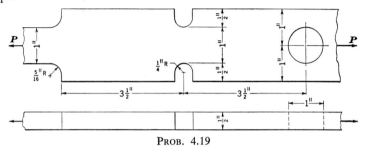

PROB. 4.19

4.20 Determine the maximum stress developed in the member represented in the accompanying illustration.

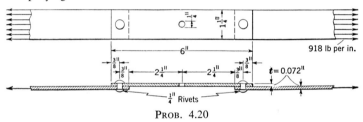

PROB. 4.20

4.21 The machine part shown in the accompanying illustration is made of structural steel. Determine the factor of safety with respect to failure by (a) any inelastic action and (b) fracture.

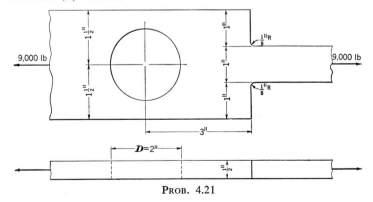

PROB. 4.21

4.22 An axial load applied to a 2017-T4 aluminum-alloy machine part develops a stress which fluctuates between 9000 and 23,000 psi tension. Determine the factor of safety of the member with respect to failure by slip.

4.23 A cylindrical boiler with an internal diameter of 6 ft is made of structural-steel plate ¼ in. thick. A factor of safety of 3.00 with respect to failure by slip must be maintained. Determine the maximum allowable internal pressure. Assume that the welded joint has an efficiency of 90 per cent.

4.24 A certain structural-steel rod 12 in. long is to carry, at different times, an impact load of 100 ft-lb and a slowly applied load of 150,000 lb. What is the minimum permissible diameter of the rod if it is to have a factor of safety of 3 with respect to failure by slip?

4.25 Determine the allowable working stress in each of the following materials, using a factor of safety of 4 with respect to failure by slip: (a) annealed copper; (b) cast aluminum; (c) cold-rolled nickel; (d) Monel metal.

4.26 Specify a working stress for each of the following materials under repeated loading, using a factor of safety of 6: (a) annealed copper; (b) cold-rolled aluminum; (c) magnesium; (d) aluminum alloy 2017-T4.

5 Qualities Other Than Strength

5.1 Importance of Other Qualities

In section 1.3 durability, appearance, and economy were cited as the three primary factors to be considered in selecting the most suitable material for a given use. In chapters 3 and 4 the factors related to one phase of durability, namely strength, or resistance to failure under load, were discussed.

However, the relative importance of strength in the design of a structure may easily be overemphasized; or, at least, other important properties may receive less than their proper share of attention. To be sure, a material must have sufficient strength to carry the loads which will be put upon it during its life, but in many products these loads are so small that almost any of the common structural materials would be satisfactory. For example, the loads on the interior wall of a building are often so small that—from the standpoint of strength alone—wood, stone, concrete, steel, brick, tile, or glass might be used. Appearance and economy, as well as the other phases of durability, then become the controlling elements in selecting the most suitable material. In Table 5.1 are listed the principal qualities other than strength which may be involved in the selection of a material for a given use, and also the properties used to evaluate them.

5.2 Durability

Durability, in general, denotes the presence of those qualities of a material which enable it to function properly and to resist destruction over a long period of time. Just as there is no single property which will measure the resistance of a material to failure under all kinds of loadings, so there is no single property which serves as an absolute measure of durability under all circumstances, because there are many forms which the destructive forces may take.

In addition to resistance to failure under load, durability may involve resistance to weathering, resistance to freezing and thawing action, resistance

TABLE 5.1

CHARACTERISTICS OF MATERIALS OTHER THAN STRENGTH

Characteristics	Measured By	Units
Resistance to disintegration ...	Durability	None
Change in dimensions	Modulus of elasticity	Psi
	Poisson's ratio	None
	Coefficient of thermal expansion	Per deg F [or C]
	Rate of shrinkage	Per hr
	Rate of creep	Per hr
Limiting unit strain	Elasticity	None
	Percentage elongation	None
Workability	Ductility	None
	Malleability	None
	Plasticity	None
Hardness	Percentage wear	None
	Brinell number	Kg per sq mm
	Rockwell number	None
	Knoop number	None
	Scleroscope number	None
	Vickers number	None
Weight	Specific weight	Lb per cu ft
	Density	Slugs per cu ft
	Specific gravity	None
Particle size	Mean diameter	In. or microns
	Particles per unit area	Per sq in. [or sq mm]
Energy retention	Mechanical hysteresis	In.-lb per cu in.
	Electrical hysteresis	None
	Damping capacity	None
Electrical resistance	Resistivity	Ohms per cc
Thermal capacity	Specific heat	Btu per lb per deg F
Thermal conductivity	Thermal conductivity	Btu per hr per sq ft per in. per deg F
	Coefficient of transmission	Btu per hr per sq ft per deg F
Acoustical absorption	Coefficient of absorption	None
	Coefficient of reflection	None

to corrosion, resistance to rotting, resistance to abrasion, or resistance to changes in properties, depending on the environment in which the material is to be used.

Many data have been published giving average useful lives of various materials. The engineer must be very careful in his use of such data in predicting the life of a product, making sure that there are no important differences between the environment (and other conditions) for which the data were given and the conditions under which the product is actually to be used. Such items as range of temperature, range of humidity, or smoke content in the atmosphere may have a pronounced effect upon durability. For example, the famous obelisk known as Cleopatra's Needle, which had withstood well over thirty centuries of Egyptian climate without apparent deterioration, had to be coated with paraffin to prevent the inscriptions from becoming entirely illegible after only a few years in New York.

5.3 Change in Dimensions

For many products a relatively small alteration in size or shape will prove harmful, even though the strain produced is not sufficient to cause inelastic action. A change in the dimensions of a member will result from a change in the load on the member, a change in temperature, or a change in moisture content. It may be caused by chemical action or by bombardment of the material with neutrons or other nuclear particles. Various properties have been defined and evaluated to assist the engineer in predicting changes in dimensions. These include: (1) modulus of elasticity, or axial stiffness under axial stress; (2) Poisson's ratio, for evaluating the strain at right angles to the applied stress; (3) coefficient of thermal expansion, for evaluating the change in dimensions due to a temperature change; (4) rate of shrinkage (or swelling) at constant temperature; and (5) rate of creep, for evaluating the change in dimensions due to plastic action under constant stress.

Modulus of elasticity. The modulus of elasticity, also known as Young's modulus (or sometimes modulus of rigidity, for shearing or torsional stresses) is defined as the rate of increase of stress with respect to strain below the proportional limit. It may be expressed in equation form as follows:

$$E = \frac{\Delta S}{\Delta \epsilon} \tag{5.1}$$

in which E = the modulus of elasticity;
ΔS = the change in the unit stress;
$\Delta \epsilon$ = the change in unit strain corresponding to ΔS.

The modulus of elasticity is therefore equal to the slope of the stress-strain diagram. Unless otherwise stated, it is taken as the slope of the initial straight-line portion of the diagram. For example, the modulus of elasticity of the steel indicated in the stress-strain diagram in Fig. 3.7 is evaluated as follows:

$$E = \frac{30,000}{0.001} = 30,000,000 \text{ psi}$$

In addition to being useful for predicting the change in length of a member under axial stress, the modulus of elasticity enters into the expression for the deflection of a beam and the expression for the load-carrying capacity of a long slender column. The deflection of a beam is inversely proportional to E, while the load-carrying capacity of a long slender column which will fail by buckling is directly proportional to E.

With the exception of nickel, which is slightly stiffer, steel has the highest modulus of elasticity of the more common engineering materials. Its value in tension or compression is approximately 30,000,000 psi, regardless of the strength or other characteristics of the steel. Tin, and magnesium and its alloys, have moduli of elasticity of approximately 6,000,000 psi; gold, silver, and aluminum and its alloys have moduli between 10,000,-000 and 11,000,000 psi; and copper and its alloys have moduli from 15,000,000 psi to 17,000,000 psi. For most of the metals, the modulus of rigidity is about 40 per cent of the modulus of elasticity.

Poisson's ratio. As a material is stressed it will deform both in the direction of the stress and at right angles to the stress. The ratio of the unit strain at right angles to the stress to the unit strain in the direction of the stress (for axial loading and stresses below the proportional limit) is called Poisson's ratio. Expressed in equation form, the relationship becomes

$$\mu = \frac{\epsilon_t}{\epsilon_s} \qquad (5.2)$$

in which μ = Poisson's ratio;
   ϵ_t = the unit strain in the transverse direction;
   ϵ_s = the unit strain in the direction of the stress.

Poisson's ratio is determined by direct measurement in a tensile or compressive test of the material. It is equal to approximately 0.30 for steel and 0.33 for most of the common nonferrous metals. Thus, if an axial stress of 30,000 psi is applied to a steel rod, the unit strain in the direction of the stress will be 0.0010, Young's modulus being taken as 30,000,000 psi. The unit strain along any line at right angles to the applied stress will be (0.30)(0.0010), or 0.00030 in. per in.; and if the applied strain is tensile, the strain at right angles to it will be compressive, and vice versa.

The ratio is useful for determining the relationship between stress and deformation in situations where there is stress in more than one direction, as in a boiler subjected to internal pressure or in a floor slab which is bending in two directions.

Coefficient of thermal expansion. The coefficient of thermal expansion is defined as the unit strain produced in a material by a change of 1 deg in temperature. Its units are therefore the reciprocal of temperature. For example, the coefficient of thermal expansion of structural steel is about 0.0000065 per deg F. Values of the coefficient for various elements are given in Table A in the Appendix.

This coefficient is useful in predicting the size of expansion joints which must be left in bridges, pavement slabs, and similar structures. It is also used in determining the "thermal stresses" developed in members which are restrained from expanding or contracting when subjected to a temperature change.

Rate of shrinkage. Several of the important engineering materials, such as wood and concrete, undergo a change in volume after the preliminary shaping operation. In timber, shrinkage is generally due to drying and is responsible for the warping of lumber which occurs under certain conditions. Volume change at constant temperature in concrete occurs as a result of change in the moisture content accompanied by chemical change in the cement paste. The rate of shrinkage is expressed as the amount of unit strain occurring per unit of time.

Rate of creep. The rate of creep, which is evaluated as the change in unit strain under a constant stress per unit of time, is indicative of the rapidity of plastic deformation under that stress. It may be evaluated as the slope of a strain-time curve, and is expressed as unit strain per hour (or per cent unit strain per 10,000 hr). If neither the stress nor the temperature is excessive, the rate of strain of many metals is approximately constant for some time after creep begins, and the strain-time curve is a straight line, as shown by the portion AB of the strain-time curve of Fig. 3.8. It is this characteristic which makes possible the determination of a creep limit by the method outlined in section 3.14.

5.4 Limiting Unit Strain

In a material subjected to axial stress, two limiting values of unit strain are important in indicating a fundamental alteration in the behavior of the material. They are the unit strain at the elastic limit and the unit strain at fracture. The unit strain at the elastic limit is known as the *elasticity*. However, for all practical purposes, the elasticity may be evaluated as the unit strain at the proportional limit. It indicates the maximum unit strain to which the material may be subjected without having inelastic action occur, and is thereby a measure of the extent of elastic action possible.

The unit strain at rupture or at the ultimate load is important in indicating the maximum strain which the material will withstand without failure by fracture. It is usually expressed as a percentage and is known as the *percentage elongation* when evaluated in a tensile test. In a compressive test the pertinent measure is the unit strain at the ultimate load. Percentage elongation is used as one measure of ductility, as discussed in section 5.6.

5.5 Workability

Workability denotes the capacity of a material for being shaped. Since all materials must be shaped in some manner before they can be utilized as structural elements, workability is one of the most important characteristics of a material. Some materials which have desirable properties for certain uses cannot be used economically because of difficulty in forming the material to the desired shapes.

Because of the difference in characteristics of different materials, many methods of shaping have been devised, and other methods not yet developed may make possible the economical utilization of some desirable materials hitherto unusable. For example, the use of wrap-around windshields for automobiles is a direct result of a development of shaping processes.

Since different materials are best shaped by radically different methods, such as forging, stamping, casting, cutting, grinding, rolling, hammering, extruding, sawing, or splitting, there can be no one property which will serve as a measure of the workability of all materials.

Ductility, malleability, plasticity, and hardness are other qualities related to workability, and, like it, frequently have considerable influence upon the cost of the finished product.

5.6 Ductility

DISREGARD

The term *ductility*, as generally used, denotes the capacity of a material for being drawn into wire. As used in engineering, it signifies a large capacity for plastic (nonelastic) deformation in tension or shear without rupture, as contrasted with brittleness, which signifies little capacity for plastic deformation without failure.

Materials are frequently characterized as ductile or brittle, the proper term depending on the relative amount of plastic deformation a material will undergo before rupture. As has been indicated previously, another distinction between ductile and brittle materials may be made on the basis of the relative ultimate strengths in tension and shear. If the ultimate tensile strength is comparatively low, the material is brittle and will fail in tension with a spiral fracture when loaded in torsion. If the ultimate shearing strength is comparatively low, the material will fail in shear at right angles to the axis when loaded in torsion. The latter action is typical of ductile materials.

There is no single property which serves as a true quantitative measure of ductility. However, the *percentage elongation* (or unit strain at rupture) in an 8-in. gage length or in a 2-in. gage length is frequently specified in standards as a check upon ductility. Since a ductile material "necks down" at the section of fracture, the percentage elongation in 2 in. will be greater than the percentage elongation in 8 in. for the same specimen. Therefore, if the ultimate elongation is to be significant, the gage length over which it is measured must be specified.   The *percentage reduction in the cross-sectional area* of a tensile specimen at the fractured section gives an indication of ductility.   Various forms of *bend tests,* such as bending a bar 180 deg around a pin having the same diameter as the bar, are also used to measure ductility.

A material which is ductile will take a considerable amount of local punishment without injury to the rest of the piece.   As this quality is very desirable in many of the shaping operations, such as rolling, extruding, drilling, punching, and cutting, ductility usually adds to the workability of a material.

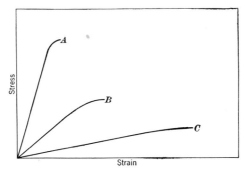

FIG. 5.1   Comparative stress-strain diagrams.

Ductility also contributes to, but does not alone control, toughness. The area under the stress-strain diagram, which is a measure of toughness, is dependent upon both strength and ductility.   Figure 5.1 shows the stress-strain diagrams for three materials.   Material A is comparatively strong and brittle, while material C is comparatively weak and ductile. Yet all three materials have the same modulus of toughness, as is shown by the fact that the areas under their stress-strain diagrams are equal.

5.7 Malleability

Malleability denotes the capacity of a material for withstanding plastic deformation in compression without fracture.   It bears some relationship to ductility, which is the capacity for withstanding plastic deformation in tension or shear.   No general method, applicable to all materials, has been devised for measuring malleability, although this property is of importance in rolling, forging, and similar operations.   Materials which are rolled, pressed, or hammered into thin shapes must be malleable.   Gold is one of the most malleable of materials.

The term malleable is also used to designate a type of cast iron which has been given a specific heat treatment. Malleable cast iron is malleable only by comparison with other cast irons.

5.8 Plasticity

~~Plasticity denotes in a general way the capacity of a material for being molded or worked into shape under pressure, and is related to viscosity.~~ Metals become more plastic as the temperatures increase toward the melting points; concrete and similar materials are plastic before they harden; and bituminous materials become plastic at summer temperatures. However, each of these manifestations of nonelastic action requires a different technique of measurement, so no single property has been devised for comparing the plasticities of all materials.

5.9 Hardness

The term *hardness* is used to designate several qualities. Hardness may indicate resistance to abrasion, resistance to scratching, resistance to cutting, or resistance to shaping. It may denote strength, stiffness, brittleness, resilience, or toughness, or combinations of these qualities, its meaning depending on the material and on the use to which the material is to be subjected. Consequently, a number of techniques have been developed for obtaining a quantitative measure of hardness. Among the important indices of hardness are *percentage wear,* determined by abrasion tests, and several so-called *hardness numbers,* determined by indentation tests.

Percentage wear. For materials such as stone and brick, where resistance to abrasion is a desirable quality, hardness is determined by a wear test. For stone, one standard test consists in holding a 1-in.-diameter cylinder of the stone under a pressure of 1250 gm against a revolving horizontal table on which is a standard abrasive sand. The hardness is evaluated as the percentage loss in weight for 1000 revolutions. Another type of wear test used for stone[1] and for brick[2] consists in placing a specified weight of the material in a drum containing steel or cast-iron spheres and rotating the unit at a specified speed. ~~The percentage loss in weight after a specified number of revolutions is taken as an index of the hardness.~~

Brinell number. In the Brinell test,[3] which is used for metals, a 3000-kg load (500 kg for nonferrous metals) is applied to a flat surface of the metal for 15 sec through a steel ball 10 mm in diameter. ~~The Brinell hardness number is evaluated as the load divided by the area of the spherical indentation remaining after the load is removed.~~

---

[1] ASTM Designations D 2 and C 131.
[2] ASTM Designation C 7.
[3] ASTM Designation E 10.

Rockwell number.   In the Rockwell test,[4] which is also used for metals, a hardened steel ball $\frac{1}{16}$ in. in diameter (Rockwell B) or a standard diamond point (Rockwell C) is pressed into the material under a load of 10 kg.   The load is increased to 100 kg for the Rockwell B or to 150 kg for the Rockwell C, and the increase in penetration for the increase in the load is measured in terms of a Rockwell hardness number.

Knoop hardness number.   The Knoop hardness number is evaluated by an indentation test[5] which differs from the Brinell and Rockwell tests in the type of indentor used.   The Knoop indentor consists of a diamond ground to pyramidal form to produce a diamond-shaped indentation with a ratio of diagonals of 7.11 to 1.   The load applied ranges from 25 to 3600 gm, the choice depending on the hardness of the material.   After the load is removed, the length of the long diagonal is measured, and the Knoop hardness number is computed as the ratio of the load to the projected area of the resultant indentation.   The principal advantage of the Knoop hardness test is that the indentor produces an impression without the ridging or sinking in near the edge of the indentation which may develop in the Brinell test, and thus a more accurate measurement is possible.   This hardness test is well adapted for soft materials as well as hard materials, and is useful in evaluating the hardness of thin specimens.

Vickers hardness number.   The Vickers hardness test utilizes a pyramidal diamond indentor and a light load.

The Brinell test, the Rockwell test, the Knoop test, and the Vickers test, as well as several similar tests, such as the Monotron test, measure the resistance of the material to indentation.

Scleroscope number.   In the Scleroscope test, a small standard weight is dropped from a specified height onto the specimen, and the height of rebound is measured as the Scleroscope number.   This number indicates the surface hardness of the material and is, in general, related to the resilience.

Although the several indentation tests are empirical, the results obtained from them can, within limits, be correlated with one another and with other properties of the material.   For example, for the ferrous alloys (excluding cast iron), the Brinell hardness number is approximately 10 times the Rockwell C number[6] and is 7 times the Scleroscope number. Also, the ultimate tensile strength is approximately 500 times the Brinell hardness number.

[4] ASTM Designation E 18.

[5] V. E. Lysaght, "Micro-Hardness Testing of Materials," *Materials and Methods,* Vol. 22 (1945), p. 1079.

[6] A set of hardness-number conversion tables for steel is given in ASTM Designation E 48 and in *Metals Handbook.*

The indentation tests are widely used in industry as a check on the quality and uniformity of metals. Since they are nondestructive, these hardness tests may be made on the finished product. The Rockwell tests are popular for steel machine parts, where the relatively small permanent indentation is not undesirable. For gear teeth and similar parts where the Rockwell indentation would be harmful and the surface hardness is to be measured, the Sclerescope test is advantageous. The Brinell test gives an average value of hardness over a relatively large area and is therefore the most suitable hardness test for coarse-grained materials, such as cast iron.

The indentation tests cannot be successfully used interchangeably to compare the hardnesses of unlike materials. For example, the relative hardnesses of such dissimilar materials as rubber and steel, as determined by the Brinell and Scleroscope tests, would be far different, since these two methods really measure different qualities of the materials.

5.10 Weight

In many engineering applications the selection of the material may be governed almost entirely by its weight, and in numerous other applications the strength-weight ratio may be the controlling factor. For structural parts of airplanes, for example, a maximum of strength and stiffness with a minimum of weight is extremely important. For other applications, such as counterweights, a maximum of weight per unit volume is desirable. Three properties which are used to measure the heaviness of a material are specific weight, density, and specific gravity.

Specific weight. The specific weight of a material is defined as the *weight per unit volume*. Normally it is expressed in units of pounds per cubic foot (pcf). For example, the specific weight of steel is 490 pcf.

Density. Density is defined as the *mass per unit volume*. It is expressed in units of slugs per cubic foot and may be obtained from the specific weight by dividing by the acceleration of gravity. For example, the density of steel is equal to $490/32.2 = 15.2$ slugs per cu ft. In the metric system, the density in grams mass per cubic centimeter is numerically equal to the specific weight in grams weight per cubic centimeter.

Specific gravity. The specific gravity of a material is the weight of any volume of that material divided by the weight of an equal volume of water (usually at 4 C). The specific gravity of steel is therefore $490/62.4 = 7.86$. The quantity is dimensionless. Values of specific gravity for most of the elements are given in Table A in the Appendix.

For solid materials such as the metals, the specific weight, density, and specific gravity have definite numerical values, and individual samples of the material show only a small deviation from the average value for the

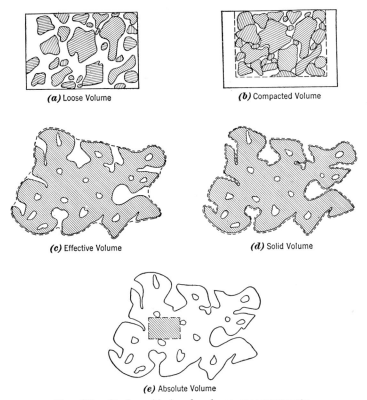

(a) Loose Volume

(b) Compacted Volume

(c) Effective Volume

(d) Solid Volume

(e) Absolute Volume

FIG. 5.2 Various kinds of volume measurements.

material. For other materials, such as wood, stone, and sand, the specific weight varies greatly, its value depending on the voids in the material and on its moisture content. The specific gravity of sand, for example, may have any one of several different values, the exact ratio depending on the degree of compaction of the sand, and on its moisture content.

Unfortunately, there is at present no consistent terminology for the different volumes which a given weight of material may be considered to be occupying. The following terminology will be used throughout this text to indicate the five different volumes recognized in engineering practice.

Loose volume. Loose volume refers to the overall volume which a granular material will occupy when simply poured into a container. There will obviously be voids between the individual particles, as shown in Fig. 5.2a. The volume of the voids may amount to 50 per cent or more of the total volume.

Compacted volume. If granular material is poured into the container and is then rodded, tamped, or vibrated, the overall volume may be reduced appreciably, as shown in Fig. 5.2b.   If the compaction is carried out in a standard manner, consistent results may be obtained for a given material.   The ASTM specifies a standard method for obtaining the compacted volume of an aggregate.[7]

Effective volume.   The effective volume of a mass of sand or other granular material is the total volume enclosed within the boundaries of the individual particles and does not include the volume between the particles. It does include the voids within the particles, as shown in Fig. 5.2c.   Obviously, the effective volume of a given particle is constant, regardless of the degree of compaction of the mass of particles.   If the sand is to be used in concrete, the most convenient form for purposes of calculation is that in which the aggregate is saturated with water but has a dry surface.   Under that condition, the aggregate will neither absorb water from the mixture nor contribute additional water to the mixture.   The volume which the aggregate contributes to the mixture under that condition is the effective volume.   That is, the effective volume of a mass of particles is the volume of water which the mass of saturated particles will displace if immersed in water.

Solid volume.   The solid volume of a mass is the volume occupied by the material, exclusive of voids between the particles and of surface voids which will absorb water.   In Fig. 5.2d the solid volume is the portion within the dotted line.   If a mass of initially dry particles is immersed in water, the solid volume is the volume of water displaced after the particles have become saturated.   The volume displaced initially is the effective volume.

Absolute volume.   The absolute volume of a material is the volume which it would occupy if it were consolidated into a mass containing neither external nor internal voids, as indicated by the shaded rectangle in Fig. 5.2e.   In literature pertaining to concrete, the term absolute volume has at times been used to designate what is here called effective volume.

For a material containing no voids, the effective volume, the solid volume, and the absolute volume are equal.

5.11 Particle Size

An important characteristic of materials is the size of the individual particles, fibers, grains, or crystals which constitute the mass of material. In addition to its pronounced effect on appearance, the particle size has a definite relationship to strength.   Other qualities being equal, a mass made up of small particles will usually be stronger than a mass composed

---

[7] Designation C 29, *Standard Method of Test for Unit Weight of Aggregate.*

of large particles, because of mutual interference to slip between adjacent grains. That is, the planes of weakness, or planes along which individual particles will fail most easily, are not usually parallel in the random arrangement of particles in most materials. Thus, when slip does occur in one particle, the path of the slip will be blocked by the adjacent particles, and the failure will not extend so far as it would have if the particles had been larger. The relatively low strength of timber in shear parallel to the grain is an example of the strength-reducing effect of an extended plane of weakness.

Properties other than strength may also be dependent upon grain size. The ductility of cast metals, for example, usually increases as the grain size is increased. The remarkable capacity of rubber or nylon for being stretched is attributed to its long-chain molecular structure.

The method used for determining the size of particles depends on the nature of the material. In metals, grain size is expressed as the average number of grains per unit of area or in terms of an arbitrary scale, and is determined from a photomicrograph of a representative portion of the material.

Granular materials, such as sand, are put through a series of standard sieves, and are graded according to sieve numbers. The sieve number corresponds to the number of openings per linear inch. A No. 200 sieve, for example, has 200 openings per inch, or 40,000 openings per square inch. The size of particles which will pass through a No. 200 sieve is difficult to determine, and at present no single standard method has been accepted as giving satisfactory results under all conditions. One approach to the problem is made by suspending the material in a liquid and determining the dispersion of light by the suspended particles.

5.12 Hysteresis

The term hysteresis is used to denote lost energy. Applied to materials, it indicates the amount of strain energy per unit volume which is lost in a cycle of loading and unloading. The cycle may be completely tension, completely compression, or any combination of tension and compression. The energy absorbed in a cycle of loading and unloading may be expended in several ways. It may be dissipated in the form of heat, or it may be utilized in producing permanent relative displacement of the particles of the material, resulting in permanent set, or it may serve to alter the properties of the material.

Since energy per unit volume may be determined from the stress-strain diagram as an area, the area between the loading and unloading stress-strain curves will represent the hysteresis. The usual stress-strain behavior when the stress exceeds the elastic limit is shown for structural steel in

Fig. 5.3, with the unloading curve approximately a straight line parallel to the initial tangent.

The area $OACO$ represents the energy which was expended in stressing a cubic inch of the material to 40,000 psi, and the triangle BAC represents the energy which each cubic inch of the specimen released upon removal of the stress. The difference, or the area $OABO$, represents the energy which was absorbed by each cubic inch. This quantity is the hysteresis, and for the cycle of loading and unloading indicated in Fig. 5.3 it is equal to approximately $40,000(0.005) = 200$ in.-lb per cu in.

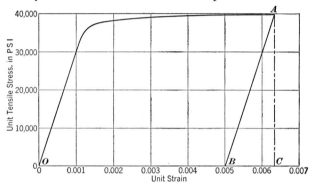

FIG. 5.3   Example of hysteresis loop for mild steel.

If the material is again loaded, its stress-strain diagram will often retrace the line BA, indicating that some of the lost energy has been utilized in increasing the elastic strength of the material.

It is evident that the quantity of lost energy in a cycle of loading and unloading beyond the proportional limit is not a fundamental property of the material, but is dependent on the amount of stress and strain applied in the cycle, and may be different for two consecutive cycles.

Even though the stress does not exceed the proportional limit, there is usually some lost energy in a cycle of loading and unloading because of heat developed throughout the material or because of other effects resulting in a slight curvature of the unloading curve, as illustrated in Fig. 2.6c. The hysteresis, measured as the area of the loop formed by the loading and unloading curves, is of importance in predicting the behavior of the material when subjected to vibration. If the hysteresis is large, the vibrations will damp out rapidly. The magnitude of the damping effect is evaluated not only by the hysteresis but also by a property called the damping capacity.

The damping capacity of a material is defined as the ratio of the energy loss per cycle of loading and unloading (the hysteresis) to the maximum energy absorbed during one cycle of the vibration. Its magnitude for a given material depends on the maximum stress developed by the vibration,

TABLE 5.2

DAMPING CAPACITY FOR A FEW MATERIALS (%)

Material	Maximum Stress (psi)		
	4500	6700	11,200
Brass	0.25	0.39	0.55
Carbon steel			
0.10% C*	2.28	2.78	4.16
0.13% C*	1.92	...	...
0.13% C†	0.60	...	...
0.19% C*	1.48	...	...
0.39% C*	0.68	...	...
0.51% C*	0.41	...	...
1.32% C*	0.41	...	...
Cast iron	28.0	40.0	...
Nickel, 99.4%	10.24	...	...
Nickel steel, 3.10%	0.60	0.64	0.92
Stainless steel, No. 18-8	0.76	1.16	3.8

* Normalized.
† Cold-drawn.

as may be noted in Table 5.2, which gives values of the damping capacity for a few materials. Experiments indicate that the damping capacity is independent of the frequency of the vibration. The relatively high damping capacity of cast iron has led to its use in crankshafts and other machine parts subjected to vibration.

5.13   Other Types of Forces

Practically all the properties discussed in the preceding sections have dealt with the capacities of materials for resisting or transmitting forces which are mechanical in nature—that is, which result from the pressure of one member against another, or from the weight of objects imposed upon the structure of which the member is a part. However, many members or machine parts are often called upon to resist or to transmit other types of forces, such as chemical, electrical, thermal, and acoustical.

The effects of all these types of forces on the materials upon which they act are related to the physical and chemical composition of those materials. To aid in predicting the behavior of materials subjected to such forces, other property terms have been devised in order to indicate the extent of the presence of qualities related to the transmission of, or resistance to, the forces.

5.14   Electrical Characteristics

Conductivity and resistance are among the most important electrical characteristics of materials. Electrical conductivity denotes the capacity for transmitting electric current, while resistance, the reciprocal of conductivity, denotes the capacity for impeding the passage of current. The resistance of a homogeneous material varies directly with its length, and inversely with its cross-sectional area.

The resistance of a wire, or other conductor, is measured in ohms. An ohm is defined as the resistance, at 0 C, of a column of mercury 106.3 cm long and 1 sq mm in cross section. The resistance of a material is measured by its resistivity, expressed as ohms (or microhms) per cubic centimeter. Annealed copper, which has a resistivity of 1.594 microhms per cubic centimeter is often used as a standard of comparison for the conductivity of other materials. Aluminum has a relative conductivity of about 0.60, while the relative conductivity of steel wire is about 0.116. The relative conductivity of pure silver, which has the least resistance of any material known, is 1.086. Values for the relative conductivities of other materials are given in Table 9.1 and in Table A in the Appendix.

If a metal wire is subjected to axial stress below the proportional limit, its electrical resistance changes. This characteristic is utilized in a device known as an *electric strain gage*. A fine wire, usually of a metal having a high resistance, is cemented to the member in which the strain is to be developed, and its resistance is evaluated. When the member is loaded, the wire is strained, and the change in its resistance may be measured by a Wheatstone bridge. From the change in resistance and the known characteristics of the wire, the magnitude of the strain may be evaluated.

The resistance of the nonmetallic materials, most of which are at least somewhat porous, is dependent on the moisture content of the material. Since the resistance of water is less than that of air, the resistance of a porous material is less when it is wet than when it is dry.

5.15 Thermal Characteristics

The specific heat of a material is defined as the quantity of heat required to raise the temperature of a unit mass of the material one degree.

In the cgs (centimeter-gram-second) system of measurement, specific heat is expressed in calories per gram per degree centigrade, where the calorie is the quantity of heat required to raise the temperature of 1 gram of water 1 degree centigrade. Thus, the specific heat of water is 1 calorie per gram per degree centigrade.

In the fps (foot-pound-second) system of measurement, specific heat is expressed in Btu per pound per degree Fahrenheit, where the Btu (British thermal unit) is the quantity of heat required to raise the temperature of 1 lb of water 1 deg F. Thus, the specific heat of water in the fps system is 1 Btu per lb per deg F. A Btu is equal to 252 calories, and a calorie is equivalent to $4.18(10)^7$ ergs, or 37 in.-lb of energy.

The thermal conductivity of a material is the time-rate of transfer of heat by conduction, through a unit thickness, across a unit area, for a unit difference in temperature. That is, in the fps system the thermal conductivity of a material is expressed as the number of Btu per hour per square foot of exposed area transmitted through a 1-in. thickness of the material when the temperature on one side of the material is 1 F higher than the temperature on the other side.

The thermal conductivity of most materials varies with the temperature, and in general it is comparatively high for those materials having a high electrical conductivity. At 500 F the thermal conductivity, in Btu per hr per deg F per sq ft per in., is about 2680 for copper, 1380 for aluminum, and 340 for soft steel. The conductivity of most insulating materials, such as those used for pipe covering, is about 0.4.

The thermal conductivity of the nonporous materials, such as the metals, is a definite quantity, while the conductivity of the more porous materials, such as plaster, wood fiber, and some of the insulating materials, is dependent on both the porosity and the moisture content of the material. Because dry air has a low conductivity, many insulating materials depend for their usefulness upon the air contained in pores or pockets within the material. If such an insulating material is brought into contact with moisture, or with air containing more moisture than the air within the material, moisture may be absorbed; and since the thermal conductivity of water, or even moist air, is considerably higher than the conductivity of dry air, the efficiency of the insulating material will be lowered appreciably.

Heat may be transmitted through a material (a) directly, by conduction, or (b) indirectly, by the passage of air through the pores and cracks in the material. The latter phenomenon is not uncommon in some types of insulating board. In addition to the loss of heat, condensation of moisture within the material may occur, if there is a difference in humidity between the two exposed surfaces. This condensation may increase the rate of heat transfer and, at the same time, induce rotting or other disintegration of the material.

The total amount of heat (in Btu) transmitted in 1 hr from the air on one side of a square foot of material or assembly of materials (such as a wall or partition) to the air on the other side, for a difference of 1 F in air temperature, is known as the coefficient of transmission.

5.16 Acoustical Characteristics

When a sound wave impinges upon a material, the energy of the wave is divided into two portions. One starts a new series of waves outward from the material, and the other passes through the material or is absorbed and dissipated in the form of heat within the material. The percentage of the original wave which is absorbed is called the coefficient of absorption, while the percentage which is reflected back into the air from the surface of the material is called the coefficient of reflection.

Reverberation is the persistence of sound in a closed room after the source of sound has been cut off, and is due to the multiple reflection of sound from the walls, ceiling, and floor. If excessive, it will create echoes, and will tend to make all sounds unintelligible, rendering the room useless for many purposes. Reverberation may be decreased by proper architectural design, by increasing the area of sound-absorbing surface, or by increasing the coefficient of absorption of the existing areas.

In general, the nonporous materials have a low coefficient of absorption, and the porous materials have a high coefficient of absorption, because of the relative amounts of air space within the materials. Wood, brick, glass, marble, plaster, and concrete—the materials generally used for walls, floors, and ceilings—all have low coefficients of absorption, generally less than 5, although the coefficients for all materials are dependent on the pitch of the sound. Draperies may have coefficients between 10 and 50, while some types of fiberboard indicate a coefficient of absorption of over 90. Holes and grooves in the surface of the material have a marked effect in increasing the coefficient of absorption.

Under the proper conditions, sound waves may induce stresses in members. If a sound wave comes in contact with a member whose natural period of vibration is equal to the period of vibration (reciprocal of frequency) of the original wave, it will induce vibrations in that member. These vibrations, of course, set up stresses which, in extreme cases, may be sufficient to cause failure of the member. For example, a glass goblet may be broken by the vibrations induced by a sustained note of the proper pitch played on a musical instrument.

5.17 Chemical Characteristics

Among the many important chemical characteristics of materials, one of great significance to the engineer is the extent and readiness with which the materials of construction enter into chemical combination with other substances that may come in contact with them. The chemical activities predicate the methods which must be used in the manufacturing processes and are an important factor in determining the final properties of the material.

The rusting of iron and steel, the corrosion of other metals, and the disintegration of boilers under the influence of certain types of feed waters are a few illustrations of chemical changes which occur in materials after manufacture and which necessitate the expenditure of millions of dollars annually for repair, replacement, and maintenance of structures.

The chemical behavior of the metals under certain conditions may be predicted by the use of the following series, known as the electromotive-force (emf) series of metals:

Metal	EMF (v)	Metal	EMF (v)
Lithium	2.96	Cobalt	0.278
Rubidium	2.93	Nickel	0.231
Potassium	2.92	Tin	0.136
Strontium	2.92	Lead	0.122
Barium	2.90	Hydrogen	0.000
Calcium	2.87	Antimony	−0.100
Sodium	2.71	Bismuth	−0.226
Magnesium	2.40	Arsenic	−0.300
Aluminum	1.70	Copper	−0.344
Manganese	1.10	Silver	−0.798
Zinc	0.762	Mercury	−0.799
Chromium	0.557	Palladium	−0.820
Iron	0.441	Platinum	−0.863
Cadmium	0.401	Gold	−1.136

Any free metal in the series will displace from a compound any metal following it in the series; for example, $Fe + CuSO_4 \rightarrow FeSO_4 + Cu$. This means that the metals preceding hydrogen in the series will be acted upon by acids, the metals forming salts and liberating hydrogen. Metals below hydrogen may also be acted upon by acids, but the action is not one of simple replacement. The ease with which the metals react to acids is greatest for the metals at the beginning of the list, and least for the metals near the end of the list. Heat may be required for the reaction to proceed.

All the metals preceding copper readily form oxides, and occur in nature as oxides, while the metals following copper do not oxidize in air and are frequently found in the uncombined state. The oxides down to manganese are difficult to reduce, while the oxides following cadmium are readily reduced. The oxides following mercury can be reduced simply by applying heat.

The electromotive potential between two of the metals in a voltaic cell varies directly with the degree of separation of the metals in the series, and with the solution used in the cell.

5.18 Radiation Absorption

With the development of nuclear reactors, there has arisen the need for evaluating the capacity of materials for resisting radiation, and for knowing the effects of the interaction of materials and radiation. Of the several types of radiation, gamma rays and neutron radiation are the ones of primary concern to the engineer because of their greater capacity for penetrating materials. Alpha particles (helium nuclei) and beta particles (electrons) have relatively little penetrating power, and therefore, although they are important under certain circumstances, they are in general less significant insofar as effects on materials are concerned.

Neutrons may be absorbed by the nuclei of the materials they penetrate, or they may be deflected and reduced in energy by so-called elastic collisions with the nuclei. In each case, the probability of interaction is measured by the *cross section* of the material. The absorption cross section for neutrons is equivalent to the reduction in area of a solid stream of neutrons one square centimeter in area by a single nucleus of the material penetrated. Expressed somewhat differently, the absorption cross section for neutrons represents the probability of interaction between a given nucleus and a neutron stream. The cross section is expressed in units of 10^{-24} sq cm, which are called barns. An area of 1 barn is of the same order as the projected area of the nucleus of an atom, but there is no evident relationship between the size of a nucleus and its absorption cross section for thermal neutrons. Cadmium, which is used as an absorbing material, has an absorption cross section of about 3000 barns for thermal neutrons (i.e., neutrons traveling at a velocity of about 2200 meters per second at ordinary temperatures).

A neutron and a nucleus may interact to reduce the energy of the neutron without altering the composition of the nucleus. The probability of this event is evaluated by the scattering cross section, which is analogous to the absorption cross section.

A quantity called the macroscopic cross section is obtained by multiplying the cross section by the number of nuclei per cubic centimeter. Evaluated in units of cm^{-1} it is useful for comparing the effectiveness of equal volumes of materials for absorbing or scattering neutrons.

Three mechanisms of interaction between gamma rays and materials have been observed: Compton scattering, pair production, and the photoelectric effect. However, from the standpoint of the over-all effect, the contributions of the three mechanisms may be added and the total expressed as an absorption coefficient for the material. As the gamma radiation penetrates a material its intensity decreases at a rate proportional to the intensity. The absorption coefficient is the coefficient by which the intensity is multiplied to obtain the rate of decrease of intensity. That is,

$$\frac{\Delta I}{\Delta x} = -\mu I \qquad (5.3)$$

in which I = the intensity of radiation, in gamma rays per unit area;

ΔI = the change in intensity;

Δx = the distance in which I changes by an amount ΔI;

μ = the absorption coefficient.

The absorption coefficient is measured in units that are the reciprocal of distance, which is usually expressed in centimeters.

The magnitude of the absorption coefficient for a given material varies with the energy of the incident radiation. In general, the magnitude of the absorption coefficient increases as the density of the absorbing material increases, with the result that the reduction of gamma radiation from one level of intensity to another involves about the same total weight of material regardless of its nature.

The effectiveness of a material for attenuating gamma radiation is sometimes evaluated by its one-half thickness, or the thickness of the material required to reduce the intensity of radiation to one-half of its initial value. Similarly, the one-tenth thickness is used to designate the thickness required to reduce the intensity to 10 per cent of its initial value.

Radiation-absorbing characteristics of materials are important because the biological tolerance of humans for radiation is low compared with the amount of radiation involved in the various nuclear-engineering devices in current use. For example, the maximum permissible dosage of thermal neutrons for an individual on the basis of a constant over-all exposure is of the order of 1000 neutrons per sq cm per sec, whereas neutron fluxes of the order of 10^{12} neutrons per sq cm per sec are common in nuclear reactors.

PROBLEMS

5.1 Determine the modulus of elasticity of each of the metals shown in Fig. 9.18.

5.2 Determine the modulus of elasticity of each wood shown in Fig. 10.6.

5.3 When subjected to an axial pull of 2000 lb, a $\frac{1}{2}$-in. round bar of aluminum stretched 0.0078 in. in a gage length of 8 in. What was the modulus of elasticity of the material?

5.4 The modulus of elasticity of a given concrete is 4,000,000 psi and the proportional limit is 2000 psi. How much would a cylinder of the concrete 3 in. in diam shorten in a length of 4 in. under a load of 10,000 lb?

5.5 If Young's modulus for a magnesium alloy is 6,500,000 psi, what is the maximum axial load which may be applied to a $\frac{1}{2}$-in. diam rod of the metal without producing a total elongation of more than $\frac{1}{16}$ in. in a length of 6 ft?

5.6 Derive an expression for the modulus of resilience in terms of the proportional limit and the modulus of elasticity.

5.7 Poisson's ratio for Duralumin is 0.33. (a) How much will the cross-sectional area of a 2-in. square Duralumin rod be changed by an axial pull of 40,000 lb? (b) How much will the volume of a 1-ft section of the rod be changed by a 60,000-lb load? (See Fig. 9.18.)

5.8 Poisson's ratio for steel is 0.30. How much will the diameter of a steel rod 2 in. in diameter change under an axial pull of 60,000 lb?

5.9 A $\frac{1}{2}$-in. round bar of aluminum stretched 0.00195 in. in a length of 2 in., and decreased 0.00016 in. in diameter, when subjected to an axial load of 2000 lb. Determine Poisson's ratio.

5.10 What must be the value of Poisson's ratio for a material to maintain a constant volume under axial load?

5.11 A 2-in. cube of a material for which Poisson's ratio is 0.33 and the modulus of elasticity is 10,000,000 psi is subjected to a total axial compressive load of 60,000 lb in the x direction. Determine the unit strain in the x, y, and z directions.

5.12 If an axial tensile load of 40,000 lb in the y direction is added to the cube described in problem 5.11, with the 60,000-lb load being maintained, what will be the final dimensions of the cube?

5.13 A 6-ft diam boiler made of plate $\frac{1}{4}$ in. thick is subjected to an internal pressure of 150 psi. Determine the unit strain in the longitudinal direction (a) on the inside of the boiler and (b) on the outside of the boiler.

5.14 A 1-in. diam bar of structural steel is held rigidly at each end of a 6-ft length. To what temperature drop may the bar be subjected without producing inelastic action?

5.15 How much will an aluminum-alloy piston $3\frac{1}{2}$ in. in diameter expand when its temperature is increased from -30 F to 140 F?

5.16 The control cables in a certain airplane are 34 ft long. If the cables are made of aluminum wire, how much will they change in length when the temperature drops 70 F?

5.17 Determine the change in length of a 400-ft-long cement kiln built of structural steel if the average temperature changes 300 F.

5.18 If a steel having the same coefficient of thermal expansion as structural steel were used for a jet engine, how much would a ring of the steel 26 in. in diameter expand when the temperature is increased from 50 F to 1200 F?

5.19 If steel rails 33 ft long are laid at 120 F with their ends touching, how much space will there be between the ends of the rails at -20 F?

5.20 If a concrete pavement slab is laid without expansion joints at a temperature of 40 F, what unit stress will be developed in the slab at 100 F?

5.21 The modulus of elasticity of a nickel steel is 23,000,000 psi and its proportional limit is 90,000 psi. Determine its elasticity.

5.22 What property is equal to one-half the product of the proportional limit and the elasticity?

5.23 Determine the elasticity of each of the following materials: (a) structural steel; (b) the concrete of Fig. 2.5; (c) hickory; (d) gray cast iron.

5.24 Determine the elasticity of each of the following materials: (a) oak; (b) cedar; (c) malleable cast iron; (d) Monel metal.

5.25 Results of a test on a Duralumin bar indicate an elasticity of 0.0025 and a modulus of elasticity of 10,500,000 psi. Determine (a) the proportional limit and (b) the modulus of resilience.

5.26 A test of a certain brass rod shows it to have an elasticity of 0.0012 and a modulus of elasticity of 16,800,000 psi. How much energy load might an 8-in. length of a $\frac{1}{2}$-in. diam rod of the brass be expected to absorb without slip?

5.27 An axial load is applied to a specimen developing a unit strain of 0.001 and storing 5 in.-lb of energy per cubic inch. If the factor of safety with respect to slip is 9 for the dynamic load determine (a) the modulus of elasticity and (b) the elasticity of the material.

5.28 Punch marks were placed 1 in. apart on the surface of a structural-steel specimen. After the specimen had been tested to failure, the distances between punch marks were 1.17, 1.17, 1.17, 1.24, 1.19, 1.44, 1.30, and 1.18 in. Determine (a) the percentage elongation in 8 in. and (b) the percentage elongation in 2 in.

5.29 Name the methods that may be used in shaping each of the following materials: (a) timber; (b) structural steel; (c) concrete; (d) armor plate.

5.30 A 0.505-in. diam test specimen measures 0.392 in. in diameter at the break after testing to rupture. Determine the percentage reduction in area.

5.31 (a) Name two practical situations requiring the use of a ductile material. (b) Name two examples of situations in which ductility would be unimportant.

5.32 If a test specimen elongated uniformly and did not neck down or undergo volume change what would be the percentage elongation for a reduction in area of 30 per cent?

5.33 Determine the relative ductilities of (a) structural steel, (b) wrought iron, (c) cast iron, and (d) annealed copper.

5.34 List the following metals in order of ductility, indicating for each an approximate numerical value of the property: (a) cold-drawn copper; (b) rolled annealed aluminum; (c) hot-rolled zinc; (d) annealed nickel.

5.35 What is the approximate ultimate tensile strength of each of the following materials if its Brinell hardness number is as indicated? (a) Armco iron, 75; (b) structural steel, 120; (c) tool steel, 220; (d) gray cast iron, 160.

5.36 Determine the ratio of elastic strength to weight for (a) structural steel, (b) X-4130 steel, (c) annealed aluminum, and (d) 75S-T aluminum alloy.

5.37 Determine the ratio of ultimate strength to weight for (a) structural steel, (b) X-4130 steel, (c) annealed aluminum, and (d) 75S-T aluminum alloy.

5.38 (a) Which nonferrous metal in Chapter 9 has the highest ratio of ultimate strength to weight? (b) Which nonferrous alloy?

5.39 By what percentage does 1 per cent of carbon increase the ratio of ultimate strength to weight for iron in the hot-worked condition?

5.40 A sample of sand which has a solid specific gravity of 2.67 weighs 110 pcf in a standard compacted condition. Determine the void space in a cubic foot of the sand.

5.41 If the sand of the preceding problem will absorb 1 per cent of moisture, what is its effective specific gravity when it is (a) dry and (b) saturated?

5.42 A container 1 ft on each side is packed with spheres ¼ in. in diameter in cubical array; that is, eight adjacent spheres in two layers form a cube with edges parallel to the edges of the container. What percentage of the space in the container is void?

5.43 (a) Could the void space in the container of problem 5.42 be decreased by a different arrangement of spheres? (b) If so, how should the spheres be arranged and what decrease in void space would result?

5.44 (a) What maximum size of spheres could be introduced in the void space of the container of problem 5.42? (b) By what maximum percentage could the void space be reduced by introducing such spheres?

5.45 An 1800-gram sample of dry sand is immersed in water. Its weight after the balance comes to equilibrium is 1080 grams. Determine the solid specific gravity of the sand.

5.46 If the absorption of the sand in problem 5.45 is 1.20 per cent by weight, (a) what did the balance record initially and (b) what is the effective specific gravity of the sand?

5.47 A bar similar to the one from which the stress-strain diagram in Fig. 3.6 was obtained was loaded to a unit deformation of 0.004 and was then unloaded. The unloading curve was parallel to the initial straight-line portion of the loading curve. Determine the hysteresis.

5.48 Assuming that all of the strain energy absorbed in breaking the bar of Fig. 3.6 was converted to heat energy without loss, determine how much the temperature of the bar would be increased. (1 Btu = 778 ft-lb = 252 calories, and 0.820 calorie is required to raise 1 cc of steel 1 C.)

5.49 Determine the approximate minimum number of particles in 1 lb of sand which has been passed through a No. 200 sieve. Assume that all particles are spherical, and that the solid material of which the sand is composed weighs 165 lb per cu ft. The average diameter of the wire in a No. 200 sieve is 0.0021 in.

5.50 If aluminum costs 20 cents per pound, at which price will copper be equally cheap for use as an electrical conductor?

5.51 What diameters of copper and aluminum wires have the same electrical resistance per foot of length as a steel wire 0.04 in. in diameter?

5.52 How many Btu per hour will be lost by conduction through a 2-in. coating of insulation covering a 4-in. pipe in a length of 10 ft, if the temperature within the pipe is 250 F and the outside temperature is 70 F? The insulation has a coefficient of transmission of 0.30.

5.53 How many foot-pounds of energy will be lost in 24 hr by conduction through the vertical walls of a room 12 ft by 20 ft, and 9 ft high, if the walls have a coefficient of transmission of 0.25, the average interior temperature is 70 F, and the average exterior temperature is −30 F?

6 Control of Properties
of Materials

6.1 Importance of Control

After giving careful consideration to the uses to which each element of a product is to be put, the loads which it must carry, the environment in which it is to function, and its relationship to the other elements in the product, the engineer is prepared to stipulate the characteristics of the material that are of primary importance for the element. The next step is to select the material best qualified to meet the requirements. This involves consideration of the potential properties of various materials. However, the properties of the material at a given temperature in the finished member are influenced by both the chemical composition and the method of fabrication. Therefore, in order to select the most suitable material and to specify the optimum method of shaping it for the particular application, the engineer must know how the properties can be controlled and what changes, if any, may be expected to occur in the material during its useful life.

6.2 Basis of Control

Many of the mechanical properties of materials, such as yield strength and hardness, are structure-sensitive. That is, their numerical values are dependent upon the arrangement of the crystals, grains, fibers, or other units of which the material is composed, and upon the arrangement of the atoms within these units. Other properties, such as modulus of elasticity and electrical resistivity, are relatively insensitive to changes in the arrangement of the units in the material.

Experience shows that the properties of a material at a given temperature are controlled by two factors: (1) the chemical composition of the material and (2) its physical organization, or the arrangement of the atoms, crystals, grains, or fibers of the material. It is also concluded that:

1. ~~The potential properties of a material at a given temperature are fixed by its chemical composition.~~ For example, there is a definite upper limit for the yield strength of iron at 68 F. This upper

limit, or potential strength, is many times the strength usually obtained in a test specimen or a fabricated member, but a fixed upper limit exists. The potential strength is a specific characteristic for each material, and is dependent upon the forces developed between atoms of the material. A change in chemical composition alters the potential strength.

2. Many of the mechanical properties actually available in a given product of a given chemical composition, at a given temperature, are established by the method used in shaping or manufacturing the material. For example, the yield strength of a piece of high-carbon steel is dependent upon the history of the piece during fabrication as well as its chemical composition. Its properties may be altered by hammering it or by stretching it above the yield strength. If it is heated and cooled slowly, its properties may be quite different from what they would be if it were heated and then cooled rapidly by immersing it in ice water.

Thus, through changes in the chemical composition of materials and through variations in the fabrication methods employed, many of the properties of materials may be altered extensively. Some of the effects may be explained by considering the atomic structure of the materials.

6.3 Atomic Structure

All materials are composed of atoms, each of which in turn consists of a positively charged nucleus of comparatively large mass, around which the negatively charged and comparatively light electrons circulate. The chemical species, or chemical nature, of the material is determined by the positive charge on the nucleus, which under normal conditions is proportional to the number of electrons associated with the atom.

The hydrogen atom, for example, consists of a positively charged nucleus consisting of one particle, or proton, around which one electron circulates. There is an electrostatic attraction between the positively charged nucleus and the negatively charged electron. There is also a gravitational attraction, the magnitude of which, like the electrostatic force, varies inversely as the square of the distance between the nucleus and the electron. There is also developed a force of repulsion between the nucleus and the electron. At a particular distance the forces balance, with the result that if the electron approaches closer to the nucleus it is repelled, and if the distance between the nucleus and electron becomes larger than the equilibrium distance, the resultant force tends to pull the electron back to position. The general nature of the variation of the forces of attraction and repulsion, and the resultant force, is shown in Fig. 6.1. The distance d_o represents the equilibrium distance.

The electron is in motion, having properties of angular momentum, spin, and kinetic energy, and maintaining an average equilibrium distance from the nucleus. Its path is not circular, nor is it constant, but under normal conditions it is maintained between two closely spaced surfaces surrounding the nucleus. This region to which the electron is restricted is known as the K shell.

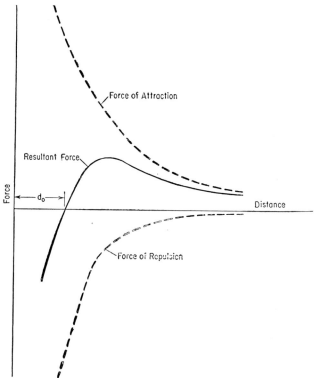

FIG. 6.1   Variation of force with distance of separation.

Helium has a nucleus consisting of two protons, or positively charged particles, and two neutrons, which are particles having about the same mass as the protons and zero charge. The two protons in the nucleus require two electrons in the K shell for balancing the charge on the atom.

The atomic number of lithium is 3, so it has three electrons. Because of forces developed between electrons, as well as forces between the nucleus and electrons, the third electron of lithium cannot circulate in the K shell. It is forced outward and establishes an orbit in the so-called L shell. Beryllium, with an atomic number of 4, has two electrons in the K shell and two in the L shell.

The L shell can contain a maximum of 8 electrons. The M shell, at a greater distance from the nucleus than the L shell, will hold 18 electrons. When it is filled, additional electrons are forced out to the N shell, which has a capacity of 32 electrons. Beyond the N shell are the O, P, and Q shells, which contain electrons for the materials with higher atomic numbers.

Since the inner shells represent conditions of minimum energy, they are normally filled first, in accordance with the principle that the most stable form is the one of minimum energy. If a material such as carbon, with two electrons in the K shell and six in the L shell, somehow loses one of the electrons in the K shell, one of the electrons in the L shell will move into the K shell to take its place. Since less energy is required in the K shell than in the L shell, the electron will give up energy as it moves in. This energy is evidenced as an X ray emanating from the atom.

In much the same way, equilibrium distances are established between the nuclei of atoms, and certain patterns or arrangements of atoms result in the stable (or equilibrium) condition. This regular arrangement gives rise to the space lattice mentioned in Chapter 1. A given chemical species at a given temperature will have a characteristic lattice with consistent distances between atoms in the unstrained condition. These distances, or lattice parameters, are actually average distances because of the thermal oscillations of the individual atoms. As the temperature is increased, the amplitude of the oscillations increases and in general the distance between atoms will increase.

This results in the well-known thermal expansion of materials. For some materials it is found that as the temperature is increased and the lattice size increases, a temperature will be attained at which another lattice arrangement will be more stable; that is, the new arrangement will involve less total energy in the lattice. At that temperature, which is known as the transition temperature, a change in the lattice form takes place. In general, the transformation is reversible, and as the material is cooled below the transition temperature, a recrystallization occurs, with the material resuming its original space lattice. For example, iron is in the body-centered cubic form at room temperature and up to about 906 C. At that temperature it transforms into the face-centered cubic form, which is stable up to 1401 C, where it again changes to the body-centered lattice, which is stable to the melting point at 1530 C.

Changes in structure may also be produced by the application of pressure.

Lattice structures for some of the elements at atmospheric pressures are given in Table 6.1. The atomic radius as tabulated in the last column is defined as one-half of the distance between the centers of nearest neighbors. The magnitudes of the atomic radii of two metals are involved in empirical rules governing their solubility.

TABLE 6.1

LATTICE STRUCTURES FOR SOME ELEMENTS

Element	Lattice Type	a (A°)	c (A°)	Interatomic Dist. (A°)
Li	bcc	3.46	...	3.00
Na	bcc	4.24	...	3.67
K	bcc	5.25	...	4.54
Rb	bcc	5.62	...	4.87
Cs	bcc	6.05	...	5.24
Cu	fcc	3.609	...	2.55
Ag	fcc	4.078	...	2.88
Au	fcc	4.070	...	2.87
Be	hcp	2.28	3.59	2.28
Mg	hcp	3.20	5.20	3.20
α Ca	fcc	5.56	...	3.93
β Ca	hcp	3.98	6.52	3.98
Sr	fcc	6.06	...	4.28
Ba	bcc	5.01	...	4.34
Zn	hcp	2.65	4.93	2.65
Cd	hcp	2.97	5.61	2.97
Al	fcc	4.04	...	2.86
In	tfc	4.59	4.94	...
Ti	hcp	2.95	4.73	2.89
α Zr	hcp	3.23	5.14	3.23
β Zr	bcc	3.61	...	3.13
α Sn	dia	6.46	...	2.80
Pb	fcc	4.93	...	3.48
V	bcc	3.01	...	2.61
α Cr	bcc	2.87	...	2.49
β Cr	hcp	2.72	4.42	2.72
γ Mn	tetfc	3.77	3.53	2.08
α Fe	bcc	2.86	...	2.58
γ Fe	fcc	3.56	...	2.57
α Co	hcp	2.51	4.11	2.51
β Co	fcc	3.55	...	2.51
Ni	fcc	3.51	...	2.48
Mo	bcc	3.14	...	2.96
Ru	hcp	2.77	4.47	...
Rh	fcc	3.78	...	2.67
Pd	fcc	3.88	...	2.74
Ta	bcc	3.29	...	2.72
α W	bcc	3.16	...	2.73
Re	hcp	2.76	4.45	2.76
Os	hcp	2.71	4.32	2.71
Ir	fcc	3.83	...	2.71
Pt	fcc	3.92	...	2.71

NOTE: A° = 1 Angstrom unit = 10^{-10} meters.

6.4 Lattice Distortion under Load

The atoms of a given solid element form a definite lattice as a result of the interatomic forces, the lattice being that for which the energy is a minimum under the given conditions. If a force is applied to one of the atoms in the lattice, it will move because the force balance is changed.

The magnitude and direction of motion will be that required to bring the forces into equilibrium again, if that is possible, and to keep the total energy of the system at a minimum.

The circles A and B in Fig. 6.2 represent two atoms that are initially in equilibrium as a result of the forces of attraction and repulsion acting between them. If a small force P is applied, the distance will be increased until the force is balanced by the net increase in attraction. However, if the force Q of the same magnitude as P is applied, the distance that atom B

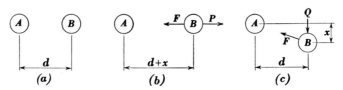

FIG. 6.2   Forces developed by atomic displacements.

travels will be greater. In effect, the force Q required to move B a given distance is less than the force P required to move B the same distance. It will be seen that a small force Q in any direction in a plane perpendicular to the line connecting the centers of the atoms will cause relative movement. That is, so far as the resistance of the atoms to relative displacement is concerned, there is a plane of weakness at right angles to the direction AB.

This same concept applies to assemblages of atoms in a space lattice, or ideal crystal. Of course, the force fields are three-dimensional and more involved than the two-atom model of Fig. 6.2, but it is found that for each lattice there are one or more planes of weakness, or planes of minimum resistance to relative motion of atoms. These planes are often called slip planes. They are the planes which contain the maximum number of atoms per unit area because fewer atomic bonds are broken or altered when slip occurs. Within the slip planes are certain directions, called slip directions, along which relative motion takes place most easily.

For the face-centered cubic space lattice the slip planes are the four diagonal planes indicated by the dotted lines in Fig. 1.2c. The hexagonal space lattice has its slip plane parallel to the basal plane, but other planes may become slip planes under special conditions. The body-centered cubic lattice has no single slip plane.

From the foregoing it becomes evident that the basic mechanism of deformation is one of shear and that the resultant displacement is not always in the direction of the applied force. For example, in Fig. 6.3a the displacement resulting from the load P will be in the direction a–a if that is the slip direction, and not in the direction of the load. In general, the applied load may be resolved into a force normal to the slip plane and two shearing forces in the slip plane—one in the slip direction and one normal to it.   Studies of single crystals have shown that there is a critical ultimate strength in shear which is independent of the normal stress.   The shearing strength is dependent on the temperature, becoming less as the temperature is increased.   This finding is reasonable in the light of the effect of increased oscillation of the atoms at higher temperatures.

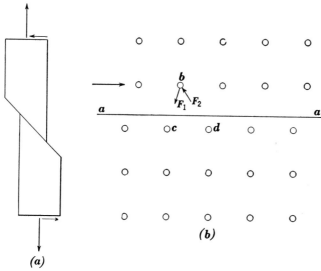

(a)

(b)

FIG. 6.3   Two dimensional models of slip.

The circles in Fig. 6.3b represent a two-dimensional model of a simple cubic lattice for which the slip plane is assumed to be perpendicular to the page and the slip direction along *a–a*.   If a force is applied to the group of atoms above *a–a*, the group will tend to be displaced to the right and resistance will be developed as a result of the changes in all inter-atomic distances which cross the line *a–a*.   Of the many changes which are involved, two are shown as examples.   As a result of the increase in distance *b–c*, the interatomic force may change by the amount F_1, and as a result of the decrease in the distance *b–d*, that interatomic force may change by the amount F_2.

By evaluating these forces in general terms as functions of the displacements and equating them to the applied force, a theoretical stress-strain diagram may be developed for the material.   In its simplest form and with certain approximations this becomes

$$S = A \sin \frac{2\pi x}{d} \qquad (6.1)$$

in which S = shearing stress;

        A = ultimate strength;

        x = displacement;

        d = atomic spacing.

Thus when x equals d the stress is zero, which corresponds to the condition of the upper block of atoms being displaced one atom distance to the right, where they would again be in equilibrium.

The quantity x/d is unit strain, ϵ. Hence, equation 6.1 may be written

$$S = A \sin 2\pi\epsilon \qquad (6.2)$$

If this is differentiated with respect to ϵ, there results

$$\frac{dS}{d\epsilon} = 2\pi A \cos 2\pi\epsilon \qquad (6.3)$$

However, for small values of ϵ the modulus of elasticity in shear is $dS/d\epsilon$. Hence, for ϵ equal to zero,

$$E = 2\pi A \qquad (6.4)$$

or

$$A = \frac{E}{2\pi} \qquad (6.5)$$

Equation 6.5 indicates that the ultimate strength in shear should be about 16 per cent of the modulus of elasticity. In other words, iron has a theoretical ultimate strength in shear of approximately 1,750,000 psi. This value is much higher than that normally obtained. In fact, bulk commercial metals have strengths in the order of one per cent of the theoretical strength. However, experiments on tiny wires of materials have given strengths approaching their theoretical strengths.

The discrepancy between the theoretical strength, which is a function of the ideal space lattice and interatomic forces, and the actual strength, which is a function of the actual lattice and actual forces, is explained on the basis of lattice imperfections. The imperfections in the lattice, known as dislocations, result from atoms slightly misplaced as a result of some unbalance in forces as the atom came to its final position in the lattice. The dislocations are of several kinds, but each is a point of weakness in the lattice, resulting in a relatively large strain at a relatively low stress level.

It would be expected that strengths would agree with the theoretical values if the dislocations could be eliminated from the structure.

6.5 Increasing the Lattice Strength

The critical shearing stress for a given crystal may be increased by introducing atomic displacements within the space lattice, to disrupt the

continuity or smoothness of the slip plane.   This may be accomplished by
(1) chemical means or (2) physical means.

Chemical displacements.   If an atom of a foreign material can be
introduced into the space lattice of a material, on or adjacent to a slip
plane, the atom will disrupt the symmetry of the slip plane and set up
forces which tend to increase the resistance to shear.   For example, the
introduction of a larger foreign atom at a regular lattice point, as shown in

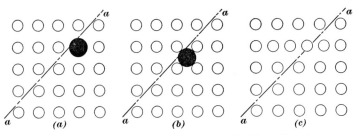

FIG. 6.4   Effect of additional atoms in blocking slip planes.

Fig. 6.4a, or between atoms, as in Fig. 6.4b, will increase the resistance to
slip along several planes such as the one having the trace *aa*.   It is evident
that relatively few foreign atoms properly dispersed throughout the lattice
may have a pronounced effect in increasing the shearing strength, and that
the maximum effect will be obtained when about one-half of the atoms are
of one material and the remainder of the atoms are of the other material.
Experimental findings verify these conclusions.   The conditions under
which a given material will retain or dissolve atoms of another metal, and
the conditions under which it will reject the atoms of another material, are
discussed in section 6.10.

Physical displacements.   Atomic displacements resulting in a warped
slip plane may be induced by physical means.   This is generally accomplished by distorting or straining the material above its proportional limit.
Irregularities and dislocations of individual atoms practically always exist
along the boundaries of a given crystal.   One theory is that, as the material
is strained above the proportional limit, these atoms are forced inward,
becoming distributed throughout the crystal, distorting the slip planes, and
thereby increasing the resistance of the material to slip.   For example, an
extra atom in one row, as indicated in Fig. 6.4c, will increase the resistance
to slip along planes such as *aa*.

For some materials the effect is permanent at room temperature but
may be removed by annealing or heating the material to higher temperatures.   For other materials, such as zinc, the strain-hardening effect dis-
appears after storage for a few hours at room temperature.   In other

words, the zinc is self-annealing at room temperature. Apparently, as the temperature approaches the melting point, the increased mobility of the atoms enables them to readjust themselves to the normal unstrained condition, and tends to nullify the effect of strain hardening. The strain-hardening effect is much more pronounced in crystals having a face-centered cubic space lattice than in those which have a hexagonal space lattice.

Thus, the properties of a member may be altered by changing the characteristics of each crystal in the member. Control is possible by physical or chemical means, each process having an effect upon the continuity of the slip planes and thereby altering the resistance to slip. In addition, the fact that almost every material as used for engineering purposes consists of an assembly of a large number of crystals, rather than a single crystal, provides the engineer with another powerful tool for controlling the properties of the resulting structural member. Again the methods of control may be classified as (1) chemical and (2) physical.

Chemical control of properties. The addition of a second material to a given base material may result in (a) a homogeneous assembly of crystals having a uniform composition, each containing atoms of both materials, or (b) a mixture of crystals of two or more typical compositions, each composition having entirely different properties. The effect of condition a in increasing strength has already been considered. The effect of condition b depends on the relative characteristics of the components produced. Steel, for example, consists of hard, brittle crystals composed of iron and carbon interspersed among relatively soft and ductile iron crystals. The effect of the hard crystals is to increase greatly the strength of the mass. A steel containing only $\frac{1}{2}$ of 1 per cent of carbon will be more than twice as strong as the material would be if the carbon had not been added.

Physical control of properties. Physical control is manifested in control of (a) orientation of slip planes and (b) size of crystals. Since the individual crystals are not isotropic but have definite properties in definite directions, the properties of a structural member can be controlled by controlling the orientation of the crystals. For example, since the component crystals are weak in shear, the member may be strengthened by so arranging the crystals that, instead of having their usual random orientation, they are aligned in such a way that the applied load has a zero or minimum component in the slip direction. Figure 6.5a is a two-dimensional representation of random orientation of crystals in a short compression member with the planes of weakness indicated. Obviously, the resistance to a vertical load may be increased by orienting the crystals as shown in Fig. 6.5b. The most unfavorable orientation is that indicated in Fig. 6.5c. If the crystals are arranged so that their glide directions as well as their slip planes are parallel, the mass will have essentially the same properties as a single crystal, and will have different properties in different directions; but if the crystals have a random orientation, the properties of the mass will tend to become the average of the properties of an individual crystal in different directions, and the mass will tend to have the same properties in all directions.

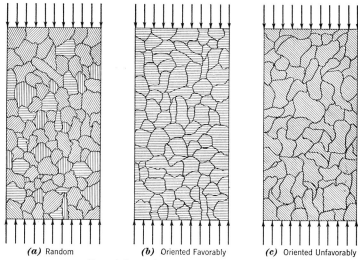

(a) Random   *(b)* Oriented Favorably   *(c)* Oriented Unfavorably

Fɪɢ. 6.5   Orientation of slip planes.

Various types of shaping operations, such as forging, rolling, and drawing, have a pronounced effect in orienting crystals.   At least some degree of orientation is produced by every shaping operation, even though its effect may be highly localized.

It is an established fact that a material composed of many small grains or crystals will be stronger and harder than the same material would be if it were composed of a few relatively large crystals.   In the fine-grained material, the individual slip planes are relatively small and the amount of slip which may occur within the boundaries of any one grain is limited by the restraint offered by the adjacent grains which have slip planes in other directions.   Slip cannot become general in the material until the load on the member has been increased sufficiently to make the shearing component of stress on some of the less favorably oriented grains equal to the critical shearing stress.

Thus, a soft, large-grained aluminum-alloy specimen will characteristically fail with a cone-cup fracture when axially loaded in tension. Failure becomes general over a comparatively large conical surface at the cross section of minimum strength, and the material exhibits ductility.   In contrast, a hard, fine-grained aluminum alloy specimen, when loaded in tension to the ultimate, gives the appearance of having failed on a single transverse plane by the two halves separating in tension. Examination of the surface reveals that the failure actually took place in shear on thousands of small surfaces corresponding to the planes of weakness of the individual crystals. Since slip is not general on a single surface, the material exhibits little ductility.

Consequently it is possible to control, within limits, certain characteristics of a piece of metal, such as strength and ductility, by controlling its grain size.

The size of the resultant crystals may be controlled (a) by altering the rate of cooling while the material is solidifying from a liquid state or (b) by mechanical working. Both methods provide feasible control because most metals are solidified from a liquid state at some stage in the manufacturing process, and mechanical working is involved in shaping most members. Evidence indicates that, if small crystals are formed without warping the slip planes, the resultant material will be as ductile as it was in the coarse-grained form; but, if the production of fine grains results in warped slip planes, the ductility is decreased. In any case, the ductility of a polycrystalline material is appreciably less than the ductility of a single crystal in shear and is greater than the ductility of a single crystal in tension. In a material composed of many crystals, the probability of random orientation is relatively greater than in a material composed of only a few crystals, and the properties of the polycrystalline material tend to approach the average value of the properties of the single crystal in the various directions.

The foregoing facts may be summarized as follows. Control of properties is possible by control of chemical composition, control of rate of cooling, or control of shaping operations.

1. *Control of chemical composition.* No engineering material is a chemically pure element, and its properties depend on the nature and amount of impurities or added elements present.

2. *Control of rate of cooling.* Alteration of the rate of cooling may change the crystal size and the chemical composition of individual crystals.

3. *Control of shaping operations.* Materials may be given definite directional properties or they may be made nearly isotropic by proper manipulation of shaping operations.

Control is effected by altering the characteristics of the individual crystals, and by altering their relationship to each other.

Various techniques of physical and mechanical control will be considered in more detail, first from the standpoint of the cooling characteristics, or changes which take place during solidification and further cooling, and then from the standpoint of the shaping operations as they apply to materials in general. Specific characteristics of individual materials are discussed in later chapters.

6.6 Effects of Changes of Temperature

Many of the engineering materials, particularly the metals, are melted, or at least heated to incipient fusion, during the manufacturing or shaping processes. Experience has shown that the manner in which the cooling process is carried out has, in many cases, a pronounced effect upon the properties of the resultant material. The technique of hardening metals by heating and quenching them has been known and used for centuries as an empirical process. However, modern metallurgists have discovered some of the general scientific principles underlying many of the phenomena associated with changes in temperature, and are using them to control with a high degree of precision the properties of the metals they produce.

Although these general principles have been utilized chiefly in connection with metals, they may form a basis of approach to problems of manufacture of other materials, such as vitrified clay products and glass, which also undergo transformations in properties with changes in temperature.

6.7 Temperature-Time Characteristics

The freezing of pure metals is in most respects analogous to the freezing of water. For example, if molten lead is cooled slowly, it will begin to solidify at 327 C (621 F) and will remain at that temperature until the entire mass is solid, after which the temperature will again decrease. Curve a in Fig. 6.6 represents a temperature-time curve (a curve in which temperatures during the cooling process are plotted against time) for lead. The slope of the line gives the rate of cooling. Curves b and c represent similar curves for aluminum and antimony, respectively. The freezing point of aluminum is 659 C (1218 F) and the freezing point of antimony is 630 C (1166 F). Curve d represents the temperature-time curve for a mixture of lead and aluminum. All of the aluminum solidifies at 659 C, and all of the lead at 327 C, regardless of the relative amounts of each.

Curve e is for a mixture of 5 per cent of antimony and 95 per cent of lead. The mixture does not start to solidify at the freezing point of antimony or even at that of lead, but remains a liquid to a temperature below the freezing points of both component materials. When freezing does begin, the temperature does not remain constant as it did with the previous materials, but continues to decrease at a slower rate, and the metal continues freezing to a temperature of 228 C (442 F). If the mixture con-

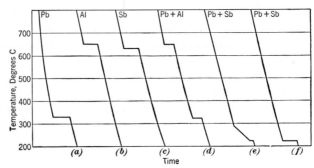

FIG. 6.6   Typical cooling curves.

tained 13 per cent antimony and 87 per cent lead, the entire mass would behave as a pure metal and all would solidify at 228 C, as indicated by curve *f*.   The explanation of these phenomena lies in the nature of the compositions which are formed by the two metals.

EQUILIBRIUM DIAGRAMS

6.8 Classification of Equilibrium Diagrams

The behavior of a mixture of metals upon cooling may be shown graphically by what is known as an equilibrium diagram, sometimes called a composition diagram or a constitution diagram.   This is a diagram in which temperatures are plotted as ordinates and compositions as abscissas. Three characteristic types of diagrams exist, namely layer type, solid-solution type, and eutectic type.   These indicate three characteristic actions which may occur when two liquids are mixed and frozen.   There are various combinations of the three elementary types.

The equilibrium diagrams to be discussed in this chapter cover the basic types which may exist when there are two fundamental constituents, and these diagrams involve only the liquid and solid phases under conditions of atmospheric pressure.   Equilibrium diagrams treating three fundamental constituents have important industrial applications, and diagrams including the gaseous phase and pressures other than atmospheric are used in special problems.   The basic principles are the same in all diagrams, however.

The diagrams are divided into areas (or volumes) and show the type of material existing under the conditions indicated by the location of the area with respect to the axes of reference.   The boundary lines between the adjacent areas indicate changes occurring in the material as it passes from one area to the other.   The changes may be *changes of state* (liquid to solid, etc.) or may be *changes in composition* (from a mixture to a compound, etc.).   The diagrams are determined experimentally.

6.9   Layer Type of Equilibrium Diagram

The simplest type of equilibrium diagram is obtained when the two materials are mutually insoluble and form neither chemical compounds nor solutions.   Lead and aluminum are two such metals, and their equilibrium diagram is shown in Fig. 6.7.   Temperatures in degrees are plotted as ordinates, and compositions as abscissas.   Thus the left boundary represents pure aluminum; the right boundary, pure lead.   The horizontal line at 659 C represents the boundary between the liquid mixture and a mixture of liquid lead and solid aluminum.   It indicates the temperature at which solidification of the mass begins and is sometimes called the liquidus.   The horizontal line at 327 C represents the boundary between a mixture of liquid lead with solid aluminum and the completely solidified mass.   It indicates the temperature at which solidification ceases, and is known as the solidus.

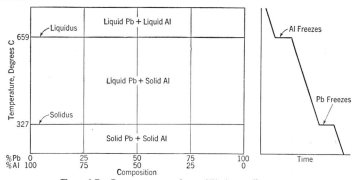

Fig. 6.7   Layer type of equilibrium diagram.

If any mixture of lead and aluminum is slowly cooled from 700 C, the aluminum begins to freeze at 659 C, the temperature remaining constant until all the aluminum is in the solid state.   Then the temperature decreases, with no change in the state of the mass, to 327 C.   At 327 C, regardless of the composition of the mixture, the lead solidifies.   Below 327 C the mass consists of solid lead and solid aluminum, unmixed.   At the right in Fig. 6.7 is shown a temperature-time diagram.

A diagram like that in Fig. 6.7 is known as a layer type of equilibrium diagram—because the diagram has a layer-like appearance, not because the materials will solidify in layers.   Whenever lead and aluminum are the two metals considered, they will separate, unless mixed continually, because of the great difference between their specific gravities.   Gold and lead also have a layer type of diagram; but, because of the small difference in specific gravities, the solid mass may consist of crystals of gold imbedded in a matrix of lead.   The crystals of gold solidify first, and the lead fills in the remaining spaces.

6.10 Solid-Solution Type of Equilibrium Diagram

~~The second type of equilibrium diagram—the solid-solution type—is obtained when the two materials are mutually soluble.~~ Copper and nickel are two such materials, and their equilibrium diagram is shown in Fig. 6.8. The left boundary represents pure nickel, and the right, pure copper. Pure nickel solidifies at 1452 C (2646 F), and pure copper at 1083 C (1981 F). The upper of the two curved lines indicates the temperature at which solidifi-

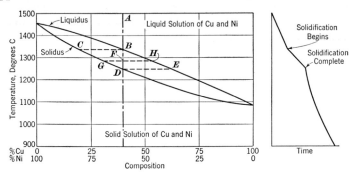

FIG. 6.8   Solid-solution type of equilibrium diagram.

cation begins, and is again called the liquidus. It indicates a change from the liquid state to a combination of liquid and solid. The lower line, the solidus, shows the temperatures at which solidification is complete. It is the boundary between the solid state and the solid plus liquid states.

After the boundary lines have been established, any change of state that occurs during cooling may be predicted from the diagram. For example, a mixture composed of 40 per cent copper and 60 per cent nickel at 1500 C would be represented as the point A. If such a mixture is cooled, no change takes place until a temperature of about 1340 C is reached (point B). At this temperature a solution composed of 20 per cent copper and 80 per cent nickel (point C, found by projecting a horizontal line from the liquidus to the solidus) solidifies. The remaining liquid contains slightly over 40 per cent copper and cannot solidify until the mass has cooled slightly. Then a solution containing slightly over 20 per cent copper solidifies, again enriching the resultant liquid in copper, and lowering the freezing point.

By the time the temperature has dropped to 1290 C, for example, the entire mixture is represented by the point F. The composition of the solid portion of the melt is given by the point G, and the composition of the liquid portion is given by the point H. The proportion of the melt which is solid may be determined by taking the ratio of the distance FH to the total distance GH; and the proportion which is still liquid is given by the ratio of *GF* to *GH*.   The composition of the liquid which solidifies at *F* is between the compositions given by the points *C* and *E*.   The selective freezing of the solid solution continues until the entire mass has become solid (point *D*).   The last drop of liquid to solidify contains about 65 per cent copper, and freezes at about 1250 C (point *E*).

If the cooling is slow, the material which solidifies first will take on additional copper from the material which solidifies later, so that the resultant solid will be entirely homogeneous, all crystals containing 40 per cent copper and 60 per cent nickel.   However, if the cooling is rapid, some of the transformations in the solid state may not have time to take place, and the final solid will not be homogeneous, the amount of transformation depending on the rate of cooling.   If the cooling were very rapid, the resultant mass might be composed of crystals of all compositions between 20 per cent copper and 65 per cent copper.   The average composition of the entire mass would, of course, still be 40 per cent copper and 60 per cent nickel, and it would have a uniform appearance because of the thorough mixing of the various solid solutions.   The crystals would be smaller than in the mixture which was slowly cooled.   Also, the properties of the crystals containing 20 per cent copper would be different from those containing 60 per cent copper, with the result that the slowly cooled and rapidly cooled solutions would have different properties even though they both contained a total of 40 per cent copper and 60 per cent nickel.

The structure and some of the properties of a solid solution may be explained in terms of its space lattice.   Two metals will form a solid solution in all proportions if atoms of the solute can replace atoms of the solvent in the space lattice of the latter.   The replacement usually occurs at random, as indicated in Fig. 6.9a, but it may occur according to a definite pattern for certain combinations of materials, giving rise to what is known as an *ordered lattice*, also called a *superlattice*.   For example, an alloy containing equal numbers of nickel atoms and gold atoms has a body-centered cubic space lattice.   When a superlattice forms, the gold atoms will occupy the corner positions, and the nickel atoms will occupy the center position (or vice versa), as indicated in Fig. 6.9b.   In an ordinary solid solution the atoms are located at random.   It is evident that the formation of a superlattice is possible only if atoms of the solvent and atoms of the solute are present in the proper proportions.   Thus, the gold-nickel superlattice would have the chemical composition AuNi.   Other superlatices involving two metals are $AuCu_3$, $PtCu_3$, $PdCu_3$, $FeNi_3$, $MnNi_3$, CuZn, CuBe, CuPd, AgMg, AgZn, AgCd, NiAl, FeCo, and CuAu.   These superlattices, or bimetallic compositions, are not chemical compounds in the usual sense.   There are also compositions, such as $MnFeNi_3$, which involve three metals.

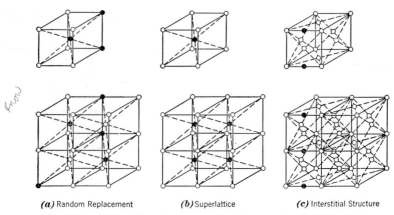

(a) Random Replacement   *(b)* Superlattice   *(c)* Interstitial Structure

FIG. 6.9   Unit cells and groups of cells in typical solid solutions.

Two metals will not be mutually soluble by substitution in all proportions unless they have the same type of space lattice and unless the sizes of
the two lattices are approximately equal.   That is, the forces which the
neighboring atoms exert on a given atom must be substantially the same
in solute and solvent for the replaced atom to remain in equilibrium.   It
has been found that, if the two metals do have the same type of space lattice
and if the difference in atomic size is not more than 8 per cent, the metals
will usually be mutually soluble in all proportions.   In addition, the
liquidus tends to be convex upward.   If the difference in atomic size is
between 8 and 15 per cent, the metals are still mutually soluble but there
is generally a tendency toward a minimum in the liquidus.   That is, the
liquidus is convex downward and tends to become tangent to the solidus
at a temperature lower than the freezing point of either of the constituents.
The behavior begins to approach that of a eutectic, which will be described
in the next section.

If the difference in atomic size exceeds 15 per cent, the metals are
usually not mutually soluble in all proportions.   In this case it is possible
for a solution to be formed over a limited range of compositions by replacement or else by the atoms of the solute occupying positions between the
atoms of the solvent.   This structure, indicated in Fig. 6.9c, is known as
an interstitial solid solution.   It can occur only if the atoms of the solute
are sufficiently small to fit in the spaces between the atoms of the solvent.
Carbon, hydrogen, boron, and nitrogen have a limited solubility of this
type in some of the metals.   The solvent and the solute need not have the
same type of space lattice.   For example, atoms of carbon (which has a
hexagonal space lattice) may be dissolved in this fashion in iron (which
has a face-centered cubic lattice) to form austenite.   However, the solubility is limited to a maximum of 1.7 per cent carbon.

Since the atoms of different materials are not identical, the introduction of an atom of the solute into the space lattice of the solvent creates a local disturbance or "warping" of the slip plane or planes in its vicinity, resulting in an increase in the strength and hardness.   This effect tends to be a maximum at some intermediate composition, approximating equal numbers of atoms of solvent and solute.

In general, electrical resistivity is a minimum at some intermediate composition.   Most of the solid solutions are relatively soft and ductile. Many of them are useful for engineering purposes because of their ease of shaping, their electrical characteristics, or their resistance to corrosion. The superlattice arrangement of atoms represents a more stable condition than the random arrangement.   In the superlattice condition, a material has a higher specific heat, a lower electrical resistivity, a higher tensile strength, and greater hardness than when in the disordered state. In general, there exists for each composition a limiting temperature above which a superlattice cannot exist.   If the material is quenched (cooled rapidly) from the critical temperature range to room temperature, the formation of the superlattice may be retarded in some cases, and its formation may be accelerated by reheating the material to a temperature below the critical value and allowing the alloy to cool slowly.   When this control is possible, as for example in the composition AuCu, quenching will produce a softer metal than slow cooling, and the strength and hardness of the quenched material may be increased by annealing.   This type of control of properties is useful when it is desirable to have the material soft and ductile for shaping, and have it stronger and harder for subsequent use.

6.11   Eutectic Type of Equilibrium Diagram

The third basic type of equilibrium diagram—the eutectic type—is obtained when the two materials form a eutectic.   A eutectic is that mechanical mixture of two materials which has the lowest freezing point of any combination of the materials.   It has a definite chemical composition and a definite freezing temperature, but it is not a chemical compound. Microscopic examination of an individual grain of a eutectic shows it to be a mixture of particles of one constituent in a matrix of the other.

Lead and antimony are two materials which form a eutectic, and their equilibrium diagram is shown in Fig. 6.10.   The eutectic, which has a freezing point of 228 C, is composed of 87 per cent lead and 13 per cent antimony.   The liquidus extends from the freezing point of antimony on the left-hand border diagonally down to the eutectic temperature at the eutectic composition and up to the freezing point of lead on the right-hand border.   The solidus extends from the freezing point of antimony almost vertically to the eutectic temperature, across the diagram horizontally almost to pure lead, and then up to the freezing point of lead.   The area between the solidus and the right-hand border corresponds to a solid solution of lead and antimony.   However, lead, which has a face-centered cubic space lattice, can dissolve only about 2 per cent of antimony since the latter has a hexagonal space lattice.   In the discussion which follows, the term α-lead will denote this solid solution.   Similarly, antimony will dissolve only a small percentage of lead, and this solid solution, which corresponds to the area between the solidus and the left-hand border, will be called α-antimony.

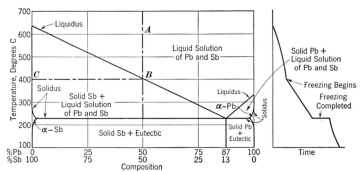

FIG. 6.10   Eutectic type of equilibrium diagram.

If a mixture of 50 per cent lead and 50 per cent antimony is cooled slowly, freezing begins at 400 C (point *B*) with crystals of α-antimony being formed (point *C*, again determined by projecting a horizontal line from the liquidus to the solidus).   This action increases the percentage of lead in the liquid, lowering its freezing point.   The selective freezing of α-antimony continues until the eutectic is reached, when all of the remaining liquid solidifies in the form of the eutectic.   Thus, the resultant solid is composed of grains of α-antimony in a matrix of the eutectic, the entire mass still having an average composition of 50 per cent lead and 50 per cent antimony.

Each grain of the eutectic consists of a mixture of 87 per cent lead and 13 per cent antimony, the structure being revealed under the microscope as tiny particles of antimony in a matrix of the lead.   A combination of 94 per cent lead and 6 per cent antimony, which composition has been used for battery plates, solidifies as grains of α-lead in a matrix of the eutectic.   In general, the eutectic has a much smaller particle size than either of its constituents alone, and therefore has a higher ultimate strength and greater hardness than the individual constituents.   For example, the eutectic of lead and antimony has an ultimate tensile strength of about 6000 psi as compared with about 2000 psi for antimony and 2500 psi for lead.   If the ductile constituent dominates in the eutectic, as it does in the lead-antimony combination, the eutectic will not usually be brittle, but if the brittle component predominates in the eutectic, then the eutectic will be brittle.

Eutectics are widely used for engineering purposes because of their low melting points or because of their relatively high tensile strengths and their hardness. For example, many of the solders, which must have low melting points, are composed in part of eutectics, while most of the ferrous alloys depend for their strength and hardness upon a eutectoid structure. The term *eutectoid* is used when the mixture is formed from a solid solution, while the term *eutectic* is used when the mixture is formed from a liquid solution.

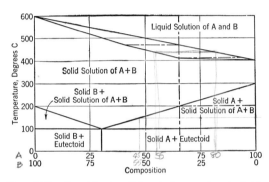

FIG. 6.11   Combined solid solution and eutectoid.

6.12   Combination Types of Equilibrium Diagrams

Combinations of the three fundamental types of equilibrium diagrams also exist. Figure 6.11 shows the equilibrium diagram for two materials which exist as a solid solution in one range of temperature but undergo changes as the temperature is decreased. The upper part of the diagram is similar to the solid-solution type, and the lower part is similar to the eutectic type.

If a mixture containing 65 per cent metal *A* and 35 per cent metal *B* were slowly cooled from 500 C or above, it would begin to solidify at 470 C, the solid containing about 40 per cent *A*. The liquid then becomes richer in *A,* and the freezing point is lowered. The selective freezing continues to 410 C, at which temperature the mass is completely solid. From 410 to 200 the mass is composed of a solid solution of 65 per cent *A* and 35 per cent *B*. At a temperature of 200 the solid solution undergoes a transformation, pure *A* separating out. This action changes the composition of the solid solution, and it cools slightly before more *A* separates out. The selective separating of *A* continues until the eutectoid, composed of *A* and *B,* is formed at 100. The mass then consists of a mixture of the eutectoid and *A*. No additional changes take place with additional cooling to room temperature.

6.13 Reheating and Cooling

The equilibrium diagrams in Figs. 6.7 to 6.11 are drawn for the condition of slow cooling, but are, in general, reversible. That is, if the solid composition is heated, it will begin to liquefy when the temperature reaches the solidus, and will be completely liquefied when the temperature reaches the liquidus. The first material to solidfy will be the last to liquefy, and vice versa. For some materials, including the iron-carbon alloys, the reaction temperature is a few degrees higher upon heating than upon cooling.

As has been indicated in the discussion of solid solutions, and as is also true for the eutectic, the changes which occur upon cooling require some time. If the material is *quenched* by immersion in a cooling agent such as water, the transformations may only partially occur and some of the characteristics of the material at high temperatures may be retained at room temperatures.

Alteration of the rate of cooling is one of the phases of control of properties by *heat treatment,* which is discussed further in the following chapter.

6.14 Applications of Equilibrium Diagrams

As the properties of metals and many other materials are dependent on the treatment they receive during the cooling process, and as the equilibrium diagram serves to indicate the nature of the material formed, the importance of the equilibrium diagram in indicating properties becomes evident.

For example, in the system described in section 6.12, the solid solution of *A* and *B* may have properties different from the mixture of the eutectoid and pure *A*. If the properties of the eutectoid are desirable, and the properties of the solid solution are undesirable, the engineer will know that the alloy of *A* and *B* cannot be used above 100 C without the possibility of damage, for above 100 C the eutectoid and solid *A* will be reconverted to the solid solution.

Conversely, if the solid solution is the desirable form for the alloy, the engineer will be concerned with devising some means for preventing the change of the solid solution into the eutectoid. This might be accomplished in one of two ways. A third element might be found, which, when added to the alloy, would halt the transformation or would lower the temperature of transformation below the working temperature of the alloy without introducing any undesirable properties. Nickel will effect the latter change for the iron-carbon alloys.

The second method of preserving the solid solution is by alteration of the rate of cooling.   The diagram as shown in Fig. 6.11 is for slow cooling. If the solid solution is quenched through the critical range (range of transformation from solid solution to eutectoid and pure A), the transformation of the solid solution to the eutectoid will not have time to occur, and the solid solution will be retained at room temperature.   However, if the alloy is again heated above the critical range and is allowed to cool slowly, it will transform to the eutectoid, and the advantage of the rapid cooling will be lost.

SHAPING OPERATIONS AND THEIR EFFECTS UPON PROPERTIES

6.15   Classification of Shaping Operations

Many different operations have been developed for shaping the various engineering materials, and each influences the properties of the final product.   The production techniques may be classified in the four following groups: (1) casting, which involves pouring the material in a liquid form into a mold of suitable shape and allowing it to solidify; (2) working, which involves hammering or pressing the material to the desired form while it is in a plastic, but solid, condition; (3) synthesizing, or building up the final shape by fastening together two or more simpler shapes; and (4) finishing, which includes a large number of special processes designed to bring the shape to its desired dimensions, to improve its appearance, or to increase its durability.

Each of these four major operations may be subdivided into several distinct processes.   The products resulting from these processes may be designated as indicated in the following list:

A. Castings
  1. Sand castings
  2. Plaster-mold castings
  3. Permanent-mold castings
  4. Die castings
  5. Investment-mold castings
  6. Shell-mold castings
  7. Flexible-mold castings
B. Wrought shapes
  1. Hot-rolled shapes
  2. Cold-rolled shapes
  3. Drop forgings
  4. Smith forgings
  5. Press forgings
  6. Machine or upset forgings
  7. Cold headed parts
  8. Stampings
  9. Extrusions
 10. Impact extrusions
 11. Drawn wire and tubing
 12. Cupped shapes
 13. Spinnings
 14. Pierced shapes
C. Synthesized or built-up members
  1. Riveted or bolted assemblies
  2. Weldments
  3. Brazed assemblies
  4. Laminations
  5. Powder-metallurgy parts
D. Finished surfaces
  1. Sawn
  2. Planed
  3. Ground
  4. Polished
  5. Surface-hardened
  6. Shot-peened
  7. Plated
  8. Coated

6.16 Castings

Casting is well adapted for the formation of parts of either simple or complex shape, if a number of the parts are to be produced. Many alloys have been developed for this purpose, including ferrous alloys, copper alloys (brass and bronze), aluminum alloys, magnesium alloys, and zinc alloys. Materials which are too hard to shape in the solid state except by grinding (Alnico, for example) are shaped by casting. The process is also used for concrete, some ceramic products, and widely used for plastics.

The most widely used of the casting processes for the formation of metal parts is sand casting, the normal annual production in the United States being in excess of 20,000,000 tons. The manufacture of a sand casting involves first the preparation of a wooden or metal pattern which has the shape of the finished product and is of the proper size, due allowance being made for shrinkage and machining when the latter is necessary. The pattern is placed in a container called a "flask," and sand containing a binder is packed around the pattern. The mold is separated in two parts, the pattern is removed, and the mold is dried or sometimes baked. The mold is then reassembled, and "cores" are placed in the mold where hollow spaces or openings are desired in the casting. Metal inserts known as "chills" are sometimes placed in the mold to accelerate the cooling at points where greater hardness may be desired. The molten metal is poured into the mold and allowed to solidify, after which the sand mold is removed. The casting is cleaned, and usually machined to bring it to the desired dimensions, as the commercial tolerance on size varies from $\frac{1}{16}$ in. to $\frac{3}{16}$ in. Sand casting is well adapted to the production of a wide range of sizes, from parts weighing less than an ounce to parts like steel car frames weighing more than 70 tons, and forging-press bases weighing over 200 tons. It is not satisfactory for members with thin sections, $\frac{1}{8}$ in. being the usual minimum practical thickness. Intricate shapes are readily produced by sand casting.

If a smoother finish on the casting is essential, plaster of Paris, instead of sand, may be used for the mold, producing what is known as a plaster-mold casting. The use of a plaster mold permits the casting of sections as thin as $\frac{1}{32}$ in., and the dimensional tolerance is usually within $\pm$ 0.005 in. A typical surface finish is 125 rms, which means that the root mean square of the deviations from a plane surface is 125 microinches. The elimination of machining tends to offset the higher cost of the mold and enables plaster-mold castings to compete with sand castings for the production of small (up to about 15 lb) shapes. Aluminum, magnesium, yellow brass, aluminum bronze, beryllium bronze, silicon bronze, manganese bronze, and other nonferrous alloys which have melting points less than 2100 F are used for plaster-mold castings.

If a large number of parts which are to have accurate dimensions (± 0.01 in.) without machining are required, the cost of preparing "permanent molds" may be justified.   These molds are normally made of an alloy cast iron, and an individual mold may be used as many as 30,000 times.   Permanent molds are suitable for the manufacture of castings from a wide range of metals, among the most important of which are aluminum alloys, copper alloys, iron, steel, and magnesium alloys.   The metal in a permanent-mold casting is finer grained than that in a sand-mold casting as a result of the more rapid rate of cooling.   Permanent-mold castings less than 0.10 in. in thickness have been satisfactorily produced, but the shapes cannot be so complex as those for some of the other types of castings the molds for which are destroyed in removing the castings.   The majority of permanent-mold castings range from 0.1 to 10 lb in weight.

One modification of permanent-mold casting is *centrifugal casting*, which was developed for the production of cast-iron pipe, but which has been adapted to the production of many other shapes.   In casting pipe centrifugally, the mold, which is a hollow cylinder, is located with the axis nearly horizontal and is rotated about the axis.   The molten metal is fed into the rotating cylinder, and flows radially outward against the mold because of the centrifugal force developed.   Any desired thickness may be built up by controlling the amount of metal fed into the mold.   The impurities will be found nearest the center of rotation since they are, in general, lighter than the casting metal, which flows to the outside by centrifugal action.   If shapes other than cylindrical are being cast, the molds are symmetrically arranged in a horizontal plane about the axis of rotation, which is vertical.   The molten metal is fed in near the axis of rotation and is forced outward into the molds by centrifugal force.   The speed is usually between 150 and 300 rpm, although it may be as high as 1500 rpm.

Another modification of the permanent-mold process is the continuous-casting technique which has been adapted for use with the cuprous alloys, aluminum, and special steels.   Molten metal is dumped into a reservoir called a tundish, which has an open-end mold and rolls at the bottom. The metal solidifies in passing through the mold and is withdrawn in a continuous ribbon by the rolls.   The length of the ribbon is limited only by the supply of molten metal.   Continuous-casting machines producing steel billets from 4 in. by 4 in. to 6 in. by 24 in. are in operation.

Molds, or forms, for concrete are normally made of wood or metal and are discussed in the chapter on concrete.

A high degree of dimensional accuracy in the resultant casting may be obtained by using hardened alloy-steel molds and injecting a definite quantity of the casting metal into the mold under a high pressure—sometimes as much as 25,000 psi.   The resulting product is known as a die

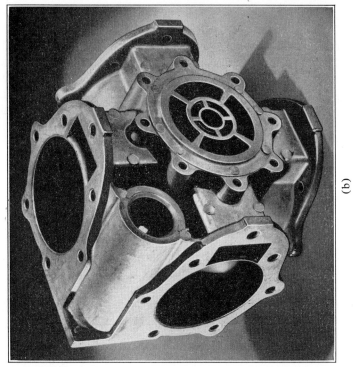

(b)

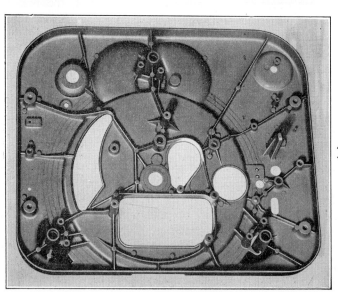

(a)

FIG. 6.12   Examples of die castings.   (a) Phonograph record-changer.   (b) Pump
casing.   (Courtesy New Jersey Zinc Company)

casting. About 75 per cent of the die castings produced are of zinc alloys, although aluminum alloys, copper alloys, and magnesium alloys are also suitable for this purpose. The chemical composition of the metal must be carefully controlled to eliminate impurities which might cause corrosion of the molds. Castings weighing less than 0.05 gm have been produced by this method, and formation of parts only 0.015 in. thick is feasible. Zippers are normally made by die casting, and the production of intricate shapes, including chains, to close tolerances is possible. The die castings shown in Fig. 6.12 are indicative of the shapes which may be produced by this method.

Investment-mold casting or precision casting, formerly used exclusively in the jewelry industry, has recently been adapted to the formation of small machine parts and other shapes which must be accurate in size or which are made from materials difficult or impossible to machine. The process consists in preparing a master mold which may be constructed in several sections. The mold is filled with wax, polystyrene or other plastic, or mercury which hardens or is frozen, forming a replica of the shape to be cast. The mold is removed, and the wax, plastic, or frozen mercury casting is used as a pattern for forming a second mold which may be made of plaster or of a ceramic material with a high melting point. When this mold, known as the investment mold, has hardened, it is heated and the molten wax, plastic, or mercury is poured out. The casting material is then poured into the mold and allowed to solidify in the usual manner, after which the mold may be broken and removed. This procedure permits the formation of very complicated and irregular castings because neither the pattern nor the mold finally used needs to be preserved. Sections as thin as $\frac{1}{32}$ in. may be cast satisfactorily, and tolerances as low as $\pm$ 0.002 in. are possible.

Smoother surfaces can be cast by this method, particularly when frozen mercury patterns are used, than by any other method. The surface finish that can be produced is about 40 rms. Plaster-mold castings and die castings have a finish of about 50 rms, and permanent-mold castings will vary from 100 to 125 rms. Precision castings may be formed of practically any metal. Although most investment castings weigh only a few pounds, the method has been applied to products weighing over 100 lb. One feature of the frozen-mercury patterns is that two parts can be bonded by merely pressing them together, thus permitting the formation of complex patterns. When mercury is used for the intermediate casting, the process is known as the Mercast process.

The first step in the preparation of a shell-mold casting consists in preparing a pattern of aluminum, iron, or bronze. A mixture of sand and a two-stage phenolic resin is packed around the pattern and the assembly is baked in a mold-making machine. The pattern is removed and the sand-plastic shell is reassembled to form the mold. Although difficulties are encountered in casting some metals by this process, it is in general quite versatile. It is suitable for castings weighing up to several hundred pounds.

At the present time tolerances as low as ± 0.002 in. on small dimensions are attained by some foundries. In one instance an austenitic chromium-nickel steel support ring for a jet engine is held to a tolerance of 0.010 in. in an 11-in. diameter. Excellent control of complex shapes is possible with this process.

The structure of shell-mold castings is more uniform than the structure of sand castings because the greater permeability of the shell molds permits gas to escape, thereby preventing or reducing blowholes. In addition, the shell is a comparatively good insulating material, resulting in a lower rate of cooling in the casting.

The process is also known as the Croning process. It was invented by Johannes Croning in Germany about 1937.

Flexible molds provide an inexpensive means of producing plastic parts for which a high tolerance of dimension is not required. The mold is prepared by pouring fluid vinyl-resin-based plastisol around a pattern, leaving one side open, and curing it at an elevated temperature for a few minutes. The pattern may then be popped out of the flexible mold by bending it, leaving it ready to receive the casting material, such as an epoxy gel. Relatively few runs may be made with a flexible mold, but its low cost makes it competitive for many applications.

6.17 Properties of Castings

As has been indicated, the mechanical properties of any structural member or machine part are dependent on the chemical composition of the material and on the size and orientation of the slip planes in the final product. For a casting of a given chemical composition, the physical condition of the crystals is dependent on the rate of cooling and on the volume changes which occur during the cooling. These factors are in turn dependent on the size and shape of the casting and on the material of which the mold is composed. For example, if a large casting of a solid cylindrical or rectangular shape is allowed to cool slowly as it normally would in a sand mold, heat flows outward from the casting through the mold, which is at a lower temperature, and solidification begins at the outside of the cylinder since that region first reaches the freezing temperature. The next material to solidify is that adjacent to the outside skin, and in general the additional material will solidify as an extension of the crystals which have already begun to form. That is, crystals tend to grow from the outside radially toward the center of the piece, the

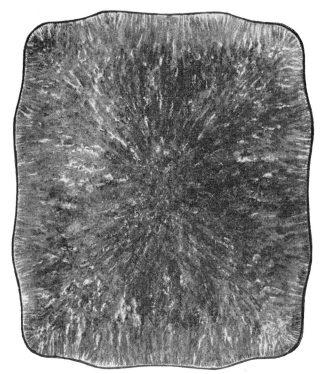

FIG. 6.13   Cross section of ingot of medium-carbon steel.
(Courtesy Drop Forging Association)

process resulting in selective, rather than random, orientation of slip planes. Figure 6.13, which is a photograph of the cross section of an ingot of medium-carbon steel, shows the directional characteristics of the crystals.

Near the center of the casting, solidification takes place more slowly, and the crystals tend to be larger and to have a random orientation. As a result, the properties are not constant across the section; the material near the outside tends to be stronger and harder than that near the center. While this characteristic is not necessarily objectionable (in fact, a member with a hard surface to resist wear, and a more ductile core to resist impact, may be highly desirable), it requires careful selection of samples in evaluating the properties of a cast metal.

If the cross section of the casting is thin, solidification will take place more rapidly and a more nearly homogeneous structure will result. A metal mold, which has a higher thermal conductivity than a sand or plaster mold, will tend to produce a finer-grained and more uniform casting. The structure of the casting is also influenced by the chemical composition of the material. If the resultant material consists of a solid solution or a eutectic in combination with a metal or solid solution, the grain size will depend on the temperature range of solidification (the distance between the liquidus and solidus on the equilibrium diagram) of the specific alloy. A large temperature range of solidification will tend to produce a coarser-grained material. A high latent heat also promotes grain growth because it decreases the rate of cooling.

In many castings the grain size is nearly uniform throughout the member, and the crystals have random orientation except at the surface. However, since the crystals at the surface are usually unfavorably oriented for resisting stress concentration, abrupt transitions in cross section and sharp re-entrant corners are particularly objectionable in castings.

The volume change which accompanies cooling from temperatures above the melting point has an important bearing upon the properties of a casting. Most of the engineering materials shrink as they cool, and the volume change accompanying a drop of several hundred degrees in temperature may be equivalent to that induced by a stress of several thousand pounds per square inch. In the ordinary casting the material around the outside solidifies first, enclosing a definite volume, while the material in the center is still in a liquid form. If the material in the center shrinks as it solidifies, it will tend to occupy less volume than that already enclosed by the solid skin, thereby inducing radial tensile strains in the piece which will lower its resistance to applied stress or which may even cause the piece to crack before it has cooled to room temperature. This defect may be prevented in part by proper design of the mold—usually by providing a "riser" or pool of molten metal which will flow into the space which is solidifying last. One advantage of plaster molds in comparison with metal molds is that the plaster molds will break or crush readily as the casting shrinks, permitting adjustment of the shrinkage strains.

Cooling strains cannot be entirely eliminated from a casting during the initial cooling process, but they may be subsequently removed by proper heat treatment. Annealing to remove initial strains has not been found entirely successful in die castings, as it may result in the formation of blisters due to entrained gas near the surface.

As compared with the other methods of shaping materials, casting usually produces a material which is more nearly isotropic and which has a lower tensile strength than can be obtained by some of the procedures which produce a preferred orientation of crystals. Investigations of vibration characteristics indicate that a material has a much higher damping capacity when cast than when shaped by other methods. This has led in some instances to the replacement of forged crankshafts by cast crankshafts. Even though cast crankshafts are much more brittle, they have more satisfactory operating characteristics because of high damping capacity.

FIG. 6.14   Hot rolling of steel rods.   (Courtesy Republic Steel Corporation)

The defects which may be present in castings and which tend to lower their strength include porosity or blowholes due to entrained air or gas, segregation of constituents, and initial strains due to unequal shrinkage rates. Nonhomogeneity may be detected by magnetic methods, such as magnaflux, or by X rays.

6.18 Rolling

Most of the structural-steel shapes such as angles, channels, and I beams are formed by rolling, and the method is also used for forming bars of various shapes, sheet material, plates, and strip from a wide variety of materials. The process may be carried out with the material at an elevated temperature, in which case it is known as hot rolling; or it may be done at temperatures approaching ordinary room temperatures, in which case it is called cold rolling. The general procedure is the same in each case, but the properties of the resultant materials are somewhat different.

In the rolling operation a billet, or large casting, is passed between two rolls, which operation reduces its cross section and increases its length. In the formation of most rolled stock this process is repeated several (12 or 15) times, each pass through the rolls reducing the cross section and bringing the shape more nearly to that finally desired. Figure 6.14 shows the hot rolling of steel rods. The rolls are normally made of chilled cast iron or alloy steel and produce a relatively smooth surface which for many uses requires no additional finishing or machining. Mirror finish is possible in steel, copper, or brass by using carefully shaped and hardened rolls— sometimes made of tungsten carbide, which is extremely hard and about twice as stiff as steel. A tolerance of ± 0.001 in., or 0.0003 in. for stainless steel, may be maintained on the dimensions. Finishing rolls operate at speeds up to 5000 fpm or more.

A modification of the rolling operation known as the *unitemper process* has recently been introduced. In it the shape to be formed is held between gripping rolls which stretch as well as press the material into the desired shape. It has been utilized for forming strip and sheet material, and results in a product of finer and more even grain and with more uniform hardness than results from the use of the standard rolling process.

6.19 Properties of Rolled Sections

The alteration in shape of a billet by rolling is accomplished by applying sufficient pressure or stress to cause plastic deformation. Such plastic deformation alters the properties of the material, temporarily at least, by reducing the size and altering the orientation of the crystals, and by other mechanical effects, such as elongation of the grains, blowholes, cavities, and inclusions, which tend to produce a "fibered" structure. In general, those metals which have a cubic space lattice tend to be oriented with the slip direction parallel to the direction of rolling. Metals which crystallize with a hexagonal space lattice may have their longitudinal axes either parallel or almost perpendicular to the direction of rolling, the position depending on the metal, the temperature during rolling, and the extent of reduction of the cross section in rolling.

For each metal there exists a critical temperature, or temperature range, above which the metal will recrystallize from a strained state and below which it will tend to retain its crystal boundaries. An increase in temperature above the critical range provides the heat necessary to increase the mobility of the atoms, permitting recrystallization. If the metal is rolled at a temperature well above the critical temperature, recrystallization and grain growth will occur, and the principal effect of rolling will be to alter the shape of the material; the properties will be effected but little. If the rolling takes place at a temperature below the critical temperature, the crystal form imposed by the rolling will be maintained and the properties will be altered. In general, the tensile strength is increased and the ductility is decreased by cold rolling or rolling below the critical temperature. In addition, the severe strain imposed during the cold rolling will induce residual strains in the material, and these may later cause cracking, as well as reduction of the ductility and toughness of the material. The residual strains may be removed by annealing.

If the rolling takes place at a temperature just above the critical temperature, the crystals will be reduced in size, thereby increasing the strength, but the ductility of the metal will not be decreased. As the temperature of the metal soon reaches the critical temperature in cooling, there is not sufficient time for readjustment of crystal boundaries to occur, and the fine-grained structure which makes for strength and ductility is retained. However, the increase in strength is not so great as the increase which may be produced by cold rolling.

For most metals the critical temperature is well above room temperature, but for others, such as lead and zinc, it is below room temperature. For the latter, the effects of strain hardening are not permanent, but disappear in a few days at room temperatures as the metals anneal.

Many observations have been made of the structure of metals following their recrystallization. For example, metals which crystallize in the hexagonal system retain the structure developed during rolling. Under controlled conditions a cubic structure, in which one face of the cube lies in the plane of rolling and one axis is parallel to the direction of rolling, may be produced with certain face-centered cubic lattices. Copper, gold, aluminum, and some alloys will assume this orientation if a well-developed deformation texture is obtained before recrystallization. The tendency for the cubic formation to result from recrystallization may be inhibited by cold reduction less than 50 per cent, by a low annealing temperature, or by the addition of certain alloying elements.   Material which has recrystallized in this form has marked directional properties and is unsuited for some subsequent shaping processes, such as cupping or deep drawing.

The strength of copper in which the cubic structure has been induced is about 20 per cent greater at an angle of 45 deg with the direction of rolling than in the direction of rolling or at an angle of 90 deg with it.   The ductility is about 400 per cent greater at 45 deg than at 0 deg or 90 deg.

The tensile strength of face-centered cubic metals is slightly greater in the transverse direction than in the direction of rolling, and the same is true of a cold-rolled steel sheet.   The strength may be a maximum at 45 deg with the direction of rolling if the reduction has been large.   An increase in tensile strength is accompanied by an increase in the elastic strength and a decrease in ductility.   The tensile strength of hot-rolled steel is slightly greater in the longitudinal direction than in the transverse direction.

Metals which crystallize in the hexagonal system, such as zinc, have a higher strength and a lower ductility in the transverse direction than in the direction of rolling.   Comparative stress-strain diagrams are shown in Chapter 9.

Cold rolling tends to produce a smoother and more shiny surface than hot rolling.   Hot-rolled steel acquires a coat of iron oxide, or "mill scale," because of rapid oxidation at the rolling temperatures.

Defects which may be present in both hot-rolled and cold-rolled shapes include seams, broken surface, scabs, blisters, inclusions of foreign material, roll marks, uneven gage, and rough corners.   These may be controlled or entirely eliminated by proper care during the shaping operation.

6.20   Forging

Forging is probably the oldest known method of shaping metals, and it is well adapted for the formation of parts ranging in weight from a fraction of a pound to several tons if the shape is not too complex.   In general, the operation consists in placing a heated billet or slab of the material in a die having the proper shape, and pressing or hammering the metal into place in the die with a suitably shaped punch, hammer, or die.   Several different machines have been devised for producing forgings.

Board drop-forging is a procedure in which a hammer which may weigh as much as 5000 lb is lifted and allowed to fall on the metal being shaped. Sometimes the hammer is so arranged that, in addition to the forces developed by its impact in dropping, steam or air pressure is applied behind the hammer.   Large shapes may be produced by drop forging, but the

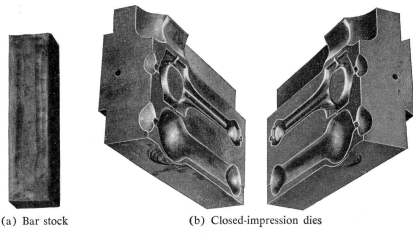

(a) Bar stock   (b) Closed-impression dies

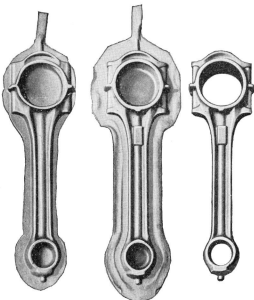

(c) Steps in forging
FIG..6.15   Drop-forged connecting rod.   (Courtesy Drop Forging Association)

method has also been used satisfactorily for shaping parts which weigh less
than 1 oz.   Smooth surfaces are produced with tolerances of ± 0.010 in.
or less, the exact amount depending on the care used in shaping the die.
Crankshafts, connecting rods, steering knuckles, and many other machine
parts are shaped by drop forging.   The dies involved in producing a
drop-forged connecting rod are shown in Fig. 6.15.

Smith forging employs smith hammers or open-frame hammers to produce flat forged stock. In this process the dies, instead of having depressions shaped to form the finished product, are flat, so the operation is one of reducing the cross section of the shape and improving the properties of the material. Smith forging is sometimes used as an operation preliminary to shaping by drop forging. Smith forgings or flat die forgings range in size from less than 1 lb to 20 tons.

Press forging utilizes steam, air, or oil pressure behind half of the die instead of utilizing the force due to dropping the upper half of the die. In preparing a press forging the heated billet or slug is placed in the die and then pressure is exerted so as to cause the metal to flow into the desired shape. This technique is one of the most important forming methods available and is well adapted for shaping nonferrous metals, such as aluminum alloys and bronze, as well as ferrous metals. Closer tolerances are available in press forgings than in drop forgings, but shapes which may be produced by this process are more limited because of the necessity of carefully controlling the flow of the metal in the die.

Machine forging, also called *upset forging,* is commonly used to produce aircraft-engine cylinders, bolt blanks, rivets, upset rods, and similar shapes. The stock, usually in the form of "wire" or rod, is inserted into a die designed to grip the material, with a portion of the wire projecting beyond the grips. Then a "header" is moved against the projecting metal, forcing it into a die which shortens it axially and expands it laterally. If the metal is not preheated the process is called *cold heading.*

Hollow forgings may be produced by having the header in the form of a punch. The tolerances produced by this method of shaping are closer than those resulting from the press-forging process, and a smooth surface is obtained. Carbon steel, stainless steel, copper, and copper alloys are the principal metals shaped by machine forging or cold heading. Stock for cold heading normally ranges from $\frac{1}{8}$ in. to 1 in. in diameter, but upset forgings weighing hundreds of pounds have been produced.

Stamping, also called *pressforming,* is a modification of the forging process and is often used to make sheet-metal parts, such as automobile fenders, cowling, and many airplane parts. Dies for stampings are usually made from a metal having a relatively low melting point and are shaped by casting, economical replacement being possible when they become worn. Lead and zinc have been used for dies, and a zinc-base alloy, known as Kirksite, is widely used. In forming some parts, rubber is used as the punch, forcing the sheet metal into place in the metal die. The rubber punch has many operational advantages, permitting more rapid change of dies and eliminating the need for careful registry of the halves of the die.

Both water and oil have been used as the forming medium to produce complicated shapes with even greater accuracy than rubber.

Stock up to $\frac{3}{4}$ in. in thickness may be formed by stamping, and dimensional tolerances of 0.002 in. or less may be maintained. Although the process has been applied widely to forming aluminum-alloy shapes, it may be utilized in a variety of metals, including brass, bronze, zinc, magnesium, nickel, carbon steels, and stainless steels.

6.21   Properties of Forgings

Forging and rolling have the same general effects upon the properties of the metal. With a properly designed die, operated under correct conditions, forging produces a stronger product than casting, because of the

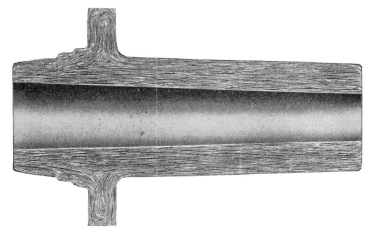

FIG. 6.16   Structure of upset forging.   (Courtesy Drop Forging Association)

mechanical working which the material receives. As the metal is forced into position, it is stressed above the proportional limit and refinement of grain or strain hardening results. Individual crystals of the metal are elongated, giving the material a grain-like appearance similar to wood. Figure 6.16 shows the flow lines, which may be brought out by etching, developed in a rear-axle housing formed by machine forging. For most metals the tensile strength is increased in the direction of the flow lines. Hence the forging may be designed so that the metal flows in the direction of the principal stresses developed during load. If the forging is carried out within the proper temperature range, the grain size of the metal is reduced by the mechanical working, and the increased strength is obtained with no decrease in ductility.

6.22 Extrusions

Many shapes of constant cross section are formed by a process known as extrusion. The technique consists in applying sufficient pressure to a rod or blank of the material to force it through a die or opening, the cross section of which forms the outline of the piece being shaped. The material is extruded through the die in the form of a ribbon of constant cross section, which is then cut to the desired lengths. All types of cross sections, hollow as well as solid, may be formed by this process, provided the wall thicknesses of the hollow portions can be about equal in order to avoid longitudinal planes of weakness. Stepped extrusions, or extrusions having sharp changes in cross section, are also produced. They are particularly useful for members such as airplane-wing spars which are tapered to conserve weight without sacrifice of strength.

A modification of the extrusion process is used for the production of small, thin-walled parts such as collapsible tubes. These parts, known as *impact extrusions,* are formed by placing a small disc or blank of the material on a suitably shaped die. Another die is forced down upon the blank, causing the material to flow upward along the sides of the die, thus forming the hollow tube. Machines have been developed which are capable of forming several hundred impact extrusions per hour.

A number of metals, including lead, copper, aluminum, magnesium, nickel, steel, zinc, and their alloys, are suitable for forming extruded parts. In general, metals are extruded at elevated temperatures, although low-carbon steel can be extruded at room temperature. Many clay products, such as brick, drain tile, and hollow building blocks, are formed by extruding the plastic clay through a suitable die before burning. Plastics may also be formed into strips and tubing by extruding.

6.23 Properties of Extrusions

It is evident from the manufacturing process that a metal extrusion will have definite directional properties. The high pressure required to force the metal through the die develops stresses well above the elastic limit, thereby inducing strain hardening in the finished product. The amount of refinement of grain or of strain hardening developed is dependent on the magnitude of the pressure as well as on the temperature of the material at the time of forming. In general, the properties of extrusions are comparable to the properties of rolled sections.

Possible defects in extrusions include blowholes due to pockets of entrained gas, longitudinal laminations or planes of weakness due to improper design of the die, and cracks, which may be due to formation at too low a pressure or temperature.

6.24   Drawn Wire and Tubing

Most wire, and some rods and tubing, are produced by a process known as drawing.   In this operation a rolled rod or tube pointed on one end is pulled through a die having an opening smaller than the original cross section of the rod.   The operation may be repeated a number of times in producing a wire of small diameter, and in some cases the wire is annealed between passes through successive dies in order to relieve some of the high strains produced in the drawing operation.   Scale must be removed, and suitable lubricants must be used.   The dies are normally carbides of tungsten, cobalt, boron, titanium, or tantalum, but diamond dies are used for fine wires.   Platinum wire as fine as 0.000017 in. in diameter is manufactured by this process.

A higher tensile strength may be produced by drawing than by any other known method of shaping.   For example, a steel which has an ultimate tensile strength of 60,000 psi in the hot-rolled condition may be drawn to a strength of 300,000 psi, and glass fibers having strengths in excess of 1,000,000 psi have been produced by drawing.   In each case there is a corresponding decrease in ductility with the increase in tensile strength.

6.25   Cupped Shapes

Cylindrical vessels and seamless steel tubing may be produced by a process known as cupping.   In this operation a disc of the hot metal is placed on a die having an opening equal in diameter to the external diameter of the finished product.   A ram or plunger having an external diameter equal to the internal diameter of the finished product is pressed against the blank, forcing the metal through the die into the desired cylindrical form.   The technique is quite similar to that involved in stamping or pressforming.   Since this cupping process involves shaping of the material by developing plastic deformation, it is apparent that directional properties will be imparted to the metal and that the strength will be increased while the ductility is decreased.

In one modification of this method, the metal is forced into the desired shape by exploding a charge of dynamite on one face of the blank.

6.26   Spinning

Many thin-walled vessels are advantageously shaped by a process called spinning.   In this operation a blank of the material in the form of a disc or a cup is clamped to a wooden or metal die.   The inside surface of the die corresponds to the exterior surface of the shape to be formed, or vice versa.   The die and the blank are rotated in a lathe at a high speed and the metal is forced into the die cavity by means of a ram or suitable tool. Tolerances of 0.015 in. or less may be maintained on dimensions.

This procedure is well adapted for the low-cost production of thin-walled shapes (that is, shapes up to $\frac{3}{16}$ in. thick) in the form of surfaces of revolution. Aluminum, steel, copper, brass, bronze, nickel, magnesium, and other metals may be shaped by spinning. Sections having diameters over 180 in. and depths of 72 in. have been formed by this method. In some instances the metal is hot-spun. Since strain hardening occurs during the shaping operation, the strength of the metal is increased.

6.27 Pierced Shapes

Most seamless steel tubing is produced by a process known as piercing. In this operation a heated rod of the metal is forced longitudinally over a fixed die, the external diameter of which is equal to the internal diameter of the tube. At the point where the die pierces the rod being shaped, the rod passes between rolls which are spaced to fix the external diameter of the tube. In this process, directional properties are imparted to the metal, but since the operation is carried out above the critical temperature of the metal the effect is one of grain refinement rather than strain hardening.

6.28 Riveted or Bolted Assemblies

Complex shapes may be fabricated by constructing the shape in simple elements and joining the elements by various techniques. One of the standard techniques consists in fastening the elements together by rivets, bolts, screws, nails, pins, or other fasteners. This method has long been regarded as standard, and is widely used. For example, a large cargo plane or bomber contains over a million rivets.

While the method has many advantages, and permits the formation of parts from simple rolled or extruded sections rather than by casting or other more involved procedures, it has some inherent disadvantages. The connection is relatively bulky and heavy and is practically always weaker than the original section, because of the removal of material in the original section. However, it does permit disassembly for repair or inspection.

6.29 Welding and Brazing

With the impetus of World War II, welding was developed from a somewhat questionable repair method to an accepted production technique. A number of processes have been evolved, all of which give reliable and predictable results under carefully controlled conditions. The development of inspection techniques, such as X-ray and gamma-ray radiography, which permit examination of a completed welded joint, has contributed materially to the acceptability of this method of fabrication.   The joining techniques which have been evolved may be classified into three groups: (1) pressure processes; (2) nonpressure processes; (3) brazing.

The weldability of several of the more common metals is indicated in Table 6.2.

TABLE 6.2

WELDABILITY OF METALS

Material	Resist.	Elec. Arc	Oxyacet.	Brazing
Low-carbon steel	E	E	E	E
Medium-carbon steel (0.30 to 0.45 %C)	W	W	W	E
High-carbon steels	D	D	D	S
Low-alloy steels	E	E	E	E
3xx stainless steels	E	E	E	E
4xx stainless steels	W	W	W	S
Cast iron	S	W	W	D
Aluminum and its alloys	W	E	S	W
Magnesium and its alloys	S	W	W	S
Copper and its alloys	D	W	W	E
Nickel and its alloys	E	E	W	E
Titanium	W	D	N	D
Lead	N	W	W	N
Zinc	D	N	W	N
Tungsten	D	S	N	E
Molybdenum	W	S	N	E
Gold, silver, platinum	D	W	D	E

NOTE: E, easily welded or brazed; W, can be welded or brazed; D, difficult to weld or braze; S, special precautions necessary; N, not used.

In the pressure processes the parts are joined by the combined action of heat and pressure.   The heat may be supplied by external means ranging from a blacksmith's forge to the exothermic reaction involved in the Thermit process,[1] or may be produced internally by resistance offered in the joint to the passage of electric current.   The heat may or may not be sufficient to melt the parts to be joined, but, together with the pressure, it is sufficient to develop an intimate contact between the members being joined.   The pressure may be applied mechanically as a steady force or may be applied by a series of blows, as in forging.

In the nonpressure process the parts are joined by the addition to the joint of molten material of like chemical composition.   The molten metal may be the iron produced in the Thermit process, but generally comes from melting a specially prepared rod by an a-c or d-c electric arc or by the combustion of a suitable mixture of gases, one of which is usually

[1] A finely divided mixture of aluminum and ferric oxide is ignited, producing molten iron and aluminum oxide.   Temperatures in the neighborhood of 2700 C may be obtained.

acetylene. The heat developed at the joint is normally sufficient to melt a small portion of each part being joined, thus assuring an intimate mechanical connection between the weld metal and the base metal.

Brazing consists in joining parts by the addition of a molten nonferrous filler metal having a melting point above 540 C but below the melting point of the metals being joined. The metals being joined are not melted by the brazing operation, and the brazing metal must adhere to them sufficiently to develop the necessary strength in the joint. Originally, brass (whence the term brazing) was used as the filler metal, but in modern practice it has been almost entirely replaced by other alloys, among the most important of which are a series of bronzes. Copper, nickel, silver, and various alloys have been used as brazing metal to meet various special conditions. Many different methods, including torch, electric arc, induction heating, and resistance heating, have been used for melting the filler metal. A recent development consists in assembling the parts to be joined, placing the solid filler metal in the form of a rod or other suitable shape in the proper position, and heating the unit in a furnace. This technique is economical of filler metal, time, and heat, and it is rapidly gaining adoption as a production process.

A number of alloys having a melting point below 540 C have been developed for joining parts. These alloys are known as solders. In most cases they are used primarily to produce an air-tight or liquid-tight joint rather than to produce a mechanically strong junction. Lead is the most commonly used solder base; hence, the solders normally have a low ultimate strength and a low creep limit.

The properties of a welded or brazed joint depend on the geometry of the joint, the extent of forging, whether or not fusion of the base metals occurs, and impurities which may be present. Welded connections may be defective because of incomplete joining which leaves seams between the two pieces; because of oxide inclusions due to overheating during welding; because of cooling strains developed in the material; or because of the alteration in the properties of the metal adjacent to the joint. Since lower temperatures are involved in brazing, brazed assemblies are less subject to residual distortion and to oxidation. Machine welding, which is used extensively, has eliminated many of these difficulties by affording proper control of the amount of material added, the pressure, and the temperature. Spot-welding and seam-welding machines are particularly valuable in the airframe industry, where thin sections, requiring good control of operations, are prevalent. In complicated parts where the elimination of cooling strains may become important, much may be done to improve the quality of the resultant product by controlling the sequence of the welding operations. Metals which are prone to oxidize readily may be welded satis-

(a) 2017-T4 rivet in 2025 Alclad aluminum-alloy sheet, ×5

(b) Spot weld of 2024 aluminum alloy, ×5

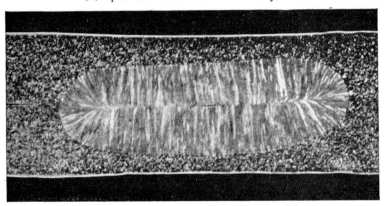

(c) Spot weld of 18-8 stainless steel, ×15

Fig. 6.17   Cross sections of riveted and welded joints.

factorily by shielding the area involved with an inert gas.   This is usually done by forcing a stream of inert gas over the heated area, but in some applications it has been desirable to surround the work with a transparent plastic envelop filled with the inert gas and do the welding inside the envelop.   Under properly controlled conditions the strength of a welded joint may exceed the strength of the base metal.   However, the allowable stresses in welded connections are normally lower than those in the base metal.

Figure 6.17 shows cross sections of riveted and welded connections. Differences in the structure of the material at the junction are clearly visible.

6.30   Laminated Construction

A section which is built up or increased in width or thickness by fastening together parallel members is known as a lamination. The technique of developing laminated members has received a great impetus in the wood-products industry. The production of plywood and other laminated timber members is described in the chapter on timber.

Laminated construction permits the use of nonisotropic material to produce a more nearly isotropic product. A sheet of plywood, for example, in which the grain in any layer is at right angles to that in the adjacent layer or layers, is more nearly isotropic than any one layer. Since metals are much more nearly isotropic than wood, lamination has little if any advantage over other methods of shaping as far as improvement of properties is concerned, except for increasing resistance to corrosion. One minor use of laminated metal construction is in bimetallic temperature controls. For this purpose, two thin strips of metals having different coefficients of thermal expansion are fastened together. A temperature change will cause the lamination to curl, and the resultant deformation may be utilized to operate an electrical relay.

Laminated construction is used in safety glass, the resultant sheet consisting of a tough, resistant, and transparent sheet of plastic cemented between two pieces of plate glass. The glass supplies resistance to abrasion, and the plastic is tough, preventing broken glass from flying when the pane is broken.

In any laminated construction it is evident that the properties of the product will depend on the orientation of the layers, and on the characteristics of the cementing material or other device used to hold the assembly together, as well as on the properties of the component units.

6.31   Powder-Metallurgy Parts

The technique of producing parts by pressing together and heating metal powder was known to the Egyptians as early as 3000 B.C. and it was also used by the Incas. The process was virtually forgotten until 1829, when it was employed as a method for forming platinum. Commercial development began about 1909, when the process of manufacturing tungsten wire for lamp filaments was patented. Within the last few years the process has been adapted to the fabrication of many small parts which could not otherwise be produced. In 1953, about 13,000 tons of iron were consumed in the manufacture of powder-metallurgy parts.

One form of the process consists in placing the material to be shaped, in the form of a fine powder, in a die of suitable conformation and applying pressure to consolidate the mass. The resultant briquette is usually placed in a sintering furnace for a short time at a temperature below the melting point of the material.   In some cases the product is placed in a sizing press or coining machine for accurate sizing after sintering.   Tolerances may be held to 0.0005 in.

Another application consists in feeding the powdered metal to a set of rolls, to form a porous sheet.   This is sintered, and may be rerolled and annealed to obtain the desired properties.   Copper, cupro-nickel, brass, bronze, Monel metal, and stainless-steel sheet have been produced by this method.

The powder may also be mixed with a liquid to form a slurry, cast in a plaster mold, allowed to dry, and then sintered.   Porous metal or plastic sheet, suitable for filters, is made by depositing a suitable layer of the powdered material on a flat surface and sintering.

The properties of the resultant product depend on the chemical composition of the powder or powders used, on the size, shape, and gradation of the particles of the powder, on the construction of the die and the pressure used during consolidation, and on the subsequent heat treatment. The ultimate tensile strength of steel products made from powder has been found to range from 200,000 psi for sintered and coined parts to 6000 psi for porous sheet material.

For some parts a commercially pure powder is used, and for others a mixture of powders or of a powder and a binder is desirable.   Most powders used will pass a 100-mesh sieve and from 35 to 50 per cent of the sample will pass a 325-mesh sieve.   The shape of the particles of powder varies from flat discs to spheres or needles, the form depending on the method used to produce them.   The grading, or distribution of particle size, of the powder is important.   Empirical findings indicate that a normal-distribution type of grading is preferable for most uses, as it results in a product containing less voids.   However, for some uses, such as self-lubricating bearings or filters, controlled voids are essential.

The movement of the material during consolidation also influences the properties.   For example, if a cylindrical part is formed by pouring the powder into the mold and consolidating it with a punch moving downward, the density and hardness of the product will be greatest at the top and become progressively less toward the bottom.   This longitudinal variation in properties is due to the friction developed between particles and between the powder and the die.   If the die is designed so that the cylinder is formed with two punches, one moving inward from each end, the resultant product will be comparatively hard and dense at each end and softer toward the middle of the length.   Friction developed during consolidation results in heat which in most cases has a beneficial effect on the product.

Sintering serves to amalgamate the product, making it harder and stronger, even though the temperature is not high enough to cause fusion.

The strength of the product apparently results primarily from the intimate contact developed between the particles during consolidation. Some advantages are obtained from applying the pressure and heat simultaneously. However, at the present stage of development few general principles have been developed; most information is of an empirical nature.

In present-day practice, powder metallurgy is best adapted to the production of small parts, although bearings weighing 228 lb have been successfully fabricated by the method. Many presses operate at pressures of 20,000 psi, although pressures up to 100,000 psi have been used. Parts have been produced in a single press at the rate of 240,000 per hr.

Units made by the powder-metallurgy process include billets for tungsten wire less than 0.001 in. in diameter and having an ultimate tensile strength of 590,000 psi; oilless bearings, part metal and part graphite, or porous metal, later filled with oil under pressure; cutting tools of tungsten carbide or molybdenum carbide, or tantalum carbide with nickel or cobalt as a cementing medium, permitting cutting speeds more than ten times those previously possible with the best high-speed steels; jet engine blades containing copper to improve the strength and increase the damping capacity; heavy metals, such as a tungsten-cobalt-nickel combination with a specific gravity 50 per cent greater than that of lead; gears; Alnico magnets; brushes for electrical equipment, made of copper and graphite; and electrical contact points, made of a mixture of two metals such as tungsten and silver or copper, in which the silver or copper provides the conductivity and the tungsten the resistance to high temperatures, resulting in a product with high conductivity and unusually high resistance to pitting or burning. Glass parts are also made by sintering compacts of powdered glass.

Powder-metallurgy parts made of a mixture of two materials retain the characteristics of each material, instead of developing new characteristics as they might if the materials were fused to produce a compound or eutectic of the constituent metals. Sheet produced by rolling powder has randomly oriented grains, in contrast with sheet rolled from bar stock. The random orientation is advantageous in material that is to be deep-drawn, spun, or cupped.

6.32 Finished Surfaces

The properties of a given structural member are in a large degree dependent on the characteristics of the surface. In most structural members the maximum stress occurs at the outside surface, and the surface is the portion at which deterioration due to either physical or chemical characteristics starts. In general, a smooth surface is essential for parts subjected to repeated loading, since any scratch or crack may result in a marked decrease of the endurance limit because of stress concentration. In addition, a smooth surface often presents a better appearance than a rough surface, although special finishes may be desirable to produce certain effects. The most effective technique for producing a smooth surface depends on the characteristics of the material.

Chemical etching or machining has been developed as a production method of removing metal more economically than is possible by conventional machines when special shapes are involved. It is particularly useful in producing webbed parts, tapered sections, and integrally stiffened "waffle" panels. As applied to aluminum alloys, the method consists in masking the portions not to be cut and immersing the part in a hot alkaline solution. The metal is dissolved chemically at a rate dependent on the temperature and the etching solution. Cuts up to 2 in. in depth appear to be possible at this time. With proper modification of the solution the process is also used for shaping steel and titanium products.

Special methods have been developed for machining those hard metals, carbides, and ceramics that are difficult to form. These methods include electrolytic grinding, electrosparking, electroarcing, and ultrasonic machining. In drilling a hole by electrolytic grinding, for example, a rotating disc is brought close to the part to be drilled. An electrolyte flows through the gap and a low-voltage direct current is applied between the part and the rotating disc. The material that is removed flows away in the electrolyte. In the electroarcing process the work is made the anode, and the tool the cathode, in a low-voltage (25-v) direct-current circuit. The metal is vaporized or cracked off as a result of thermal stress, and flows away in a stream of dielectric coolant. The method is rapid, but leaves some evidence of burned metal. This roughness of finish may be reduced by increasing the voltage, in which case the process is sometimes called electrosparking. Finishes as low as 26 rms are claimed for the process, as compared with 60 rms for electroarcing and 5 rms for electrolytic grinding.

Ultrasonic machining utilizes a tool that is made to vibrate at the tip at frequencies in the order of 25,000 cps. The tool is pressed against the work and a suspension of an abrasive such as boron carbide in water flows around and under the tip of the tool. Material is eroded and the tool sinks into the work, forming a hole having the same cross section as that of the tool.

Wood is usually first shaped by sawing; then it may be planed to produce a smoother surface, and finally may be sanded to remove remaining irregularities. Metal parts that are not fabricated to final dimensions in the initial forming process may be further shaped on a lathe, milling machine, or similar device which removes metal by cutting away the surface. This operation may leave objectionable tool marks but these may be removed by grinding; by polishing, which consists in grinding by using a very fine abrasive; or by superfinishing, which consists in removing all surface irregularities projecting above an established base plane. None of these processes will produce a perfectly flat or smooth surface, but the height of irregularities may be reduced to a few millionths of an inch.

Special surface treatments may be provided to increase still further the resistance of a member to destruction. A wooden surface may be oiled, painted, or varnished to repel moisture which might result in decay. The surface of a metal member which is subject to corrosion may be protected by covering the metal with a thin layer of a material less subject to corrosion. While paint may be used for this purpose, it is relatively weak structurally and offers but little resistance to abrasion. Metallic coatings are usually more satisfactory. Zinc is commonly used for protecting steel parts, in which case the part is said to be *galvanized.* Tin plate, consisting of a thin coating of tin on a sheet of steel, has been widely used in the foods industry. Lead, cadmium, and silver are also used as plating materials. For those applications in which a hard, wear-resistant surface coating is necessary, nickel plate or chromium plate is well adapted. Plating is applied by dipping the base metal into a bath of the plating material, or by electrolysis. Concrete and bituminous materials are sometimes used as protective coatings for steel. Sheet material of various aluminum alloys, as widely utilized in the aircraft industry, may be protected by a coating of pure aluminum. The standard Alclad sheet consists of a base sheet of strong aluminum alloy covered by a coating (about 10 per cent of the total thickness) of structurally weak, but chemically resistant, aluminum.

A process known as *shot peening* has been developed for increasing the surface resistance of materials subjected to repeated loading. It has been found that plastic deformation induced by compression normal to the surface will have a marked influence in increasing the endurance limit with respect to stresses parallel to the surface. In the shot-peening operation the surface is bombarded with hardened steel pellets to produce the necessary plastic deformation.

6.33 Selection of Materials and Processes

It is evident that the selection of the best material and most suitable method of fabrication of a given structural member or machine part may not be a simple process. In making that selection the engineer must have the answer to two questions: (1) What properties are required of this member? (2) What materials have those properties? In many cases, several materials and processes may appear about equally well adapted for producing a unit which will be structurally satisfactory. Considerations other than strength are of paramount importance in some circumstances. Weight, appearance, or cost may be the controlling factor.

In other situations, no known material or method of fabrication may be satisfactory. Hence, new materials and new shaping processes are constantly being devised to meet urgent requirements. It is imperative that every engineer know something about the range of properties available in the principal engineering materials, and the effect of production upon those properties. Hence, the following chapters are devoted to a brief consideration of the principal materials, metallic and nonmetallic, which have proven useful for engineering purposes.

PROBLEMS

6.1 In what shells are the electrons located (a) in the carbon atom and (b) in the oxygen atom?

6.2 In what material are the following shells filled with electrons? (a) The K and L shells; (b) the K, L, and M shells. *(a) Neon (b) tin*

6.3 A single crystal of a material having a face-centered cubic space lattice is subjected to axial stress parallel to one edge of the lattice. Evaluate the normal and shearing stresses on one of the planes of weakness.

6.4 A single crystal of a metal having a face-centered cubic space lattice is subjected to biaxial stress normal to the planes of two pairs of the sides. Determine the normal and shearing stresses acting on one of the planes of weakness.

6.5 Determine the theoretical ultimate shearing strength of tungsten.

6.6 Nickel and silver do not mix in any proportions. Construct an equilibrium diagram for the two, labeling all portions of the diagram.

6.7 Construct and label completely the equilibrium diagram for the materials lead and indium, which form a solid solution in all proportions.

6.8 Platinum (freezing point 1774 C) and gold (freezing point 1063 C) form a solid solution in all proportions. A mixture containing 50 per cent gold begins to freeze at 1550 C and becomes entirely solid at 1200 C. Draw the complete equilibrium diagram, labeling all areas.

6.9 Lead and gold are mutually insoluble. Construct their equilibrium diagram.

6.10 Bismuth and antimony form a solid solution in all proportions. Construct the equilibrium diagram.

6.11 Draw the equilibrium diagram, and label all areas, for the copper-palladium system. The two metals form a solid solution in all proportions.

6.12 Draw the equilibrium diagram, and label all areas, for the copper-platinum system. The two metals form a solid solution in all proportions.

6.13 Silver and gold form a solid solution in all proportions. Construct the equilibrium diagram.

6.14 Draw the equilibrium diagram for the nickel-platinum system, which is a solid solution in all proportions.

6.15 Construct the equilibrium diagram for the nickel-cobalt system. These two metals are mutually soluble in all proportions.

6.16 Copper (freezing point 1083 C) and gold (freezing point 1063 C) form a solid solution in all proportions. The equilibrium diagram has a minimum freezing point of about 890 C when the solution contains 18 per cent copper. Construct the equilibrium diagram.

6.17 Gold and thallium form a eutectic containing 28 per cent gold at 120 C. Construct the equilibrium diagram, labeling all areas, and describe the changes which occur when a mixture containing 50 per cent gold cools from 1100 C to room temperature.

6.18 Silver and copper form a eutectic containing 72 per cent silver at 1435 F. Construct the complete equilibrium diagram.

6.19 Lead and silver form a eutectic containing 5 per cent silver at 300 C. Construct the complete equilibrium diagram.

6.20 At 508 F, cadmium and zinc form a eutectic containing 83 per cent cadmium. Construct the complete equilibrium diagram and describe the changes that take place in a mixture containing 40 per cent cadmium as it solidifies.

6.21 Describe the changes which occur when a mixture of 20 per cent SiO_2 and 80 per cent Al_2O_3 cools from 2000 C to room temperature. The equilibrium diagram for the system is given in Fig. 12.2.

6.22 Describe the changes which occur when a mixture of 40 per cent SiO_2 and 60 per cent Al_2O_3 cools from 2000 C to room temperature.

6.23 Sand (SiO_2) and titanium dioxide, with freezing points of 1750 C and 1820 C, respectively, form a eutectic containing 10 per cent TiO_2 at 1540 C. Assume that a mixture containing 80 per cent SiO_2 begins to solidify at 1720 C. Draw the complete equilibrium diagram.

6.24 Two materials, R and S, with freezing points of 1800 C and 100 C, respectively, form a eutectic containing 30 per cent R at 800 C. At 500 C the eutectic decomposes to form a compound T, composed of 65 per cent R and 35 per cent S, which is stable below 500 C. Draw the complete equilibrium diagram.

6.25 Silicon and gold (freezing points 1420 C and 1063 C, respectively) form a eutectic containing 94 per cent gold at 370 C. Draw the equilibrium diagram and label all areas.

6.26 Cadmium and bismuth (freezing points 321 C and 271 C, respectively) form a eutectic containing 40 per cent cadmium at 140 C. Draw the complete equilibrium diagram.

6.27 Describe the changes which occur as a solder containing 40 per cent tin and 60 per cent lead cools slowly from 400 C to room temperature. (See Fig. 9.7.)

6.28 Describe the changes which take place in a mixture of 80 per cent tin and 20 per cent lead as it cools slowly from 400 C to room temperature. (See Fig. 9.7.)

6.29 Describe the changes which occur in an alloy which contains 20 per cent copper and 80 per cent aluminum as it cools slowly from 1000 C to room temperature. (See Fig. 9.3.)

6.30 Draw and label completely the equilibrium diagram for salt and water (freezing points 850 C and 0 C, respectively), which form a eutectic containing 23.5 per cent NaCl at −22 C.

6.31 Describe the changes which occur as a mixture of 75 per cent copper and 25 per cent nickel is cooled slowly from 1500 C to room temperature.

6.32 Describe the changes which occur in a mixture of 95 per cent lead and 5 per cent antimony as it cools slowly from 700 C to room temperature.

6.33 What production method would be suitable for shaping about 500 small parts of irregular nonsymmetrical cross section? The parts weigh a fraction of a pound each and are tapered along their length with a flange at the large end. Tolerances of ±0.003 in. must be maintained.

6.34 A series of thin-walled cup-shaped parts $1\frac{3}{4}$ in. long and $\frac{3}{4}$ in. in diameter with straight sides are to be fabricated to ±0.007 in. What production method would be the most suitable if the cost is relatively important?

6.35 A large number of straight-sided hollow cylinders with an outside diameter of 1 in. and a wall thickness of 0.24 in. are required. What production method would be the most suitable if tolerances of ±0.002 in. are to be maintained?

6.36 Several thousand gears varying from $\frac{1}{4}$ in. in diameter to $2\frac{1}{2}$ in. in diameter, with bossed hubs, are to be produced with tolerances of 0.080 in. What methods of production would be suitable?

6.37 Specify a satisfactory production method for a relatively small number of hollow cup-shaped parts 4 in. in diameter. The outside surface of the part is ribbed. Tolerances of ±0.020 in. must be maintained.

6.38 Several hundred long and relatively slender parts of irregular cross section are to be produced, with the dimensions of the cross section changing abruptly at three points throughout the length. Rigidity and light weight are required. Specify a suitable production method.

7 The Iron-Carbon System

7.1 Variation in Properties

No other class of materials exhibits so great a possible variation in properties as does the iron-carbon system even exclusive of the alloy steels. The wide range of properties available makes possible the use of iron-carbon alloys in almost all fields of engineering, wherever materials having strength and ductility are required.

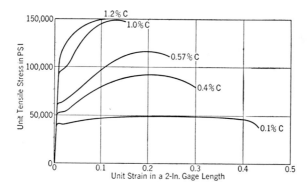

FIG. 7.1   Stress-strain diagrams for typical hot-worked iron-carbon alloys.

A difference of 2 or 3 per cent in the carbon content, a difference in heat treatment, and a difference in the amount of mechanical working during the shaping process may cause the ultimate tensile strength to vary from 20,000 psi to 300,000 psi; the elongation at failure may be varied from 50 per cent to 0.1 per cent, and the elastic strength may be varied from 10,000 psi to 270,000 psi.

The stress-strain diagrams in Fig. 7.1 show some of the variations in properties obtainable with a change in carbon content of slightly more than 1 per cent. It can be seen that higher carbon contents will give lower strengths and ductilities. If a larger scale were used for the graph, the series of stress-strain diagrams would also show that the modulus of elasticity is practically unaffected by the change of 1 per cent in the carbon content despite the enormous change in strengths. The usual limits of

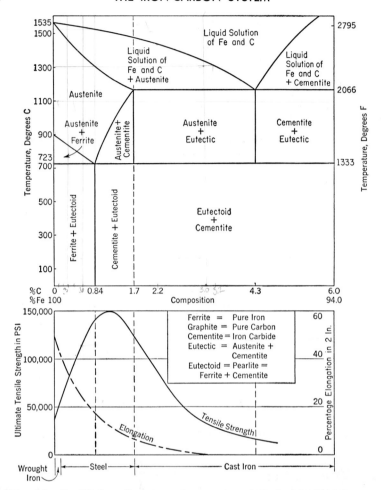

FIG. 7.2   Equilibrium diagram and properties of the iron-carbon system.

Young's modulus for the iron-carbon alloys are from 28,000,000 psi to 32,000,000 psi until the carbon content exceeds about 1.5 per cent, whereupon the modulus decreases. The alloys weigh about 490 lb per cu ft for carbon contents of up to about 1.5 per cent. Cast iron, containing from 2 to 4 per cent carbon, weighs about 450 lb per cu ft.

7.2 Equilibrium Diagram

Some of the methods which can be used in controlling the variations in strength, ductility, and other characteristics may be explained with the aid of the equilibrium diagram for a portion of the iron-carbon system, a simplified version of which is shown in Fig. 7.2. The temperature range shown is from 0 C to 1535 C (2795 F), the melting point of pure iron. The range of carbon content shown is from 0 to 6 per cent, which is the range for those materials which are of use to the engineer; alloys containing more than 6 per cent carbon are too weak and brittle to be of value. Wrought iron contains between 0 and 0.12 per cent carbon; steel, less than 1.7 per cent; and cast iron, over 1.7 per cent.

The diagram is a combination of the solid-solution, eutectic, and eutectoid types. It presents only the condition of slow cooling that would occur normally in air, and is valid only for combinations of iron and carbon without other alloying elements.

An increase in the rate of cooling of the material by immersing it in oil or water, or the addition of an alloying element such as nickel, silicon, or chromium, will change the diagram, as will be discussed later.

7.3 Action of Alloys in Cooling

The ordinary rolled section of structural steel, such as an I beam, contains about 0.2 per cent carbon. If steel of this composition is cooled slowly from above 1535 C, it will remain liquid until a temperature of about 1520 C is reached, when crystals of a material containing about 0.1 per cent carbon begin to form. Their formation increases the carbon content of the remaining liquid, which solidifies further as the temperature drops. The selective freezing continues until a temperature of about 1470 C is reached, by which time the entire mass has solidified. The mass consists of a solid solution of carbon in iron and is known as *austenite*. At that temperature the iron is in the form known as gamma iron (γ iron), which has a face-centered cubic space lattice. The carbon atoms are located interstitially in the iron lattice, as indicated diagrammatically in Fig. 6.4b and Fig. 6.9c. In this temperature range the iron can hold up to 1.7 per cent carbon in solution.

As the temperature continues to drop, the solid solution remains unchanged until the temperature has decreased to about 850 C. At this time a remarkable transformation occurs. The steel, which has cooled to a light red, begins to liberate heat. There is also an increase in volume, indicating that an internal adjustment is taking place. Investigations show that at this stage in the cooling, known as the recalescence period, the space lattice of the iron changes from the face-centered cubic form of γ iron to a body-centered cubic form, called alpha iron (α iron). Since the solubility of carbon in α iron is limited to about 0.03 per cent under the most favorable conditions, the carbon which was dissolved in the γ iron will begin to be rejected from a portion of the austenite. However, the remaining austenite, which at the 850 C temperature will dissolve almost 1 per cent of carbon, will absorb free carbon. The result is that crystals

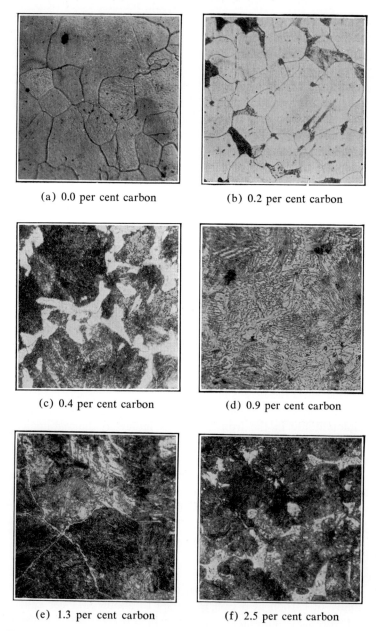

(a) 0.0 per cent carbon

(b) 0.2 per cent carbon

(c) 0.4 per cent carbon

(d) 0.9 per cent carbon

(e) 1.3 per cent carbon

(f) 2.5 per cent carbon

FIG. 7.3   Effect of carbon upon structure of ferrous metals (all ×500).

of α iron, also known as ferrite, begin to be precipitated from the austenite. The selective precipitation of ferrite continues, with the remaining austenite absorbing more carbon, until the temperature reaches 723 C (1333 F). At that temperature the carbon and part of the iron combine chemically to form iron carbide, Fe_3C, known to metallurgists as *cementite*.

The cementite, instead of forming in separate grains, combines mechanically with some of the ferrite and appears in flat sheets interspersed with similar sheets of ferrite within individual grains. These grains are known as *pearlite* because of their iridescent or pearl-like appearance in white light. Pearlite, which is a mechanical mixture of ferrite and cementite, is the iron-carbon eutectoid containing 0.84 per cent carbon. From the lower critical temperature to room temperature, steel containing 0.20 per cent carbon consists of a mixture of grains of ferrite and pearlite. The appearance of the resultant mass is indicated in Fig. 7.3b.

Figure 7.3a is a photomicrograph of iron containing no carbon. The individual grains are easily distinguished. The few black spots are impurities, primarily MnS. In Fig. 7.3b the grains of ferrite are evident as white areas, while the dark areas are crystals of pearlite. In Fig. 7.3c, which is a photomicrograph of a steel containing 0.4 per cent carbon, is shown the great increase in the relative amount of pearlite (the dark areas). The few light areas are ferrite. Figure 7.3d shows a photomicrograph of pearlite and illustrates the lamellar characteristic of the individual grains. The alternate parallel plates of ferrite and cementite which comprise a grain of pearlite are in the order of 0.000020 in. thick, although the thickness varies considerably.

If the initial liquid is hypereutectoid, as in the case of the steel shown in Fig. 7.3e, which contains 1.3 per cent carbon, the cooling characteristics will be similar to those of structural steel except that, when the austenite begins to decompose at about 1000 C, cementite is precipitated instead of ferrite. At room temperature the resultant mass will be composed of crystals of cementite and the eutectoid, pearlite.

A liquid containing 3 per cent carbon (cast iron) will start to solidify at about 1350 C, austenite being formed. Solidification will be complete at 1130 C, the solid consisting of austenite and the eutectic. At 723 C, which is the temperature at which the γ iron is transformed to α iron, the mixture will break down to form pearlite and cementite, plus some uncombined carbon (graphite). The eutectic is known as *ledeburite*.

If the initial carbon content is as much as 5 per cent, solidification will begin at about 1200 C, cementite being formed first, and will be complete at 1130 C, the solid being cementite and the eutectic. The eutectic must, therefore, be composed of austenite and cementite. At 723 C this will also break down to form pearlite, cementite, and graphite.

7.4 Constituents at Room Temperature

The preceding analysis shows that, after slow cooling, the iron-carbon products at room temperature consist of combinations of ferrite, pearlite, cementite, and graphite. Since pearlite is ferrite and cementite, the essential basic constituents are ferrite, cementite, and graphite—in other words, iron, iron carbide, and carbon.

Since the properties of these three materials are not at all similar, the properties of the resultant material will depend very much on the relative proportions of the three. The ultimate tensile strength of ferrite is about 40,000 psi, and its ultimate elongation in 2 in. is about 50 per cent. Graphite, by comparison, is weak and very brittle, while cementite is much harder but is also much more brittle than ferrite.

7.5 Variation of Strength and Ductility with Carbon Content

If a small quantity of carbon is added to pure iron in the molten state, the carbon will combine with part of the iron to form cementite at room temperature, making the resultant material stronger in tension but less ductile. This effect upon the properties increases with increasing carbon content up to about 1 per cent carbon. As more carbon is added, the resultant steel becomes more brittle, and the fractures obtained from a tensile test indicate failures in tension rather than in shear—that is, the fractures are nearly square across the specimen, rather than the typical cone-cup fractures of mild steel. The ultimate strength as obtained from a tensile test begins to decrease as the carbon content is increased above about 1 per cent. As the carbon content is increased further, a saturation point is reached and the excess carbon will appear as free graphite, both the tensile strength and the ductility being decreased.

A cast iron containing 4 per cent carbon will have an ultimate tensile strength of only about 20,000 psi. The compressive strength, however, is not affected so seriously by the increased graphite because the failure is not controlled by the tensile strength of the material, and the cast iron containing 4 per cent carbon may have an ultimate compressive strength as high as 80,000 psi.

Since the ductilities of both cementite and graphite are less than that of ferrite, ductility decreases rapidly with an increase in carbon content, the elongation in 8 in. decreasing from about 50 per cent for pure iron to about 0.1 per cent for cast iron containing 5 per cent carbon.

The properties of the iron-carbon alloys at room temperatures are dependent not only on the percentage of carbon but also on the size of the crystals and on the degree of dispersion of the carbon. Small crystals and highly dispersed carbon tend to increase the strength and hardness. The size of the crystals may be controlled by the shaping operations used in fabricating the member, and both the size of the crystals and the degree of dispersion of the carbon may be controlled by modifying the rate of cooling or by subjecting the material to additional cycles of heating and cooling after the initial cooling to room temperature.

7.6 Isothermal Transformations and Quenching

Transformations which occur in the iron-carbon alloys during cooling, as described in section 7.3, are for the normal condition of cooling in air. The changes which occur, particularly the transformation of γ iron to

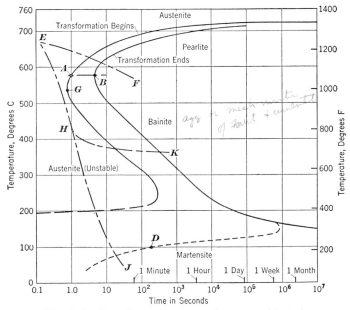

Fig. 7.4   Transformation curves for eutectoid steel.

α iron, are not instantaneous, and the products formed are dependent on the actual temperature (or temperature range) at which the transformation occurs.   For example, if austenite is allowed to transform at the lower critical temperature, the temperature being held constant until complete transformation occurs, pearlite will be formed as described.   However, if austenite is cooled to a temperature in the neighborhood of 100 C in the short time interval before transformation begins, the resultant product will have properties much different from those of pearlite.   The curves in Fig. 7.4 show the time required for the transformation of austenite to begin and the time required for the transformation to be complete at various temperatures.   At low temperatures a very long time is required for complete transformation.   The dotted portion of the curve indicates the approximate length of time for virtual completion of the transformation. These curves are called S curves, IT (isothermal transformation) curves, or TTT (time-temperature-transformation) curves, and those shown in Fig. 7.4 are for the eutectoid composition. The shapes of the curves, and their positions along the time scale, change with an alteration in carbon content. Either an increase or a decrease in the carbon content will shift both curves to the left. The curves are also affected by the presence of other alloying elements.

Above 723 C austenite is stable; but below that temperature, modification due to the transformation of γ iron to α iron will occur. Under normal conditions of cooling, the transformation of austenite to pearlite is completed at about 690 C. If the temperature of the austenite is suddenly decreased from above 725 C to (for example) 580 C, and is held at 580 C, transformation begins in 1 sec (point A) and is complete in a few seconds (point B). The resultant product is pearlite.

If the temperature of austenite is suddenly decreased from above 725 C to 100 C, transformation will begin at about 200 C. Although the transformation will continue for a long period of time, it will be virtually complete after a few minutes (point D). The resultant product is called martensite. It is fine-grained, and the carbon (in solution or in the form of iron carbide) is more uniformly dispersed than in pearlite. As a result, it is very hard and brittle, having an elastic strength of about 150,000 psi and an ultimate tensile strength of approximately 200,000 psi. Martensite is suitable for some articles, such as razor blades and files, but is too brittle for most purposes.

If the transformation of austenite takes place at a temperature between about 530 C and 200 C, the resultant product is known as bainite. It is much more ductile than martensite of equal hardness. At present bainite is produced commercially by a patented process called Austempering. A material having essentially the same strength as bainite, but somewhat less ductility, may be obtained by the annealing of martensite.

In general, the idealized isothermal transformation described, in which the temperature is lowered instantaneously to the desired value and is then held constant, can be approached only in small thin specimens and is not yet feasible for the usual shapes involved in commercial production. To obtain isothermal transformation the material must be placed in a controlled-temperature environment which lowers the temperature of the piece very rapidly. Neither air nor any other gas is satisfactory as it will not remove the heat from the piece rapidly enough, so a bath of molten salts or metal (such as lead) is used. However, if the member is thick, isothermal transformation cannot be attained because the center of the piece will cool more slowly than the outside. As a result, actual cooling curves attained under commercial conditions will be something like the line *EF* in Fig. 7.4, with the process yielding pearlite as the end product. However, if the piece is relatively thin and is quenched in a cold liquid such as ice water or brine, a curve such as *EHJ* may result. Then, when transformation occurs, the resultant product will be martensite. It is evident that, if martensite is to be produced, the cooling curve must lie to the left of the S curve until the desired temperature is reached. That is, it must lie to the left of point *G* (sometimes called the knee of the curve). Bainite may be produced by quenching to an elevated temperature, and then reducing the rate of cooling to give a cooling curve similar to *EHK* in Fig. 7.4.

The purpose of quenching is to lower the temperature of the piece to the desired value before transformation starts, in order to produce a fine-grained product and one with more highly dispersed carbon than would be possible with the normal slow cooling. Martensite is brittle because of severe initial cooling strains. These may be relieved by annealing or reheating the material to a suitable temperature.

7.7 Effects of Reheating

In general, the effects of reheating a metal are the reverse of those obtained in slow cooling. For example, a steel containing 0.20 per cent carbon and consisting of pearlite and ferrite is reconverted to austenite as the α iron is transformed to γ iron in the critical range. However, for this steel the temperatures of transformation are about 30 C higher for heating than for slow cooling. Changes in the carbon content, and the presence of other alloying elements, affect the temperature differential. If the material being reheated was formed by quenching, other effects may be observed. As has been stated, quenching is accompanied by severe distortion of the piece because of the volume changes involved in the transformation of γ iron to α iron, as well as the shrinkage due to cooling. The outside of the piece cools rapidly, becoming rigid, and resists further changes in shape. The inside cools more slowly and tries to change its volume within the rigid outside layer, and this process produces strains which may be sufficiently great in some cases to cause the material to crack or shatter. As the quenched material is reheated, the rigidity of the outside layer decreases and thus some readjustment is permitted to take place.

As atomic readjustment occurs, warping of the slip planes decreases, with the result that the strength is decreased and the ductility is increased. This tendency is further augmented by some increase in grain size. As would be expected, the amount of the effect in a given quenched steel depends on the temperature to which the material is heated and on the length of time it is kept at that temperature. Although the atomic readjustment may occur at temperatures well below the critical one, the most pronounced effect is near the critical temperature.

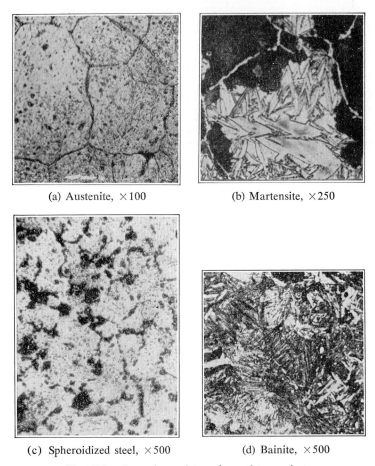

(a) Austenite, ×100   (b) Martensite, ×250

(c) Spheroidized steel, ×500   (d) Bainite, ×500

FIG. 7.5   Austenite and transformation products.

If the material is heated and held at a temperature slightly below the critical temperature for several hours, the cementite which was dispersed throughout the martensite will agglomerate in particles that are more or less spherical in outline, instead of in plates or thin sheets as in pearlite. This structure is illustrated in Fig. 7.5, which is a photomicrograph of a carbon steel that was quenched and reheated.   The spheroids of cementite are clearly outlined.   If the annealing continues at a sufficiently high temperature, all of the cementite in the martensite will be converted to the spheroid form, and the product will be a material which is relatively soft and ductile.   In fact, for a given carbon content, this product is the softest and most ductile form obtainable with a given iron-carbon alloy.

It is evident that, within limits imposed by a given carbon content, a

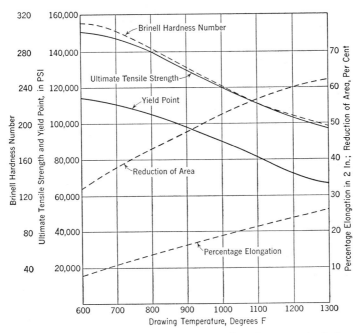

Fig. 7.6   Effect of drawing temperature on properties of water-quenched steel containing 0.45 per cent carbon. (Average values for ½-in. to 1½-in. rods.)

wide range of strengths and ductilities is available in the final product. The technique of producing a material which is to have properties other than those of pearlite is to quench austenite and then to anneal (normalize, temper, or draw) it to relieve the initial strains and to decrease the brittleness.

Various names have been applied to the transformation products of austenite produced by annealing. Some authors use the terms *troostite* and *sorbite* for materials having strengths and ductilities available with two progressive degrees of annealing.

Transformations take place more slowly during annealing than during quenching, and the properties of the final product may be closely controlled. Figure 7.6 indicates the range of properties available in one steel by annealing. Control is also possible by altering the chemical composition. For example, a steel having an ultimate tensile strength of about 120,000 psi could be produced from a steel having a carbon content of about 0.65 per cent by quenching it in water, or the higher strength could be produced by increasing the carbon content to about 0.80 per cent and cooling the material slowly. The specified tensile strength could also be obtained with a lower carbon content by adding certain alloying elements or by cold-working the material. Which of these four processes would be the best to use in a given situation depends on the other properties desired in the material, as these processes do not affect all properties in the same manner.

A number of technical terms have been developed in industry to designate various heat-treating operations which are used to impart specific properties. Some of the more commonly used terms are described in the following sections. The definitions of the terms were prepared jointly by the American Society for Metals, Society of Automotive Engineers, American Foundrymen's Association, and American Society for Testing Materials.[1]

7.8 Quenching

Quenching is defined as "a process of rapid cooling from an elevated temperature, by contact with liquids, gases, or solids."

As has been pointed out in connection with Fig. 7.4, the product resulting from the transformation of austenite depends on the rate of cooling below the critical range. The rate of cooling is dependent on the size of the piece being quenched, and on the nature of the quenching medium. While the quenching medium may be either a gas or a liquid, it is usually a liquid.

A relatively low rate of cooling may be obtained by submerging the piece in a bath of molten lead (327 C or 621 F, or higher). A higher rate of cooling may be obtained by using an oil, many grades of which are available. Mixtures of glycerin and water may be used where a still higher rate of quenching is desired, and ice water gives about the highest rate of cooling available. Under some circumstances a bath of oil on water is desirable, the piece to be quenched being first immersed in the oil and then submerged in the water.

Quenching must be done carefully, to avoid warping or cracking of the metal being treated. If a large axle, for example, is submerged horizontally in the quenching bath, the side entering first will be cooled rapidly and will shrink, causing the axle to warp. To avoid the possibility of a permanent warp being present in members of that type, they are usually immersed vertically. Even then, if the member is large, there is possibility of damage; for, as the material on the outside cools below the critical range, it will shrink and circumferential tensile strains and radial compressive strains will be set up. At the same time, the adjacent layer of material within is cooling through the critical range and is *expanding* as the transformation of austenite occurs. The resultant strain is often sufficient to crack the member or, in extreme cases, to cause it to explode. Even if

---

[1] ASTM Designation E 44.

the member does not crack, severe strains may remain upon cooling, and these will weaken the member greatly and will offset the beneficial properties induced by the quenching.

7.9 Hardening

Hardening is defined as "any process of increasing the hardness of metal by suitable treatment, usually involving heating and cooling." For example, the hardness of a piece of steel which is in the pearlitic state may be increased by heating it above the critical range, thus converting it into austenite, and then quenching it, producing bainite or martensite. This increase in hardness when martensite is produced will normally be accompanied by an increase in the tensile strength and a decrease in the ductility. The brittleness of the martensite may be reduced by annealing.

A special type of hardening, called casehardening (sec. 7.11), is used to produce a hard surface on a member without altering the properties of the core.

7.10 Annealing

Annealing is defined as "a process involving heating and cooling applied usually to induce softening. The term is also used to cover treatments intended to (a) remove stresses, (b) alter mechanical or physical properties, (c) produce a definite microstructure, and (d) remove gases."

Annealing is normally applied to members which have previously been quenched, and which are thereby subjected to quenching strains. As described in section 7.7, the reheating involved in annealing permits internal readjustment which may be accompanied by grain growth (extending to spheroidizing) if prolonged. Several types of annealing have been defined.

Full annealing. Full annealing is defined as "a softening process in which an iron-base alloy is heated to a temperature above the transformation range and after being held for a proper time at this temperature is cooled slowly to a temperature below the transformation range." The objects are ordinarily allowed to cool slowly in the furnace, although they may be removed from the furnace and cooled in some medium which assures a slow rate of cooling.

In practice, the temperature is usually held about 55 C above the upper critical temperature for about an hour, for each inch of thickness of the heaviest piece being annealed. This process permits the steel to become converted into austenite, which is transformed to pearlite upon subsequent slow cooling. The cooling is usually done in the annealing furnace so that the rate of cooling will be less than it would be in air. The process increases the softness and ductility of the piece and removes strains which might be present from previous quenchings or from shaping processes.   If the temperature is excessive, there will be an increase in the grain size, which is generally undesirable.

Process annealing.   Process annealing is defined as "a process, commonly applied in the sheet and wire industries, in which an iron-base alloy is heated to a temperature close to, but below, the lower limit of the transformation range and subsequently cooled."   This process is applied for the purpose of softening for further cold working.   The temperature range for process annealing is generally from 550 C (1022 F) to 650 C (1202 F).

Normalizing.   Normalizing is defined as "a process in which an iron-base alloy is heated to a temperature above the transformation range and subsequently cooled in still air at room temperature."   This treatment is rather similar to full annealing, but the material is allowed to cool somewhat more rapidly.   It is not often used with steels containing more than about 0.8 per cent carbon because of the tendency for the formation of objectionable crystals of cementite and increase in grain size.

Patenting.   Patenting is defined as "a process of heat treatment applied to medium- or high-carbon steel in wire making prior to the wire drawing or between drafts.   It consists in heating to a temperature above the transformation range, followed by cooling to a temperature below that range in air or in a bath of molten lead or salt maintained at a temperature appropriate to the carbon content of the steel and the properties required of the finished product."

Spheroidizing.   Spheroidizing is defined as "any process of heating and cooling steel that produces a rounded or globular form of carbide in the structure."   Spheroidizing methods frequently used are:
1. Prolonged heating at a temperature just below the lower limit of the transformation temperature range, with subsequent slow cooling.
2. Subjecting an object to a temperature which rises and falls alternately between a point within the transformation range and a point just below that range.   This method gives good results with small high-carbon-steel objects.
3. Heating an object to a temperature above the transformation range and then, after holding that temperature for a suitable time, cooling the object very slowly in the furnace.   This method is applicable to tool steel only.
4. Quenching in oil from the minimum temperature at which all carbide is dissolved, followed by reheating to a temperature slightly

below the transformation range.   This method is applicable to tool
steel containing a carbide network.

These processes, which develop the spheroid structure visible in Fig. 7.5,
result in an unusually soft and ductile product.

Tempering.   Tempering, also known as drawing, is defined as "a
process of reheating hardened or normalized steel to a temperature below
the transformation range, followed by any desired rate of cooling."   The
process is essentially one of converting martensite, produced by quenching,
into a softer and more ductile transformation product, austenite.   The
temperature employed depends entirely on the initial hardness of the piece,
and the degree of hardness finally desired.   It is evident that a comparatively high temperature for sufficient time to permit transformation will
result in a comparatively soft and ductile material.

Malleableizing.   Malleableizing is defined as "a process of annealing
white cast iron in which the combined carbon is wholly or in part transformed to graphitic or free carbon, and, in some cases, part of the carbon
is removed completely."

White cast iron is cast iron which has been quenched or cooled so
rapidly that the portion of the carbon which normally (under conditions
of slow cooling) is liberated as free carbon upon decomposition of the
eutectic at about 723 C (1333 F) is retained in the combined form with
the iron, as cementite.   The malleableizing operation liberates the carbon
in the form of rounded nodules consisting of many small crystals.   This
treatment greatly increases the ductility of the cast iron.

Graphitizing.   Graphitizing is defined as "an annealing process applied
to certain iron-base alloys, such as cast iron or some steels with high
carbon and silicon contents, by which the combined carbon is wholly or in
part transformed to graphitic or free carbon."

7.11 Casehardening

Casehardening, which is one of the special types of hardening, is
defined as "a process of surface hardening involving a change in the composition of the outer layer of an iron-base alloy followed by appropriate
thermal treatment."

The purpose of casehardening is to produce a member or machine
part which has a hard, wear-resisting surface, without reducing the toughness of the member.   This is accomplished by increasing the carbon content of a thin surface layer which may be hardened in the conventional
manner, or by adding nitrogen which combines with the iron near the surface to form a hard layer.   Since only a surface layer is affected by the
treatment, the core retains its ductility and toughness.

Low-carbon steels, such as SAE 1020, SAE 1117, NE 8024, and NE 8620, are suitable casehardening alloys. These steels are more easily machined than are the high-carbon alloys or other alloys which would be required to develop the same surface hardness by the usual quenching and drawing sequence. The resultant saving in time during manufacture gives the casehardened steels an economic advantage. Tests indicate that, in addition to having greater ductility and toughness, casehardened steels have a higher endurance limit than deep-hardened steels of equal hardness. Four general processes have been developed for producing casehardened steels.

Carburizing. Carburizing is defined as "a process of casehardening in which carbon is introduced into a solid iron-base alloy by heating above the transformation temperature range while in contact with a carbonaceous material, which may be a solid, liquid, or gas." Carburizing is frequently followed by quenching to produce a hardened case. As the process was formerly carried out, the metal (often wrought iron) and the carbonaceous material, consisting of bone, leather, coke, charcoal, or similar material, were packed together in a steel container and heated in a furnace. At the elevated temperature (900 C to 960 C), carbon gradually penetrated the ferrous metal, producing a skin or case of high-carbon alloy. In the middle temperature range, a $\frac{1}{16}$-in. case was produced in about 8 hr. However, the variability of the amount and character of the carbonaceous material resulted in a variable product. Later, standardized charcoal mixtures were developed for use as the source of carbon, and these increased the uniformity of the product.

The latest techniques, which are highly successful, utilize a liquid or a gas, instead of a solid, as the source of carbon. In gas carburization the parts to be carburized are placed in a furnace into which is fed a carefully controlled mixture of gases. The active element, which normally comprises only 1 or 2 per cent of the total gas content, is often methane, although ethane, propane, natural gas, or a manufactured product may be used. At the elevated temperature (820 C to 930 C), the carbon in the gas is dissociated and enters into combination with the iron. By maintaining a carefully balanced atmosphere of gases and by careful temperature control, the properties of the carburized part may be held within narrow tolerances. At 930 C a 0.050-in. case is produced in about eight hours. Since the material is heated above the critical range, austenite is produced and the part must be quenched to harden it. That is, the carburizing process does not automatically produce a hard surface; it only increases the hardenability, or capacity of the member for being hardened.

Decarburization is also possible by the same process. For example, if the atmosphere contains an excess amount of carbon dioxide, the CO_2 will dissociate into carbon monoxide and oxygen, which will remove carbon from the iron-carbon alloy.

Cyaniding. The liquid carburizing process is known as cyaniding, or the salt-bath treatment. Cyaniding is defined as "a process of case-hardening an iron-base alloy by the simultaneous absorption of carbon and nitrogen by heating in a cyanide salt." Cyaniding is usually followed by quenching to produce a hard case. The pieces to be carburized are immersed in the bath of molten salt, the active component of which is sodium cyanamide, calcium cyanamide, or some other cyanide salt. The usual temperature range for cyaniding is from 870 C to 960 C. At 930 C a case 0.065 in. thick will be produced in about eight hours.

Nitriding. Nitriding is defined as "a process of casehardening in which an iron-base alloy of special composition is heated in an atmosphere of ammonia or in contact with nitrogenous material. Surface hardening is produced by the absorption of nitrogen without quenching." As is indicated in the definition, either a gas nitriding process with ammonia or a liquid salt bath may be used to supply the nitrogen. The nitrogen, which dissociates at the elevated temperatures involved, is absorbed by the steel, producing a hard, brittle case. The process does not require such a high temperature as the carburizing process or the cyaniding process; it is usually carried out at approximately 520 C, although temperatures as high as 650 C are sometimes used. Since these temperatures are below the critical range, the α iron is not transformed to γ iron. Hence there is much less distortion of the piece than occurs in the other processes. Full hardening is developed without quenching, and this is an additional advantage. The principal disadvantage of the process is the relatively long time involved in treatment. About 30 hr are required to produce a case 0.020 in. thick.

Carbonitriding. This is "a process of casehardening an iron-base alloy by the simultaneous absorption of carbon and nitrogen by heating in a gaseous atmosphere of suitable composition, followed by either quenching or cooling slowly as required." Ammonia combined with city gas or some other source of propane is normally used to provide the nitrogen and the carbon. Whether or not quenching is required depends on the relative amounts of carburizing and nitriding developed.

7.12 Austempering

A patented technique for the production of a strong carbon steel is known as Austempering. It consists in quenching the iron-carbon alloy in a medium which is held at a temperature between 200 C (392 F) and

480 C (896 F) so that the temperature of the piece remains essentially constant during the transformation process. The quenching medium (molten salts or other suitable material) must reduce the temperature of the metal very quickly so that the cooling curve will fall to the left of the knee of the S curve. As will be noted from the S curves of the eutectoid composition (Fig. 7.4), this procedure will produce bainite, which is a strong, ductile, fine-grained material. After the transformation has been completed, the material is removed from the quenching bath and is cooled to room temperature. The interrupted quenching, in addition to improving the structure of the material, decreases the possibility of developing high quenching strains such as would be produced by quenching below 100 C.

7.13 Martempering

Another of the techniques which have been developed for producing a strong ductile steel by interrupted quenching is known as Martempering. The purpose of the operation is to produce martensite in which the usual quenching strains are virtually eliminated. While details of the process vary somewhat, the part to be tempered is usually quenched in such a manner as to produce a cooling curve similar to *EH* in Fig. 7.4. However, before the transformation is completed, the part is placed in liquid salts or molten lead at a temperature of about 200 C (392 F) until the temperature has become equalized throughout the piece, and it is then cooled in air. The result is a fine-grained martensite without undue cooling stresses. During World War II, one plant produced over 3,000,000 Martempered parts without a single rejection for quenching cracks or warpage.

7.14 Flamehardening and Induction Heating

Two special processes which have been developed for aid in heat-treating operations are *flamehardening* and *induction heating.* Either process serves to reduce the amount of time required in a hardening or tempering sequence and to provide better metallurgical control.

In addition to making possible the heat treatment of members that are too large to be placed in furnaces, flame hardening is particularly well adapted for producing a hard surface over a limited area which has been machined. For example, it is successfully used in the production of gears to obtain hardened teeth which will resist wear without developing a brittle structure throughout the entire gear. In the flamehardening process a gas flame (often oxyacetylene) is directed against the surface to be treated, rapidly increasing its temperature to the desired range (above the critical temperature), and the member is then quenched by water or oil jets to produce the desired hardness. The heating is sufficiently localized to prevent serious distortion.

The use of induction heating in the manufacture of small parts was extended greatly during World War II. The piece to be heated is placed in an induction furnace, or a furnace surrounded by a coil through which a medium-frequency or high-frequency alternating current is passed. The temperature of the charge in the furnace increases rapidly. For example, a temperature rise of 1280 C (2304 F) may be produced throughout a steel rod $1\frac{3}{8}$ in. in diameter in 8 sec or less. Forging stock $5\frac{1}{4}$ in. in diameter has been heated by this process through a similar temperature range in 7 min. In the usual furnaces, the frequencies used vary from 600 cycles per second to about 20,000 cycles per second although frequencies of 2,000,000 cycles per second have been utilized.

Induction heating has the advantage of producing a uniform temperature throughout the member very rapidly, is clean, and reduces waste due to formation of mill scale and other oxides. The method is used for heating nonmetallic materials as well as metals.

7.15 Cold Treatment

As noted in Fig. 7.4 the complete transformation of austenite at temperatures below about 150 C requires a long time. This characteristic has led to certain difficulties in connection with gages and other parts in which low tolerances are required. For example, martensite would normally be regarded as a suitable material for a gage because of its hardness and resistance to wear. However, it has been found that the dimensions of gages produced by quenching austenite to form martensite change over a period of time following manufacture. The errors introduced by the volume change that takes place because of the continued transformation of austenite to martensite amount, in some cases, to as much as twenty times the tolerances of the gages. Obviously, a gage in which such a change in dimensions has occurred is unfit for further use.

It has been found that gages of martensitic composition can be stabilized by subjecting them to a cold treatment. While the details of the procedure involved are not standardized and are subject to considerable discussion and modification, they consist essentially in subjecting the gage to temperatures of -100 F or lower, followed by heating to a temperature slightly above room temperature. The cycle of cooling and heating may be repeated several times, as it has the effect of accelerating the volume change, thereby stabilizing the instrument. In addition to fixing the dimensions of the gage, cold treatment increases the hardness, strength, and ductility of the material.

7.16 Hardenability

When the sources of many raw materials, including metals used for alloying with steel, were shut off or became inadequate near the beginning of World War II, industry was faced with the necessity of developing new steels to be substituted for those in common use. Many new alloys were developed from available materials, but the evaluation of all their charac-

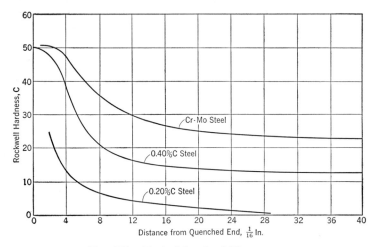

FIG. 7.7   Typical hardenability curves.

teristics would have been practically impossible because of the amount of time required. As a matter of expediency, the usability of each of the proposed substitute alloy steels was evaluated on the basis of the hardenability of the metal, as measured by the *Jominy end-quench test.* The hardenability test gives an index of the capacity of the steel for being hardened by quenching. It indicates the *maximum hardness* which may be developed by quenching, and the *depth to which the material may be hardened.* Since the tensile strength and a number of other characteristics of steels are rather closely related to hardness, the hardenability data give preliminary indications of the worth of substitute alloys. The test is now regarded as standard.

In the Jominy test a standard specimen 1 in. in diameter and about 4 in. long is heated to the proper hardening temperature in an atmosphere which inhibits scaling and decarburization. The specimen is then hung with its longitudinal axis vertical and is quenched by a stream of water directed against the lower face for at least 10 min. This treatment produces a high rate of cooling at the lower end and a low rate of cooling at the upper end. For example, at a temperature of 1300 F the cooling rate varies from approximately 600 F per sec at the lower end to 40 F per sec at the top.

After the specimen is quenched, its Rockwell C hardness is measured at $\frac{1}{16}$-in. intervals along its length, and a hardenability chart is prepared by plotting hardness against distance from the end. The index of hardenability is reported as the distance from the quenched end within which the designated hardness is obtainable.

Typical hardenability curves are shown in Fig. 7.7. They indicate the relative maximum hardnesses which may be developed in the steels, as well as the depths to which a given degree of hardness may be developed. With proper interpretation, data from a Jominy end-quench test supply useful information regarding the properties obtainable by various heat treatments. Hardenability is being made a basis for specifying steel, as outlined in section 8.46, in which the so-called H steels are described.

PROBLEMS

7.1 Determine the elastic strength of each of the steels shown in Fig. 7.1.

7.2 If the modulus of elasticity of each is 30,000,000 psi, determine the modulus of resilience of the steels shown in Fig. 7.1.

7.3 Determine the modulus of toughness of each of the steels for which the stress-strain diagrams are given in Fig. 7.1.

7.4 Each wire in a certain cable is to carry a static tensile load of 1000 lb, with a factor of safety of 4 with respect to failure by fracture. (a) Which of the materials indicated in Fig. 7.1 would be best suited for the use, and (b) what would be the required diameter?

7.5 Describe the changes which occur in pure iron as it is slowly cooled from 1550 C to room temperature.

7.6 Describe the action of a steel containing 0.84 per cent carbon as it is slowly cooled from 1600 C to room temperature.

7.7 What changes will occur in a steel containing 1.5 per cent carbon as it is slowly cooled from the molten state to room temperature?

7.8 (a) What two compositions will produce an iron-carbon alloy having an ultimate tensile strength of approximately 100,000 psi when slowly cooled? (b) Which of the two will be the better adapted to absorbing dynamic loading?

7.9 A certain steel containing 0.40 per cent carbon was slowly cooled through the critical range. (a) What will be its approximate ultimate tensile strength and elongation? (b) How may its tensile strength be increased?

7.10 If the yield point in tension is assumed to be 70 per cent of the ultimate strength, what will be the approximate modulus of toughness for a pearlitic steel containing 0.80 per cent carbon?

7.11 What is the critical range for steel containing (a) 0.40 per cent carbon, (b) 0.80 per cent carbon, and (c) 1.5 per cent carbon?

7.12 (a) How many pounds of carbon are contained in a cubic foot of cast iron containing 5 per cent carbon? (b) How many cubic feet? The specific gravity of carbon may be assumed to be 2.40.

7.13 Determine the critical cooling rate for the production of pearlite.

7.14 Between what limits must the cooling rate lie to insure the production of bainite?

7.15 What is the maximum cooling rate which will insure the production of martensite?

7.16 By approximately how much may the ultimate tensile strength of a steel containing 0.84 per cent carbon be increased by quenching it, as compared with cooling it slowly?

7.17 Outline the procedure to be followed in shaping and preparing for use, the cutting edge of a broken steel chisel containing 0.80 per cent carbon.

7.18 (a) At what maximum safe temperature may a tool of martensitic structure be used? (b) If that temperature is exceeded, how may the tool be reconditioned?

7.19 A low-carbon-steel rod for which ductility is the most important property was accidentally quenched at a temperature of 650 C. (a) Was the material damaged? (b) If so, how may the damage be remedied?

7.20 Describe the changes which occur in the properties of a pearlitic steel containing 0.60 per cent carbon as it is heated to 900 C, immersed in molten lead, and subsequently cooled to room temperature.

7.21 Describe the changes which occur in the properties of a pearlitic steel containing 0.40 per cent carbon as it is heated to 900 C, quenched in ice water, reheated to 600 C for several hours, and cooled in air.

7.22 What will be the final properties of a martensitic steel containing 1.00 per cent carbon if it is subjected to a full annealing process?

8 Manufacture and Properties
of Ferrous Metals

8.1 Uses of Ferrous Metals

Wrought iron, steel, and cast iron, which are known as the ferrous metals, are among the most widely used engineering materials because of their availability, high strength, workability, and durability. In 1955 about 125,000,000 tons of steel ingots and steel for casting were produced in the United States. This amount is approximately equal to the annual production in the world prior to 1939. At that time the United States was the leading producer, with Germany, Japan, and Great Britain following in order of production.

Despite its importance at the present time, iron did not come into extensive use until comparatively recently. In the form of meteoric iron, it was discovered in prehistoric times, but was then probably not available in sufficient quantities to compete with the more abundant and easily worked copper and copper alloys, or if it was used, the evidence has rusted away because iron, in contrast with copper, oxidizes readily. In an Egyptian cemetery oxidized remains of iron beads dating back to 4000 B.C. have been found, and a piece of iron was found in the Great Pyramid of Gizeh. The latter was presumably made about 3100 B.C.

It is thought that iron was first produced from its ores by heating the ore in a charcoal fire. The resulting metal, wrought iron, which could be shaped by heating and hammering, was used for small tools. Later it was discovered that if the wrought iron was packed in a carbonaceous material and heated, the resulting metal was stronger and harder. Thus, steel was first produced. The famous Toledo steel used for swords was made in this way.

During the Middle Ages the art of forging iron and steel reached a surprising degree of perfection through the efforts of swordsmiths, locksmiths, and armorers. The first complete documentary evidence of stack furnaces for the smelting of iron indicates that twenty-nine blast furnaces and forges were in operation in the lower Rhine valley in 1444. These produced pig iron and bars of refined iron.

Production of all the ferrous metals was on a relatively small scale until after the development of the blast furnace in the eighteenth century.   In 1728 rolled sheet iron was produced, but it was not until 1783 that rolled rods and bars made their appearance.   The development of industry has both depended upon and fostered the utilization of iron.

With the experience gained in the production of tools, machine parts, and other small objects, engineers were able to extend the use of iron to larger structures.   In the latter half of the eighteenth century, cast iron was used in the construction of arch bridges, and the early part of the nineteenth century marked the beginning of the use of wrought iron in suspension and truss bridges.

Not until after the invention of the Bessemer converter in 1855 did steel become of importance as a structural material.   Then, with its superior qualities, it soon supplanted wrought iron and cast iron for general construction.   At the present time it is the most widely used of the three ferrous metals, finding application in practically every field of engineering activity.

Wrought iron is still extensively used for general blacksmith work, decorative metalwork, and gas and water pipes.

Cast iron is used for pipes, hardware, farm implements, and machine parts which are not subjected to high tensile stresses or to dynamic loading. It is comparatively cheap, readily cast into complex shapes, and easily machined.   About one-fifth of the pig iron made annually in the United States is used in the form of cast iron.

The ferrous-metals industry is one of the most important in the United States.   Not only does it provide the metal for a wide variety of structures, machines, and implements, but it in turn depends upon a number of sup- porting industries.   On the average, the production of a ton of steel requires the following items in addition to labor and equipment: 2800 lb of iron ore, 1600 lb of coal, 825 lb of limestone, 16,000 lb of air, 480,000 lb of water, 87,000 lb of gas, 4300 lb of steam, and 27,000,000 Btu of heat.

8.2   Ores

Hematite (Fe_2O_3) is the principal iron ore, but magnetite (Fe_3O_4), siderite ($FeCO_3$), and limonite ($Fe_2O_3 + nH_2O$) are also used in the production of iron and steel.   Taconite is becoming industrially important as the richer sources of ore are depleted.   Sulfur, phosphorus, silica, and clay are the principal impurities which may be present in the ores.

Deposits of hematite in northern Minnesota (Lake Superior or Mesabi Range region) have for years furnished a large percentage of the iron ore used in the United States.   Other ore-producing regions in North America are Michigan, Alabama, Utah, New York, Colorado, Wyoming, Sault Ste. Marie, Newfoundland, Cuba, and Mexico.   In 1956, 24 per cent of the

141,000,000 tons of iron ore used in the United States was imported, principally from Canada and South America.

Extensive deposits of high-grade magnetite are found in Sweden. Swedish steel has long been considered to be among the best steels produced.

Deposits of siderite are found in the Ruhr Valley in Germany, and in Austria. There are also large deposits of high-grade hematite in Brazil.

As most of the ores are found at or near the surface of the earth, they are mined by stripping off the overburden of earth and removing the ore with steam shovels, either directly, as may be done with many of the softer hematite and limonite deposits, or after the ore has been loosened by blasting.

After mining, the ores are usually crushed to pass a 1-in. sieve to facilitate processing, and may be heated to burn off the sulfur or to drive out the water.

8.3 Processing

Since the important iron ores occur as oxides, or may be transformed into oxides by heating, the process of obtaining iron must be one of reduction, or removal of the oxygen.   The reduction is followed by refining to remove as much of the impurities as is feasible and to adjust the carbon content to produce the grade of material desired.   The product obtained from the reduction process is called *pig iron* and is essentially a crude cast iron.   During the refining process, the carbon content is altered to produce wrought iron, steel, or cast iron as desired, and other elements usually are added to impart desirable properties to the final product.

The intensive drain on our iron-ore deposits during World War II called attention to the fact that reserves of the Mesabi Range were being depleted very rapidly, and this stimulated the development of other sources.   One of the most abundant iron ores in North America is taconite, a hard, heavy, gray-green quartz containing about 20 to 30 per cent iron.   For years, research workers sought methods of concentrating the iron ore in the taconite deposits to the point where the ore could be used economically.

The process which was evolved for processing taconite consists in crushing and grinding the hard rock to a fine powder and separating the iron oxide magnetically from a water slurry.   Then, since the material cannot be fed into the blast furnace in the finely divided form without being almost entirely lost with the flue gases, it is formed into mud pellets about one-half inch to one inch in diameter.   These are fired at about 2300 F to sinter sufficiently to withstand subsequent handling.   The resulting material, which is about 65 per cent iron, can then be fed into a blast furnace in the same way that the conventional ore is handled.

8.4 Production of Pig Iron

The iron ore is reduced by heating it with carbon. The oxygen in the ore combines with part of the carbon to form gases, leaving the iron in the uncombined state. Since an excess of carbon must be provided to prevent the iron from reoxidizing at the high temperatures involved, the iron will absorb carbon, forming cast iron. A flux is added to help in removing the impurities.

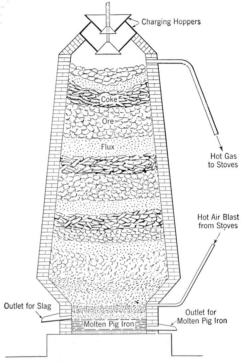

FIG. 8.1   Principal features of blast furnace.

The process is carried out in a blast furnace, the principal features of which are indicated in Fig. 8.1. The 258 blast furnaces in operation in the United States at the end of 1952 had a total rated capacity of over 68,000,000 tons per year. The average blast furnace, which has a capacity of about 700 tons of pig iron per day, is approximately 20 ft in diameter and 80 ft high. The larger furnaces have a capacity of 1600 tons per day.

The upper part of the stack of a blast furnace is constructed of steel lined with firebrick. The lower portion, called the "bosh," is usually constructed of brickwork from 2 to 3 ft thick, since it is the hottest part of the furnace, while the cylindrical part of the bottom, known as the crucible, is cast steel lined with about 3 ft of firebrick.

In operation, the charge, consisting of about 60 per cent iron ore (or as much as 40 per cent scrap iron), 25 per cent coke (or other high-carbon fuel), and about 15 per cent limestone, is fed in at the top of the stack and gradually works down toward the bottom.   The furnace is kept filled, and the operation is continuous—individual furnaces have processed as much as 1,500,000 tons before being shut down for relining.   Air, preheated to 500 or 600 C, is forced in near the bottom of the furnace under a pressure of about 15 psi.   The oxygen in the air combines with the coke to form carbon monoxide, increasing the temperature at the bottom of the furnace to about 1600 C or 2900 F.   The blast of air also helps maintain a steady current of hot gases upward through the furnace.

As the ore starts to work down the stack, it comes in contact with the ascending gases, which contain carbon monoxide.   At the temperatures near the top of the stack (about 300 C or 572 F), the iron oxide is reduced by the carbon monoxide to metallic iron.   Apparently little reduction is accomplished by the coke directly, even though the ore is in contact with it.   The fuel does not burn until it comes in contact with the air near the bottom of the furnace.   Under the action of the intense heat in the lower portions of the furnace, the iron is melted and collects in the crucible or hearth at the bottom of the stack.

As the iron reaches the molten state, it will absorb from $3\frac{1}{2}$ to 4 per cent carbon and also some of the impurities present in the ore.   All of the phosphorus present in the ore and fuel will be absorbed by the iron, greatly impairing its quality for many uses unless subsequently removed. Manganese and silicon will also be absorbed by the iron, but are not undesirable.   Unless a sufficient quantity of limestone is present, the sulfur will also be taken on by the iron, making it brittle at high temperatures.

The lime (CaO), which is produced from the limestone, and part of the sulfur, the silicon dioxide, and other materials will be fused together to form a *slag,* which also settles to the bottom of the furnace and floats on top of the iron in the crucible.   The slag and pig iron are drawn off separately at about 6-hr intervals through temporary openings punched in the side of the crucible.

If the blast furnace is operated in conjunction with a steel mill, the molten pig iron may be either taken directly to the furnaces or placed in a storage tank and kept molten until needed; otherwise, it is cast into pigs weighing about 100 lb.

The slag, which is composed principally of oxides of silicon, aluminum, calcium, and magnesium, is utilized in the manufacture of some grades of cement, mineral wool, roofing material, paint, or concrete, or it may be used as ballast for railroad tracks.   The hot gases emitted from the top of the blast furnace contain some carbon monoxide and are used in pre-heating the air which is forced in at the bottom of the furnace.

In 1952, about one-third of the world total of approximately 152,000,-000 tons of pig iron was produced in the United States.

CAST IRON

8.5 Production of Cast Iron

Cast iron is produced by remelting pig iron and pouring it into molds of the desired shape. The purpose of the remelting is to reduce the amount of impurities and to secure a more uniform product than would be obtained by casting the pig iron directly as it came from the blast furnace.

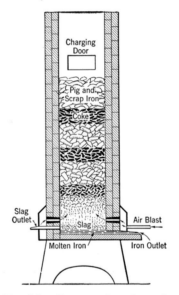

FIG. 8.2   Cross section of cupola.

There are two types of furnaces in general use for the remelting of pig iron. In the production of most of the ordinary gray cast iron, such as is used for machine parts, a *cupola* is used, while an *air furnace* is more commonly used for the better grades of gray cast iron, and cast iron which is to receive heat treatment. In some cases a small *open-hearth furnace* (similar to the open-hearth furnaces used in making steel) is used to produce a high-grade cast iron.

A cupola, shown in Fig. 8.2, consists of a stack lined with firebrick, and operates on the same general principle as a blast furnace. While the sizes of cupolas vary considerably, a common size is about 6 ft in diameter and about 20 ft high, having a capacity of approximately 20 tons of cast iron per hour.   The furnace may be operated continuously, but generally a charge is completely melted and removed from the furnace before any new charge is added.

The charge consists of about 20 per cent coke (or other high-carbon fuel) and 80 per cent pig iron.   Scrap iron consisting of the residue from other heats, broken pieces, or old cast-iron parts may also be added. While in some melts the scrap-iron content may be equal to the pig-iron content of the charge, such a high proportion often results in an inferior product, and for the better grades of cast iron the amount of scrap iron is usually limited to about one-fourth of the total metal.   The pig iron in a given charge usually comes from several different blast furnaces, and a much more uniform grade of cast iron is produced than if all of the charge came from one blast furnace.   A small amount of limestone may also be added to reduce the sulfur content of the cast iron and to remove some other impurities.

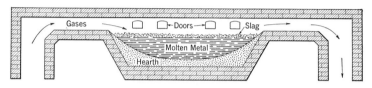

FIG. 8.3   Diagram of a reverberatory furnace.

The action in a cupola differs from that in a blast furnace in that the cupola produces no particular chemical change in the iron; a small amount of iron may be oxidized and some sulfur may be absorbed from the fuel. The principal function of the cupola is to give a more uniform product and to eliminate some impurities.   Other elements, such as nickel, may be added to the melt if an alloy cast iron is desired.   The final carbon content of the cast iron varies from $1\frac{1}{2}$ to about $3\frac{1}{2}$ or 4 per cent, the amount depending on the pig iron used and on the use to be made of the product.

The air furnace is an example of the type known as *reverberatory furnaces*.   As shown in Fig. 8.3, a reverberatory furnace consists of a flat, wide compartment known as the *hearth,* with an adjacent compartment containing the grate upon which the fuel is burned.   The roof of the furnace is lined with firebrick to aid in reflecting heat downward onto the hearth.   The hot gases from the burning fuel are conducted across the top of the metal on the hearth, heating it by direct contact and by reflected heat from the roof.   A jet of air is introduced between the grate and the hearth to maintain the circulation.   If liquid or gaseous fuel is used, it may be burned directly above the charge.   Air furnaces range in capacity from 5 to 40 tons.

The charge, consisting of a mixture of pig iron and scrap, is placed on a bed of silica sand on the bottom of the hearth. Limestone may be added if necessary. Under the action of the heat from above, the charge is melted. Some of the impurities forming the slag rise to the top and form a protective coating above the iron, preventing it from oxidizing and from absorbing additional sulfur from the fuel. This makes possible better control over the properties of the resultant cast iron than can be obtained in the cupola where the fuel and iron are in direct contact. The temperature of the furnace may also be more closely regulated. However, the air furnace requires about twice as much fuel as the cupola, in addition to being more expensive to build. Therefore, the cast iron produced by the air furnace is more costly than that produced by the cupola.

A recent development in the production of cast iron is the so-called *duplex process,* in which the material is given a preliminary treatment in the cupola and is then transferred to an electric furnace. Since it is possible to maintain a constant temperature in the electric furnace, this process results in a superior grade of cast iron. In the electric furnace it is also possible to superheat the material, giving it better casting characteristics, and to adjust the analysis accurately.

After treatment in the cupola or electric furnace, the molten metal is cast into forms having the desired shape by following one of the processes outlined in section 6.13. Sand castings are utilized principally for the production of cast iron.

8.6   Types of Cast Iron

Aside from the variations which may be introduced by chemical means (the addition of alloying elements), the properties of cast iron may be altered by physical means (control of the rate of cooling). As was noted in the discussion of the equilibrium diagram, when cast iron is allowed to cool slowly a part of the carbon combines with the iron to form iron carbide or cementite (Fe_3C), and the remainder solidifies as free carbon or graphite.

A decrease in the rate of cooling will decrease the amount of combined carbon and increase the amount of free carbon, and will also increase the size of the resultant crystals. Thus, a piece of slowly cooled cast iron consists of crystals or flakes of graphite, which are usually long and thin, in a matrix of pearlite and cementite. The general appearance of gray cast iron under the microscope is indicated in Fig. 8.4a. Graphite is very weak, so the presence of many graphite flakes will make the cast iron weak and brittle. The free carbon gives the cast iron a dark color, from which comes the name *gray cast iron.*

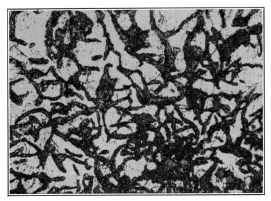

(a) Gray cast iron, ×500

(b) White cast iron, ×50

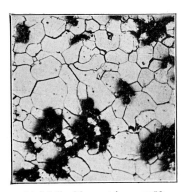

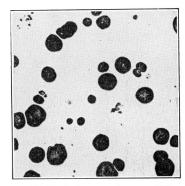

(c) Malleable cast iron, ×50   (d) Nodular cast iron, ×100

FIG. 8.4   Microstructure of cast iron.

An increase in the rate of cooling will have two effects: a decrease in the amount of free graphite and a decrease in the size of the crystals. If the molten cast iron is cooled very rapidly, practically all of the carbon will be retained in the iron in the form of cementite. The cementite itself is hard and brittle, so the net effect is to produce an iron which is strong and hard but also very brittle. Because of the absence of graphite, the iron has a lighter appearance than gray cast iron and is called *white cast iron*. White cast iron is shown in Fig. 8.4b.

Chilled iron is cast iron which has been cooled rapidly by lining part of the mold with metal. A railroad-car wheel often has its wearing surface chilled to make the surface resistant to wear, while the rest of the wheel is cooled more slowly to reduce brittleness.

Rapid cooling also has the effect of setting up high initial stresses, which are undesirable but which can be removed by annealing.

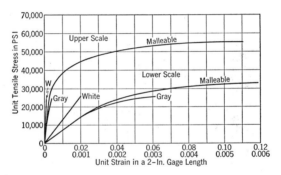

FIG. 8.5   Typical stress-strain diagrams for cast iron.

An extended annealing produces what is known as *malleable cast iron*. As outlined in section 7.10, the castings are packed in iron oxide, iron ore, or other material containing oxygen and are heated to about 700 C (1292 F) for a few days. Some of the combined carbon is converted into graphite, but it is formed in very small particles, known as *temper carbon*, instead of in relatively large flakes. The amount of carbon transferred from the combined state to temper carbon depends on the temperature and time of malleableizing. Usually the operation is continued until practically all of the carbon is converted. The malleable cast iron then consists of crystals of pure iron interspersed with particles of temper carbon, as shown in Fig. 8.4c. For some applications, from 0.3 to 0.8 per cent combined carbon is desirable in addition to the uncombined or temper carbon. The resulting product is known as pearlitic malleable cast iron. Malleable cast iron has both greater strength and greater ductility than gray cast iron, as is indicated in Fig. 8.5. In fact, a good grade of malleable cast iron has properties that compare favorably with those of forged steel. Complex shapes may be produced more economically in malleable cast iron than in forgings.

8.7 Properties of Cast Iron

The physical properties of cast iron can be varied through a wide range by varying the amount of combined carbon, as indicated in section 8.6. The presence of other elements, either in the form of impurities which cannot be removed or as definite added alloys, has an appreciable effect on the properties of the final product. The ultimate tensile strength of gray cast iron can be varied from less than 10,000 psi to over 70,000 psi. The typical stress-strain diagrams for gray, white, and malleable cast irons in Fig. 8.5 indicate some of the relative properties of the three.

Malleable cast irons are designated by a code in which the first three numbers indicate the tensile yield strength in hundreds of psi and the last two digits indicate the percentage elongation. Thus 32518 denotes a minimum yield strength of 32,500 psi and an elongation of 18 per cent, while 70002 denotes a minimum yield strength of 70,000 psi and 2 per cent elongation.

The compressive characteristics of cast iron are dependent on the same factors as the tensile characteristics, but the values run somewhat higher. The ultimate compressive strength of gray cast iron, as determined from tests on small specimens, ranges from 50,000 to 200,000 psi, while the compressive strength of malleable cast iron may run as high as 275,000 psi. The modulus of rupture is approximately twice the tensile strength.

A type of cast iron known as Meehanite metal and produced under patented processes that control the distribution of free carbon in the metal has been developed to provide irons having specific properties. A few typical values of Meehanite are given in Table 8.1.

One important characteristic of cast iron is its relatively high damping capacity, which is advantageous for situations where the member is subjected to some vibration or fluctuation of load.

Because of the effect of the rate of cooling upon properties, the material near the center of a large gray-iron casting will have properties different from those of the material near the surface. In general, the material near the outside will cool more rapidly, and will therefore be harder and more brittle than the slowly cooled iron at the center. Tests[1] have demonstrated that the ultimate tensile strength of the material at the center of a 4-in. casting may be only 75 per cent of the strength of the material at the

[1] R. S. McPherran, "Effect of Section and Various Compositions on the Physical Properties of Cast Iron," *Proceedings of the American Society for Testing Materials,* Vol. 29, pp. 76-82.

TABLE 8.1
PROPERTIES OF CAST IRONS

Property	Meehanite Metal						ASTM Class		Malleable
	GM	GA	GE	HD*	SC*	CC†	20	60	(35018)
Ultimate tensile strength, psi	55,000	50,000	30,000	33,000	27,000	42,000	20,000	60,000	57,000
Ultimate compressive strength, psi	200,000	175,000	120,000	145,000	130,000	160,000	89,000	175,000	90,000
Ultimate shearing strength, psi	55,000	48,000	30,000	34,000	28,000	42,000	27,000	60,000	48,000
Modulus of rupture in bending, psi	93,000	89,000	61,000	67,000	37,000	77,000	47,000	90,000	......
Modulus of rupture in torsion, psi	64,000	60,000	35,300	......	......	......	......	......	58,000
Endurance limit, psi	25,000	22,000	13,700	16,000	20,000	19,000	8,000	30,000	26,000
Modulus of elasticity, psi $\times 10^6$	23.0	21.0	12.0	17.5	17.5	19.0	11.0	20.0	25.0
Specific weight, pcf	466	463	438	......	......	......	437	456	455
Brinell hardness number, min	217	207	174	202	300	187	110	275	130
Coefficient of thermal expansion, $\times 10^{-6}$ per deg F	6.91	6.87	6.66	7.09	6.74	6.81	6.70	6.70	6.6
Thermal conductivity, Btu/hr/sq ft/in./ deg F	355	350	290	325	278	325	319	348	......
Damping capacity in torsion, per cent/ cycle at 20,000 psi	21.0	24.0	32.0	27.0	......	26.0	......	......	......

* Heat-resisting type.
† Corrosion-resisting type.

outside of the casting. The average tensile strength of a bar 2 in. in diameter may be less than one-half of that of a $\frac{1}{2}$-in. bar.[2]

8.8 Uses of Cast Iron

Because of the ease with which they may be formed, shapes of gray cast iron may be produced more cheaply than steel shapes formed by other processes. However, because of its comparatively low tensile strength, and its brittleness, gray cast iron is generally used only for members in which the tensile stresses are low and which are not subject to dynamic loading. Gray cast iron is extensively used for machine frames and beds; pipes; casings and housings for stationary equipment; cylinder heads; dies; molds; and rollers.

As has been indicated, chilled iron is suitable for wear-resisting surfaces such as railroad-car wheels. It has also found extensive application in plows. Because of its extreme hardness, white cast iron may be used where resistance to abrasion and wear are desired.

Malleable cast iron is useful for small parts requiring some ductility. Pipe fittings, parts for farm machinery, and housings, pedals, and similar automobile parts are made of malleable cast iron.

8.9 Physical Defects in Cast Iron

There are several types of physical defects which if present in cast iron, will weaken it. Blowholes, cracks, segregation of the impurities, and coarse-grain structure are the most common sources of difficulty.

Blowholes. Blowholes are gas pockets which remain in the solid iron because there was not suitable opportunity for the gas to escape. A porous molding sand aids in the reduction of blowholes. A high sulfur content promotes the formation of blowholes.

Surface cracks. Small surface cracks may be produced if the mold is so designed that the iron does not have an opportunity to shrink properly as it cools. Cracks may also be formed at sharp re-entrant angles in a casting because of the tendency of the crystals to form with their long axes normal to the surface, resulting in a plane of weakness at a corner.

Impurities. Impurities, such as sulfides and phosphides, tend to collect in separate masses, introducing brittle spots and points of stress concen-

[2] R. Schneidewind and E. C. Hoenicke, "A Study of the Chemical, Physical and Mechanical Properties of Permanent Mold Gray Iron," *Proceedings of the American Society for Testing Materials,* Vol. 42, pp. 622-34; H. L. Campbell, "Relation of Properties of Cast Iron to Thickness of Castings," *Proceedings of the American Society for Testing Materials,* Vol. 37, pp. 66-69.

tration within the mass of iron. The carbon and silicon may also segregate, creating spots of varying hardness in the cast iron, making it difficult to machine.

8.10 Effect of Other Elements

Sulfur, phosphorus, manganese, and silicon are nearly always present in cast iron, because they are present in the iron ore; and it is very difficult, if not impossible, to remove them in the ordinary commercial processes.

Sulfur. Sulfur, which combines with the manganese or the iron to form a sulfide, makes the cast iron brittle (hot short) at high temperatures. It also increases shrinkage. Hence it is usually limited to less than 0.1 per cent in specifications for cast iron.

Phosphorus. In amounts of more than 2 per cent, phosphorus makes the iron brittle and, in addition, weakens it. However, since it also has the effect of increasing the fluidity and of decreasing the shrinkage, it is desirable in making sharp castings for ornamental parts where strength is unimportant.

Manganese. The manganese content is usually less than 2 per cent, in which quantities it has little effect upon the strength of cast iron. Sulfur combines with it, and manganese and carbon form a carbide (Mn_3C) which unites with the iron carbide. This action decreases the amount of free carbon, and increases the shrinkage and hardness of the iron, making it more resistant to abrasion and increasing the difficulty of machining it.

Silicon. The silicon content in most cast irons is from 0.5 to 3.0 per cent. Silicon combines with the iron, replacing carbon, and thus promotes the formation of graphite. The result is a softer, weaker, more machinable cast iron. Three parts of silicon are approximately equivalent to one part of carbon in affecting the tensile strength of cast iron. Silicon also increases the fluidity of the cast iron and decreases shrinkage. With a silicon content of more than 6 per cent the effect of iron silicide becomes evident, making the material harder. Cast iron with a high silicon content (about 15 per cent) is acid-resistant.

Nickel. Nickel in amounts from 0.5 to 3 per cent has the effect of retarding the chemical combination of iron and carbon under rapid cooling, and of retarding the formation of large graphite flakes. These effects result in increased strength, hardness, and ductility and make nickel cast iron suitable for crankshafts, pistons, gears, dies, brake drums, cylinder heads, and similar parts.

Chromium. Chromium is sometimes added as an alloying element in cast iron in amounts up to 1 per cent. It has the effect of increasing the percentage of combined carbon, thus increasing the strength and hardness of the cast iron. It is frequently used in combination with nickel.

Both copper and molybdenum increase the tensile strength and hardness of cast iron.

WROUGHT IRON

8.11 Definition of Wrought Iron

The American Society for Testing Materials defines wrought iron as a "ferrous material, aggregated from a solidifying mass of pasty particles of highly refined metallic iron, with which, without subsequent fusion, is incorporated a minutely and uniformly distributed quantity of slag." The carbon content of wrought iron is usually less than 0.12 per cent, and the slag content is from 0.6 to 3 per cent.

8.12 Production of Wrought Iron

The production of wrought iron from pig iron involves the removal of carbon. This may be done by the *puddling process* or by the *Aston process*.

Puddling process. In the puddling process a small reverberatory furnace, similar to the air furnace shown in Fig. 8.2 and having a capacity of about 600 lb, is used. The charge consists of a good quality of pig iron and some iron oxide or slag to assist in the formation of a protective coating of slag on the top of the melt. Soft coal is commonly used as the fuel.

The charge melts at a temperature of about 1200 C (2192 F), as may be seen from the equilibrium diagram. Iron oxide is then mixed in with the molten metal. This removes the silicon and manganese and part of the phosphorus, forming a basic slag. With most of the impurities removed, the oxygen in the iron oxide then combines with the carbon in the pig iron, forming carbon monoxide.

As the carbon content of the iron is reduced, its melting point is increased, as is evident from the equilibrium diagram. If the temperature of the furnace is then kept just below the melting point of pure iron, 1535 C (2795 F), the iron will solidify when its carbon content is reduced to practically zero. The particles of solid iron are collected on the end of a long rod and removed from the furnace in the form of "muck balls" weighing from 200 to 300 lb apiece. The muck balls contain some liquid slag, most of which is removed by squeezing the balls and rolling them into "muck bars." These muck bars are then cut to short lengths, stacked, heated, and rolled into commercial shapes or "merchant bars." Often they are restacked, heated again, and rerolled to improve the quality.

Aston process.   In the Aston process, developed about 1930, a *Bessemer converter* is used.   This converter, shown in Fig. 8.6, is a short stack lined with firebrick, and built so that it can be rotated about a horizontal axis.   There are in the bottom a number of openings, called tuyères, through which air can be forced.   The average converter is about 8 ft in diameter and 15 ft high, and has a capacity of about 15 tons.

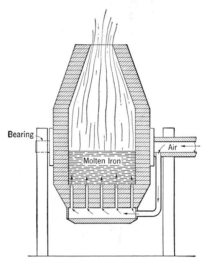

Fig. 8.6   Cross section of Bessemer converter.

The molten pig iron is placed in the converter, which is in an upright position, and air is blown up through the mass.   The oxygen in the air first combines with the impurities, burning them out, and then combines with the carbon in the molten pig iron, leaving an iron which is comparatively pure but which contains gases.   To remove the absorbed gases, the iron is poured into a ladle of molten slag which is at a temperature well below the freezing point of iron.   The sudden reduction in temperature liberates the gases with explosive violence, shattering the iron into tiny, slag-coated globules which settle to the bottom of the ladle in a spongelike mass.   The iron is then squeezed to remove the slag, and rolled into commercial shapes.

8.13   Types of Wrought Iron

In addition to the wrought iron produced by the processes just described, there are other types of nearly pure iron which are manufactured for specific purposes.   Charcoal iron and sponge iron are two examples of these other types.

Charcoal iron is made from steel scrap, wrought-iron scrap, or pig iron by heating the metal on a hearth in direct contact with a charcoal fire. The carbon in the iron is oxidized by bringing the metal in contact with an air blast on one side of the hearth. The nearly pure iron which is produced is suitable for electrical apparatus, boiler tubes, bolts, and other uses where a high resistance to corrosion is desired. Charcoal iron is tough and can be readily welded.

Sponge iron, another type of nearly pure iron, is produced directly from the iron ore by using a small blast furnace. The charge consists of a high-grade ore, iron oxide, and some carbonaceous material. By providing just the proper amount of air required to oxidize the carbon without oxidizing the iron, a nearly pure iron is produced. It is suitable as a raw material for high-grade steel.

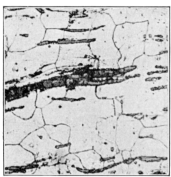

FIG. 8.7   Photomicrograph of wrought iron.

8.14 Properties of Wrought Iron

Wrought iron may be distinguished by the presence of the slag which has not been entirely removed. The slag, which is essentially ferrous silicate, is in the form of microscopic fibers running parallel to the direction of rolling, as is shown in Fig. 8.7. Some of the properties of wrought iron under load are evident from the stress-strain diagram in Fig. 8.8. The ultimate compressive strength varies from about 30,000 to 40,000 psi in small sections, and the ultimate shearing strength is about 40,000 psi. Wrought iron weighs about 480 pcf and has a coefficient of thermal expansion of 6.73×10^{-6} per deg F. The Rockwell B hardness number is about 55.

The properties of wrought iron are somewhat dependent on the nature and duration of the rolling operation. Continued working down to the critical temperature reduces the grain size and increases the ductility and toughness. If the rolling is continued below the lower critical range, the ductility will be decreased because of the induced strains.   The rolling gives the wrought iron its directional properties.   The ultimate tensile strength is from 20 to 60 per cent higher in the direction of rolling than in the transverse direction.

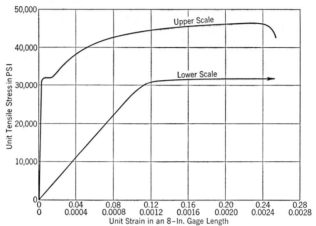

Fig. 8.8   Typical stress-strain diagram for wrought iron in tension.

Alloy wrought iron containing up to 3 per cent nickel is sometimes used where a metal having a high tensile strength is desired.   Wrought iron containing 3 per cent nickel will develop a yield point of approximately 45,000 psi, an ultimate tensile strength of about 60,000 psi, and an elongation in 8 in. of 22 per cent.   In general, wrought iron has a high resistance to corrosion.   This characteristic is sometimes attributed to the presence of many fine fibers of slag, which tend to block the path of progressive mechanical action.   Photomicrographs of wrought iron stressed above the yield point indicate that in the relatively softer iron the slag is effective in blocking the slip planes.

Wrought iron is easily welded, and because of its high workability it is extensively used for ornamental iron work.   Its high resistance to corrosion makes it useful for piping, boiler plates and tubes, sheet metal, and similar applications.   Wrought iron is also used extensively in certain locomotive and car parts.

STEEL

8.15   Definition of Steel

"Steel is that form of iron which is malleable at least in some one range of temperature, and, in addition (a) is either cast into an initially malleable mass; or (b) is capable of hardening greatly by sudden cooling; or (c) is both so cast and so capable of hardening."[3]   The carbon content of steel varies from 0.05 per cent to 1.8 per cent.

8.16   Production of Steel

The production of steel from pig iron involves the removal of as much of the impurities as practicable, the adjusting of the carbon content to the desired value, and the addition of such alloying elements as may be required to alter the properties.

While several methods have been developed for producing steel, they may be considered under two general groups: those used for producing large quantities of low-carbon steel, or *tonnage steel,* such as structural steel, and those used for producing steel in smaller quantities to meet special needs, such as tool steel.

At the present time the *open-hearth process* is used almost exclusively for producing tonnage steel, although the *Bessemer process* and the *duplex process* are in that class.   For the production of the special steels, which are generally high-carbon steels or alloy steels, the *open-hearth, cementation, crucible,* or *electric-furnace* process may be used.

Steel-production processes may also be classified as *acid* or *basic,* according to the nature of the charge.   The pig iron normally contains phosphorus, which tends to give the charge an acid reaction.   If no basic materials are added, and if the lining of the furnace is acid or neutral, the charge remains acid throughout the process, and the phosphorus will be retained in the steel, making it brittle at ordinary temperatures.   However, if limestone (which is basic) is added to the charge, it will react with most of the phosphorus in the iron to form a material which is retained in the slag.   The addition of limestone results in a basic charge, requiring a basic lining for the furnace, and produces a less brittle metal.

8.17   The Bessemer Process

The development of the Bessemer process, so named after Sir Henry Bessemer, inventor of the Bessemer converter in 1855, is unquestionably one of the most outstanding industrial developments in recent times insofar as its effect upon engineering is concerned, for it made possible the manufacture of steel on a large scale.   Since the properties of steel are in general superior to those of wrought iron for construction purposes, the increased availability of steel gave an impetus to construction.   The increased demand resulted in the production of better steel, which in turn made possible many new uses for the metal, thereby developing new industries.

[3] H. M. Howe, *The Metallography of Steel and Cast Iron* (New York: McGraw-Hill Book Company, Inc.).

FIG. 8.9   Bessemer converter in action.   (Courtesy A. M. Byers Company)

The general features of the Bessemer converter were discussed in section 8.12 in connection with the Aston process for making wrought iron. The essential method of operation in the Bessemer process is the same as in the Aston process.   Molten pig iron (a uniform mixture of iron from several blast furnaces) is placed in the converter and air is blown through the mass, igniting some of the impurities.

The increase in temperature ignites the carbon which is combined with the iron, and it burns out in about 12 min (Fig. 8.9), leaving iron containing some phosphorus, sulfur, iron oxide, and absorbed gases.   The molten iron is dumped into a ladle, and is recarburized by adding a small quantity of molten pig iron with a high carbon and manganese content. Aluminum or some other material is added to "kill" the steel (that is, remove the gases).

The carbon combines with the iron, while the manganese combines with the oxygen and sulfur which were in chemical combination with the iron, rendering them less harmful.   The manganese oxide goes into the slag, and the manganese sulfide which remains dissolved in the iron does not make the steel so brittle as the iron sulfide would.   Soda ash may be added to reduce the sulfur content of the steel.   After the recarburization the steel is poured into molds known as ingot molds to solidify.

The process just described is the *acid* Bessemer process.   Since the phosphorus is not removed from the steel while it is in the converter, an acid lining (usually silica brick) is required for the furnace.

If the phosphorus content of the pig iron is sufficiently high and the silicon content is low, the *basic* Bessemer process may be used.   This differs from the acid process in that limestone is added to the charge and the time of operation is lengthened.   The phosphorus combines with the limestone and is retained by the basic slag which is formed.   A low silicon content is necessary to keep the slag basic, and the furnace must be lined with magnesite, dolomite, or other basic refractory brick.

The basic process is used in Europe, but most American ores have too low a phosphorus content for the basic Bessemer process, and too high a phosphorus content for the acid process to be completely satisfactory; so the Bessemer process has been almost entirely replaced by the open-hearth process.   Where Bessemer converters are used in the United States, the acid process is employed.

8.18   The Open-Hearth Process

The open-hearth process, also known as the Siemens-Martin process, in honor of the two men who were instrumental in developing it, utilizes a reverberatory furnace, of the same general type as the air furnace used in making cast iron.   Open-hearth furnaces are built in capacities up to 100 tons.   The average-size furnace has a capacity of about 60 tons.

In the open-hearth process, as generally employed in the United States, the charge, consisting of pig iron, steel scrap, and iron ore, is made basic by adding calcined limestone (CaO).   The iron ore furnishes oxygen to aid in the removal of impurities.   The fuel used to supply the heat is usually producer gas, although other fuels are more suitable under some circumstances.   The furnace is lined with firebrick made from dolomite (CaO · MgO), lime (CaO), magnesia (MgO), or other basic material. Under the influence of the intense heat the charge is melted and the lime removes phosphorus and other impurities from the iron to form the slag. The slag floats on the surface of the melt, protecting the steel beneath from further oxidation.   The process is continued until the iron is nearly pure, about 8 hr being required.   Since the carbon content of the product is low, carbon must be added.   This is usually done after the steel has been removed from the furnace, the addition being in the form of pig iron rich in carbon and manganese, as in the Bessemer process.

The process just outlined is the basic process.   If the pig iron used has a low phosphorus content, the acid process may be used, the principal difference being that limestone is not added to the charge and that the lining of the furnace must be silica, or a similar material which has an acid reaction.   Since there is no lime in the charge to remove the phosphorus, whatever phosphorus is in the charge will remain in the steel.

The basic process is the one most used in the United States because of the appreciable phosphorus content of the American ores, although the acid open-hearth process is extensively used in Europe.   Steel produced by the acid open-hearth process has been generally regarded as superior to the steel produced by the basic process.   This is largely due to the fact that a higher grade of pig iron is required for the acid process.

8.19 Comparison of Bessemer and Open-Hearth Processes

The open-hearth process has been regarded as superior to the Bessemer process and consequently many specifications prohibit the use of Bessemer steel.   However, recently developed control equipment and fluxing techniques for removing impurities have greatly improved the quality and uniformity of Bessemer steel.   When properly controlled the Bessemer process will produce steel equal in quality to that obtained from an open-hearth process.

Split-second control is not necessary in the open-hearth process, since it requires a longer time.   Also, since air does not come in direct contact with the steel, as it does in the Bessemer process, there is less danger of oxidation.   However, examination of the steel will not reveal which process was used in its manufacture.   The Bessemer process is cheaper, because no added fuel is required, and it is more rapid.   The usual capacity of the Bessemer converter is about 25 tons in 12 min, as compared with 60 tons in about 8 hr for the average open-hearth furnace.

8.20 Duplex and Triplex Processes

A combination of the acid Bessemer process and the basic open-hearth process, known as the *duplex* process, is used to advantage in many plants. In the duplex process the pig iron is first put through the Bessemer process to remove most of the manganese and silicon and is then put into the open-hearth furnace for removal of phosphorus and further purification.   In this way a shorter period in the open-hearth furnace is required.

Two *triplex* processes have recently been put into operation.   In one of them the steel is given a preliminary treatment in the Bessemer furnace, further refining in the open-hearth furnace, and final treatment in the electric furnace.   In the other triplex process the pig iron is treated in the cupola, reduced in the Bessemer furnace, and refined in the electric furnace.   The principal advantage of triplex processes is the increased production made possible by the use of the Bessemer converter, which reduces the steel more rapidly than it could be reduced in the open-hearth furnace.

In 1951, about 90 per cent of the steel ingots produced in the United States were made by the basic open-hearth process.   Nearly 5 per cent were made by the Bessemer process, and over 6 per cent by the electric-furnace process.

8.21 Electric-Furnace Process

Since the electric furnace affords a means of obtaining the high temperature and careful control necessary in the manufacture of steel, it has been adopted in many instances for the production of high grade alloy steel.

There are two general types of electric furnaces, the *arc* type and the *induction* type.

The arc type of furnace consists of a well-insulated chamber in which the charge is placed and into which the carbon electrodes extend, as shown in Fig. 8.10.   The electrodes may be kept above the surface of the charge or they may be inserted in the charge.   In the former type the heat produced by passing the current from one electrode to the other is reflected down onto the surface of the charge.   In the second type, which is more common, the charge itself forms one electrode.   Either single-phase or three-phase current may be used.

The induction furnace consists of an insulated chamber around which is wound a coil.   The charge is placed in the chamber and high-frequency current is passed through the surrounding coil, which functions as the pri-

FIG. 8.10 Pouring a charge from an electric furnace. (Courtesy Republic Steel Corporation)

mary winding of a transformer, with the charge itself serving as the secondary. The eddy currents induced in the charge develop sufficient heat to melt it.

In both the arc and induction furnaces the charge consists of a high-grade ore or scrap steel (100 per cent scrap may be used), with a flux to remove the impurities. Since the charge is not contaminated with fuel or with air, and since the temperature may be carefully regulated, a very high grade of steel suitable for castings and forgings is produced in the electric furnace.

The principal disadvantage of the electric furnace is its high operating cost, but where power is sufficiently cheap to make it economical it is very satisfactory.

In 1951 the steel-making capacity of electric furnaces in the United States was about 7,000,000 tons annually.   The capacity of individual furnaces ranges up to 100 tons.

8.22 Other Processes

The open-hearth, Bessemer, and electric-furnace processes all reduce the carbon content of the charge to practically zero.   The additional carbon needed to obtain the desired properties in the steel is added to the ladle as the charge is removed from the furnace.

Two other processes have been developed for converting wrought iron to steel by increasing the carbon content while the charge is in the furnace. One of the processes is called the *cementation process,* and the other is known as the *crucible process.*

The cementation process consists in heating the prefabricated wrought-iron shapes in a carbonaceous atmosphere at a temperature below the melting point of the iron.   The source of carbon may be charcoal or other solid carbon, or it may be methane or other gases.   As the wrought iron is heated in the presence of carbon, the iron absorbs the carbon and steel is produced.   The amount of carbon absorbed at a given point in the iron is a function of the temperature and time of treatment, as well as the distance to the point from the surface of the member.   Since no impurities are removed during the recarburization, a high grade of wrought iron must be used as the base material.

The crucible process, which antedates the Bessemer and open-hearth processes (having been developed about 1740), consists in melting a charge of high-grade wrought iron and powdered charcoal, together with any other alloying elements which may be desirable.   The charge is usually placed in a clay or graphite crucible holding about 100 lb.   As the charge is heated, the iron dissolves the carbon, forming a homogeneous melt which is cast into appropriate molds.   Castings, forgings, and rolled shapes may be produced by this method.   As is the case in the cementation process, no impurities are removed, and therefore a high grade of wrought iron must be used.

8.23 Shaping Operations

As the steel comes from the Bessemer converter, open-hearth furnace, or electric furnace, it may be cast directly into the desired shape or it may be cast into ingots weighing from 3 to 60 tons.   After solidification, the ingots are given a preliminary shaping by being rolled or forged into billets which may then be reduced to final dimensions by rolling, forging, drawing, or any of the operations discussed in Chapter 6.   Each of the operations will affect the crystalline structure, thereby altering the properties of the final product.   Figure 8.11 shows typical stress-strain diagrams for specimens of low-carbon steel shaped by some of the common techniques.

Casting is widely used for the production of frames for locomotives, cars, and other large equipment, and for the production of complex shapes which would involve large amounts of waste if other shaping techniques were employed.   Rolling is used for the production of plates, sheets, rods,

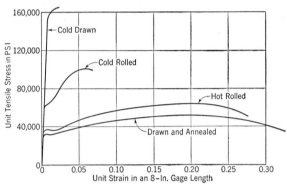

FIG. 8.11   Effect of shaping operations upon carbon steel.

and the common structural shapes such as angles, channels, and I beams. Figure 6.14 is a photograph of a rolling mill in action.   Most of the steel shapes formed by rolling are hot rolled, but cold rolling is employed where dimensions must be held to relatively close tolerances.   Cold rolling gives the steel a shiny surface, and a higher strength than does the hot-rolled process.   Forging is commonly used for the production of cannon, sheeting, thick plate, and various machine parts.   Steel wire and small rod are produced by drawing.   The extrusion process has recently been adapted to the shaping of steel.   Steel parts may be assembled by conventional practices of riveting, bolting, or welding.

IMPURITIES IN STEEL

8.24   Use of Elements Other Than Iron and Carbon

The strength, ductility, and related properties of the iron-carbon alloys are affected by the presence of other elements.   Those whose presence is generally regarded as harmful are sulfur, phosphorus, oxygen, hydrogen, and nitrogen.   Other elements, such as nickel, aluminum, chromium, silicon, vanadium, molybdenum, manganese, and tungsten, are used to impart desirable properties to the ferrous metals.   Steel containing an appreciable amount of any of the latter elements is called *alloy steel*. About one-fifth of the annual production of steel in the United States is alloy steel.

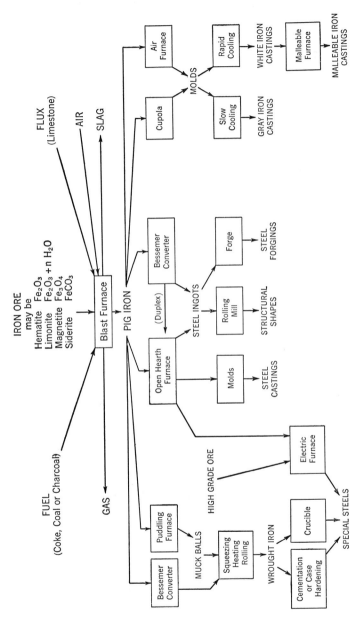

FIG. 8.12   Processes and products in the ferrous-metals industry.

8.25   Sulfur

Sulfur has the same effect on steel as on cast iron, making the metal hot short.   As a result, sulfur may be harmful in steel which is to be used at elevated temperatures or, more particularly, may cause difficulty during hot rolling or other shaping operations.   However, steel with a high sulfur content cuts smoothly in machining, so the stock for small shapes requiring machining, such as screws, may have a higher sulfur content than would be permissible in structural steel.

Since the cost of removing all of the sulfur from steel would make the steel too expensive for general use, sulfur is practically always present. Most specifications for structural steel limit the amount of sulfur to less than 0.05 per cent.

8.26   Phosphorus

Since phosphorus makes steel cold short (brittle at low temperatures), it is undesirable in parts such as railroad rails, which are subjected to impact loading when cold.   However, it has the beneficial effect of increasing fluidity, which tends to make hot rolling easier and also tends to increase the sharpness of castings.   It increases strength, hardness, corrosion-resistance, and electrical resistivity.   Since cast iron is brittle anyway, phosphorus is sometimes added to make the castings clean-cut.   Most specifications for structural steel limit the phosphorus content to less than 0.05 per cent.

8.27   Oxygen

During manufacturing processes, and particularly when the iron is in the liquid state, any free oxygen combines readily with the iron to form iron oxide.   In the finished steel or iron, the iron oxide usually appears in the form of tiny inclusions distributed throughout the metal.   Since these inclusions introduce points of weakness and increased brittleness, they are objectionable.   Inclusions may also cause concentration of stress, which is highly undesirable if the material is to be subjected to repeated loading, for they promote the formation of cracks which may result in progressive fracture.

The possibility of the formation of iron oxide is much less in those processes, such as the electric-furnace process, in which the molten metal does not come in contact with the air.   The presence of materials more readily oxidized than iron in the charge also helps prevent the formation of the iron oxide.

Oxygen and other gases may be removed from the steel by adding a small percentage of aluminum, usually less than 0.05 per cent.   The addition is generally made to the ladle as the molten steel comes from the furnace.   However, a high aluminum content promotes the formation of graphite, which may be undesirable.   Other deoxidizers and scavengers are often added to the ladle to improve the steel.   Among these are calcium and silicon; calcium, manganese, and silicon; manganese and titanium; and zirconium.

8.28   Hydrogen

Ionized hydrogen, such as is produced when steel is immersed in sulfuric acid to remove mill scale before cold drawing, makes steel brittle. The hydrogen may be removed by heating the steel for a few hours, or it will gradually work out of the steel at ordinary temperatures.   When present, hydrogen increases the hardenability of the steel.

8.29   Nitrogen

Nitrogen has a hardening and embrittling effect upon steel. This may be objectionable, or it may be desirable in producing a hard surface on the steel.   This characteristic is used to advantage in the nitriding process by exposing the steel to ammonia gas at about 600 C (1112 F) to produce a hard, wear-resisting surface without lowering the ductility of the center of the piece.

Nitrogen is used, in small percentages, as an alloying element in certain chromium steels.   It apparently forms nitrides with chromium or with chromium and iron, increasing the tensile strength without decreasing the ductility.   It promotes the formation of austenite.

8.30   Necessity for Alloying Steel

The purpose of adding alloying elements to carbon steel is to impart to the finished product desirable physical or chemical properties which are not available in carbon-steel parts fabricated by standard procedures. Aside from properties involving electrical, magnetic, or thermal characteristics, the desirable properties for most engineering purposes fall into three classes: (1) high tensile strength or hardness without brittleness; (2) resistance to corrosion; (3) high tensile strength or high creep limit at elevated or subzero temperatures.

Tensile strength or hardness.   High-strength carbon steels are produced by (a) cold working or (b) heat treating.   Cold working, as a technique for increasing strength, is limited by its nature to a few simple shapes, such as wire, tubing, and rod.   So, for the majority of uses, the only practical method of producing a high-strength carbon steel is to subject it to a suitable heat treatment.   As has been shown, the beneficial effect of heat treatment is produced by the dispersion of carbon (in the form of carbides) throughout the piece.   That is, if the hard particles of carbide are well distributed throughout the material, they tend to inhibit the sliding which develops initially in the relatively soft grains of ferrite.   For example, if all of the carbon in a steel member containing 1 per cent carbon were concentrated in one grain, the strength of the steel would be no greater than that of pure iron because the iron surrounding the grain of carbon would slip readily along its planes of weakness.   However, if the same amount of carbon were uniformly dispersed throughout the steel in solution as a carbide, the resultant distortion of the space lattice and the planes of weakness would be sufficiently great to prevent sliding until a relatively high stress had been developed.   Hence, the steel containing 1 per cent carbon may develop a strength many times that of the ferrite which constitutes 99 per cent of its weight.

It has been shown that the dispersion of the carbon is attained only by quenching the steel at a rate greater than the critical one.   The relatively high rate of cooling necessary is easily attained in a thin section, such as a watch spring, but it cannot possibly be developed in a relatively thick section because of the comparatively low thermal conductivity of steel.   That is, a thin section of steel can be cooled rapidly to the temperature of the surrounding medium, but a thick section of steel raised to the same temperature will contain much more heat.   For this heat to be removed from the material, the surrounding medium must cool the outside of the piece to a sufficiently low temperature for the heat to flow from the inside to the outside very rapidly.   The relatively low thermal conductivity of steel prevents the heat from flowing at a sufficiently high rate to reduce the temperature at the inside of the section at a rate anywhere near the critical one.   As a result, the outside of the piece may be hardened but the inside remains soft because of its comparatively low rate of cooling.   The overall strength of the part is considerably less than that which could be obtained if the piece were thin in cross section.

It has been found, however, that the addition of relatively small quantities of certain elements other than carbon makes possible the production of a steel having uniformly dispersed carbides throughout the entire cross section, even though the cross section be comparatively large.   The presence of dispersed carbides results in a strong, hard material.   The alloying elements make possible such a structure because of one or more of the three following effects:

1. The knee of the S curve is moved to the right, thereby decreasing the critical cooling rate, and making it possible for the heat to flow from the center of a large member at a sufficiently high rate to develop a satisfactory structure there.

2. The knee of the S curve is depressed (lowering the critical temperature) to facilitate the removal of heat from the inside of a member of thick cross section.   In some cases the critical temperature may be depressed to below room temperature, making possible the development of an austenite structure without quenching.
3. Stable hard carbides are formed, which supplement the iron carbide in its keying action along slip planes.

Of great importance is the fact that *the addition of small percentages of two or more alloying elements usually has a much greater effect than the addition of a larger total percentage of only one alloying element.*   This fact made possible the development of satisfactory substitute steels during World War II, when supplies of standard alloying elements such as nickel and tungsten were critical.

Insofar as strength and hardness are concerned, the sole effect of adding an alloying element to steel is to make possible in a thick cross section the development of the same structure and properties which are available in a thin section of carbon steel.   For this purpose the specific alloying element used to produce the effect is immaterial (within limits).   For example, molybdenum and tungsten are interchangeable in the production of a high-speed tool steel.

Resistance to corrosion.   The carbon steels are relatively susceptible to corrosion.   When steel is subjected to an environment containing oxygen and moisture, it oxidizes readily, forming the familiar iron rust.   The coating of oxide formed on the surface is weak and easily displaced, exposing additional metal to rust.   When certain alloying elements, such as chromium, are added to the steel, they will oxidize to form a tough adherent film which will protect the surface from further damage.   When the alloy is added for the purpose of resisting corrosion (as contrasted with developing strength and hardness), the chemical nature of the alloying element is of prime importance.

Resistance to abnormal temperatures.   While carbon steel is widely adaptable for many uses under ordinary conditions, it is not satisfactory for use at abnormal temperatures.   At low temperatures, such as those encountered in liquid-air equipment, it becomes excessively brittle; and, at temperatures in the vicinity of 1200 F and upward, encountered in jet engines and certain refining equipment, the elastic strength and creep limit are too low for efficient use.

Certain alloying elements, including nickel, chromium, and columbium, have been found to impart desirable characteristics to the steel at the extreme temperatures encountered in many engineering applications. Here, also, the nature of the alloying element used is of prime importance.

TABLE 8.2
COMPOSITION OF MORE-COMMON SAE AND AISI STEELS
(PER CENT)

No.	C	Ni	Cr	Mo	Si	V (min)	Mn	S (max)	P (max)
1020	.18–.23	....	....	....	....	....	.30–.60	.050	.040
1040	.37–.44	....	....	....	....	....	.60–.90	.050	.040
1095	.90–1.05	....	....	....	....	....	.30–.50	.050	.040
1113	.10–.16	....	....	....	....	....	1.00–1.30	.24–.33	.07–.12
1330	.28–.33	....	....	....	.20–.35	....	1.60–1.90	.040	.040
2317	.15–.20	3.25–3.75	....	....	.20–.35	....	.40–.60	.040	.040
2330	.28–.33	3.25–3.75	....	....	.20–.35	....	.60–.80	.040	.040
2345	.43–.48	3.25–3.75	....	....	.20–.35	....	.70–.90	.040	.040
2515	.12–.17	4.75–5.25	....	....	.20–.35	....	.40–.60	.040	.040
3115	.13–.18	1.10–1.40	.55–.75	....	.20–.35	....	.40–.60	.040	.040
3130	.28–.33	1.10–1.40	.55–.75	....	.20–.35	....	.60–.80	.040	.040
3140	.38–.43	1.10–1.40	.70–.90	....	.20–.35	....	.70–.90	.040	.040
3240	.38–.45	1.65–2.00	.90–1.20	....	.20–.35	....	.40–.60	.040	.040
3310	.08–.13	3.25–3.75	1.40–1.75	....	.20–.35	....	.45–.60	.025	.025
4042	.40–.45	....	....	.20–.30	.20–.35	....	.75–1.00	.040	.040
4130	.28–.33	....	.80–1.10	.15–.25	.20–.35	....	.40–.60	.040	.040
X4130	.25–.35	....	.80–1.10	.15–.25	....	....	.40–.60	.050	.040
4140	.38–.43	....	.80–1.10	.15–.25	.20–.35	....	.75–1.00	.040	.040

4340	.38–.43	1.65–2.00	.70–.90	.20–.30	.20–.35	.....	.60–.80	.040	.040
4615	.13–.18	1.65–2.00	.....	.20–.30	.20–.35	.....	.45–.65	.040	.040
4640	.38–.43	1.65–2.00	.....	.20–.30	.20–.35	.....	.60–.80	.040	.040
4815	.13–.18	3.25–3.75	.....	.20–.30	.20–.35	.....	.40–.60	.040	.040
5150	.48–.55	.....	.70–.90		.20–.35	.....	.70–.90	.040	.040
52100	.95–1.10	.....	1.30–1.60		.20–.35	.....	.25–.45	.025	.025
6120	.17–.22	.....	.70–.90		.20–.35	.10	.70–.90	.040	.040
6150	.48–.55	.....	.80–1.10		.20–.35	.15	.65–.90	.040	.040
71600*	.50–.70	.....	3.00–4.00			.....	max .30	.035	.040
8620	.18–.23	.40–.70	.40–.60	.15–.25	.20–.35	.....	.70–.90	.040	.040
8630	.28–.33	.40–.70	.40–.60	.15–.25	.20–.35	.....	.70–.90	.040	.040
8640	.38–.43	.40–.70	.40–.60	.15–.25	.20–.35	.....	.75–1.00	.040	.040
8720	.18–.23	.40–.70	.40–.60	.20–.30	.20–.35	.....	.70–.90	.040	.040
9255	.50–.60	.....	.....		1.80–2.20	.....	.70–.95	.040	.040
9315	.13–.18	3.00–3.50	1.00–1.40	.08–.15	.20–.35	.....	.45–.65	.040	.040
9260	.55–.65	.....	.....		1.80–2.20	.....	.70–1.00	.040	.040
9440	.38–.43	.30–.60	.30–.50	.08–.15	.20–.35	.....	.90–1.20	.040	.040
9450	.48–.53	.30–.60	.30–.50	.08–.15	.20–.35	.....	1.20–1.50	.040	.040
9747	.45–.50	.40–.70	.10–.25	.15–.25	.20–.35	.....	.50–.80	.040	.040
9830	.28–.33	.85–1.15	.70–.90	.20–.30	.20–.35	.....	.70–.90	.040	.040

*Contains 15.00-18.00 per cent tungsten.

8.31 Classification of Alloy Steels

Alloy steels may be classified either on the basis of chemical composition and heat treatment or on the basis of usage and physical properties. A number of years ago the Society of Automotive Engineers worked out a system for the classification and identification of a group of the steel alloys more commonly used in the automobile industry. The system of classification has also been adopted by the American Iron and Steel Institute. The SAE or AISI classification is not a substitute for a chemical formula but is merely a shorthand system for the designation of steels of specific chemical compositions. The classification index consists of a number containing four or five digits. The first two digits of the number denote the characteristic alloying element or elements and the approximate alloy content according to the following system:

10xx	Plain carbon	5xxx	Chromium
11xx	Free-cutting carbon	5xxxx	Chromium
13xx	Manganese (1.75%)	61xx	Chromium (0.80 or 0.95%), vanadium (0.10 or 0.15%)
2xxx	Nickel (3.50 or 5.00%)		
31xx	Nickel (1.25%), chromium (0.65 or 0.80%)	86xx	Nickel (0.55%), chromium (0.50%), molybdenum (0.20%)
33xx	Nickel (3.50%), chromium (1.55%)	87xx	Nickel (0.55%), chromium (0.50%), molybdenum (0.25%)
40xx	Molybdenum (0.25%)	92xx	Silicon (2.00%), manganese (0.85%)
41xx	Molybdenum (0.20%), chromium (0.95%)		
43xx	Molybdenum (0.25%), chromium (0.50 or 0.80%), nickel (1.80%)	93xx	Nickel (3.25%), chromium (1.20%), molybdenum (0.12%)
		94xx	Nickel (0.45%), chromium (0.40%), molybdenum (0.12%)
46xx	Molybdenum (0.25%), nickel (1.80%)	97xx	Nickel (0.55%), chromium (0.17%), molybdenum (0.20%)
48xx	Molybdenum (0.25%), nickel (3.50%)	98xx	Nickel (1.00%), chromium (0.80%), molybdenum (0.25%)

The last two digits of the classification number indicate the approximate carbon content (usually ± 0.03 per cent) in hundredths of one per cent. The second digit, except for the 1000, 4000, 8000, and 9000 series, indicates the approximate percentage of the principal alloying element. Thus, "SAE 1020" indicates a steel containing about 0.20 per cent carbon, and "SAE 2340" designates a steel containing about 0.40 per cent carbon and approximately 3 per cent nickel.

The series are subject to constant revision as needs arise. Compositions of a few of the more common SAE and AISI steels are given in Table 8.2.

The classification of steel by chemical composition has not been entirely satisfactory to the users because of the variability of the product as a result of variations in heat treatment. Two steels having the same SAE number and the same nominal heat treatment may develop quite different properties because of differences in rate of cooling due to minor variations in the technique employed and to differences in the thickness of section. Hence, consideration is being given to the idea of the consumer specifying minimum properties rather than an SAE number. While this system has definite advantages to the user, there has not as yet been developed a system of designation comprehensive enough to cover all needs. A step in this direction is the designation of gray cast iron by the ASTM according to class (such as class 20, 30, 40, 50, and 60), the minimum ultimate tensile strength being 1000 times the class number, and the designation (as previously mentioned) of malleable cast irons by a class number such as 35018, in which the 35 indicates an elastic strength of 35,000 psi and the 18 indicates a minimum percentage elongation in 2 in.

In addition to the steels covered by the SAE and AISI designations, there have been developed a number of special steels, usually known by trade names, to meet general requirements for certain classes of usage. In many cases strength is not the only criterion of selection. Some of the special classes of usage are

1. High-strength low-alloy;
2. Corrosion resistance;
3. Retention of hardness at red heat (for high-speed tool steels);
4. Resistance to oxidation and creep at high temperatures;
5. Retention of ductility at low temperatures;
6. Special electrical, magnetic, and thermal characteristics.

The general effects of the alloying elements and a few of the properties of typical alloy steels are discussed in the following sections. Because of the extremely large number of alloys which have been developed, the treatment herein cannot be comprehensive and is intended to provide a survey of the types of steels available and the general effects of the more common alloying elements. A number of excellent compilations[4] of properties of specific alloys have been published, and other information is available in technical magazines as well as in trade literature available from manufacturers.

8.32 Carbon

As is shown in Fig. 7.1, the effect of a small amount of carbon (up to about 1.2 per cent) on iron is to increase the strength and decrease the ductility. A carbon content of more than about 2 per cent promotes the

[4] *Mechanical Properties of Metals and Alloys,* Circular C447, U. S. Department of Commerce, National Bureau of Standards (Washington, D. C.: GPO, 1943); S. L. Hoyt, *Metals and Alloys Data Book* (New York: Reinhold Publishing Corporation, 1952).

TABLE 8.3

PROPERTIES OF FERROUS METALS
(AVERAGE VALUES)

| Material* | Strength (psi × 1000) | | | | | | Elong. in 2 In. (%) | Hard. (Bhn) |
	Tension Ult.	Tension Elas.	Comp. Elas.	Shear Ult.	Shear Elas.	Endur. Lim.		
Commercially pure iron ...	42	19	19	30	12	26	48	69
Wrought iron	55	30	30	38	18	25	35	100
SAE steels								
1020—Hot-rolled	60	35	35	43	21	30	35	120
—Cold-drawn	80	60	60	60	36	38	18	150
—QW 1625, D 400..	80	50	...	...	...	...	20	163
—QW 1625, D 1300.	70	35	...	...	...	...	32	140
1040—Cast	70	32	...	...	...	...	20	...
—Hot-rolled	90	52	...	80	36	...	20	180
—QW 1500, D 1050.	102	87	87	90	52	57	23	210
—QW 1500, D 800..	121	92	...	...	...	...	17	248
1095—Hot-rolled	140	78	...	...	...	...	6	265
—QO, D 850	188	97	97	100	58	98	10	380
—QO, D 400	282	174	174	...	96	112	8	488
2317—Hot-rolled	90	...	...	...	...	...	...	181
—QO 1650, D 300..	181	157	...	...	...	...	14	375
—QO 1500, D 1300.	78	47	...	...	...	...	29	140
2330—Hot-rolled	112	...	...	...	...	...	...	232
—QO 1475, D 400..	240	210	...	...	...	...	12	490
—QO 1475, D 1300.	83	55	...	...	...	...	23	167
2345—Hot-rolled	138	...	...	...	...	...	...	281
—QO 1450, D 400..	270	230	...	...	...	...	11	540
—QO 1450, D 1200.	112	91	91	90	54	67	24	248
2515—Hot-rolled	102	...	...	...	...	...	...	214
—QO 1450, D 200..	190	156	...	...	...	...	15	387
—QO 1450, D 1200.	105	80	...	...	...	...	30	200
3115—Hot-rolled	90	...	...	...	...	...	...	182
—QO 1550, D 200..	158	122	...	...	...	...	12	330
—QO 1550, D 1300.	80	45	...	...	...	...	30	130
3130—Hot-rolled	112	...	...	...	...	...	...	233
—QW 1500, D 400..	245	215	...	160	100	...	10	490
—QW 1500, D 1300.	94	66	...	...	...	...	28	187
3145—Hot-rolled	138	...	...	...	...	...	...	281
—QO 1500, D 400..	260	220	...	...	...	...	8	510
—QO 1500, D 1300.	102	71	...	...	...	...	20	217
3240—QO 1475, D 400..	275	240	...	240	130	...	9	550
—QO 1475, D 1200.	130	110	...	110	70	...	22	275
3310—Hot-rolled	120	...	...	...	...	...	...	250
—QO 1525, D 200..	220	185	...	...	...	...	12	440
—QO 1525, D 1300.	105	80	...	...	...	...	28	210
4130—Hot-rolled	108	70	...	95	60	...	...	221
—QW, D 400	240	212	...	...	...	...	10	480
—Normalized	76	45	...	87	35	43	32	145
X4130—Annealed	85	60	...	...	...	...	30	180
—QW, D 400	255	220	...	...	...	...	10	480
—Normalized	119	70	...	...	...	...	25	220

TABLE 8.3 (*Continued*)

	Strength (psi × 1000)						Elong.	
Material*	Tension		Comp.	Shear	Endur.		in 2 In.	Hard.
	Ult.	Elas.	Elas.	Ult.	Lim.	Elas.	(%)	(Bhn)
SAE steels (*Continued*)								
4140—QW, D 1100	140	116	116	...	63	64	16	250
4340—Hot-rolled	175	...	...	...	...	...	...	382
—Annealed	112	...	...	...	...	...	...	228
—QO 1500, D 400..	290	265	...	...	...	...	10	575
4615—Hot-rolled	90	...	...	...	...	...	...	181
—Annealed	73	48	...	...	...	...	33	147
—QO 1425, D 300..	134	105	...	...	...	...	18	302
4640—QO, D 500	250	222	...	...	...	...	10	480
4815—Hot-rolled	97	...	...	...	...	...	...	214
—Annealed	87	...	...	...	...	...	...	191
—QO 1525, D 300..	182	160	...	...	...	...	13	375
5150—QO 1525, D 600..	260	235	235	...	123	100	11	512
—QO 1525, D 1200.	150	130	...	...	...	...	22	290
6120—Hot-rolled	95	...	...	...	...	...	...	198
—Annealed	72	...	...	...	...	...	...	...
—QO 1500, D 300..	145	130	130	...	72	92	16	332
6150—Annealed	103	70	...	...	...	...	27	217
—QO 1575, D 1000.	185	175	...	...	...	...	13	388
—QO 1575, D 400..	300	261	...	...	...	...	2	601
71660—Hot-rolled ,......	130	67	...	...	...	...	12	228
9255—QO, D 700	240	215	...	...	...	...	8	480
C 0.40, Mn 1.20								
—QO 1500, D 200..	252	220	...	238	190	112	8	500
—QO 1500, D 1200.	120	80	...	115	75	50	25	250
Stainless steel "18-8"								
—Annealed	80	35	35	...	18	35	55	150
Gray cast iron								
No. 20 (ASTM).....	20	...	80†	...	...	9	...	110
No. 60 (ASTM).....	60	...	145†	...	...	24	...	275
Alloy cast iron-1.15% Ni...	50	...	156†	...	...	20	...	...
Malleable cast iron	54	36	36	...	18	30	10	120

* QO = quenched in oil, QW = quenched in water, D = drawn, and numbers following such letter symbols indicate temperatures in degrees F.

† Ultimate strength.

formation of graphite, lowering both the strength and the ductility. A carbon content in excess of 5 or 6 per cent results in a metal of very low strength that has no commercial value.

8.33 Nickel

Nickel is one of the most important alloying elements for steel and cast iron because it provides increased resistance to corrosion and improves the physical properties. It forms a solid solution with iron, reducing the capacity of the iron to combine with carbon. This action results in the tendency of high-carbon nickel steels to contain free graphite, especially if the steels are annealed.

The effect of nickel upon the equilibrium diagram is to lower the transformation lines and to move the eutectoid to the left. The structure of the nickel-carbon steels at room temperature, under the condition of slow cooling, is shown in Fig. 8.13.

When a nickel-carbon steel containing 1 per cent carbon is cooled slowly to room temperature, martensitic structure is obtained if the nickel content is a little more than 5 per cent, and austenitic steel is obtained with a nickel content of about 13 per cent. Thus, the same constituents can be produced in a steel containing 1 per cent carbon by adding 6 or 7 per cent nickel and allowing the alloy steel to cool slowly as can be produced by quenching the carbon steel. However, the nickel-carbon steel will be

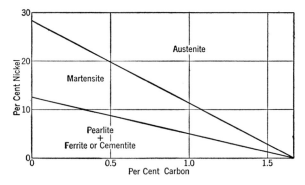

FIG. 8.13   Constitution of nickel steels.

free from the initial strains which are induced in the carbon steel by quenching.

The average effect of nickel in amounts up to 8 per cent is as follows:[5] 0.01 per cent Ni increases the elastic strength 40 psi, increases the tensile strength 42 psi, and decreases the final elongation in 8 in. 0.01 per cent. A steel containing 13 per cent nickel is too hard to be machined by ordinary methods.

Average properties of some of the most commonly used SAE nickel steels are given in Table 8.3.

Figure 8.14 shows some of the properties of the iron-nickel alloys. As will be noted, almost the entire range of the alloys is useful for some purpose.

There are several distinct groups of iron-nickel alloys with or without other elements:

[5] R. R. Abbott, "The Role of Nickel in Alloy Steels," *Proceedings of the American Society for Testing Materials*, Vol. 17, No. 2, p. 9.

Structural nickel alloys.   Structural nickel alloys contain up to about 5 per cent nickel and include the SAE nickel steels as well as some others which have been developed for general construction rather than machine parts.   As will be noted, the effect of the nickel is to increase the tensile strength appreciably without impairing the ductility.   Hence steels of this type are useful for long-span bridges, shafting, axles, gears, bearings, and other machine parts.   The effect of heat treatment upon one of the SAE nickel steels is shown in Fig. 8.15.

The TTT diagram given in Fig. 8.16 for the 2340 nickel steel shows the effect of the nickel in lowering the transformation temperature and in delaying the onset of the transformation.   It will be noted that the hardness at the completion of the isothermal transformation is greater when the transformation takes place at a low temperature than at a high temperature. Therefore, in order to produce a steel of a given hardness a somewhat lower rate of cooling may be used for a nickel steel than for a carbon steel. Hence less cooling strain will be developed in the nickel steel, and more-complete hardening is possible in thick sections.

Low-temperature alloys.   Steels having a nickel content of 8 to 10 per cent have unusually high resistance to impact at subnormal temperatures and are, therefore, useful in the manufacture of low-temperature equipment such as refrigeration units and liquid-air equipment.

Alnico alloys.   Alloys containing from 14 to 28 per cent nickel have a marked increase in magnetic capacity in comparison with low-nickel alloys of carbon steel.   With the addition of aluminum and in some cases other alloying elements, materials having a very high magnetic capacity have been developed.   Five sets of such alloys are in common use and are known in general as Alnico.   They contain from 8 to 12 per cent aluminum, 14 to 28 per cent nickel, 0 to 24 per cent cobalt, and 0 to 6 per cent copper.   The carbon content is relatively low, and the balance is iron. All these alloys are very hard and are too brittle to be shaped by fabrication processes other than casting and grinding, or else by powder-metallurgy techniques.   An Alnico magnet is capable of lifting many times its own weight.

The Alnico alloys are not equal in magnetic capacity to the platinum-cobalt alloys (containing more than 76 per cent platinum) but they are, of course, much cheaper.

High-temperature alloys.   Steels containing from 25 to 35 per cent nickel have a high resistance to oxidation at elevated temperatures and are therefore used for parts of internal-combustion engines, for electrical resistance wire, and for some parts of jet-propulsion units that operate at tem-

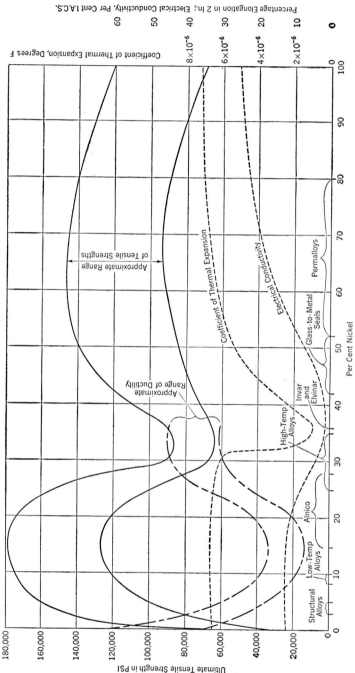

FIG. 8.14 Effect of nickel on properties of commercial iron-nickel alloys. (Small percentages of other elements may have a marked effect on properties.)

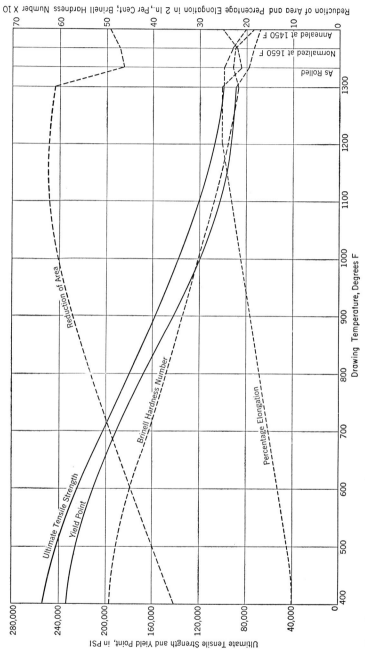

FIG. 8.15 Effect of heat treatment on properties of an oil-quenched nickel steel (SAE 2340). ($\frac{1}{2}$-in. to $1\frac{1}{2}$-in. specimens.)

peratures up to about 1500 F.   This group of alloys has a modulus of
elasticity of about 23,000,000 psi.   The material is austenitic in structure
and is therefore nonmagnetic.   The serviceability at high temperatures is
increased by the addition of chromium.   One steel which has given satisfactory service for some parts of jet engines contains 25 per cent nickel,
16 per cent chromium, and 6 per cent molybdenum.   For temperatures
in the 1500 F to 1800 F range, nickel-base alloys are used, and above
1800 F the base is usually cobalt.

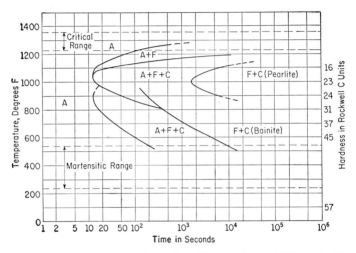

FIG. 8.16   Time-temperature-transformation diagram for a 2340 steel. (Data from
International Nickel Co.)

Invar and elinvar.   As will be noted in Fig. 8.14, there is a marked
decrease in the coefficient of thermal expansion as the nickel content
approaches 36 per cent.   This characteristic has led to the development
of a series of alloys for use in standard bars, various measuring devices,
and other equipment in which thermal expansion would introduce difficulties.   Two of these alloys are known as invar and elinvar.

Glass-to-metal seals.   Alloys containing from 42 to 52 per cent nickel
may be produced with the same thermal-expansion characteristics as many
of the commercial glasses.   Such alloys are therefore very useful in
making glass-to-metal seals.   For example, the lead-in wires in light globes
and vacuum tubes must have the same coefficient of thermal expansion as
the glass, to prevent cracking as the unit heats in service.   A number of
commercial alloys have been developed for this purpose.   One of the first
to be developed is known as platinite and contains 46 per cent nickel.

High-nickel steels. Steels containing from 40 to 60 per cent nickel retain a relatively high strength and ductility at low temperatures, and are useful for the construction of liquid-air machines and similar equipment designed to operate at subzero temperatures, where ordinary carbon steel becomes brittle. A steel containing from 55 to 60 per cent nickel, with about 1 per cent manganese and from 0.30 to 0.40 per cent carbon, has an ultimate tensile strength of about 114,000 psi, an elastic strength of 57,000 psi, and an elongation of 40 per cent at the boiling point of liquid air (-190 C or -310 F).

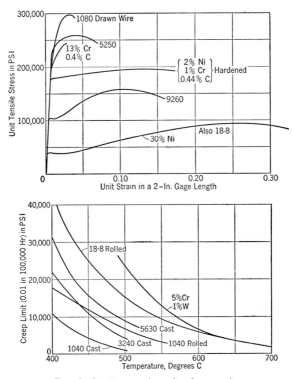

Fig. 8.17   Properties of a few steels.

Permalloys. If the nickel content is more than 30 per cent, the magnetic permeability of the iron-nickel alloys increases. Hence alloys containing from 45 to 50 per cent nickel to 80 per cent nickel are useful as magnetic shields, laminated cores for transformers, and certain detecting devices in which high permeability with low magnetizing forces is essential. The alloy containing 47 per cent nickel is extensively used for this purpose, having a permeability about twenty times that of ordinary soft iron. Where the need for permeability is sufficiently great to offset the additional cost, alloys containing 80 per cent nickel are extremely useful. Their permeability is about 160 times that of iron. In this group of alloys a small percentage of molybdenum or a small percentage of chromium and copper is frequently added to increase the electrical resistance.

8.34 Chromium

Chromium is one of the important alloying elements because of its unusual effectiveness in imparting corrosion-resisting characteristics to steel at both ordinary and elevated temperatures. Recent advances in forming techniques, particularly for the stainless steels, have greatly increased the adaptability of chromium alloys. Chromium combines readily with both iron and carbon, forming a double carbide, and has the effect of lowering the transition temperatures in cooling. In amounts up to 3 per cent, chromium has the effect of reducing the crystal size. The resultant structure of the chromium-carbon steels after slow cooling is indicated in Fig. 8.18.

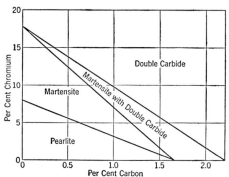

FIG. 8.18   Constitution of chromium steels.

With a carbon content of 0.8 per cent, from 3 to 8 per cent chromium produces a martensitic structure. As the chromium content is increased above about 6 per cent, chromium carbide begins to form, replacing the martensitic structure, and the hardness is increased. If more than about 12 per cent chromium is present, all the carbon is in the form of iron carbide and chromium carbide.

When nickel-chromium alloys are heated above 1000 F, chromium is precipitated at the grain boundaries as chromium-rich carbides, thereby depleting the steel of the chromium available for oxidation and permitting corrosion to start at the grain boundaries. To prevent this undesirable phenomenon, the carbon content must be limited or a stabilizer must be added. Columbium may be used as a stabilizer since it has an even greater affinity for carbon than does chromium and will thus form carbides, leaving the uncombined chromium to resist corrosion.   Titanium serves the same general purpose but is not quite so effective as columbium at elevated temperatures.   Neither has an appreciable effect upon the physical properties that influence fabrication.

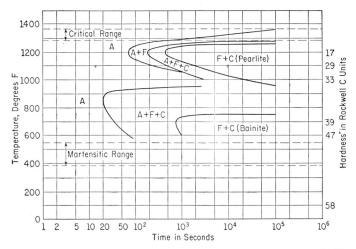

FIG. 8.19   Time-temperature-transformation diagram for a 3240 steel. (Data from International Nickel Co.)

There are two general series of chromium steels in common use in addition to the nickel-chrome alloys.   The first group consists of the steels having a chromium content of from 1 to 2 per cent, and the second group includes those containing from 10 to 27 per cent chromium.

Steel with a carbon content of about 1 per cent and a chromium content of 1 per cent is used for well-drilling tools.   With a chromium content between 1 and 1.75 per cent, the steel is suitable for such products as ball bearings, crushing machinery, tools, and safes.   A chromium content of 2 per cent produces a steel suitable for such products as crushers, dies for drawing steel, rolls used in rolling mills, and armor-piercing projectiles. Low-chromium steel, such as SAE 5150, is used for machine parts.

If the chromium content is increased to more than about 10 per cent, the resulting steel is corrosion resistant, takes a high polish, and presents a fine appearance.   Steel of this general type is often called *stainless steel*.

Nickel-chrome alloys are also of importance because they combine the beneficial effects of both nickel and chromium.   As compared with the nickel steels, the nickel-chrome steels have a higher elastic strength with the same ductility, have a greater hardness, and are more susceptible to heat treatment.

TABLE 8.4

Composition and Average Values of Properties of Some AISI Stainless Steels

Type	C (%)	Mn (%)	Cr (%)	Ni (%)	Ultimate Tensile Strength (ksi)			Yield Strength, .002 Offset (ksi)		Elong. in 2 In. (%)		Endurance Limit (ksi)		Creep Limit† (psi)	
					AN	CR*	HT	AN	CR*	AN	CR*	AN	CR*	1000 F	1500 F
301	.09–.20	2.0	16–18	6–8	100	200	...	40	150	55	10	40	85	16,000	900
302	.09–.20	2.0	17–19	8–10	75	330	105	30	270	55	15	35	70	16,000	900
303	max .20	2.0	17–19	8–10	75	145	105	30	120	...	...	...	...	16,000	...
304	max .08	2.0	18–20	8–10	75	290	104	30	270	45	15	35	70	16,000	900
309	max .20	2.0	22–24	12–15	90	200	105	45	175	45	10	35	70	16,500	1000
310	max .25	2.0	24–26	19–22	90	140	...	45	110	45	15	35	60	18,000	1100
316‡	max .10	2.0	16–18	10–14	75	220	98	30	195	55	15	35	60	25,000	3000
321§	max .10	2.0	17–19	8–11	75	235	98	30	210	50	15	35	55	17,000	900
347‖	max .10	2.0	17–19	9–12	75	220	98	30	210	50	12	35	60	18,000	900
410	max .15	1.0	11–14	max .50	70	130	200	40	98	30	10	45	90	11,000	750
430	max .12	1.0	14–18	max .50	70	110	80	40	100	30	10	35	50	8,500	700
442	max .35	1.0	18–23	max .50	80	110	...	50	90	25	10	35	50	8,500	600
446	max .35	1.0	23–27	max .50	75	110	95	40	100	23	10	45	55	6,000	...
501	min .10	1.0	4–6	.....	...	...	...	...	...	...	...	...	...	...	...
502	max .10	1.0	4–6	.....	...	...	...	...	...	...	...	...	...	...	...

NOTES: (1) All have a maximum silicon content of 1 per cent, a maximum sulfur content of 1 per cent, and a maximum phosphorus content of 0.04 per cent (except 303, for which the phosphorous limit is 0.07 per cent). (2) AN = annealed, CR = cold rolled, HT = heat treated.

* Maximum values.   † 1 per cent per 10,000 hr.   ‡1.75–2.50 per cent Mo.   § 4 × C min per cent Ti.   ‖ 8 × C min per cent Cb.

For example, a comparison of the TTT diagram for 3240 steel (Fig. 8.19) with the diagram for 2340 steel (Fig. 8.16) shows the effect of the chromium in retarding the transformation of austenite, even though the total alloy content is less.

One particular nickel-chrome alloy, known as 18-8 because it contains 18 per cent chromium and 8 per cent nickel, is widely used as a high-strength stainless steel. It retains its austenitic structure to at least -75 C (-103 F), and is therefore very useful in certain refrigeration equipment, as in the manufacture of solid carbon dioxide or the dewaxing of lubricating oils, where certain parts of the equipment must withstand high pressure at low temperatures. Because of its relatively high resistance to creep, as is indicated in Fig. 8.17, it is also suitable for use at elevated temperatures. Other important stainless steels are listed in Table 8.4.

There are three general classes of stainless steel. In one group the principal alloying element is chromium (11.5 to 18.0 per cent). The carbon content may vary from 0.08 to 1.10 per cent, and nickel is present in some of the alloys. The steels in this class may be hardened by quenching and may be softened by an annealing treatment similar to that which is used for the plain carbon steels. In the quenched condition the principal constituent is martensite, and hence the steels in this group are sometimes referred to as martensitic stainless steels. The group includes alloys 403, 406, 410, 414, 416, 420, 431, 440, 501, and 502.

Stainless steels of the second class cannot be hardened appreciably by heat treatment. The chromium content may vary from 14 to 27 per cent, and the carbon content is usually less than 0.20 per cent. The nickel content is negligible. The steels in this group, as well as those in the first class, are magnetic in the annealed condition. The principal constituent is ferrite, and hence they are known as ferritic stainless steels. Alloys 405, 430, 442, 443, and 446 are in this group.

The third class of stainless steels is also nonhardenable by heat treatment and contains from 6 to 22 per cent nickel in addition to 16 to 26 per cent chromium. The carbon content is generally less than 0.20 per cent. Other elements, such as molybdenum, titanium, and columbium, are sometimes added to increase the resistance to corrosion. The alloys in this group are the 300 series and, as may be seen from Table 8.4, they respond readily to cold working. In the annealed condition the steels are essentially austenitic because of the effect of the nickel in lowering the critical temperature, hence they are sometimes called the *austenitic stainless steels*. They are nonmagnetic unless subjected to severe cold working.

While the corrosion resistance of all three groups is relatively high, it may be increased even more by a special treatment known as *passivation*. This consists in inducing a film of chromium oxide on the surface of the steel by subjecting it to the action of a strong oxidizing agent.   A dilute solution of nitric acid is normally used for this purpose.   If the surface of the material is free from scale and clean, a much more durable corrosion-resisting coat is induced than would be obtained if the alloy were allowed to oxidize normally in the atmosphere.

The base price of stainless steels averages about one dollar per pound.

Alloys of chromium and vanadium, containing about 1 per cent chromium, 0.2 per cent vanadium, and from 0.2 to 1 per cent carbon are coming into general use for structural purposes.   The alloys are uniform in texture, are readily heat-treated and machined, and will develop tensile strengths as high as 230,000 psi.   Certain of the alloys will develop a tensile strength of 200,000 psi with an elongation of 12 per cent.   Chromium-vanadium alloys are used for shafting, springs, gears, dies, ball-bearing raceways, and other applications requiring a high elastic strength combined with some ductility.

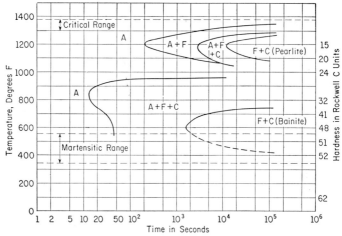

FIG. 8.20   Time-temperature-transformation diagram for a 4340 steel. (Data from U. S. Steel Corp.)

8.35   Molybdenum

The principal effect of the addition of molybdenum to an iron-carbon alloy is to shift the TTT curve to the right.   This lowers the critical rate of cooling and makes possible deep hardening with appropriate heat treatment.   A TTT diagram for the 4340 alloy is given in Fig. 8.20.   Since the composition of this alloy is essentially the same as that of 3240, except for about 0.25 per cent molybdenum in 4340, a comparison of Fig. 8.20 with Fig. 8.19 shows the effect of molybdenum in delaying the completion of transformation.   Molybdenum also tends to increase the tensile strength at elevated temperatures. For example, at 1200 F a 0.15 per cent carbon steel has an ultimate tensile strength of about 20,000 psi, and the addition of 1 per cent molybdenum increases the tensile strength to about 38,000 psi. Molybdenum tends to decarburize steel at high temperatures, so the heat treatment is best carried out in a controlled atmosphere. Molybdenum together with, or as an alternate for, tungsten is used in high-speed tool steels, the molybdenum replacing tungsten in the double carbide. One part of molybdenum is approximately equivalent to two parts of tungsten. There are three types of molybdenum alloy steel that are well adapted for high-speed tools. Each type contains about 0.85 per cent carbon and approximately 4 per cent chromium. In addition, one type contains 1.50 per cent tungsten, 8.75 per cent molybdenum, and 1.10 per cent vanadium; a second type contains 8 per cent molybdenum and 2.25 per cent vanadium; and a third type contains 4.5 per cent tungsten, 4.0 per cent molybdenum, and 1.5 per cent vanadium. All these alloys have given satisfactory service as high-speed tool steels.

8.36 Silicon

Silicon combines with carbon to form hard carbides which, when properly distributed throughout the alloy, have the effect of increasing the elastic strength without loss of ductility. Silicon steel containing up to 2 per cent of the alloying element is used for structural purposes. If the silicon content is increased to about 12 per cent, the steel becomes too hard to be machined but is acid-resistant. A steel may have its resistance to corrosion, to wear, or to heat increased by a process known as *Ihrigizing*. In this process the surface is impregnated with silicon by heating the steel in an atmosphere containing silicon. Thus, Ihrigizing is similar in many respects to the nitriding process. Alloys containing up to 2 per cent silicon, 0.6 per cent chromium, 0.7 per cent manganese, and 0.5 per cent carbon have proved satisfactory for recoil springs because of the resistance of the alloys to shock loading.

8.37 Tungsten

Tungsten forms hard stable carbides when added to steel. It raises the critical temperature, thus increasing the strength of the alloy at high temperatures. This characteristic has led to the use of tungsten as an alloying element in high-speed cutting tools. The high-speed tool steel increases the capacity of metal shaping and finishing equipment about 100 times over that possible with plain carbon steel. One of the widely used high-speed steels, known as 18-4-1, is composed of 18 per cent tungsten, 4 per cent chromium, 1 per cent vanadium, and from 0.5 to 0.8 per cent carbon. The high strength characteristic of tungsten steel at elevated temperatures has led to its use in forging dies. Alloys developed for this purpose contain about 0.3 per cent carbon, 0.4 per cent vanadium, 2 to 4 per cent chromium, and 9 to 18 per cent tungsten. The addition of tungsten alone produces a brittle steel, but with the addition of chromium the toughness is increased. Tungsten does not shift the S curve for steel, so tungsten steels are not considered deep-hardening steels.

8.38 Vanadium

Vanadium has the same deoxidizing effect upon molten steel as aluminum, but is not used so much for that purpose because of its greater cost. It has very little effect upon the equilibrium diagram, but forms very hard carbides, thus increasing the elastic strength and tensile strength of low-carbon and medium-carbon steel. It promotes a fine-grained structure and hence increases ductility. Vanadium is soluble in ferrite, increasing its hardenability. The creep resistance of steel appears to be increased by the addition of vanadium. It is extensively used in steel for springs in proportions up to 1 per cent, and is used in high-speed tool steels, usually in combination with tungsten and molybdenum.

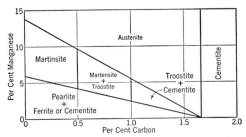

FIG. 8.21 Constitution of manganese steels.

8.39 Manganese

Manganese, like nickel, forms a solid solution with iron, but it has a much more noticeable effect than nickel (in equal percentages) in lowering the critical range of the steel. Figure 8.21 shows the resultant structure of slowly-cooled carbon-manganese-iron alloys at room temperature. With 1 per cent carbon and 6 per cent manganese, austenite is formed at room temperature.

In the cast or rolled state the resultant steel is nearly as brittle as glass because of the separation of the brittle iron-manganese carbide in a weaker network. However, by reheating to about 1000 C (1832 F) and quenching, the separation of the double carbide upon cooling is prevented and a fine-grained austenitic structure results.

There are two types of manganese steel in general use—the pearlitic and the austenitic. The martensitic steels are too brittle for general usage.

With a carbon content of about 0.5 per cent and a manganese content of 1.25 per cent, the alloy is suitable for use as rifle barrels.

If the manganese content is between 8 and 14 per cent and the steel has been quenched in water at about 1000 C, it is known as Hadfield high-manganese steel.   This grade of steel is very hard and cannot be machined satisfactorily, so it must be shaped by casting or rolling to forms which can be finished with only a small amount of grinding.   It has capacity for large plastic deformation without failure, and therefore has greater toughness than carbon steels of equal ultimate strength.   Because of its resistance to abrasion, as well as the other properties mentioned, it is suitable for frogs, switches, safes, rock-crushing machinery, and mining and milling equipment.

8.40   Boron

One of the most effective elements for increasing the hardenability of steel is boron.   From 0.002 to 0.004 per cent boron moves the S curve for the 0.40 per cent carbon steel far enough to the right for the ordinary quenching procedures to produce a fine-grained steel with well-dispersed carbon.   The resultant alloy has good ductility and toughness.   With 0.40 per cent carbon a boron content of about 0.003 per cent appears to give the most satisfactory results; if the boron content is increased to 0.007 per cent, the alloy becomes too hot short for satisfactory workability.   Boron is most effective in combination with manganese.

8.41   Columbium

When columbium is added to steel, it forms iron columbide, which has an appreciable effect in increasing the creep limit of the material at elevated temperatures, provided the columbium-carbon ratio exceeds 8. Columbium is also used as an effective stabilizing agent in stainless steel, since it has the effect of counteracting the grain-boundary corrosion which takes place in chromium steel at elevated temperatures.

8.42   Copper

Copper imparts corrosion-resistance qualities to steel and in addition has a beneficial effect upon strength.   Copper-bearing steels containing up to about 0.30 per cent copper are used for structural purposes.   Copper is also utilized in conjunction with nickel in corrosion-resisting steels.

8.43   Lead

Lead in amounts up to 0.50 per cent has been found to increase the machinability of steel, and it is now utilized in screw stock and in other stock where free-machining qualities are essential.   In this respect its effect

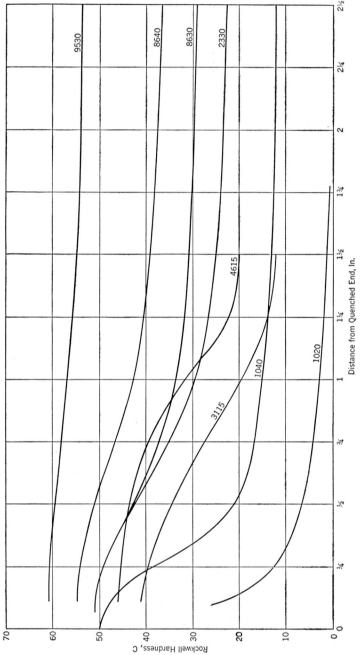

FIG. 8.22   Average hardenability curves for some SAE steels.

is similar to that of sulfur, but it has the advantage of not making the steel hot short. Strength and hardness are not affected appreciably by the addition of lead.

8.44 Titanium

Titanium is a strong deoxidizing agent, being equal in capacity to aluminum and stronger than silicon in this respect. It also forms carbides and nitrides, which may exist as solid solutions. Its effect is to decrease the grain size, thereby improving the yield strength and creep strength and decreasing the hardness. An alloy consisting of ferrite and titanium carbide has desirable deep-drawing characteristics and is unique among steel alloys in that it has no yield point. Sheet containing a small amount of titanium (less than four and one-half times the carbon content) is a satisfactory base material for enamel, in that the enamel may be applied directly in layers as thin as 0.002 in. without the use of a base coat.

8.45 Other Alloying Elements

A number of additional alloying elements have been used to produce special-purpose steels, and still others will undoubtedly be developed in the future.

Zirconium is one of the strongest deoxidizing agents known, being more effective than titanium, aluminum, or silicon. It readily combines with both sulfur and nitrogen, rendering them harmless.

Tellurium is extremely effective in increasing the resistance of steel to abrasion. As small a quantity as 5 grams per ton of steel has a marked effect upon the wear resistance.

Selenium will increase the machinability of steel.

Tantalum has the same effect as columbium in stabilizing carbon to inhibit intergranular corrosion of high-chromium steels.

8.46 Hardenability of Alloy Steels

One of the most important advances in the technology of alloy steel is the development of a method for predicting the *hardenability* (not hardness) of low-alloy steels from the chemical composition.[6] A hardenability factor, which gives the depth to which full hardness may be developed by heat treatment, may be determined for a given chemical composition by using curves and tables. The process involved in the evaluation of the hardenability factor brings out the fact that the addition of two or more elements in small amounts is much more effective than adding an equal total per-

[6] M. A. Grossman, "Hardenability of Steel Calculated From Chemical Composition," *Transactions, American Institute of Mechanical Engineers,* Vol. 150, p. 227.

centage of only one alloying element.   Hardness equivalents may be evaluated and show about the following relationship:

$$0.04V = 0.12Mn = 0.13Mo = 0.16Cr = 0.45Si = 1.10Ni$$

As indicated in section 8.40, other elements such as boron have an even greater effect upon hardenability than does vanadium.   Some elements, such as sulfur, decrease the hardenability of steel.   There is developing, a tendency to specify steels for some uses on the basis of hardenability rather than on the basis of chemical composition.   As an aid in selecting steels having proper hardenability characteristics, the American Iron and Steel Institute has developed and published a series of hardenability bands for certain steels, known as the H steels.

DETERIORATION OF FERROUS METALS

8.47   Nature of Deterioration

In general, the mechanical properties of the ferrous metals tend to remain constant; aging has little effect upon them.   However, these metals are subject to corrosion and, unless protected in some way, may disintegrate entirely in a short time.   Damage amounting to millions of dollars is caused annually in the United States by chemical attack, primarily corrosion.

Not only are the stresses in a load-carrying member increased by virtue of the decreased cross-sectional area due to corrosion, but in addition the stresses may be raised appreciably by the surface irregularities produced by the chemical attack.   For example, a small amount of pitting on the surface of a member may reduce its effective endurance limit to less than half the true endurance limit of the material.

8.48   Action in Corrosion

Corrosion is usually regarded as an electrolytic action.   While the exact chemical reactions which take place in a specific situation may be complicated, the fundamental action is dependent on the presence of three materials: the metal, moisture, and the corrosive agent, which is often oxygen.

Moisture is necessary as the medium in which the electrolytic action takes place, and oxygen, in addition to combining with the iron to form the familiar rust, combines with the liberated hydrogen which would otherwise halt the reactions.   Of course, the temperature and the presence of other chemicals may have an accelerating or retarding effect, but the nature and rate of corrosion are controlled primarily by the relative proportions of metal, moisture, and oxygen.   The four principal environments which promote corrosion are the atmosphere, water immersion, soil, and chemicals.

Corrosion in air represents one extreme condition in which an abundance of oxygen is present, and in which the rate of corrosion depends on the available moisture.   An abundance of rainfall permits rapid corrosion particularly if smoke or other industrial gases are present in the air.   In an arid region, where there is but little moisture in the air, corrosion will take place at a greatly reduced rate.   In air corrosion the attack is usually manifested by uniform shallow pitting over the entire exposed surface. Four atmospheres in order of increasing severity are normal indoor conditions, rural, industrial, and marine.

Corrosion under water represents the other extreme condition: an abundance of moisture but only a limited supply of oxygen.   Corrosion in boiler tubes and hot-water supply systems has necessitated large expenditures for replacement in the past.   In some instances the corrosive action has been materially reduced by removing the dissolved oxygen from the water, while in other cases the corrosion has been due primarily to impurities in the feed water.   In this type of corrosion the surface usually exhibits relatively large scattered pits rather than a uniform disintegration.   That is, the action is concentrated, rather than general, and works rapidly through a thin plate or tube.   Some metals corrode much more rapidly in sea water than in fresh water.

Corrosion in soil is representative of a third condition, in which there is more nearly an equal balance between moisture and oxygen.   With the wide variety of salts and acids which may be present in soil, the type and rate of corrosion of metals in contact with the ground may be expected to vary within wide limits.   The corrosive action of the soil may also be augmented by stray electric currents in the ground, particularly in the vicinity of street-car tracks.

Corrosion by chemicals is a common industrial problem.   In this type of corrosion a wide variety of actions can take place, depending on the nature of the chemicals in contact with the metal.   Oxidizing agents, in particular, cause difficulty.

8.49   Methods of Preventing Corrosion

There are two general methods of preventing corrosion: by internal treatment to produce a corrosion-resistant material, or by placing a protective coating on the surface.

Certain alloying elements such as copper and chromium may be added to the steel.   They function by forming a hard, dense, adherent film of oxide on the surface which prevents further corrosion.   Unprotected iron also forms a film of oxide on the surface, but it is porous and mechanically weak and soon rubs off, exposing the metal beneath to the corrosive action

The principal protective coatings used for iron and steel are concrete, paint, zinc, tin, aluminum, copper, nickel, stainless steel, cadmium, and other metals.   A 2-in. layer of good concrete provides a very satisfactory corrosion-resistant coating for structural steel.   Paint is the most common protective coating and, if properly applied so that there is a good bond between the paint and metal, it affords satisfactory protection until it wears out.   Most paints are mechanically weak and last only a few years.   For some purposes, particularly where resistance to acids is involved, porcelain enamel coatings are used.   Steel containing a small percentage of titanium is particularly well adapted to this treatment; a smooth porcelain coating only 0.002 in. thick will give complete protection.

Dipping, sherardizing, and *electroplating* are the processes used for depositing zinc on iron or steel, after which it is said to be *galvanized*.

In the dipping process the steel, after being cleaned, is lowered into or drawn through a bath of molten zinc.

In the sherardizing process the zinc is volatilized and then condensed on the steel.   This process seems to result in a stronger bond between zinc and steel than is obtained by dipping.

The process of depositing zinc by electrolysis is becoming increasingly popular.

Galvanizing provides satisfactory protection unless the coating cracks. Even if the coating does crack, the zinc will afford protection for a time. Since it is above iron in the electromotive-force series of metals, it will go into solution more readily than the iron.   It will therefore decrease the deterioration of the iron until it is entirely exhausted.

The familiar tin can is an example of steel protected by tin plating. The coating is usually applied by dipping the sheet metal into a bath of molten tin.   The coating must be carefully applied, since any defect in the coating will cause rapid corrosion as a result of the electrolytic action which is set up.   Tin is below iron in the electromotive-force series, so the iron will go into solution more actively than the tin.   Consequently, if there is a defect in the tin coating so that the iron can dissolve, it will do so, protecting the tin from deterioration.   Iron may rust for some distance around a pinhole in an otherwise perfect tin plating.

Other metals such as nickel, chromium, and cadmium provide excellent protective coatings for iron and steel, but are used only on small objects because of expense.   They are usually applied by electrolysis.

In addition to the rusting or oxidation of single metals in the presence of moisture and oxygen, corrosion may occur—and at an accelerated rate —when two dissimilar metals are associated.   The intensity of the electrolytic action is dependent on the nature of the two metals involved, and on their relative areas.   A modified electromotive-force series, which includes some of the more common alloys, follows:

Magnesium	Lead-tin solder	Copper-nickel alloys
Magnesium alloys	Stainless steel 304, 316	Nickel (passive)
Zinc	(active)	Inconel (passive)
Aluminum 5052, 3004,	Lead	Stainless steel 410, 430,
3003, 1100, 6061, 6053	Tin	304 (passive)
Alclad	Muntz metal	Titanium
Cadmium	Manganese bronze	Hastelloy C
Aluminum alloy 2117,	Naval brass	Monel metal
2017, 2024	Nickel (active)	Stainless steel 316 (pas-
Mild steel	Inconel (active)	sive)
Wrought iron	Yellow brass	Silver solder
Cast iron	Aluminum bronze	Silver
Chromium iron	Red brass	Graphite
Ni-Resist	Copper	Gold
Stainless steel 410, 430	Silicon bronze	Platinum
(active)		

The metals at the beginning of the list are those most readily attacked, and those near the end of the list are least readily attacked.   For example, if magnesium and zinc are associated, the magnesium will be attacked; but, if zinc and iron are associated, the zinc will be attacked.   In general, the *rate* of corrosion varies directly with the ratio of the area of the material which is not attacked to the area of the other material.   For example, a unit consisting of an aluminum rivet in a brass plate would be attacked more rapidly than a unit consisting of a brass rivet in an aluminum plate.

8.50 Value of Principles

Many problems remain to be solved before ferrous metals can be produced and used with the maximum effectiveness possible.   Improvements in manufacture, heat treatment, design, fabrication, and protection from corrosion are being made every day, and must continue to be made in the interests of effective use.   To the engineer who would keep abreast of the changes in the field, as well as to the engineer who is helping to bring about improvements, a sound working knowledge of the principles involved is essential.   When those principles are known and understood, the achievements of the metallurgist in producing a material with desired properties, and of the designer in putting that material to new and helpful uses no longer appear as works of black magic but are revealed as the simple fulfillment of natural laws.

PROBLEMS

8.1 How many pounds of iron are there in a ton of hematite if no impurities are present?

8.2 Approximately how many tons of each of the raw materials in the charge would be required to supply the blast furnace of Fig. 8.1 for a day?

8.3 Show in tabular form the effect of the shaping operations upon the elastic strength, ultimate strength, and toughness of carbon steel.

8.4 A certain close-fitting machine part has an effective length of 6 in. It is to carry a steady tensile load of 15,000 lb and a dynamic load of 10 ft-lb, but the loads are not applied at the same time. (a) Decide whether cold-rolled or hot-rolled carbon steel (Fig. 8.11) would be the better if the weight of the part is to be a minimum. (b) Determine the required cross-sectional area, using a factor of safety of 3.

8.5 Which has the greater resistance to fracture under dynamic loading—drawn and annealed or hot-rolled carbon steel (Fig. 8.11)?

8.6 What diameter of hot-rolled structural-steel rod will have the same resistance to failure by fracture under steady load as a cold-drawn wire 0.1 in. in diameter (Fig. 8.11)?

8.7 How much may the modulus of toughness of a cold-drawn carbon-steel wire be changed by annealing (Fig. 8.11)?

8.8 Compare values of as many of the properties of wrought iron and hot-rolled structural steel as may be determined from their stress-strain diagrams.

8.9 Outline the steps in the transformation of iron ore into a material suitable for the base of a heavy stationary engine.

8.10 Starting with iron ore, outline the steps in the production of a 36-in. water pipe.

8.11 Outline the principal steps which would be followed in converting pig iron into an automobile fender.

8.12 Indicate the changes which occur in the ultimate strength and ductility of pig iron during each step of its transformation into a wire for a cable of a suspension bridge.

8.13 Outline the processes which would be used in the production of a knife blade.

8.14 A 2340 steel has been held at 1500 F for several hours. At what average rate (deg per sec) must it be quenched to produce a martensitic structure?

8.15 Compare the properties of a cast steel containing 0.40 per cent carbon and 3 per cent nickel with the properties of a steel containing 0.40 per cent carbon and 30 per cent nickel.

8.16 A 3240 steel is quenched from 1500 F to 1100 F in 15 sec. What treatment should follow to produce (a) a pearlitic structure, (b) a bainite structure, and (c) a martensitic structure?

8.17 A certain steel contains 0.40 per cent carbon and 5 per cent manganese. What changes would occur in its properties with the addition of 8 per cent manganese? Should the two be given the same heat treatment?

8.18 Specify a ferrous metal or alloy suitable for each of the following uses: (a) railroad-car wheels; (b) blades in a centrifugal pump; (c) pressure vessel to operate at −50 C; (d) lathe tool to operate at red heat; (e) safe.

8.19 Specify a ferrous-metal alloy suitable for each of the following uses: (a) jaws of a stone crusher; (b) tank for storing acid; (c) automobile springs; (d) roller bearings; (e) heavy machine base.

8.20–8.25 In the following problems, (a) select from the data given in Chapter 8 the material most suitable for the given use, and (b) determine the minimum required area of the piece, based on a factor of safety of 3.   Other factors being equal, select as the most suitable material that one which will result in the smallest volume of material required.   Where two or more loadings are indicated, the member must be made strong enough to support each separately, but not simultaneously.

| Prob. No. | Load in Tension | | | Temp. (C) | Length of Piece (in.) | Criterion of Failure |
	Continuous (lb)	Slowly Applied (lb)	Dynamic (ft-lb)			
8.20	....	20,000	10	10	8	Slip
8.21	....	180,000	10	10	36	Slip
8.22	20,000	....	....	650	10	Creep
8.23	5,000	....	40	10	6	Fracture
8.24	....	20,000	20,000	15	10	Fracture
8.25	5,000	15,000	10	15	8	Fracture

8.26 If gold were cheap, would it be satisfactory as a protective coating for steel?

8.27 (a) From a chemical standpoint, would aluminum make a satisfactory protective coating for the ferrous metals? (b) Why?

9 Nonferrous Metals

9.1 Introduction

Metals other than iron and steel are used for engineering purposes, either as commercially pure metals or as alloys. The nonferrous metals are, in general, subject to change in properties by mechanical working, but are less affected by heat treatment than are the ferrous metals. Several of them are more resistant to corrosion than are the ferrous metals, because the oxides which are formed as corrosion begins will form a tough protective film on the surface of the metal, preventing further chemical action. Therefore, these particular nonferrous metals are often used in situations where ferrous metals would be rapidly damaged by corrosion. Other nonferrous metals are used in stiuations where their density, electrical conductivity, strength, stiffness, or other properties make them more economical than ferrous metals.

Nonferrous metals are also used where other qualities, such as light weight, electrical properties, or appearance, may make them more desirable than iron or steel. The nonferrous metals are more frequentiy used in the form of alloys than in the form of commercially pure metal. In general, they have lower endurance limits and lower moduli of elasticity than the ferrous metals.

The nonferrous metals of greatest commercial importance are copper, aluminum, lead, zinc, tin, nickel, and magnesium. Those of secondary importance are bismuth, antimony, beryllium, silver, cadmium, and mercury. Others, such as chromium, cobalt, tungsten, molybdenum, and vanadium, are of importance chiefly for alloying with steel. The importance of uranium, zirconium, and titanium has increased greatly in the last decade.

COPPER

9.2 History of Copper

Because copper was originally found in the form of the chemically uncombined metal which is soft enough to be hammered into shape easily, it was the first of the metals to be used by man for other than ornamental purposes.   Excavations in Chaldea have disclosed hammered copper implements and weapons which were made about 4500 B.C. or earlier.

Later, about 3100 B.C., methods of casting copper were discovered, making possible new uses for the metal.   It is apparent that new uses developed very slowly, however, for the early copper castings which have been found are similar in shape to stone implements in use at the same time.

Smelting of copper from the ore, and manufacture of bronze from copper ores and tin ores, started about 2500 B.C.   The more desirable properties of bronze made it the most generally used metal for several centuries.   Many types of small tools and implements of bronze have been found, even including saws for cutting stone.   However, after the discovery of iron, about 1400 B.C., bronze was gradually replaced, because of the superior qualities of the ferrous metals for many uses.

9.3   Copper Ores

Copper occurs in the free state, called native copper, or in the form of oxides or sulfides, the latter frequently containing iron.   *Cuprite* (Cu_2O), *copper glance* (Cu_2S), and *copper pyrites* ($CuFeS_2$) are among the important ores, although many others are mined.   Most of these ores are low grade, containing only about 2 per cent copper.

Arizona, New Mexico, Montana, Utah, Nevada, and Michigan are the principal copper-producing states.   The Michigan ores are native copper, while those of the Rocky Mountain region are primarily sulfides.   In addition to the United States, the important copper-producing countries of the world include Chile, Northern Rhodesia, Russia, Belgian Congo, West Germany, and Canada.   The prewar copper production in the United States was about one-third of the world total of approximately two and three-quarter million tons, and over twice as great as that of any other country.

9.4   Preparation of Copper

The particular process used to remove copper from its ores depends on the type of ore; and since there are many types of ore, there are many processes, each differing from the others in detail.   In general, the sulfide ores present the most complex problem.   After the necessary preliminary mechanical treatment, such as concentrating, washing, and grinding, the processes are carried out in three principal steps: *roasting,* to convert or partially convert the sulfide to an oxide; *reducing,* to remove the oxygen and remaining sulfur from chemical combination with the copper; and *refining,* to purify the free copper.   The sequence of roasting, reducing, and refining is sometimes referred to as the *dry process,* as contrasted with the *wet process* in which copper is extracted by dissolving the ore in appropriate reagents and treating it with chemicals to precipitate the metallic copper.

Roasting.   The roasting operation, the purpose of which is to burn out some of the combined sulfur, was formerly carried out by simply piling the ore, mixed with a combustible material, in heaps and burning it in the open.   The modern roasting furnace is a type of reverberatory furnace, in which the ore is brought to a red heat to ignite the impurities.

Reduction.   Reduction is a more difficult operation and is usually carried out in two steps—smelting and converting.

The smelting may be done in a blast furnace or in a reverberatory furnace.   The primary function of the smelting operation is that of concentration.   It does not even complete the separation of sulfur from the copper, there being produced a mixture of copper sulfide (Cu_2S) and iron sulfide (FeS), called matte, and also slag and gases.   The operation is usually carried out in such a way that the matte contains about 50 per cent copper.

The converting is then done by putting the molten matte into a converter similar to the Bessemer converter.   As air is blown through the matte, the iron is oxidized and combines with the silicon present to form a slag, which is removed.   As the blow continues, the sulfur in the copper sulfide is oxidized, leaving free copper, known as blister copper, which is cast into molds.   The operation requires about 2 hr.

Refining.   Refining is usually accomplished by an electrolytic process, although a fire-refining process is sometimes used.   In the electrolytic process the bars of blister copper are used as the anodes, and the cathodes are thin sheets of copper.   A solution of sulfuric acid or acid copper sulfate is used as the electrolyte.   During electrolysis, pure copper is deposited upon the cathode plates.   This can then be remelted and shaped as desired. The two principal forms in which pure copper is used are wire and sheet. The sheet is rolled and the wire drawn, with or without subsequent annealing.

9.5   Properties of Copper

Copper is a comparatively soft, ductile metal, which has a face-centered cubic space lattice.   Some typical stress-strain diagrams for copper are shown in Fig. 9.1.   These indicate the marked effect of cold working upon the tensile properties, and the increase in ductility resulting from annealing. Other properties are given in Table 9.1.

The outstanding properties of copper are its high resistance to atmospheric corrosion and its high electrical conductivity.   The electrical con-

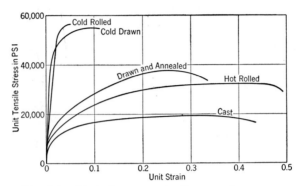

FIG. 9.1   Typical stress-strain diagrams for copper.

ductivity is greatly influenced by the purity of the copper. For example, only 0.4 per cent arsenic, a common impurity in copper ore, will reduce the conductivity of copper 50 per cent. The average prewar price of copper in the United States was about 13 cents per pound.

TABLE 9.1

PROPERTIES OF NONFERROUS METALS

Metal	Endur. Lim. (psi)	Shear. Str. (psi)	Creep Lim.* (psi)	Wt. (lb per cu ft)	Poiss. Ratio	BHN
Aluminum	....	....	....	168.5	0.33	...
Cast	....	....	9,000	....	....	...
Cold-rolled	8,500	13,000	....	....	....	44
Annealed	5,000	9,600	....	....	....	23
Copper	....	....	....	557	0.33	...
Cast	10,000	....	....	....	....	...
Cold-rolled	16,000	24,000	....	....	....	103
Cold-drawn	10,000	10,000	....	....	....	...
Annealed	10,000	....	....	....	....	...
Soft sheet	11,000	21,000	....	....	....	42
Lead	....	....	0	710	0.43	...
Cast	....	....	....	....	....	4
Rolled	400	....	....	....	....	...
Magnesium	....	....	....	108.6	0.342	...
Cast	....	14,000	....	....	....	30
Rolled	....	14,000	....	....	....	37
Extruded	8,000	16,000	....	....	....	35
Nickel	....	....	....	555	0.31	...
Cast	....	....	....	....	....	85
Cold-rolled	40,000	75,000	54,000	....	....	90
Hot-rolled	24,000	....	....	....	....	115
Annealed	28,000	52,000	....	....	....	95
Tin	....	....	0	454	0.33	...
Zinc	....	....	....	440	0.11	...
Rolled	....	19,000	....	....	....	...

* Based on a creep of 0.01 in 10 years at 360 C.

Copper is marketed in five forms, in the first four of which the copper content must exceed 99.9 per cent. The five forms are electrolytic copper, phosphorized copper, silver-bearing copper, oxygen-free high-conductivity copper, and arsenical copper.

Electrolytic copper is characterized by high electrical and thermal conductivity and excellent workability.

Phosphorized copper contains from 0.006 to 0.050 per cent phosphorus, which was added to remove all oxygen. The presence of phosphorus reduces the thermal and electrical conductivity from 4 to 25 per cent, but increases the toughness somewhat.

Silver-bearing copper is copper to which a small quantity of silver has been added to increase the annealing temperature, thereby making the material useful for commutators and other electrical equipment with operating temperatures up to 700 F. The addition of silver does not impair the electrical or thermal conductivity.

Oxygen-free high-conductivity copper has an electrical conductivity of 101 per cent IACS and a thermal conductivity equal to that of electrolytic copper.

Arsenical copper is copper to which 0.45 per cent arsenic has been added to increase the resistance to scaling at elevated temperatures and to increase the tensile strength 20 per cent above that available in electrolytic copper. As previously noted, arsenic reduces the electrical conductivity to about 45 per cent in this grade. The thermal conductivity is likewise reduced from 223 to 102 Btu per sq ft per hr per ft per deg F.

9.6 Uses of Copper

About one-half of the copper produced in the United States is used in drawn wire, and much of the remainder is used in alloys.

Because of its high resistance to corrosion, copper is used in the form of sheet and plate. It is also used extensively in alloys, as a base metal or as an added metal. A small percentage of copper increases the corrosion resistance of many other metals.

9.7 Alloys of Copper

Literally thousands of alloys containing copper have been developed. The use of copper as a corrosion-resisting agent in steel has already been discussed. Many other useful series of alloys of copper containing various elements to increase tensile strength and hardness have been developed. Other series of alloys which utilize the desirable electrical characteristics are important. For example, a combination of high tensile strength and high electrical conductivity is desirable in many cases. One alloy, developed to meet that need, contains 50 per cent copper and 50 per cent iron.

In the form of No. 18 wire it will develop a tensile strength of about 180,000 psi and has a relative electrical conductivity of 30 per cent.

A metal which has been found to impart desirable strength characteristics to copper is beryllium. The magnitude of the effect which a small percentage of beryllium has upon copper is almost comparable to the pronounced effect of carbon upon iron. Copper containing only 2 per cent beryllium can be made to develop an ultimate tensile strength of 200,000 psi with appropriate heat treatment and mechanical working. The alloy is particularly useful because of its high endurance limit. It has been widely adopted for springs, gages, and similar parts which are subjected to repeated load under conditions where resistance to corrosion is important. Unfortunately, the alloy cannot be used at temperatures above about 390 F because of the annealing effect at elevated temperatures.

Another alloy of copper suitable for the same uses as the beryllium-copper alloys is one containing 60 per cent copper, 20 per cent manganese, and 20 per cent nickel. It can be made to develop an ultimate tensile strength of 200,000 psi, has a high endurance limit, and offers excellent resistance to corrosion.

Silicon and *titanium* have also been used in small amounts separately or together to increase the strength of copper. The mechanism by which these alloys influence the strength of copper is known as precipitation hardening and is discussed in more detail in section 9.13. The addition of *tellurium* increases the machinability of the copper-aluminum alloys.

Other important alloys containing copper, such as duralumin, brass, bronze, and Monel metal, are discussed in the sections on aluminum, zinc, tin, and nickel, respectively. Properties of a few of the copper alloys are given in Table 9.5.

ALUMINUM

9.8 History of Aluminum

From the time of its discovery, about a hundred years ago, until the discovery in 1886 of the present electrolytic process for its commercial production, aluminum was little more than a chemical curiosity. Since that time it has become one of the important engineering materials. This rapid progress of its application may be ascribed largely to its many suitable properties, particularly its light weight combined with a relatively high strength, especially in alloys.

9.9 Aluminum Ores

Although aluminum is the most widely distributed of the metals, comprising 7.85 per cent of the earth's crust, the only commercial ore is bauxite, a ferruginous hydrate of alumina containing about 60 per cent alumina

(Al_2O_3). In 1952 Arkansas produced about 95 per cent of the total for the United States. Alabama, Florida, and Georgia produced the remainder. Surinam supplied 25 per cent of the world production of about 12,800,000 tons of bauxite, the United States supplied 13 per cent, British Guiana, 19 per cent, and France, 9 per cent.

During the same period the United States led the world in the production of metallic aluminum, with about 42 per cent of the world total of over 2,000,000 tons. Canada produced about 22 per cent, Russia, 12 per cent, and West Germany and France less than 10 per cent each.

About 87 per cent of the bauxite mined in the United States is used in the aluminum industry. The remainder is taken by the chemical industry and for the manufacture of abrasives, cement, and refractory materials.

9.10 Production of Aluminum

Bauxite deposits are found in beds and lenticular masses. If the ore is near the surface it is mined by open-pit methods; if it is deep in the ground, it is taken out through tunnels and shafts. The ore is usually crushed and dried at the mine as a preliminary step in the purification process. Production of pure Al_2O_3 is the next step.

The most common process consists in digesting the bauxite with sodium hydroxide, forming sodium aluminate from which pure aluminum hydrate is precipitated after the impurities (which are not soluble) have been removed by filtering. The hydrate is calcined to remove the chemically combined water and form pure Al_2O_3. Reduction of the Al_2O_3 to aluminum is accomplished in an electrolytic reduction cell using cryolite (a fluoride of sodium and aluminum) as the electrolyte. The heat necessary to keep the mass molten is supplied entirely by the current. The anodes are specially prepared carbon, and the bottom of the cell, which is also carbon, serves as the cathode on which the molten aluminum collects. The molten aluminum is tapped from the cell and poured into molds.

The pig metal is then remelted to remove dross, electrolyte, etc., and is poured into ingot molds of various shapes as a preliminary step to working. The metal is then shaped by rolling it into sheet, bar, or standard sections, by drawing it into wire, or by forging, casting, or extruding it. In the case of the strongest alloys of aluminum, the shaping process must be followed by a specific heat treatment to produce the desired properties. Commercial aluminum sheet (given the trade designation 1100) must have an aluminum content of not less than 99 per cent.

9.11 Properties of Aluminum

The outstanding characteristics of aluminum are its light weight and comparatively high strength. Other characteristics of importance are its high electrical conductivity, its resistance to atmospheric corrosion, and its ability to form useful alloys by the addition of other metals. Figure 9.2 shows the effect of mechanical working and annealing upon aluminum. Values of other mechanical properties are given in Table 9.1.

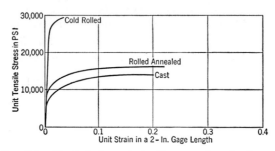

FIG. 9.2   Typical stress-strain diagrams for aluminum.

Aluminum, like other metals crystallizing in the face-centered cubic lattice, is ductile. It is resistant to many usually corrosive agents and is widely used for equipment in the chemical industry. It is, however, attacked by hydrochloric acid, although resistant to strong nitric acid. Aluminum is attacked rapidly by strong alkalies.

The resistance of aluminum alloys to corrosion varies to some extent with their composition, although all retain in large measure this quality of pure aluminum. The alloys formed by the addition of chromium or of magnesium, manganese, and silicon in the proportions to form the silicide are fully equal in corrosion resistance to commercial aluminum, while those containing copper or nickel show some loss. The latter alloys are usually given a protective coating if they are to be exposed to the weather. The protection may be aluminum paint, but in the case of sheet metal a surface layer of pure aluminum affords practically complete protection.

The average cost of refined aluminum was about 20 cents per pound in 1952.

9.12   Uses of Aluminum

About half of the aluminum produced is used in the form of light-weight alloys, while the other half is used as the pure metal in the form of rolled sections, tubes, sheets, bars, or wire. Rolled, drawn, extruded, or forged aluminum has found application in all branches of engineering where a light-weight, reasonably strong, corrosion-resistant material can be used to advantage. While many examples could be given of the profitable application of aluminum to engineering structures, the most noteworthy instances are those in which the use of aluminum has made possible the construction of something which would be otherwise unfeasible. For example, a 240-ft dredge boom, a 150-length of which is made of aluminum alloy, has been built. A shovel dipper with a capacity of 32 cu yd was made possible by the high strength-weight ratio of aluminum alloys. Aluminum is also being used for bridge floors to decrease the dead weight on the bridge. Aluminum alloys have played an important part in the development of modern aircraft. Railroad cars, buses, and truck bodies are made from aluminum or its alloys. Electrical transmission lines of aluminum cable, reinforced with steel to improve its strength, are in general use. Aluminum is also widely used for domestic purposes, particularly for kitchen utensils.

9.13   Alloys of Aluminum

Since pure aluminum is relatively soft and weak, it is not well adapted for structural purposes. However, a number of other metals may be added to aluminum to form alloys which have greater strength and hardness than pure aluminum. The most commonly used alloying elements are copper, manganese, silicon, and magnesium. Iron, nickel, zinc, chromium, and titanium are used to a lesser degree. For the production of castings, alloys of aluminum are used instead of the pure metal, because of their superior casting qualities as well as the more advantageous mechanical properties.

Two tools, cold working and heat treatment, are available for altering the properties of aluminum alloys. Cold working has the same general effect upon the alloys of aluminum as upon pure aluminum or upon the steel alloys—that is, cold working increases the strength and hardness and decreases the ductility. Alteration in properties by heat treatment is possible with some of the aluminum alloys, but not all. In addition, the effect of a given heat treatment upon an aluminum alloy is quite different from the effect of that treatment upon the iron-carbon alloys. However, the objective of heat treatment is the same—to distribute throughout the mass of the material a series of finely divided hard particles which tend to prevent slipping along the planes of weakness in the softer metal. The mechanism by which this is accomplished is known as solution heat treatment and may be explained by reference to Fig. 9.3 for the copper-aluminum system.

Pure aluminum (left-hand border of Fig. 9.3) exists in only one crystalline form, in contrast with iron, which exists in three forms. Hence any modification in the properties of the copper-aluminum alloys depends on variations in the solubility of the copper at different temperatures. It will be noted that the solubility of copper in aluminum is limited to a maximum of about 5 per cent and that this solubility occurs at about 540 C. As the temperature decreases, the solubility decreases. If a liquid alloy containing between 4 and 5 per cent copper is allowed to cool, crystals begin to form when the temperature reaches the line *AB*—the liquidus. The composition of the initial crystals is not the same as that of the liquid, but is much lower in copper, as may be seen by projecting a horizontal line to the solidus *AC*.

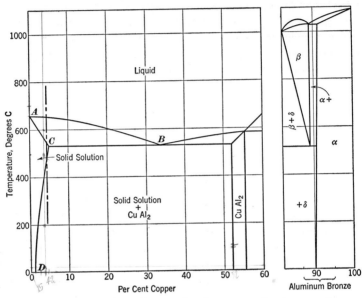

FIG. 9.3 Equilibrium diagram for the copper-aluminum system.

When the mass has cooled to the temperature indicated by the intersection of the composition line with the solidus *ACB*, it will be entirely solid, consisting of a solid solution of copper and aluminum. When the temperature decreases to the value given by the intersection of the composition line with *CD*, the solubility of copper is decreased and particles of CuAl$_2$, which is a comparatively hard material, begin to be precipitated from the solid solution.[1] Further reduction in temperature results in the formation of more CuAl$_2$ until equilibrium is finally attained at room temperature.

If the rate of cooling during the decomposition of the solid solution is slow, the CuAl$_2$ will tend to form in relatively large crystals, as would be expected. If the rate of cooling is rapid, the solid solution—without CuAl$_2$—will be retained at ordinary temperatures. However, the solid solution is not in equilibrium under those conditions, and crystals of

---

[1] Metallurgists are not in agreement concerning the composition of the precipitate. However, from the standpoint of properties, the important fact is that a comparatively hard material is formed from part of the solid solution.

$CuAl_2$ will form very slowly. A period of several months may be required to stabilize the composition, but the material thus formed will be stronger than the alloy which was allowed to cool slowly because of the more favorable distribution of the $CuAl_2$. The partial decomposition of the solid solution to form $CuAl_2$ may be accelerated by reheating to a temperature below the critical range *CD,* after quenching.

Under the usual commercial conditions the cooling rate is such that the $CuAl_2$ is formed in relatively large crystals which are not so effective as a hardening agent as though they were dispersed throughout the alloy. Therefore, alloys of this type are usually subjected to a heat treatment to increase the strength of the material.

The alloys are reheated and held at a temperature above the critical range for a sufficient length of time to permit the $CuAl_2$ to go into solution again. The material is then quenched, resulting in a supersaturated solid solution which is relatively soft and ductile. The process is known as "solution heat treatment."

At ordinary temperatures the $CuAl_2$ would gradually be precipitated. Usually the aging is accelerated by "artificial aging," or "precipitation heat treatment," which consists in reheating the alloy to a temperature below the critical range, usually about 300 C (572 F), to enable the $CuAl_2$ to be formed rapidly.

In contrast with the carbon steels, the low-copper alloys of aluminum are made soft and ductile by quenching, and are made stronger and more brittle by annealing at about 180 C. The soft, ductile solid solution cannot be preserved indefinitely at room temperatures, because of the formation of $CuAl_2$. Refrigeration is sometimes used to delay the precipitation in order to retain the alloy in a soft, ductile form suitable for shaping.

The right-hand portion of Fig. 9.3 shows the equilibrium diagram for the high-copper alloys of aluminum which are known as aluminum bronze. Two components, α and δ, exist at room temperature upon slow cooling. The component α is a solid solution which is strong, ductile, and relatively soft and is unaffected by heat treatment. With higher percentages of aluminum, the eutectoid δ is formed. The eutectoid is hard and is too brittle to be worked cold but it can be hot worked readily. Since the boundary between α and $\alpha + \delta$ is not vertical in the diagram, it is evident that the alloys which will tend to cross the boundary in cooling (the alloys containing between 7 and 10 per cent aluminum) are subject to change in properties by heat treatment. The transformation of the eutectoid δ into the softer solid solution α may be halted by quenching the alloy or cooling it rapidly through the critical range of transformation, with the result that the quenched alloy is stronger than the slowly cooled alloy. In this respect the two-phase, or duplex, aluminum bronzes are similar to steel. The maximum tensile strength of the aluminum bronzes is obtained with an aluminum content of about 10 per cent. This strength is approximately 60,000 psi in the annealed condition and may be raised to 125,000 psi by cold working.

Aluminum bronze has a high resistance to corrosion even in sea water, making it a valuable metal for various naval uses. It is also extensively used for castings.

Aluminum-silicon alloys containing 10 to 14 per cent silicon are often used for making castings. The alloys can be used to cast thin sections, and are corrosion-resistant and malleable. However, their properties are not altered appreciably by cold working.

Iron or *nickel* is usually added in amounts up to 5 per cent to refine the grain and strengthen the product. *Manganese* is added as a scavenger for gases.

Alloys of aluminum containing up to 7 per cent *magnesium* have been found to be particularly resistant to corrosion, as well as being easily worked. They are sometimes known as magnalium. The alloy containing 3.75 per cent magnesium (alloy G4A) is used where maximum resistance to corrosion is required.

The highest combination of static and impact strength yet available in aluminum castings is obtained with a magnesium content of 10 per cent (alloy G10A). The metal has been successfully used in large power-shovel dippers. Magnesium is the one alloying element which increases the tensile strength of aluminum alloys with practically no decrease in ductility.

A *manganese* content of 1 or 2 per cent increases the ultimate strength of aluminum. Alloys of this type (3003) have been used for many years for about the same purposes as commercial aluminum. The metal is about as corrosion-resistant as aluminum, but its properties are not affected by heat treatment.

Nickel has about the same effect as manganese in alloying with aluminum. Alloys containing 2 or 3 per cent nickel have been used to a limited extent in the form of sheeting and tubing.

Zinc alloys readily with aluminum, producing, if the zinc content is less than 40 per cent, a solid solution which is easily worked, but which is weak. Aluminum-zinc alloys containing less than 25 per cent zinc are used for light castings. If the zinc content exceeds about 25 per cent, the strength of the alloy is decreased by mechanical working. The aluminum-zinc alloys are among the few metals exhibiting a well-defined yield point. From 5 to 6 per cent zinc is used in 7075, which is a high-strength alloy.

Beryllium and *cobalt* (in combination with copper) impart superior

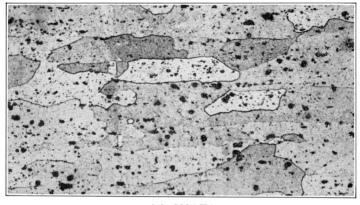

(a) 2024-T4

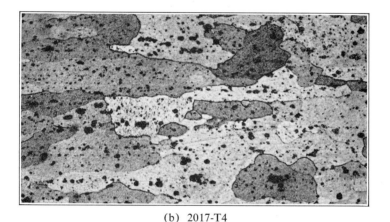

(b) 2017-T4

FIG. 9.4 Photomicrographs of aluminum alloys (×500).

strength properties, as well as resistance to oxidation, to the aluminum alloys.

The commercial alloys of aluminum may be classified in three groups.

1. Wrought alloys with properties controlled by heat treatment. Each of these alloys is designated by a number, indicating its chemical composition, followed by the letter F, O, W, or T. The letter F denotes the as-fabricated condition, with no special treatment to alter properties; the letter O designates the soft condition (annealed and recrystallized); W indicates an unstable temporary condition following solution heat treatment and is specific only when the period of aging is indicated; and T represents heat treatment and aging to produce a stable temper other than F, H, or O.

Numbers are added to denote the specific commercial treatment.   The number T2 applies to annealed castings; T3 means solution-heat-treated, cold-worked, and aged; T4, solution-heat-treated and naturally aged; T5, aged only; T6 solution-heat-treated and artificially aged; T7, solution-heat-treated and stabilized; T8, solution-heat-treated, cold-worked and artificially aged; T9, solution-heat-treated, artificially aged and cold-worked; T10, artificially aged and cold-worked.   Additional numbers denote special variations.

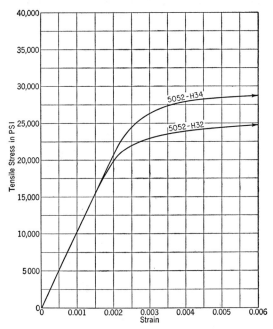

FIG. 9.5   Effect of working upon properties of sheet
aluminum alloy.

The principal commercial alloys in this class are 2014, 2017, 2024, 6151, 6053, and 7075.   The term, duralumin, was formerly used to designate alloy 2017, but is now rather loosely used to denote copper-aluminum alloys in general, and is considered obsolete by the strictly technical press. The alloy 2024, which normally has an ultimate tensile strength of about 60,000 psi in the T4 condition, may be made to develop strengths as high as 72,000 psi by special heat treatment combined with cold working. Photomicrographs of 2017-T4 and 2024-T4 are shown in Fig. 9.4.

2. Wrought alloys with properties controlled by cold working.   Each alloy in this group is designated by a number and a letter.   The letter F or O denotes the fabricated or soft condition, and the letter H followed by

TABLE 9.2

Nominal Composition and Weight of Wrought Aluminum Alloys

New Desig.	Old Desig.	Si (%)	Fe (%)	Cu (%)	Mn (%)	Mg (%)	Cr (%)	Ni (%)	Zn (%)	Ti (%)	Others Each (%)	Others Total (%)	Al (min)	Weight (lb/in.³)
1030	AE1S	...	...	...	...	...	...	...	...	...	...	...	99.30	0.098
1050	AD1S	...	...	...	...	...	...	...	...	...	...	...	99.50	0.098
1070	AC1S	...	...	...	...	...	...	...	...	...	...	...	99.70	0.098
1090	FB1S	...	...	...	...	...	...	...	...	...	...	...	99.90	0.098
1095	AA1S	...	...	...	...	...	...	...	...	...	...	...	99.95	0.098
1099	BA1S	...	...	...	...	...	...	...	...	...	...	...	99.99	0.098
1100	2S	1.0 [Si+Fe]	...	0.20	0.05	...	...	...	...	...	0.05	0.15*	99.00	0.098
2014	14S, R301	0.50–1.2	1.0	3.9–5.0	0.40–1.2	0.20–0.8	0.10	...	0.10	0.15	0.05	0.15	Rem.	0.101
2017	17S	0.8	1.0	3.5–4.5	0.40–1.0	0.20–0.8	0.10	...	0.25	...	0.05	0.15	Rem.	0.101
2024	24S	0.50	0.50	3.8–4.9	0.30–0.9	1.2–1.8	0.10	...	0.25	...	0.05	0.15	Rem.	0.101
2117	A17S	0.8	1.0	2.2–3.0	0.20	0.20–0.50	0.10	...	0.25	...	0.05	0.15	Rem.	0.099
3003	3S	0.6	0.7	0.20	1.0–1.5	...	...	...	0.10	...	0.05	0.15	Rem.	0.099
3004	4S	0.30	0.7	0.20	1.0–1.5	0.8–1.3	...	...	0.10	...	0.05	0.15	Rem.	0.098
4032	32S	11.0–13.5	1.0	0.50–1.3	...	0.8–1.3	0.10	0.50–1.3	0.25	...	0.05	0.15	Rem.	0.097
5052	52S	0.45 [Si+Fe]	...	0.10	0.10	2.2–2.8	0.15–0.35	...	0.20	...	0.05	0.15	Rem.	0.097
5053	53S	0.5–0.91	0.35	0.10	...	1.1–1.4	0.15–0.35	...	0.10	...	0.05	0.15	Rem.	0.096
6061	61S	0.40–0.8	0.7	0.15–0.40	0.15	0.8–1.2	0.15–0.35	...	0.25	0.15	0.05	0.15	Rem.	0.097
6151	A51S	0.6–1.2	1.0	0.35	0.20	0.45–0.8	0.15–0.35	...	0.25	0.15	0.05	0.15	Rem.	0.098
7072	72S	0.7 [Si+Fe]	...	0.10	0.10	0.10	...	...	0.8–1.3	0.20	0.05	0.15	Rem.	0.097
7075	75S	0.50	0.7	1.2–2.0	0.30	2.1–2.9	0.18–0.40	...	5.1–6.1	...	0.05	0.15	Rem.	0.097
8112	K112	1.0	1.0	0.40	0.6	0.7	0.20	...	1.0	...	0.05	0.15	Rem.	0.097

NOTE: Values are maximum, unless shown as average.

* Not more than 0.05 per cent of any element, nor a total of more than 0.15 per cent.

TABLE 9.3

CHARACTERISTICS OF CAST ALUMINUM ALLOYS

New Desig.	Old Desig.	Nominal Composition (%)*						Heat Treat.	Cast. Method†	Weight (lb/in.³)
		Cu	Si	Mg	Zn	Ni	Others			
C4A	195, C1	4.5	...	...	...	...	...	Yes	S	0.100
CG100A	122, CG1	10.0	...	0.25	...	...	...	Yes	S & P	0.105
CN42A	142, CNZ1	4.0	...	1.5	...	2.0	...	Yes	S & P	0.102
CS42A	B195, CS4	4.5	2.5	...	...	...	...	Yes	P	0.101
CS43A	108, CS5	4.0	3.0	...	1.0	...	...	Yes	S	0.099
CS104B	138, CS21	10.0	4.0	1.0	...	1.0	...	No	P	0.105
CS72A	C113, CS22	7.0	2.5	...	2.5	...	...	No	S & P	0.104
CS66A	152, CS23	6.5	5.5	0.4	...	...	...	Yes	P	0.104
G4A	214, G1	...	...	4.0	...	...	...	No	S	0.095
G8A	218, G2	...	...	8.0	...	...	...	No	D	0.094
G10A	220, G3	...	...	i0.0	...	...	...	Yes	S	0.092
GS42A	B214, GS1	...	1.8	4.0	...	...	...	No	S & P	0.094
GZ42A	G21	...	...	4.0	1.8	...	...	No	P	0.094
S5A	43, S1	...	5.0	...	...	...	...	No	S & P	0.096
S12A	13, S9	...	12.0	...	...	...	...	No	D	0.097
SC64A	A108, SC1	4.5	5.5	...	...	...	...	No	P	0.100
SC54A	85, SC2	3.5	5.0	...	...	...	...	No	D	0.101
SC84A	380, SC6	3.5	8.5	...	...	...	...	No	D	0.100
SC64B	319, SC8	3.7	6.3	...	1.0	0.5	...	Yes	S & P	0.101
SC64C	319, SC9	3.7	6.3	0.5	1.0	0.5	0.8 Mn	Yes	S & P	0.101
SC51A	355, SC21	1.3	5.0	0.5	...	...	...	Yes	S & P	0.098
SC122A	RX13, SC41	1.5	12.0	0.7	...	...	0.7 Mn	Yes	P	0.099
SC82A	RX8, SC42	1.5	7.8	0.4	...	0.2	0.4 Mn	Yes	S	0.098
SG70A	356, SG1	...	7.0	0.3	...	...	...	Yes	S & P	0.095
SG100A	360, SG2	...	9.5	0.5	...	...	...	No	D	0.095
SN122A	A132, SN41	1.0	12.0	1.0	...	2.5	...	Yes	P	0.098
ZG61A	F40E, ZG41	...	...	0.6	5.5	...	0.5 Cr	Yes	S	0.099

* Balance aluminum.

† S = sand, P = permanent mold, D = die.

a number denotes cold working. The number 1 following the letter H designates an alloy hardened by straining only. The number 2 designates strain hardening followed by partial annealing, and the number 3 denotes strain hardening followed by a low-temperature annealing to stabilize the alloy. A second number designates the degree of strain hardening, on a scale in which 8 is a standard hard condition. The number H12, for example, denotes a metal strain-hardened to the one-quarter-hard degree. An additional number is sometimes added to indicate special characteristics. The principal commercial alloys in this class are 3003, 3004, and 5052. Figure 9.5 indicates the effect of cold working upon the properties of 5052.

3. Cast alloys. Each cast alloy of aluminum is designated by a system consisting of one or two letters indicating the principal alloying elements, and from one to three numbers indicating the approximate percentages of the principal elements. In this system C denotes copper; N, nickel;

TABLE 9.4

TYPICAL PROPERTIES OF ALUMINUM ALLOYS

New Desig.	Old Desig.	Tension Yield Str. (ksi)	Tension Ult. Str. (ksi)	Elong., 2" (%)	Hard. (Bhn)	Shear Yield Str. (ksi)	Shear Ult. Str. (ksi)	Fatigue Endur. Lim. (psi)
3003–O	3S–O	6	16	40	28	4	11	7,000
3003–H14	3S–½H	18	21	16	40	12	14	9,000
3003–H18	3S–H	25	29	10	55	14	16	10,000
3004–O	4S–O	10	26	25	45	6	16	14,000
3004–H34	4S–½H	27	34	12	63	14	18	15,000
3004–H38	4S–H	34	40	6	77	18	21	16,000
2014–T6	14S–T	58	68	13	130	38	45	16,000
2017–O	17S–O	10	26	22	45	7	18	11,000
2017–T4	17S–T	37	60	22	100	22	36	15,000
2024–T4	24S–T	46	68	22	105	..	41	18,000
2024–T36	24S–RT	57	73	..	116	..	42	.....
	27S–T	50	65	11	115	30	39	13,000
X2219–T6	.....	35	62	16	...	..	..	.....
6151–T4	A51S–T	40	48	20	95	26	32	10,500
5052–O	52S–O	14	29	30	45	9	18	17,000
5052–H34	52S–½H	29	37	14	67	16	21	19,000
5052–H38	52S–H	36	41	8	85	20	24	20,500
6053–O	53S–O	7	16	35	26	5	11	7,500
6053–W	53S–W	20	33	30	65	12	20	10,000
6053–T4	53S–T	33	39	20	80	20	24	11,000
7075–T4	75S–T	80	88	10	150	..	47	22,500
S5A	43, S1	9	19	6	40	..	14	6,500
C4A–T4	195–T4, C1	16	31	9	65	..	24	6,000
C4A–T6	195–T6	22	36	5	80	..	30	6,500
C4A–T62	195–T62	31	40	2	95	..	31	7,000
G4A	214, G1	12	25	9	50	..	20	5,500
G10A–T4	220–T4, G3	25	45	14	75	..	33	7,000
SG70A–T4	356–T4, SG1	16	28	6	55	..	22	.....
SG70A–T6	356–T6	22	32	4	70	..	27	8,000
SG70A–T51	356–T51	20	25	2	60	..	18	6,000

NOTE: Average values as obtained from tests on specimens ½ in. in diameter.
Yield strength based on a set of 0.20 per cent.
Yield strength in compression equals, or is slightly higher than, yield strength in tension.
Endurance limits based on 500,000,000 cycles of completely reversed stress.

G, magnesium; S, silicon; and Z, zinc. Thus C4A contains about 4 per cent copper, ZG61A contains 6 per cent zinc and 1 per cent magnesium, and SN122A contains 12 per cent silicon and 2 per cent nickel as the principal alloying elements. Grades are designated by the terminal letters A, B, and C. Alloy A has lower impurity limits than B, and C is a die-casting alloy. Heat treatments are designated by the same system that is used for the wrought alloys.

The chemical compositions of several of the important alloys of aluminum are given in tables 9.2 and 9.3, and average values of mechanical properties are given in Table 9.4.

Wrought-alloy products may be produced by rolling, extrusion, drawing, or forging, while cast-alloy products may be shaped in sand molds or permanent molds or may be die-cast. The alloys of aluminum are in general somewhat less resistant to corrosion than is pure aluminum; so aluminum parts—particularly 2024-T4 sheet, which is used for aircraft—are frequently given a thin coat of pure aluminum to resist corrosion. Coated sheet is known as Alclad. Steel sheet may also be Alclad.

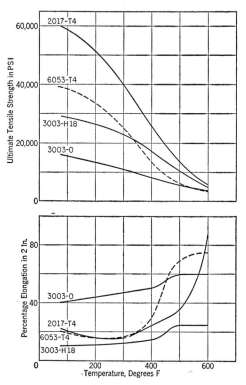

FIG. 9.6   Effect of temperature upon strength and ductility of aluminum alloys.

Aluminum-alloy structures may be fabricated by welding, brazing, or riveting, using steel rivets or rivets of alloy 2017, 2117, or 6053. Small rivets can be driven cold, although in the case of 2017 they are re-heat-treated and then driven before they age-harden. If several hours elapse between heat treatment and fabrication, the rivets may be stored in a refrigerator during the interval, to prevent age-hardening. Larger sizes are driven hot, the rivet being heated to the critical temperature. The extraction of heat by the surrounding metal and the heading tools serves as a quench. Upon aging, the rivets develop properties of the heat-treated alloy. Aluminum alloys may be joined by welding, but it is usually desirable to join strong alloy members by riveting because of the annealing which occurs during welding. The alloys cannot be cut satisfactorily with torches.

The effect of temperature upon the tensile strength and ductility of the more common aluminum alloys is shown in Fig. 9.6.

LEAD

9.14 Historical Background of Lead

The first evidences of the use of lead are found in ruins dating about 3000 B.C. At one time, about 1300 B.C., lead was used for currency. Sheets of lead were used for writing and commemorative tablets, and the metal was used for coffins. The chief engineering use in early times was for water pipes. Excavations at Pompeii and Herculaneum have disclosed many remnants of lead pipe.

9.15 Lead Ores

Lead sulfide (PbS), or *galena,* is the most important ore of lead. Other forms in which lead occurs are the carbonate and sulfate. Missouri produces about one-third, and Idaho and Utah produce about 19 and 13 per cent, respectively, of the lead ore mined in the United States. The United States produced 24 per cent of the 1952 world total of 1,800,000 tons of lead. Australia, Mexico, Russia, Canada, and West Germany are the other principal lead-producing countries.

9.16 Preparation of Lead

The extraction of lead from the lead sulfide ore is accomplished by converting the sulfide to an oxide, reducing the oxide to the metal, and then refining the metal. The removal of the sulfur, or roasting, is accomplished by heating the crushed ore and blowing air through it. The residue, or *sinter,* usually contains from 4 to 8 per cent sulfur. The reduction of the lead is accomplished in a blast furnace, with coke as the reducing agent. The particular refining process through which the lead is next put depends on which impurities are present.

9.17 Properties of Lead

Lead is the most dense of the common metals, having a specific gravity of 11.34. In a short-time tensile test, lead will develop a yield strength of about 1600 psi and an ultimate strength of about 2400 psi, but under a long-time steady load it may fail at a stress as low as 800 psi.

Lead is malleable in that it can be rolled into thin sheets (lead foil), but it is not ductile in the sense of being capable of being drawn into a thin wire. It will creep under a tensile stress as low as 150 psi. At 250 psi, rolled lead creeps at about 0.1 per cent per year. Its endurance limit is 470 psi for 10^7 cycles.

Upon exposure to the air, lead forms a thin protective coating of lead oxide which prevents further corrosion. Lead is relatively resistant to acids.

Lead pipe is often made by extruding or forcing the lead through a rigid die under pressure. Lead is marketed principally in the form of rolled sheets or pipe.

The average 1952 price of the metal was about 15 cents per pound.

9.18 Uses of Lead

Because of its workability and resistance to corrosion, lead is used for pipes and conduits. It is used in sheet form for lining vats, for tanks and chambers, and for auxiliary roofing purposes. For products that must have strength and acid resistance, lead-clad steel and lead-clad copper are proving satisfactory. Because of its chemical and electrical characteristics, lead is widely used in storage batteries. Lead oxides are used in the manufacture of certain types of paint and glass.

Lead is widely used as a radiation shielding material. Because of its density, it is effective in attenuating gamma rays and X rays. One inch of lead has approximately the same shielding effectiveness with respect to gamma rays as one foot of concrete.

9.19 Alloys of Lead

Lead alloys readily with tin to produce the various grades of solder and pewter, which are harder than pure lead. They are discussed further in section 9.25, and the equilibrium diagram for the lead-tin system is given in Fig. 9.7.

Antimony also increases the hardness and brittleness of lead, but in small percentages decreases its creep limit. One per cent of antimony increases the tensile strength of the metal in the rolled condition to 3050 psi, and 9 per cent increases it to 4700 psi. Alloys containing from 10 to 25 per cent antimony represent the useful range of combinations of these two metals. Their equilibrium diagram was given in Fig. 6.10, indicating the formation of a eutectic containing 13 per cent antimony. This eutectic is considerably softer than the crystals of antimony which will be present if the antimony content exceeds 13 per cent.

If the antimony content is from 13 to 17 per cent, the alloy is suitable for use as a bearing metal. The hard crystals of antimony will resist wear, while the soft eutectic forms a suitable matrix, readily adjusting itself to inequalities in pressure. However, this type of structure is not necessary for a good bearing. Experiments have shown that a number of pure metals have low friction characteristics, and that, when attached in a thin film to a more rigid backing material, they function satisfactorily. Lead, tin, cadmium, silver, indium, and bismuth have all been used for bearings in the unalloyed form.

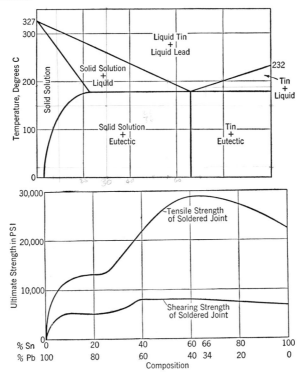

FIG. 9.7   Characteristics of tin-lead system.

Alloys of lead and tin in various proportions, with from 10 to 20 per cent antimony, are also used as bearing metals. Their ultimate tensile strengths are in the order of 10,000 psi. These alloys expand slightly upon cooling, making them suitable for castings where a sharp, accurate impression is desired. Several alloys of this type are used in making type metal.

Wood's metal, containing 50 per cent bismuth, 24 per cent lead, 14 per cent tin, and 12 per cent cadmium, and Lipowitz' metal, containing 50 per cent bismuth, 27 per cent lead, 13 per cent tin, and 10 per cent cadmium, are useful for safety plugs in automatic sprinkler systems, since they will melt at about 70 C (158 F) and 60 C (140 F), respectively.

Shot is made from a lead-antimony or lead-arsenic alloy, and slugs for small arms are usually made from an alloy containing 10 per cent of antimony.

The endurance limit and creep limit of lead are increased by the addition of small percentages of calcium. Sheathing for cables is frequently made of an alloy containing 1 per cent or less of calcium. The metal has an age-hardening effect upon lead, through the mechanism of precipitation. Copper and tellurium also increase the endurance limit and creep limit of lead.

TIN

9.20 History of Tin

There is evidence to indicate that tin was first known about 2000 B.C. However, it did not come into general use until about 1500 B.C., at which time there was an increase in the demand for tin, or rather for the tin ore to be used in making bronze. About 500 B.C. the Phœnicians discovered tin in England, and started the tin trade which was later taken over and developed into an extensive enterprise by the Romans. The metal continued to be used principally as a constituent of alloys until recently, when it has been employed in the form of a thin protective coating for other metals.

9.21 Tin Ores

Tin does not occur in the free state to any extent, but is obtained from the oxide *cassiterite* (SnO_2).

Although tin ore is found in South Dakota, Wyoming, and South Carolina, production from these sources is negligible. Of the 100 tons of tin ore produced in North America in 1952, over 80 tons came from Alaska, and the remainder from Colorado. The prewar world production of tin, which was largely controlled by an agreement among the principal tin-producing countries, was about 232,000 tons and in 1952 was 173,000 tons. The Federated Malay States have extensive deposits of tin ore, and contribute about 33 per cent of the world total. During World War II, Bolivia supplied most of the tin ore smelted in the United States. Indonesia, Thailand, China, and Nigeria are other important sources of tin ore. The Cornish tin mines in England are still producing an appreciable tonnage.

The average New York market price of tin was $1.25 per pound in 1952.

9.22 Preparation of Tin

Tin ore usually occurs in detrital or alluvial deposits and may be mined by hand labor, gravel pumps, hydraulic jets, or dredging. Since the tin-ore content of the deposits is small, it must be concentrated by screening and sluicing. Sometimes the ore must be roasted and treated with hydrochloric acid, to remove impurities such as iron. Following this treatment, the oxide is reduced to metallic tin by smelting it in a blast furnace with coal and limestone or by heating it in a reverberatory furnace.

The tin may be refined by electrolysis or by being heated to just above 232 C (450 F), at which temperature the tin melts and is drained off, leaving the impurities which have higher melting points. After being refined, the tin is cast into pigs.

Tin plating may be applied by electrolysis or by dipping. In the latter process, the sheet metal (usually steel), to be coated is carefully cleaned, immersed in a bath of the molten tin, removed, and allowed to drain. A second dipping is sometimes given to provide additional protection. The dipping must be carefully done to exclude bubbles and to prevent other defects which might cause a discontinuity in the coating. However small, any break in the tin plating offers an opportunity for corrosion to begin.

Recent improvements in the electrolytic process for the deposition of tin upon steel and other metals have made it the preferred technique, since a more uniform coating results from this process than from the dipping process. However, it must be polished before it will have the same general appearance as the dipped tin plate.

9.23 Properties of Tin

The ultimate tensile strength of tin in the annealed condition is about 2200 psi, the yield strength for an offset of 0.002 is about 1300 psi, and the elongation in 2 in. is about 45 per cent. A 30 per cent reduction in area by cold rolling increases the tensile strength and the yield strength to about 2800 psi and 2000 psi, respectively, and decreases the percentage elongation in 2 in. to about 35 per cent. Cast tin has an endurance limit of only about 340 psi. The effect of the cold working is only temporary, as normal room temperatures have an annealing effect.

One of the important properties of tin is its resistance to corrosion. This property makes it suitable for use as plating. It is not affected by hydrogen, and is but little affected by air at ordinary temperatures even in the presence of moisture.

The metal undergoes an allotropic modification at 18 C (64 F), the ordinary white tin becoming unstable and changing into a powdery gray form with an accompanying increase in volume below 18 C. Under usual conditions this change is quite slow, but exposure to very low temperatures will accelerate the process. The phenomenon is sometimes called "tin disease," as it normally spreads from a nucleus and can be transmitted from one piece of tin to another. The gray tin will revert to crystals of white tin again upon being heated above 18 C.

9.24   Uses of Tin

The use of tin as a protective coating in the form of either tin plate or *terneplate* (a lead-tin alloy coating) accounted for 38 per cent of the total use of tin in the United States in 1952. About 25 per cent went into bronze and brass. Solder was the next most important use, accounting for 20 per cent of the total. Collapsible tin tubes, tin foil, Babbitt metal, type metal, and tin castings for special uses are other applications.

9.25   Alloys of Tin

There are several hundred commercial alloys containing tin, as it has a marked effect in increasing the strength and hardness of many metals. Copper and lead are the metals with which it is most commonly combined, although it alloys readily with most of the metals.

The term *solder* is applied to the lead-tin alloys that have a low melting point and are suitable for joining metals. The tin content of prewar solders ranged from 30 per cent to 70 per cent, the amount depending on the properties desired in the solder. The equilibrium diagram for the tin-lead system is given in Fig. 9.7. It indicates that the solder containing 66 per cent tin would solidify the most rapidly and would consequently have the finest crystalline structure. Tin has been largely replaced by silver in the production of solder; an alloy containing 95 per cent lead, 3 per cent tin, and 2 per cent silver is considered to be as satisfactory as the lead-tin solders.

Pewter is also an alloy of tin and lead, usually containing about 80 per cent tin. Tin foil contains about 8 per cent zinc.

The name *bronze* has been used for a number of different alloys, but is correctly applied only to the copper-tin alloys. One period of early history is known as the Bronze Age because of the extensive use of bronze by primitive peoples.

Some of the properties of the annealed copper-tin alloys are shown in Fig. 9.8. In quantities less than about 15 per cent, tin dissolves in copper to form a solid solution; the effect of the added tin in increasing the tensile strength is evident in Fig. 9.8. If the tin content exceeds about 15 per cent, an additional brittle constituent, δ, is formed. The effect of δ in decreasing the tensile strength is also evident. Therefore the commercial alloys of copper and tin in which strength is desired contain not more than 15 per cent tin, and usually contain from about 1 to 10 per cent. The alloys may be strengthened by cold working, a tensile strength of 100,000 psi being developed in sheet bronze. Sheet bronze has an exceptionally

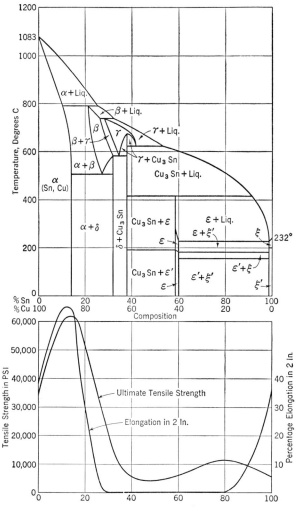

FIG. 9.8 Properties of copper-tin alloys.

high endurance limit and is useful for springs, diaphragms, and similar parts which are subjected to repeated loading in corrosive environments.

Many of the most suitable bearing metals contain tin. An alloy composed of 93 per cent tin, 3.5 per cent antimony, and 3.5 per cent copper represents a suitable type of alloy for aircraft-engine bearings. Alloys of this general type are known as Babbitt metal. The microscope reveals a network of hard copper-tin crystals embedded in a softer and tougher tin-base matrix. Their ultimate tensile strength is about 9000 psi and they have a relatively low endurance limit—less than 4000 psi for 2×10^7 cycles.

Gun metal, one of the best-known bronzes, contains about 10 per cent tin, and *bell metal* contains from 23 to 27 per cent tin.

Government bronze, or *admiralty metal,* contains 88 per cent copper, 10 per cent tin, and 2 per cent zinc.   It is widely used for valves and gears.

Phosphor bronze is any bronze to which some phosphorus has been added in amounts less than 4 per cent.   It serves mainly to reduce any copper oxide which may be present.   With 4 per cent tin it is suitable for turbine blades and for springs which are subject to corrosive forces.   With 10 per cent tin it is used for gears in which resistance to corrosion is an important factor.   A tin content of 20 per cent makes a phosphor bronze suitable for bearings that are subjected to high pressures and run at low speeds.   Lead in amounts up to 4 per cent is sometimes added to phosphor bronze to make a bearing metal.

ZINC

9.26   History of Zinc

Although zinc as a metal was not isolated until 1509, brass, an alloy of copper and zinc, was known and used as early as 600 B.C., when it was found that the addition of some zinc ore to molten copper hardened the copper.

9.27   Zinc Ores

The most important ore of zinc is the sulfide (ZnS), or *sphalerite,* although zinc may occur as a carbonate or oxide.

In 1952 about 14 per cent of the zinc ore produced in the United States came from the tristate district of Kansas, Missouri, and Oklahoma.   Montana supplied about 12 per cent; Idaho, 11 per cent; New Jersey, 9 per cent; Colorado, 9 per cent; Tennessee and Virginia, 9 per cent; and New Mexico, 8 per cent.

The world output of zinc was nearly 2,200,000 tons, of which the United States produced 37 per cent.   Other important producers were Canada, 9 per cent; Belgium, 8 per cent; Russia, 8 per cent; Germany, 7 per cent; Poland, 4 per cent.

The price of zinc in St. Louis at the end of 1952 was 12.5 cents per pound.

9.28   Preparation of Zinc

Zinc is extracted from the ore by a process of roasting, reducing, and refining.   The ores are ground and heated in a reverberatory furnace until the zinc sulfide is transformed into zinc oxide.   The oxide is reduced by placing it in fire-clay vessels with carbon (often coal), and heating it.   The oxygen and carbon combine to form a gas, and the zinc is left in the

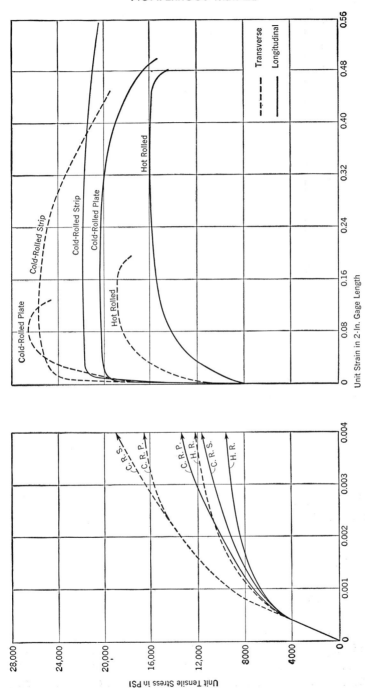

Fig. 9.9 Stress-strain diagrams for rolled zinc. (Results are dependent on the speed of testing.)

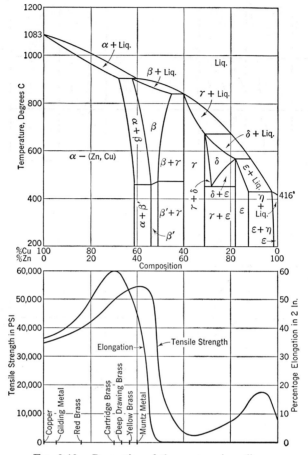

FIG. 9.10 Properties of the copper-zinc alloys.

uncombined state. At the temperature attained, the zinc is converted to the gaseous state. The gas is collected and condensed in cooling chambers. A second volatilization, or else a liquefaction in which the temperature is carefully controlled, serves to separate the zinc from additional impurities. Electrolytic processes are used for the production of zinc in the Montana and Idaho plants which produce about 19 per cent of the zinc refined in the United States.

9.29 Properties of Zinc

Zinc is brittle at ordinary temperatures, but between 100 C and 150 C it becomes sufficiently malleable to be rolled into thin sheets and sufficiently ductile to be drawn into wire. The tensile strength of cast zinc may be

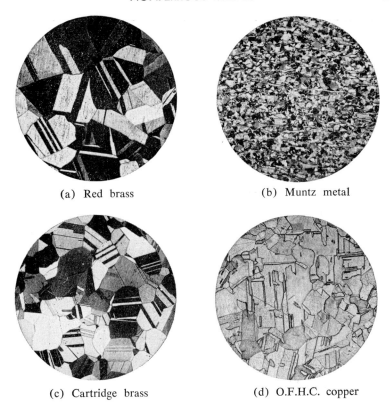

(a) Red brass   (b) Muntz metal

(c) Cartridge brass   (d) O.F.H.C. copper

FIG. 9.11 Photomicrographs of annealed copper and copper-zinc ($\times 50$). (Courtesy Revere Copper and Brass, Inc.)

tripled by rolling or drawing it. Typical stress-strain diagrams for zinc are shown in Fig. 9.9. Zinc is resistant to corrosion in moist air by virtue of the formation of a compact coating of basic zinc carbonate which protects the metal beneath.

9.30 Uses of Zinc

Nearly one-half of the zinc produced in the United States is used for galvanizing. Die castings consume over one-fourth of the zinc used, while about one-sixth is alloyed with copper. Zinc is also used in batteries, as protective sheeting, and for certain special shapes such as fruit-jar covers.

Zinc oxide is used for making paint, as it will not discolor so easily as lead oxide. Zinc chloride is useful as a wood preservative.

9.31 Zinc Alloys

The equilibrium diagram and some of the properties of the copper-zinc alloys are shown in Fig. 9.10. As indicated on this diagram, the com-

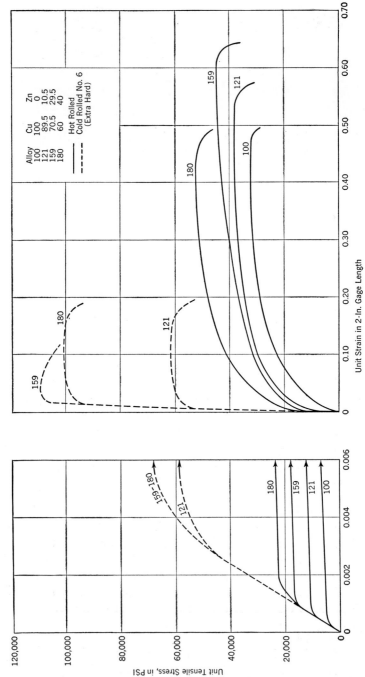

FIG. 9.12 Typical stress-strain diagrams for copper and copper-zinc alloys.

mercial alloys known as *brass* are marketed under a number of trade names. The equilibrium diagram shows that the alloys containing up to about 38 per cent zinc are in the form of a solid solution, and a photomicrograph on one such alloy—red brass—in the annealed condition is shown in Fig. 9.11a. The difference in color of the individual crystals is due to the difference in reflection of light from the crystal faces, which are oriented in different directions. The individual crystals are chemically identical. Figure 9.11b shows a photomicrograph of annealed Muntz metal which contains 60 per cent copper. As will be noted on the equilibrium diagram, this is a two-phase composition—that is, both α and β solid solutions are in equilibrium at room temperature. Figure 9.11c and Fig. 9.11d are photomicrographs of cartridge brass and oxygen-free high-conductivity copper. Stress-strain diagrams for some alloys are shown in Fig. 9.12. They indicate the effect of cold working upon the properties of the alloys. As will be noted in Fig. 9.10, the addition of more than about 38 per cent zinc results in the formation of the β phase, which has a higher strength but lower ductility than α brass. It has been found that an alloy composed of a mixture of α brass and β brass has excellent hot-working qualities. The series of brasses has a wide variety of uses, ranging from jewelry and hardware to ship sheathing, condensers, and heat-exchanger units. Practically all the shaping processes outlined are applicable to the various brasses.

The abrupt decrease in both strength and ductility as the zinc content exceeds about 50 per cent may be attributed directly to the change in structure, as indicated in the equilibrium diagram. The commercial alloys contain less than 50 per cent zinc.

Brass members (and bronze members as well) often fail in service by cracking with no apparent cause, that is, with no abnormal loads on the member. Such failures are known as "season cracking" and are due to initial strains in the material, augmented by corrosion, or by additional strains resulting from normal loads or from temperature changes. The initial strains are usually due to cold working or quenching, and may be removed by proper annealing at a temperature sufficiently low to discourage grain growth. The proper annealing temperature will depend on the composition and previous treatment of the metal.

Copper and zinc are often alloyed with one or more other metals. *Manganese bronze,* containing about 60 per cent copper and 38 per cent zinc, with about 1 per cent each of tin and iron and less than 0.5 per cent manganese, has an ultimate tensile strength of about 75,000 psi and a compressive strength as high as 150,000 psi. It is easily worked and is resistant to corrosion in salt water, and is therefore suitable for use in pumps, valve stems, marine engines, and similar parts.

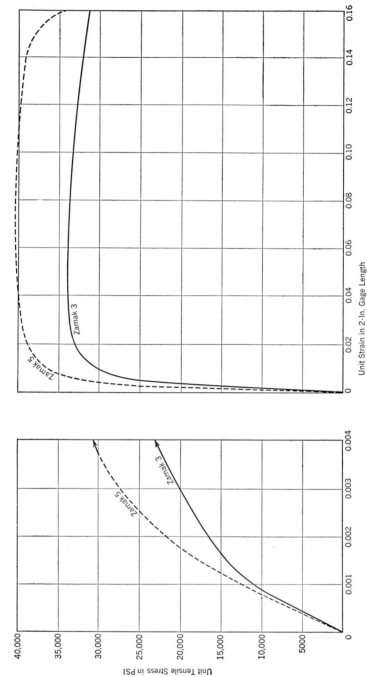

Fig. 9.13　Typical stress-strain diagrams for Zamak alloys. (Results for a given alloy are dependent on the speed of testing.)

Naval brass is similar to manganese bronze, but contains no iron. It is somewhat weaker, but more ductile, than manganese bronze and is suitable for the same general range of uses.

Sterro metal, Delta metal, and *Tobin bronze* are rather similar to manganese bronze, containing a small amount of iron.

Alloys containing from 75 to 85 per cent copper, 5 to 17 per cent zinc, and 8 to 10 per cent tin are very useful for general purposes where a corrosion-resistant metal with an ultimate tensile strength of about 40,000 psi and an elongation of 25 per cent is desired.

Zinc will alloy with many other metals. The alloy with aluminum has already been mentioned. An alloy consisting of zinc with about 25 per cent tin is used for foundry patterns, although in general the zinc-tin alloys are very weak.

Another important alloy of zinc is *Kirksite,* which has recently been developed for use as dies in forming sheet aluminum. The alloy has a low melting point and its properties are such that it may readily be cast to the desired shape. It is sufficiently hard to permit an individual die to be used several thousand times before the dimensional tolerances are exceeded. Kirksite has an advantage over alloy steels for dies, in that the material may be shaped readily and salvaged with practically no loss by simply recasting it.

A series of zinc alloys known as *Zamak* have been developed for die casting. They contain from $3\frac{1}{2}$ to $4\frac{1}{2}$ per cent aluminum, less than 0.10 per cent each of magnesium and iron, and copper in amounts varying from a trace up to $3\frac{1}{2}$ per cent. Typical stress-strain diagrams for Zamak alloys are given in Fig. 9.13. These alloys are widely used for die-cast parts, such as zippers, grilles and other automobile hardware, and many other intricate shapes. A typical zinc-alloy die casting is shown in Fig. 6.12.

NICKEL

9.32 History of Nickel

Nickel was not produced as a metal in commercial quantities until about the beginning of the nineteenth century, although alloys of nickel and copper were used for coinage over 2000 years ago.

9.33 Nickel Ores

The principal ore of nickel is the sulfide NiS, or *nickel pyrite.* The principal nickel-producing area in the world is the Sudbury district of Ontario, Canada, with 73 per cent of the 1952 world production of 173,000 tons coming from that area. Russia is the next largest producer, with about 14 per cent. The United States produces a very small amount recovered from various copper ores, and also produces some secondary nickel from scrap.   The 1952 price averaged 51 cents per pound.

9.34 Preparation of Nickel

Since the ore of nickel is a sulfide, the metal is extracted by the usual process of roasting, reducing, and refining.   As iron and copper are frequently present with the nickel, the reducing operation is somewhat complicated, the details of the process depending on the nature and amount of the impurities.   Refinement is usually accomplished by electrolysis.

9.35 Properties of Nickel

Nickel is very malleable and ductile, and therefore it can be rolled into thin sheets or drawn into fine wires.   The ultimate tensile strength of nickel, which is about 60,000 psi, may be increased to over 100,000 psi by cold rolling, as is indicated in Fig. 9.14.

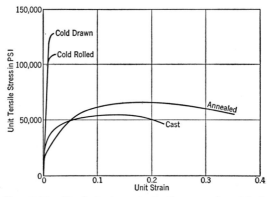

Fɪɢ. 9.14   Typical stress-strain diagrams for nickel.

9.36 Uses of Nickel

The most common uses of nickel are in alloys and as a protective coating for other metals.   It is marketed in the form of rods, sheets, tubes, and wire; and is used for special parts, such as heating coils, pumps, rolls, condensers, and other equipment where a high degree of resistance to corrosion and heat is desired.

The United States uses over 100,000 tons of nickel each year.   About 27 per cent of the nickel consumed in the United States is used in making stainless steel; 21 per cent is used in making other ferrous alloys; 39 per cent is used in nonferrous alloys; about 7 per cent is used in nickel plating.

9.37 Alloys of Nickel

Nickel in small quantities (usually about 3 per cent) is added to steel to produce a high-strength structural steel.   As was indicated in the discussion of alloy steels, the nickel alters the equilibrium diagram for the iron-carbon alloys, making possible the production of a strong and ductile material. Other important alloys of nickel with steel, such as stainless steel, invar, and platenite, are discussed in Chapter 8.

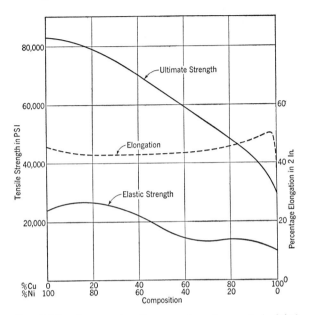

FIG. 9.15   Average tensile properties of annealed nickel-
copper alloys.

Nickel alloys readily with copper, forming a solid solution in all proportions, as was shown by the equilibrium diagram in Fig. 6.8. The variation of the tensile strength and ductility of the nickel-copper alloys with their composition is shown in Fig. 9.15. The strength and hardness of the nickel-copper alloys are increased by cold working, but the alloys are not subject to changes in properties by heat-treatment other than changes resulting from some improvement in grain size and structure as a result of annealing.

One of the important groups of nickel-copper alloys is Monel metal, which contains from 60 to 70 per cent nickel, 26 to 36 per cent copper, 1 to 3 per cent iron, and small percentages of manganese, silicon, and carbon. A special type of Monel metal, known as "K" Monel metal, contains, in addition, from 2 to 4 per cent aluminum. The addition of aluminum to the nickel-copper alloy makes possible the alteration of properties by heat treatment, because of the copper-aluminum combination. Hence, K Monel metal may be strengthened and hardened by heat treatment as well as by cold working.   Ultimate tensile strengths of 200,000 psi have been developed in K Monel metal.

Monel metal is useful because of its resistance to corrosive liquids and also, as shown in Fig. 9.16, because of its retention of properties at high temperatures.   In addition, it has a pleasing appearance and does not tarnish under normal atmospheric conditions.   Monel metal has a tensile strength of about 70,000 psi when cast and about 90,000 psi when hot-rolled.   Ultimate tensile strengths of 175,000 psi may be obtained with cold working.   Its ductility is about equal to that of steel.   Other properties are given in Table 9.5.   Because it undergoes little change in properties at subzero temperatures, Monel metal is useful for liquid-air equipment.

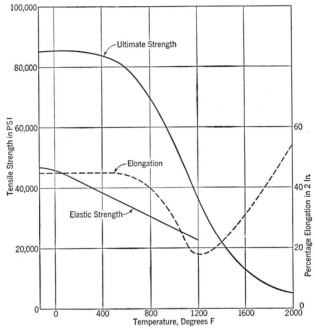

FIG. 9.16   Effect of temperature upon properties of hot-rolled
Monel metal.

Nickel-copper alloys containing from 40 to 45 per cent nickel have a relatively high electrical resistance, combined with a low temperature coefficient of resistance.   They are therefore suitable for rheostats and similar electrical control instruments.

The alloy containing 25 per cent nickel and 75 per cent copper is widely used for coinage, the well-known Buffalo "nickel" having this composition. The "nickel" which superseded it contained no nickel but was composed of 35 per cent silver, 56 per cent copper, and 9 per cent manganese.   The

Canadian five-cent piece is pure nickel. Tensile strengths above 50,000 psi at 1500 F have been developed with alloys containing approximately 17.5 per cent aluminum with nickel. Both NiAl and Ni_3Al phases are present.

The addition of small percentages of lead, tin, and zinc to an alloy containing about 65 per cent copper and 20 per cent nickel produces metals well suited for the production of castings which are highly resistant to corrosion and which also possess good machining characteristics.

German silver, or *nickel silver,* is valuable for its resistance to corrosion and its silvery-white color. An average composition contains about 20 per cent nickel, 30 per cent zinc, and 50 per cent copper.

Nickel-chromium alloys containing up to 20 per cent chromium have a high electrical resistivity, and this property makes them useful as heating elements in electrical heaters of various types. They may be used at temperatures as high as 1150 C (2102 F). Their resistance to deterioration at high temperatures also makes them suitable for high-temperature uses other than heating elements.

Nickel is an important constituent of several alloys having special magnetic properties. *Permalloy,* containing about 81 per cent nickel, 17 per cent iron, and 2 per cent molybdenum, sometimes with a fraction of one per cent each of carbon, silicon, cobalt, copper, and manganese, is very easily magnetized in an electric field. It is useful for cores of electromagnets and for loading submarine cables. It has a low magnetic hysteresis, so cannot be used for permanent magnets. *Alnico,* which—as its name implies—is an alloy of aluminum, nickel, iron, and cobalt, is the most powerful magnetic material known. The material is too hard to be machined, so it is shaped by casting and grinding or by powder metallurgy.

Alloys of nickel containing up to 40 per cent molybdenum have a high resistance to hydrochloric and nitric acids. With some iron and chromium added, the alloys are nearly as resistant to corrosion as the noble metals.

As was noted in Chapter 8, nickel is resistant to oxidation at high temperatures and is therefore employed extensively—generally in conjunction with chromium—as the base of alloys suitable for use as parts of jet-propulsion units, turbo superchargers, and other elements which may operate at temperatures between 1200 and 1500 F. The high-temperature nickel alloys include Hastelloy; Inconel "X" (composed mainly of 75 per cent nickel, 14 per cent chromium, 6 per cent iron, 3 per cent titanium, and 0.6 per cent aluminum); an iron-nickel alloy containing 25 per cent nickel, 16 per cent chromium, 6 per cent molybdenum, and 0.08 per cent carbon; the alloy 19-9 with small amounts of tungsten and molybdenum; and the SAE alloys 4130 and 4140.

TABLE 9.5

NOMINAL COMPOSITION AND PROPERTIES OF NONFERROUS ALLOYS

Metal	Composition (%)	Melt. Point (C)	Specific Gravity	Linear Coeff. Therm. Exp. ($C \times 10^{-6}$)	Specific Heat (cal/g)	Therm. Cond. (cgs units)	Rel. Elec. Cond. (Cu =100)	Ultimate Tensile Strength (ksi)	Endur. Limit (ksi)	Modulus of Elast. ($psi \times 10^6$) Tens.	Shear
Aluminum bronze*	90 Cu, 10 Al	1040	7.57	17.0	0.104	0.18	13.4	59–125	22	16.8	..
Bell metal*	80 Cu, 20 Sn	..	8.70	27.0	0.086	..	..	55	....	..	..
Brass											
Red*	85 Cu, 15 Zn	1030	8.75	18.7	....	0.246	37.0	42–75	....	13.0	5.0
Yellow*	67 Cu, 33 Zn	940	8.40	18.5	0.091	0.204	25.9	40–140	10–20	15.0	..
Constantan	60 Cu, 40 Ni	1190	8.88	17.0	0.098	0.054	3.5	65–120	....	22.0	..
Everdur*	95.8 Cu, 3.2 Si, 1 Mn	1000	8.46	17.0	....	0.078	6.7	55–145	..	..	..
German silver†	60 Cu, 25 Zn, 15 Ni	..	8.40	18.4	0.094	0.070	....	45	..	..	..
Government bronze	88 Cu, 10 Sn, 2 Zn	..	8.65	..	....	..	11.1	30–40	..	15.0	..
Gunmetal*	90 Cu, 10 Sn	1000	8.78	18.3	....	..	..	43	..	10.0	..
Invar	64 Fe, 36 Ni	1495	8.00	0.6	0.120	..	2.1	85	..	..	..
Lipowitz' metal	51 Bi, 25 Pb, 14 Sn, 10 Cd	60	..	..	0.0345	..	..	....	..	..	..
Magnalium*	90 Al, 10 Mg	600	2.50	24	....	..	..	40–48	7.5	10.0	..
Manganese bronze*	60 Cu, 39 Zn, 1 Sn	..	8.4	..	....	..	..	60–80	....	..	..
Manganin*	84 Cu, 12 Mn, 4 Ni	910	8.50	..	0.097	0.152	3.9	70–150	....	..	..

Monel metal*	28 Cu, 67 Ni, 3 Fe, Mn, Si, C	1300	8.90	14	0.128	0.06	4.1	60–175	22–38	25.0	9.5
Monel metal, K	31 Cu, 63 Ni, 3 Al, Fe, Mn, Si	1350	8.60	14	0.127	0.043	....	120–180	25–40	26.0	9.5
Muntz metal	60 Cu, 40 Zn	840	8.40	20.8	0.0917	0.300	28.6	50–100	22	15.0	..
Naval brass (admiralty)	70 Cu, 29 Zn, 1 Sn	935	8.17	20.2	....	0.263	24.7	45–125	....	....	..
Nichrome resistance wire	60 Cu, 12 Cr, 26 Fe, 2 Mn	1500	8.2	....	....	....	1.7	100	....	....	..
Nickel silver*	55 Cu, 25 Ni, 20 Zn	1135	8.72	....	....	....	4.0	72–110	....	....	..
Phosphor bronze	90 Cu, 9.5 Sn, 0.5 P	750	8.9	17.6	....	....	22.1	35–100	....	....	..
Silver	100 Ag	960	10.5	18.8	0.0558	1.00	108.5	45–50	....	11.2	3.8
Solder*	67 Pb, 33 Sn	181–252	9.4	25	0.04	....	10.8	10	....	....	..
Speculum metal	68 Cu, 32 Sn	745	8.60	19.3	....	....	....	....	....	....	..
Stellite*	55 Co, 40 Cr, 3 W, 2 C	1150	8.50	13.4	....	....	1.5	40–130	....	....	..
Tobin bronze	60 Cu, 39 Zn, 1 Sn, Fe, Pb	855	8.40	21.4	....	....	....	54–90	25	15.0	..
Type metal*	58 Pb, 26 Sn, 15 Sb, 1 Cu	....	....	19.5	....	....	....	....	....	4.5	..
Wood's metal	50 Bi, 25 Pb, 12.5 Sn, 12.5 Cd	66	9.70	....	0.035	0.032	3.3	....	....	....	..

* Average values for a group of alloys having approximately the same composition.
† Also known as nickel silver. The Federal Trade Commission has ruled against the name German silver for alloys containing no silver.

MAGNESIUM

9.38 History of Magnesium

Although magnesium as a commercially pure metal was first isolated by Bussy in 1830, it, like other metals, did not assume any importance as a structural material until after the discovery of a satisfactory commercial process for its manufacture. The fundamentals of a method were discovered by Bunsen in 1852, when he produced magnesium by the electrolysis of anhydrous magnesium chloride ($MgCl_2$). The perfection of several methods for the production of the metal on a large scale has made possible many economical engineering uses for magnesium and its alloys.

The technology of magnesium production and the development of structural magnesium alloys have advanced rapidly in the last few years.

9.39 Production of Magnesium

The production of magnesium consists in converting the raw material to magnesium chloride ($MgCl_2$) or magnesium oxide (MgO), which may be reduced to magnesium by electrolysis or by heat with a suitable reducing agent. Five processes have been developed for the commercial production of the metal.

Brine process. The first process commercially used for the production of metallic magnesium utilized a natural brine as the raw material. The brine, which is found in Michigan in large quantities at a depth of 1200 or 1400 ft, contains about 3 per cent magnesium chloride, 14 per cent sodium chloride, 9 per cent calcium chloride, and small quantities of other materials.

The brine is pumped from wells and is then treated with magnesium hydrate to remove certain impurities. The sodium chloride is removed by evaporation and filtration, and the calcium chloride is removed by fractional crystallization, leaving substantially pure $MgCl_2 \cdot 6H_2O$. The material is next dehydrated by heating, first in air and then in an atmosphere of HCl gas.

The dehydrated magnesium chloride, together with a small quantity of sodium chloride, is then placed in an electrolytic cell, consisting of a large cast-steel tank. The tank itself serves as the cathode, and a series of graphite bars are immersed in the tank to serve as anodes. Heat to maintain the proper temperature is supplied by an auxiliary furnace into which the cell is built. Operation is continuous, magnesium chloride being added as necessary. As the magnesium is liberated, it rises to the top of the cell, but it is prevented from burning by the thin film of the molten salt bath on the surface. The molten metal is dipped from the electrolytic cells and is cast into ingots. Magnesium produced by the electrolytic process usually contains less than 0.1 per cent of impurities.

Sea-water process. The first large plant for the extraction of metallic magnesium from sea water was developed at Freeport, Texas, with a capacity of about 36,000 tons per year. Sea water, which contains about 0.13 per cent magnesium (about 2 lb per cu yd), is pumped into large tanks and treated with calcium hydroxide which has been obtained by calcining oyster shells. The calcium hydroxide reacts with the magnesium chloride in the sea water, precipitating magnesium hydroxide. After filtering, the magnesium hydroxide is treated with hydrochloric acid to produce magnesium chloride. After filtering and dehydrating, the magnesium chloride is reduced to metallic magnesium by electrolysis in a cell similar to the one used in the brine process.

M.E.L. Process. This process makes use of magnesite ($MgCO_3$) as the raw material. The magnesite is calcined and is treated with chlorine gas to produce magnesium chloride, which is then fused and reduced in the electrolytic cell.

Ferrosilicon process. The ferrosilicon process utilizes dolomite ($MgCO_3 \cdot CaCO_3$) as the raw material. The dolomite is calcined and is heated with ferrosilicon in a vacuum at 2100 F. At that temperature pure magnesium is formed as a vapor, which is condensed at the cool end of the furnace.

Carbothermic process. The carbothermic process also makes use of dolomite as the raw material. The dolomite is calcined, reducing it to calcium and magnesium hydroxide. The magnesium hydroxide is then heated in kilns to drive off the water. This process results in almost pure magnesium oxide, which is ground and mixed with carbon obtained from coal or petroleum coke, and the mixture is briquetted. The briquettes are fed into an electric furnace which maintains a temperature between 3500 and 4000 F. At this temperature the carbon reduces the magnesium oxide, forming magnesium vapor and carbon monoxide. The magnesium vapor is shock-cooled by forcing it through a nozzle at the furnace outlet. It is again briquetted and formed into ingots by heating. The reduction process takes place in a natural-gas atmosphere to prevent ignition of the magnesium.

In some plants magnesium is transferred from the furnace to the molds by pumping it through pipes when it is in the molten state, rather than by moving it in open ladles.

Magnesium may be shaped by casting or working. For structural purposes, however, alloying elements are generally added first to improve the properties. Some of the alloys are adapted to sand casting, and others are adapted to shaping by rolling, extruding, or forging. Plate, sheet, and strip alloys are rolled; structural shapes, bars, and tubing are produced by extruding the metal through suitable dies, while special shapes may be forged or cast.

In 1952 about 39 per cent of the 44,000 tons of structural magnesium products produced in the United States was shaped by casting, and about 20 per cent went into wrought products. About three-fourths of the production was used in the defense industry. The average price of castings was slightly more than one dollar per pound, and in ingot form the magnesium sold at 25 cents per pound.

9.40 Properties and Uses of Magnesium

From the structural standpoint an outstanding property of magnesium is its light weight, the metal itself weighing 108.4 lb per cu ft, and its principal alloys 112 lb per cu ft. Since the relatively low elastic strength of the pure metal would offset any advantages it might have by virtue of its low specific gravity, pure magnesium is not used as a structural material. However, it does form a suitable base for alloying with other materials, particularly aluminum, which will increase its strength without materially increasing its weight.

One peculiar characteristic of the metal is that the yield strength in compression is only about 75 per cent of the yield strength in tension, while the ultimate strength in compression may be as much as 50 per cent greater than the ultimate tensile strength.

Magnesium is not acted upon by alkalies and normal carbonates, but is attacked by most acids and salt solutions. Upon exposure to the air, a thin film of corrosion-resistant oxide is formed on the surface. The addition of a small amount of manganese increases the resistance to corrosion. Where service conditions are severe, the metal should be protected by lacquer, paint, or enamel.

In addition to its structural uses, magnesium has other important applications in industry. The demand for magnesium to be used in flares and signals was largely responsible for the development of the magnesium industry in the United States. Because of its position in the electromotive-force series and its strong affinity for oxygen, the metal is also of importance as a scavenger and a deoxidizer in metallurgical operations, particularly in the nickel industry.

Magnesium is used in the Grignard reaction for the synthesis of many important organic chemicals. It is also used in many alloys.

9.41 Alloys of Magnesium

The major alloy systems of magnesium are based on the fact that the solubility of aluminum and zinc in magnesium increases with an increase in temperature. Thus, by adding these metals and heat-treating the alloy, the solid solution can be stabilized for room-temperature applications. The same general system of designation for heat treatment is used for the magnesium alloys as is used for the aluminum alloys. For magnesium the principal types of heat treatment are

1. HT or T4 solution treatment. This involves holding the alloy for 16 to 20 hr in the 500-800 F range, followed by cooling in air.
2. HTA or T6 solution treatment and aged. After 16 to 20 hr in the 500-800 F range, the alloy is held in the 300-400 F range for an additional 12 to 16 hr. This treatment improves the yield strength.
3. ACS as cast and stabilized. By heating the cast products to the 425-550 F range for 2 to 6 hr, stress relief is achieved.
4. HTS or T61 heat treated and stabilized. This treatment involves a combination of treatments 1 and 3. It is effective in increasing creep resistance.

Although the tensile strength is improved by alloying, the corrosion resistance is often decreased. As yet, no magnesium alloy has been developed that is better than the commercial magnesium for resistance to sea water or to water at elevated temperatures. This low corrosion resistance is one of the serious limitations of the metal and its alloys. For ordinary applications various coatings and surface treatments are available for protection of the surface.

The composition and general mechanical properties of some of the magnesium alloys are given in tables 9.6 and 9.7. Partial stress-strain diagrams of two of the alloys are presented in Fig. 9.17. The magnesium alloys are sometimes called Dowmetal, since the Dow Chemical Company pioneered the development of production and engineering applications of the metal and its alloys.

In addition to these alloys, alloys containing cerium for high-temperature uses and zirconium for high strength (ultimate tensile strength over 65,000 psi) have been developed.

The alloys of magnesium may be used at temperatures as low as −80 C (−112 F) without appreciable change in properties; they are reduced in strength at temperatures higher than about 100 C; and they are not satisfactory above about 200 C (392 F).

Magnesium alloys are easily machined. Certain operations, such as dry grinding, involve some fire hazard because of the affinity of magnesium for oxygen. Although the metal must be heated almost to its melting point, 651 C (1204 F), before it will burn, sparks falling in magnesium dust may ignite it.

The annealed alloys may be cold-bent or cold-rolled. Hard-rolled sheet is rather brittle for cold working, but may be formed at temperatures between 260 C (500 F) and 400 C (752 F). The metal becomes brittle and the grain size increases at temperatures above 425 C (797 F).

Care must be taken in riveting magnesium alloys, because electrolytic action may be set up if steel, copper, or nickel rivets are used without insulating the rivets from the plates. Magnesium-alloy rivets are not satisfactory because of their tendency to harden rapidly and to become brittle when cold-worked. However, rivets of one of the aluminum alloys 1100, 3003, or 2017 may be used. The first two, 1100 and 3003, are suitable only for low stresses. Rivets may be driven hot or cold. The surfaces to be joined are usually coated with a heavy bituminous or asphaltic sealing compound to prevent corrosion within the joint.

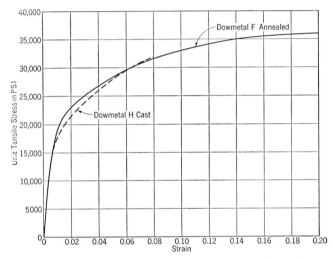

FIG. 9.17   Typical stress-strain diagrams of magnesium alloys.

Members of magnesium alloys may be joined by gas or electric resistance welding or by riveting. One of the difficulties encountered in gas welding is the necessity for complete removal of the welding flux to prevent corrosion. Buckling and warping are likely to occur in both gas and electric welding, and particular care must be used not to overheat the metal. In the *Heliarc* process a stream of helium is directed against the metal to provide an inert atmosphere during welding.

The alloys may be shaped by sand or die casting, by forging, by extruding, or by rolling. Mechanical working increases the strength and decreases the ductility, as with the other metals. Heat treatment and aging have the same effect as on the aluminum alloys.

In general, a factor of safety of 4 with respect to fracture or 2 with respect to slip is used for designing magnesium alloys to carry static loads.

TABLE 9.6

Nominal Compositions and Characteristics of Magnesium Alloys

Desig.	Composition (%)				Rel. Res. to Salt Water*	Specific Gravity (75 F)	Therm. Cond.† (100-300 C)	Uses	Coeff. of Exp. (C⁻¹ ×10⁻⁶)	Specific Heat
	Al	Mn	Zn	Zr						
C	9.0	0.2	2.0	...	...	1.82	0.16	Sand and permanent-mold castings	26	0.25
FS	3.1	...	1.0	...	...	1.77	0.23	Sheet	26	0.25
H	6.0	0.2	3.0	...	B	1.83	0.18	Sand castings and forgings. May be heat treated and aged	26	0.25
J1	6.5	...	1.0	...	...	1.80	0.19	Extrusions	26	0.25
M	...	1.5	...	...	A	1.76	0.30	Plate and sheet, extruded sections, die castings, and forgings of moderate strength	26	0.25
O1	8.5	...	0.5	...	E	1.80	0.18	Forgings and extrusions of high yield strength	...	...
R	9.0	0.2	0.6	...	...	...	...	Die, sand, and permanent-mold castings	...	...
ZK60A	...	...	5.7	0.55	...	1.83	...	Extrusions	...	...
ZK61	...	...	6	0.7	...	...	...	Sand castings	...	0.25

NOTE: See Table 9.7 for additional properties.

* Rating A is the highest. In ordinary atmosphere the various alloys are approximately equivalent and have very good resistance.

† Calories per sec per cu cm per deg C.

TABLE 9.7

AVERAGE PROPERTIES OF MAGNESIUM ALLOYS

| Designation | | Cond.* | Ult. Str. (ksi) | | | Elong., 2 in. (%) | Yield Strength Tens. (ksi) | Endur. Limit (ksi) | Hard. No. | | Rel. Elec. Cond. |
Dow Chem. Co.	Amer. Mag. Corp.		Tens.	Comp.	Shear				Brin.	Rock. E	
C	.....	AC	24	60	19	2	14	...	65	77	...
		T-2	24	60	19	2	14	...	...	75	...
		T-4	40	75	20	10	14	...	63	90	...
		T-6	40	85	21	2	23	...	84	67	...
FS	.....	O	37	75	21	21	22	...	56	83	...
		H-24	42	78	23	16	32	...	73	...	...
		AR	37	75	21	21	22	...	...	57	...
		AX	37	65	19	12	26	...	49	59	...
H	AM265	AC	29	65	18	6	14	10	50	...	15.0
		T-2	29	65	19	5	14	10	...	66	12.3
		T-4	40	70	19	12	14	10	55	83	13.8
		T-6	40	80	21	5	19	10	73	72	13.8
JI	AM57	AX	44	74	19	14	30	30	60	55	...
M	AM3	O	33	60	18	16	18	19	48	67	...
		H-24	37	...	17	7	28	...	56	...	...
		AR	33	...	...	...	...	27	...	45	...
		AX	34	56	18	9	20	27	44	77	34.5
OI	AM58	AX	48	76	22	12	32	33	60	88	11.9
		T-5	52	90	24	5	36	...	82	62	...
R	.....	AC	24	...	...	2	14	...	52	64	...
		T-4	40	...	...	11	14	...	53	77	...
		T-6	40	...	...	4	19	...	66	72	...
RC	.....	ADC	33	...	20	3	22	...	60	84	...
ZK60A	.....	AX	49	73	24	12	38	...	75	88	...
		T-5	51	76	25	10	42	...	82	...	...
ZK61	.....	T-5A	42	...	...	8	26	...	...	...	...
		T-6	47	...	...	10	30	...	...	...	...

* AC = as cast, AR = as rolled, AX = as extruded, ADC = as die-cast.

The strength-weight ratios of the magnesium alloys compare very favorably with those of some of the alloy steels. That is, a magnesium-alloy member with a given strength may be lighter than a steel member of equal strength. However, the magnesium alloys have a lower modulus of elasticity, and hence may deform more under the same load than a steel member of equal strength. The coefficient of thermal expansion of magnesium is about 0.000016 per deg F, as compared with about 0.0000065 for steel, hence there will be a greater deformation for magnesium than for steel if both undergo the same temperature change.

TITANIUM

9.42 History of Titanium

The commercial production of titanium is relatively recent. In 1946 the United States Bureau of Mines established a pilot plant for producing the metal and two years later the first commercial plant went into operation with a rated capacity of 100 lb per day. From 1949 through 1954 United States production approximately doubled each year, with over 5000 tons being produced in 1954. At the end of that year the price of sponge titanium was $4.50 per pound.

9.43 Titanium Ores

The principal ores of titanium are ilmenite ($FeO \cdot TiO_2$) and rutile (TiO_2). Prior to 1946, the principal domestic sources were Florida and Virginia, and the foreign sources were India and Norway. Extensive deposits have since been discovered in Ontario, and workable ores have been found in several states. Hematite is often associated with ilmenite.

9.44 Production of Titanium

The principal commercial production method for titanium is the Kroll process (magnesium reduction of $TiCl_4$) the end product of which is sponge metal.

If the ilmenite ore is contaminated with hematite, it is first smelted to prepare it for the Kroll process. The iron goes into pig iron and the titanium oxide collects in the slag. The slag is given an acid treatment to separate the TiO_2. If the ilmenite is not contaminated with hematite, the process of preparing the ore starts with acid treatment. The TiO_2 from the acid treatment or the rutile ore is chlorinated to produce $TiCl_4$, and refined if necessary.

The Kroll process consists in heating $TiCl_4$ in the presence of magnesium in an iron vessel with an inert atmosphere. The sponge titanium resulting from this may be purified by the iodide process. This process consists in heating the metal in a vacuum, or inert atmosphere, with iodine. Titanium tetraiodide is formed, but is dissociated by a hot filament. The purified titanium is deposited on the filament and the liberated iodine combines again with more of the impure metal. The total impurity level of the resultant metal is of the order of one-half of one per cent.

If purification of the sponge titanium is not required, the sponge is compacted, usually by melting, before fabrication. Following the melting, the metal is shaped by hot or cold working, and is available in the form of plate, sheet, strip, rod, tubing, wire, extrusions, and forgings.

Because of the affinity of the metal for oxygen, hydrogen, and other gases, casting of commercial shapes is difficult.

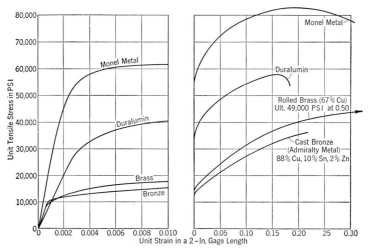

FIG. 9.18   Stress-strain comparisons of nonferrous metals.

9.45   Properties of Titanium

Commercial titanium has a melting point which is high (3135 F) in comparison with the melting points of most other engineering materials. Its value for structural purposes at high temperatures is distinctly limited by its affinity for gases. For example, above 600 F the metal absorbs hydrogen readily. This results in increased strength—but also in a marked decrease in ductility, which gives rise to serious manufacturing and service problems. Oxygen and nitrogen also are absorbed, and this also embrittles the material. On the other hand, titanium has excellent resistance to corrosion in an oxidizing atmosphere; it offers good resistance to corrosion by chlorides, sea water, and dilute alkalies; and it is cathodic to most of the metals.

The weight of titanium is about 276 lb per cu ft, which makes the metal attractive, when combined with its high strength, as an aircraft material. The modulus of elasticity of commercial titanium is about 15,000,000 psi, and the moduli of elasticity of most of its alloys are between 15,000,000 and 17,000,000 psi.

The structure-sensitive properties, such as tensile strength, show considerable variation as a result of small differences in manufacturing processes among the several producers of the metal. In the annealed condition,

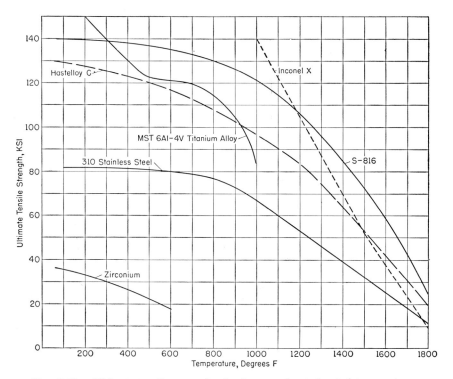

Fig. 9.19   Ultimate tensile strength of a few metals at elevated temperatures.

the 0.002 yield strength is reported between 48,000 and 80,000 psi for sheet and plate, and up to 125,000 psi for cold-drawn, full-hard wire. The tensile strength ranges from 65,000 psi to 110,000 psi for the annealed metal, and up to 145,000 for cold-drawn wire. The strength decreases as the temperature is increased as is illustrated in Fig. 9.19.

Titanium undergoes a lattice change from hexagonal close-packed (alpha) to body-centered cubic (beta) as the temperature is increased above 1625 F.

9.46 Alloys of Titanium

Those elements that are soluble in titanium may be classified in two groups.

1. The elements that *raise* the alpha-beta transformation temperature. These are known as the alpha stabilizers. The common impurities, carbon, nitrogen, and oxygen, which form interstitial alloys are in this class. Aluminum, bismuth, tin, antimony, indium, and lead are also alpha stabilizers. The alpha stabilizers strengthen the metal by solid-solution hardening, which also decreases the ductility. The resultant single-phase alloys are homogeneous, readily weldable, and not greatly embrittled at elevated temperatures. They are not subject to alteration in strength by heat treatment in the alpha range, because of the solid-solution structure. They are comparatively strong and ductile.

2. The elements that *lower* the alpha-beta transformation temperature. These are the elements that, in general, have a greater solubility in the beta phase than in the alpha phase. They are known as the beta stabilizers. Iron, the principal metal contaminant of titanium, is a beta stabilizer. Others are hydrogen, beryllium, silicon, chromium, manganese, silver, cobalt, nickel, tungsten, uranium, zirconium, vanadium, columbium, molybdenum, and tantalum. Iron and the next ten elements on the list form eutectoids with titanium, and the properties of the resultant alloys may therefore be altered by heat treatment which will control the relative amounts of the alpha and beta phases. A martensitic structure may also be produced by quenching from the beta phase. This results in increased strength, but reduced ductility, and lack of stability at elevated temperatures.

Yield strengths as high as 140,000 psi in the annealed condition and 170,000 psi in the cold-worked condition have been reported. The corresponding ultimate tensile strengths are approximately 150,000 and 180,000 psi. The elongation ranges from 2 to 20 per cent in 2 in., which is about 5 per cent less than the commercial titanium.

9.47 Uses of Titanium

The first principal use of titanium was in aircraft construction. Its favorable strength-weight ratio in comparison with other metals partially overcomes its higher cost. It is being used in sheet form for wing and fuselage covering as well as for nacelles, cowling, and bulkheads.

Titanium rivets and bolts are available. Alloy forgings are being developed for engine parts such as compressor discs and stator vanes.

TABLE 9.8

Average Properties of Annealed Titanium and Titanium Alloys

Desig.	Mfr.	Ti* (%)	Mn (%)	Al (%)	Fe (%)	Cr (%)	Mo (%)	C (%)	Tens. Str. (ksi) Yield	Ultimate	Elong., 2" (%)
RC–55	Rem–Cru	99.2	..	..	..	..	..	0.2	65	75	25
RC–70	Rem–Cru	99.0	..	..	..	..	..	0.2	80	90	20
RC–130 A	Rem–Cru	92	8	..	..	..	..	0.2MX	130	150	25
RC–130 B	Rem–Cru	92	4	4	..	..	..	0.2MX	140	150	20
Ti–140A	Titanium Metals	94	..	..	2	2	2	0.08MX	120	130	..
Ti–150A	Titanium Metals	95.8	..	..	1.5	2.7	..	0.02	120	135	12
Ti–150B	Titanium Metals	85	..	..	5	5	5	0.02	135	160	10
Ti–175A	Titanium Metals	95.5	..	..	3	1.5	..	0.02	140	172	8
MST 3Al–5Cr	Mallory–Sharon	91.5	..	3	..	5	..	0.5	135	145	..
MST 2Al–2Fe	Mallory–Sharon	95.5	..	2	2	..	..	0.5	..	140	..
RS–120	Republic Steel	93	7	..	..	..	..	....	120	130	..
RS–110	Republic Steel	94	..	..	2	4	..	....	110	120	..

*Approximate values.

The use of titanium in the chemical field is increasing because of the corrosion resistance of the metal. Vats, tanks, and tubing for containing concentrated chloride solutions, in particular, are being made of titanium in preference to stainless steel.

The principal alloying additions to titanium are iron, manganese, chromium, and molybdenum, all of which are beta stabilizers. Properties of a few of the alloys are given in Table 9.8.

ZIRCONIUM

9.48 History of Zirconium

The use of zirconium as a structural material is a recent development stimulated by the potentiality of the metal for use in nuclear reactors. When it was discovered that hafnium-free zirconium has a low cross section for thermal neutrons, intensive study of the metal was undertaken, culminating in its adoption as a structural material in the first submarine thermal reactor.

9.49 Production of Zirconium

Zircon ($ZrSiO_4$), zircite (ZrO_2), and baddeleyite (ZrO_2) are the principal ores of zirconium. Florida and North Carolina are commercial domestic sources, while Brazil, Ceylon, India, and Australia have extensive deposits.

Commercial production is complicated by the necessity for removing hafnium, which is invariably associated with the zirconium in the natural state and which is similar to zirconium chemically. The cross section of hafnium for thermal neutrons is so high that a small fraction of one per cent of hafnium in zirconium renders the metal unfit for use in nuclear reactors.

The zirconium ore is converted to zirconium cyanonitride by reacting it with carbon in a direct-current arc furnace. The product is then chlorinated and the hafnium removed. The Kroll process (magnesium reduction) is used to convert the $ZrCl_4$ to sponge zirconium. The sponge is then consolidated and may be further refined by the iodide process to yield crystal-bar zirconium.

9.50 Properties of Zirconium

Crystal-bar zirconium is comparatively soft and ductile, with a room-temperature tensile strength of 26,000 to 39,000 psi and an elongation of about 40 per cent in 2 in. The properties are sensitive to the oxygen content. The addition of 0.1 per cent oxygen to zirconium will increase the tensile strength approximately 50 per cent. Tensile strengths in the order of 90,000 psi are attained with the addition of a small amount of contaminants. The tensile strength decreases rapidly with an increase in temperature, as shown in Fig. 9.19. For example, at 600 F the tensile strength of crystal-bar zirconium is between 12,000 and 19,000 psi.

Another property that makes zirconium of importance in nuclear reactors is its high resistance to corrosion in many fluids at moderate temperatures. The metal may be exposed to water at 600 F for thousands of hours with only superficial corrosion. Its resistance to corrosion by air is excellent, and it resists corrosion by certain liquid metals at a temperature of 1500 F.

Preliminary study of zirconium alloys indicates that small additions of iron, nickel, and chromium may be beneficial at elevated temperatures.

The metal is readily worked, and its strength is increased by cold working. Tensile strengths in the order of 120,000 psi have been reported for cold-drawn zirconium wire.

Zirconium has a hexagonal close-packed lattice in the alpha phase up to about 1580 F. From above this temperature to the melting point, it is body-centered cubic. As is the case with titanium, the presence of carbon, nitrogen, and oxygen raises the transformation temperature, while hydrogen and many of the transition elements lower the transformation temperature.

SECONDARY METALS

9.51 Properties of Secondary Metals

A number of metals that may be classified as secondary from the standpoint of volume or tonnage of production are of considerable importance because they have specific properties which are useful in special situations or because of their importance as alloying elements. Others have qualities which may make them of primary importance if, as in the case of aluminum and magnesium, methods can be developed for their production at costs which will make their use economically practicable. These metals are discussed in the following sections, in alphabetical order.

9.52 Beryllium

For a number of years beryllium has been important because of its characteristic of promoting strength and hardness and increasing the endurance limit when added in small quantities to copper. It has the same effect when alloyed with iron, nickel, lead, or silver. Beryllium itself is used in making X-ray windows, cathode-ray tubes, and other specialized devices in which its characteristic of converting short-wave rays to visible light is useful. Its low absorption cross section and high scatter cross section for thermal neutrons, together with its low density, high thermal con-

ductivity, and high melting point, make it attractive as a moderating material and fuel-component material for thermal nuclear reactors.   However,
these advantageous characteristics are balanced by its brittleness, difficulty
of forming, low corrosion resistance to water, toxicity, and high cost at
present.   Improvement of production techniques would reduce some of
these obstacles to its use.

The commercial ore of beryllium is beryl ($3BeO \cdot Al_2O_3 \cdot 2SiO_2$), which
occurs as widely scattered crystals.   Brazil, Argentina, and India are the
principal world sources, and South Dakota is the principal domestic source.
Preparation of the metal by the standard process involves treatment of the
ore to convert it successively to the sulfate, hydroxide, and fluoride forms.
The BeF_2 is reduced with magnesium at 1650 F in a graphite-lined furnace.
The resultant "pebble beryllium" is purified and cast.   The metal may be
extruded or powdered and sintered.   The metal resulting from the powder
techniques is called "Q-process" beryllium, with variations in the process
leading to QMV, QT, QPT, QM, and QRM metal.   At least four other
processes for reduction of the ore have been used.

Cast and extruded beryllium has an ultimate tensile strength at room
temperature varying from 30,000 to 70,000 psi depending on the extrusion
and annealing temperatures.   It is quite brittle.   Its modulus of elasticity
is approximately 40,000,000 psi, and its coefficient of thermal expansion
is about 12.3×10^{-6} per deg C.   It is relatively light, having a specific
gravity of 1.8, and the electrical conductivity is 40 per cent of that of
copper.

Beryllium has a hexagonal close-packed structure so it would be expected to be ductile in the pure form.   However, commercially produced
beryllium has an elongation of only about 2 per cent in 2 in. at room temperature.   It is observed that traces of impurities have a marked influence
on the ductility.   Elongations of 20 per cent or more have been obtained
at 800 F.

9.53   Bismuth

Bismuth is an important constituent of many of the alloys having low
melting points.   It forms eutectics with lead, tin, cadmium, and indium,
each eutectic having a low melting point.   The eutectic containing 44.5
per cent lead has a melting point of 124 C; that containing 42 per cent tin,
138.5 C; that containing 40 per cent cadmium, 144 C; and that containing
indium, only 117 F.   The alloys containing less than 48 per cent bismuth
tend to expand upon solidification and are therefore useful for patterns
where sharp duplication of features is desirable.   The eutectic with tin,
which is known as Cerrotru, undergoes almost no volume change upon
solidification.   One of the widely used bismuth alloys is known as Cerro-

bend.   It contains 50 per cent bismuth, 26.7 per cent lead, 13.3 per cent tin, and 10 per cent cadmium, and has a melting point of only 70 C.   It has been extensively used to aid in the bending of thin-walled tubes.   If the tube to be bent is plugged at one end and filled with molten Cerrobend, which is allowed to solidify, it then may be bent without wrinkling.   After the desired shape is attained, the alloy may be remelted by simply immersing the tube in hot water and it may then be poured out.

9.54   Calcium

Calcium has two important uses: (1) as a refining agent in the production of metals, because of its high capacity for deoxidation, desulfurization, and degasification; (2) as an alloying element, because of its capacity for increasing the strength and corrosion-resistance of lead, magnesium, and nickel.   Most lead cable sheathing contains a small percentage of calcium as an alloying element.

9.55   Cerium

Cerium, in combination with certain other metals, is important as a deoxidizing and scavenging material.   It is alloyed with aluminum and magnesium to increase the strength and hardness of the latter metals.   In certain types of ductile cast iron it is used to promote the formation of round graphite particles.   An aluminum-cerium alloy has been used for pistons because of its resistance to high temperatures obtained in internal-combustion engines.

9.56   Cobalt

The use of cobalt in Alnico, an alloy very useful for making permanent magnets, has already been discussed.   Cobalt in quantities up to about 13 per cent is used with tungsten in producing high-speed cutting tools.   It is also used as a base for alloys designed to resist high temperatures.   One of these is Vitallium, which contains 65 per cent cobalt, 30 per cent chromium, and 5 per cent molybdenum.   This alloy gives satisfactory performance at temperatures up to 1500 F and is useful in jet-propulsion units.   It can be formed only by casting.   The investment-mold process is the casting process most commonly employed.

Cobalt 60, which is a radioactive isotope of cobalt, is of industrial significance because the gamma rays which it releases can be used for radiography.   Inspection of castings and weldments for flaws using Co-60 and suitable X-ray film is standard practice in many plants and in some field operations.

9.57 Indium

Although quantities of indium are relatively small, this metal has proven itself useful as a corrosion-resisting plating and as a constituent of aluminum-copper alloys. Its particular effect is to increase the age-hardening capacity of the alloys. As noted in section 9.66, it is one of the few metals well adapted for use as a bearing material in contact with iron or steel. It is relatively weak, so when it is used for bearings, as in aircraft engines, it is in the form of a thin sheet backed with a strong, rigid material.

9.58 Silver

One of the outstanding characteristics of silver is its high electrical conductivity, and it has recently found extensive application in bus bars and other heavy-duty conductors. Silver is also well adapted for use as a bearing metal and is extensively used as a lining material for various parts of chemical equipment because of its resistance to corrosion. During the tin shortage, silver was used as an alloy with lead to replace tin in solder. An alloy containing from $2\frac{1}{2}$ to 5 per cent silver gave satisfactory service and was cheaper than the conventional lead-tin solder.

9.59 Tungsten

Tungsten is one of the heavy metals, having a specific gravity of about 19.3, and is useful in the preparation of heavy alloys such as those used for counterweights in gyrorotors or as containers for radium and other radioactive materials. The metal resists oxidation at high temperature and is therefore useful for spark contacts. It is used for a series of alloys in combination with nickel up to 16 per cent, and with copper up to 20 per cent. The alloys have a reasonably high electrical conductivity and good resistance to high temperatures. Parts of these alloys are generally formed by powder-metallurgy techniques. Tungsten and copper are mutually insoluble, but compacts made of tungsten and copper powder are quite useful. A combination containing 85 per cent tungsten will develop an ultimate tensile strength of over 115,000 psi, even though the ultimate tensile strength of the tungsten is only 50,000 psi. The conductivity is about 30 per cent, the magnitude depending directly on the copper content. In general, the properties of the tungsten-copper combinations may be predicted, since they vary directly with the composition.

9.60 Radioisotopes

Uranium and plutonium are rapidly becoming of extreme importance to engineering because of their capacity for releasing a large amount of energy under controlled fission. Although industrial application of radioactive materials is in its infancy, the number of uses is increasing rapidly.

Radiography, tracers in research, and thickness gages are examples of industrial applications.

SPECIAL-PURPOSE METALS AND ALLOYS

9.61 Metallic Carbides

Because of their extreme hardness, the carbides of some of the metals, including tungsten, titanium, tantalum, and boron, are useful for tips on cutting tools and for forming gages, valve sets, bearings, guides, and other surfaces where resistance to wear is of paramount importance. In general, they are too hard to be formed by any method other than compacting or cementing.

9.62 Low-Density Products

In high-speed rotating equipment, aircraft parts, and similar products, minimum weight combined with high strength is essential. The designer of such products has three possibilities available in making his selection of materials. He may choose a metal with a low specific gravity, he may alter the geometry of the product to permit the use of a heavier metal such as steel, or he may design the product using a nonmetallic material.

TABLE 9.9

LOW-DENSITY METALS

Name	Sp Gr	Name	Sp Gr	Name	Sp Gr
Lithium	0.53	Barium	3.5	Praseodymium	6.5
Potassium	0.86	Titanium	4.5	Antimony	6.68
Sodium	0.97	Erbium	4.77	Cerium	6.9
Rubidium	1.53	Radium	5.0	Neodymium	6.98
Calcium	1.55	Germanium	5.35	Chromium	6.92
Magnesium	1.74	Yttrium	5.51	Zinc	7.14
Beryllium	1.85	Arsenic	5.73	Manganese	7.20
Cesium	1.90	Vanadium	5.87	Tin	7.28
Scandium	2.5	Gallium	5.91	Indium	7.31
Strontium	2.6	Lanthanum	6.15	Samarium	7.7
Aluminum	2.70	Zirconium	6.4		

From Table 9.9, in which specific gravities of metals lighter than iron are listed, it is evident that with the exception of aluminum and magnesium the metals are relatively rare, and as a result are expensive. The special problems associated with beryllium have been discussed in section 9.52. As has been noted, commercially pure aluminum and magnesium are relatively weak as normally fabricated. However, their strength characteristics may be markedly improved without a great sacrifice in weight, by alloying.

The over-all weight of a product may often be decreased without materially reducing its strength, by changing its shape. An I shaped section, for example, is more resistant to bending in one direction than a solid rectangular section of the same width and same weight if the two are of the same material. An appreciable saving in weight is effected in certain aircraft parts, such as ribs, by using lightening holes to eliminate material not absolutely required for strength. Honeycombing and "egg-crating" techniques are used to decrease weight without materially reducing strength and stiffness. The use of laminated products represents another procedure for increasing the strength-weight ratio of certain products. A distinct advantage results in placing the strong (but heavier) material at the sections where the stress is a maximum, attaching it to light-weight material that will fill in the regions where the stress is comparatively low.

Wood and cellulose products, glass, and plastics may often be substituted for metals to reduce weight. These materials are usually advantageous costwise. For the most part, however, they are limited with respect to the range of temperatures in which they may be used as substitutes for metals, and their dimensional stability must be carefully considered.

9.63　High-Density Products

Certain applications, such as counterweights for control surfaces of aircraft, gyros, and similar instruments, require that a maximum mass and inertia be concentrated in a minimum space. For these applications, metals are generally used. Counterweights for bascule bridges and similar parts in which space is not so critical, may be made of steel or concrete to minimize cost. Shielding for certain types of radiation requires high-density materials to minimize space (this application is discussed in section 9.65).

TABLE 9.10

HIGH-DENSITY METALS

Name	Sp Gr	Name	Sp Gr	Name	Sp Gr
Iron	7.87	Lead	11.34	Uranium	18.7
Columbium	8.57	Hafnium	11.4	Tungsten	19.3
Cadmium	8.65	Thorium	11.5	Gold	19.3
Cobalt	8.9	Thallium	11.85	Rhenium	20.
Nickel	8.90	Palladium	12.0	Platinum	21.45
Copper	8.94	Ruthenium	12.2	Iridium	22.4
Bismuth	9.80	Rhodium	12.44	Osmium	22.5
Molybdenum	10.2	Mercury	13.55		
Silver	10.5	Tantalum	16.6		

A list of the metals having specific gravities equal to or greater than the specific gravity of iron is given in Table 9.10. Of these, lead is the most generally used for the purposes under consideration, because of its relatively low cost. Mercury is readily available, but the fact that it is liquid at room temperature limits its applicability. The metals heavier than gold, as well as gold itself, are too costly for routine engineering applications other than tips of pens, phonograph pickups, and similar small-mass products. In the latter applications cited, the wearing quality, rather than density, is the significant property.

Tungsten, which is next in weight to gold, is used in a number of heavy-metal products. Pure tungsten is brittle and difficult to fabricate because of its hardness. A limited amount of shaping by grinding or cutting with diamond-tipped tools may be done, but this is expensive. Since the machinability of the metal may be increased by adding nickel and copper, the commercial tungsten-base products normally contain about 6 per cent nickel and 4 per cent copper. Fabrication by powder-metallurgy techniques is common.

The commercial tungsten alloys include Mallory 1000 Metal, Hevimet Alloy, Densalloy, and Fansteel 77 Metal. Ultimate tensile strengths range from 25,000 psi to 120,000 psi with percentage elongation in the 2 to 10 per cent range. The alloys cost from $15 to $25 per pound at 1953 prices.

9.64 High-Temperature Products

Progress in several important fields is handicapped seriously by lack of materials that have adequate strength at elevated temperatures. While the need for better high-temperature materials is particularly critical in the development of jet engines, rockets, and nuclear reactors, it is also an important factor in the improvement of diesel engines, combustion equipment, chemical processing units, and other routine industrial products. In general, the engineer is limited to metals and ceramic products for his selection. Combinations of the two, in mixtures or in the form of ceramic-coated metals known as cermets or cermels, are useful in certain applications.

In a general way, the strength of a metal at room temperature and above is related to its melting point. In considering specific examples, the effect of structural transformations and small quantities of alloying elements and impurities is very important. In addition to strength, resistance to oxidation or corrosion is normally a limiting factor for materials which are to serve at elevated temperatures. Rates of chemical processes increase as temperature is increased, thereby limiting the life of the product. However, even with these obvious limitations Table 9.11 is useful in indicating what materials may become important in developing products which will function at elevated temperatures.

In the temperature range up to 1500 F, ferrous alloys are generally the most economical. From 1500 F to 1800 F, alloys of nickel are usually employed. In the range from 1800 F to 2200 F, alloys based on cobalt are effective. For temperatures above 2200 F, operating data are limited.

TABLE 9.11
Transformation and Melting Points of Metals

Metal	Crys. Struc.	Melt. Point F	Melt. Point C
Mercury	rhbdr	−38.02	−38.9
Cesium	bcc	83.3	28.5
Rubidium	bcc	101.3	38.5
Potassium	bcc	144.14	62.3
Sodium	bcc	207.5	97.5
Indium	fc tetr	311.	155.
Lithium	bcc	356.	180.
Tin	fcc 64 F tetr[1]	449.42	231.9
Bismuth	hex rhbdr to fc rhbdr	519.8	271.
Thallium	hcp 900 C bcc	578.3	303.5
Cadmium	hcp	609.62	320.9
Lead	fcc	621.32	327.4
Zinc	hcp	786.92	419.4
Antimony	hex rhbdr to fc rhbdr	1166.	630.
Cerium	hcp to fcc	1184.	640.
Magnesium	hcp	1203.8	651.
Aluminum	fcc	1217.66	658.7
Barium	bcc	1310.	710.
Strontium	fcc	1418.	770.
Calcium	fcc	1490.	810.
Lanthanum	hcp	1535.	835.
Neodymium		1544.	840.
Praseodymium		1724.	940.
Germanium	fcc	1757.3	958.5
Radium		1760.	960.
Silver	fcc	1760.9	960.5
Gold	fcc	1945.4	1063.
Copper	fcc	1981.4	1083.
Uranium	bcc 1229 F mono	2071.4	1133.
Scandium		2192.	1200.
Manganese	bcc to cub to tetr	2300.	1260.
Beryllium	hcp	2343.2	1283.
Nickel	hcp to fcc	2645.6	1452.
Cobalt	hcp to fcc	2696.	1480.
Yttrium		2714.	1490.
Iron	bcc 900 C fcc; 1425 C bcc	2795.	1535.
Palladium		2831.	1555.
Chromium	bcc to hcp	2939.	1615.
Titanium	hcp 1625 F bcc	3074.	1690.
Vanadium	bcc	3119.	1715.
Platinum	fcc	3224.3	1773.5
Ytterbium		3272.	1800.
Zirconium	hcp 1580 F bcc	3326.	1830.
Thorium	fcc	3353.	1845.
Rhodium	fcc	3605.	1985.
Hafnium	hcp 2400 F bcc	3727.4	2053.
Columbium	bcc	4379.	2415.
Iridium	fcc	4424.	2440.
Ruthenium	hcp	4442.	2450.
Molybdenum	bcc	4748.	2620.
Osmium	hcp	4892.	2700.
Tantalum	bcc	5162.	2850.
Tungsten	bcc	6386.	3370.
Rhenium	hcp	6512.	3440.

NOTES FOR TABLE 9.11: bcc = body-centered cubic, cub = cubic, fcc = face-centered cubic, hcp = hexagonal close-packed, mono = monoclinic, rhbdr = rhombohedral, tetr = tetragonal.

[1] Temperatures indicate transition temperatures from one lattice to another, e.g., fcc 64 F tetr indicates fcc below 64 F, tetr above 64 F.

A high (25 per cent) chromium content has been found advantageous in reducing scaling at temperatures up to 2200 F. Titanium carbide has been used experimentally at 4200 F.

Brittleness is usually associated with a high melting point, and it is found that the alloys of chromium, molybdenum, and most of the other metals display this characteristic. The ceramic materials and refractories such silicides, borides, carbides, and nitrides are also brittle, thereby increasing their susceptibility to cracking under the influence of thermal strains induced by a rapid and uneven change in temperature throughout the member. Variations in thermal strains are particularly important in bimetallic elements and in cermets.

Properties of a few high-temperature alloys are given in Table 9.12.

9.65 Shielding Materials

The rapid development of nuclear reactors in recent years, and the extensive use of radioactive materials, have made it imperative to consider the effectiveness of various engineering materials for shielding purposes. The radiation from power reactors and many radioactive materials would be extremely injurious to any individual exposed to them at short range. Hence, biological shielding is a necessity for many of these devices. It is found that the effects of alpha (helium nuclei) and beta (electron) radiation are relatively unimportant because of the low penetrating power of these particles. However, gamma rays and neutrons are important because of the relatively high penetrating power of these forms of radiation.

In general the effectiveness of a material for attenuating gamma radiation is a function of the density of the material. Of the several properties that may be used to measure this quality, the half-thickness (the thickness of material required to reduce the intensity of radiation to one-half of its original value) is useful in making comparisons among materials. The half-thickness is a complex function of the energy of the gamma radiation, since in the practical range three separate processes are involved. These are pair production, the Compton effect, and the photoelectric effect. Comparative values of the resultant effect are given in Table 9.13, from which it is seen that lead, iron, and concrete are among the economical materials available for gamma shielding. Tungsten alloys are also used in certain small-scale applications, but they are too costly to use for shielding to the extent involved in a nuclear reactor.

TABLE 9.12

PROPERTIES OF HIGH-TEMPERATURE ALLOYS

Alloy	Tensile Strength (ksi)				Yield Strength (ksi)				Elongation (%)				Creep Lim. (ksi)*	
	70 F	1000 F	1500 F	1800 F	70 F	1000 F	1500 F	1800 F	70 F	1000 F	1500 F	1800 F	1200 F	1500 F
310 stainless …	82	67	32	11	40	26	19	..	55	50	37	55	8.6	1.0
321 stainless …	92	61	22	5	39	27	13	..	55	35	73	..	8.0	1.0
19–9 DX ……	130	95	39	13	102	77	33	10	26	20	43	85	..	..
19–9 DL ……	118	89	33	13	69	42	30	..	58	43	53	61	20.0	7.1
16–25–6 ……	114	93	41	18	68	42	30	..	42	35	49	59	..	..
L–605 ……	155	100	50	23	70	35	..	12	55	67	17	19	..	..
N–155 ……	116	85	37	17	57	..	33	20	43	37	39	38	..	10.3
S–590 ……	118	128	52	22	72	79	47	..	..	..	23	..	42.0	..
S–816 ……	140	121	73	25	63	46	41	..	31	27	23	20	..	11.5
Hastelloy B ……	135	109	66	24	63	42	..	..	44	31	17	30	..	..
Hastelloy C ……	130	97	51	19	54	55	..	..	38	22	36	38	..	..
Hastelloy X ……	113	94	52	21	56	42	37	17	44	45	33	43	..	..
Inconel ……	91	84	..	8	37	29	..	4	47	47	..	118	..	..
Inconel W ……	146	123	..	..	81	72	..	..	..	..	..	..	..	..
Inconel X ……	162	140	52	9	92	84	44	6	24	22	22	89	64.0	12.3
Refract 26 ……	153	142	73	..	96	91	72	..	18	17	28	..	..	..
Refract 70 ……	133	117	64	..	..	..	..	..	..	..	..	..	..	..
Nimonic 75 ……	92	..	36	..	60	..	15	..	50	..	33	..	..	..
Nimonic 80 ……	..	108	60	..	..	73	47	..	..	41	9	..	..	..
Nimonic 90 ……	148	123	64	..	90	82	52	..	39	27	8	..	..	..
Discalloy 24 …	145	125	..	..	106	94	..	..	19	16	..	..	..	..

* For creep of 0.0001 per cent per hour.

When a part, or all, of the radiation consists of neutrons, shielding is done by surrounding the source with a material having a high-neutron-capture cross section. Microscopic cross sections for thermal-neutron capture vary over a wide range. From the selected values listed in Table 9.13 it is evident that those materials that are well adapted to gamma-ray

TABLE 9.13

SHIELDING CAPACITIES FOR A FEW MATERIALS

Material	Half-thick.* (in.)	Capture Cross Sec.† (barns)
Lead	0.35	0.17
Iron	0.58	2.43
Tungsten	0.22	19.2
Ordinary concrete	4.0	....
Heavy concrete‡	0.75–1.35	....
Boron	1.90	750
Cadmium	0.55	2400
Aluminum	1.64	0.215
Copper	0.55	3.59
Magnesium	1.82	59
Water	3.85	....

* For 1-Mev gamma rays.
† For thermal neutrons.
‡ Concrete containing steel punchings or heavy aggregate.

shielding are relatively ineffective for capture of thermal neutrons, and vice versa. Cadmium is the most widely used material for capture of thermal neutrons. Neutron capture is also the basis of control of thermal reactors. In addition to cadmium, boron or boron steel is widely used for control rods.

It is sometimes said that the best shielding to use for gamma rays or neutrons is the inverse-square law. The statement is made on the basis of the fact that without intermediate shielding materials the intensity of radiation on a given area is inversely proportional to the square of the distance between the area and the source of radiation.

The values given in Table 9.13 are for thermal neutrons, or neutrons with an energy of about 0.025 electron volts. If the source consists of high-energy neutrons, it is desirable to reduce their energy to take advantage of the higher capture cross section of the shielding materials at thermal energies. Thermalizing the neutrons consists in introducing an energy-absorbing material between the source and the shield. Hydrogen is one of the most effective elements for this purpose, so hydrogeneous materials such as water, masonite, or similar cellulose-base material, and heavy water are used as moderators. Graphite is widely used for this purpose.

9.66 Bearing Metals

With the rapid increase in operating speeds of equipment, the selection of a suitable material for journal bearings is not a simple matter. However, the problem may be solved satisfactorily by the application of certain principles and the exercise of judgment. In a bearing, one material slides over another, and the surfaces of the materials in contact are never perfectly smooth. In general, each surface will have minute projections which contact the surface of the other part, even when the surfaces are lubricated. If the two parts are of the same metal and the surfaces are clean, the two parts will weld together when they contact. That is, with the same atomic spacing in each metal the lattices will match and form a continuous crystal, if no foreign atoms are interposed and if the orientation is proper. If a sufficient number of crystals weld, the bearing will freeze. In the general case where identical metals are used in the two parts, welding is taking place constantly at a series of isolated points. If sufficient force is developed by the moving part the welds will be torn loose, probably leaving roughened surfaces at which the action is almost immediately repeated until particles are torn free from both surfaces. Thus, wear ensues.

The foregoing analysis leads to the conclusion that a satisfactory bearing metal for a given part must have two characteristics. First, its lattice parameter must not match that of the given part. A larger lattice spacing or a smaller spacing will inhibit welding of the bearing metal to the moving part. It has been found in studies of pure metals in bearings that a difference in lattice size of 15 per cent is necessary if seizing is to be prevented. Even with this size difference, welding may occur, so it is also necessary that the weld be broken easily if the materials are to be satisfactory. In other words, the two metals should be selected so that the bonds developed between them are weak and brittle, rather than strong and ductile.

In order to satisfy the second requirement—that of fragile bonds—atoms on the surface of one metal should form covalent bonds, rather than metallic bonds, with the atoms of the other metal. In the covalent bond, where the valence electrons are shared, rather than being free or mobile as they are in the case of a metallic bond, a stable but brittle bond is developed. When the bond is brittle, it tends to break clean, which is a distinct advantage for bearings.

The periodic chart of the elements is useful in indicating combinations of metals in which valence bonds are formed. For example, in the elements in columns Ia through VIII the valence shells are relatively empty, whereas in the elements in columns Ib through VIIb the valence shells are fuller. Hence, for use as bearing metals in conjunction with iron or steel the latter elements are better than those in the a subgroups.

Tests have shown that the presence of lubricants does not affect the basic intermetallic action; it only affects the loads at which the bearings fail.[1] The presence of a lubricant reduces the direct metal-to-metal contact somewhat and in addition serves to conduct heat away from the minute areas of direct contact.

Steel is often one of the metals involved in a bearing, and it is found that the two criteria indicated eliminate all metals except silver, lead, tin, indium, and cadmium from consideration as good bearing materials. Of these, lead and tin are the most frequently used, but they are weak structurally so must be reinforced to carry the necessary loads. This may be accomplished by using the metals in thin sheets and backing them with stronger materials, or incorporating the stronger material into the bearing metal by employing two-phase alloys in which one phase is a strong metal that will carry the load and the other phase is one of the good bearing metals. Aluminum-tin alloys and copper-lead alloys are examples of this system. Solid solutions of two acceptable metals, such as lead-tin, and lead-indium alloys, are sometimes used to take advantage of the corrosion resistance of the alloys, which is greater in comparison with the corrosion resistance of the individual elements.

So-called "oilless bearings" are sometimes used. These are bearings, usually made by a powder-metallurgy technique, in which oil is incorporated in the pores of the bearing. The oil is drawn to the surface by capillary action as required, thereby eliminating the need for supplementary lubrication. Nylon is also useful as a bearing material. It is finding application in a wide variety of situations and requires no lubrication in contact with steel.

PROBLEMS

9.1 List ten metals in common use today which were not available for use in 1800.

9.2 How many pounds of copper are there in a ton of ore which contains 5 per cent cuprite?

9.3 Name two common metals which could be used to precipitate copper from a solution of copper sulfate.

9.4 In matte which contains 50 per cent copper, what is the percentage of (a) copper sulfide and (b) iron sulfide? (c) What is the percentage of iron?

9.5 How much static load may a No. 14 (0.064-in. diam) annealed copper wire be expected to carry in direct tension with a factor of safety of 2 with respect to failure by slip?

9.6 A cold-drawn copper wire is subjected to a static tensile stress of such magnitude that the factor of safety with respect to failure by slip is 2.5. What is the factor of safety with respect to failure by fracture?

[1] A. C. Roach and C. L. Goodzeit, "Why Bearings Seize," *General Motors Engineering Journal,* Vol. 2, No. 5 (Sept.-Oct., 1955), pp. 25-29.

9.7 Approximately how many foot-pounds of energy are required to fracture an 8-in. length of No. 4 (0.204-in. diam) cold-drawn copper wire?

9.8 If the alloy containing 50 per cent iron and 50 per cent copper has a specific gravity of 8.40, at what price per pound would it be equal in cost to annealed copper wire (a) for carrying tensile load and (b) for carrying electric current?

9.9 (a) What diameter of cold-drawn copper wire is required to carry the same static load in tension, with the same factor of safety with respect to failure by rupture, as a No. 18 (0.040-in. diam) wire containing 50 per cent copper and 50 per cent iron? (b) How will the current-carrying capacities of the two wires compare?

9.10 A cold-rolled copper member is subjected to a completely reversed repeated stress of 10,000 psi. How much steady stress may be superimposed on the repeated stress before failure would be expected to occur?

9.11 A machine part made of SAE 2345 steel is $\frac{3}{8}$ by $1\frac{1}{4}$ in. in cross section and is designed to carry a tensile impact load with a factor of safety of 2 with respect to failure by slip. If the steel is to be replaced by cast copper, what dimensions should the part have in order to carry the same load with the same factor of safety? Both parts have the same length.

9.12 (a) What diameter is required in order for hard aluminum wire (3003-H18) to carry the same static tensile load, with the same factor of safety with respect to failure by rupture, as a No. 12 (0.081-in. diam) cold-drawn copper wire? (b) What is the relative weight of the aluminum, expressed as a percentage of the weight of the copper?

9.13 (a) What diameter of aluminum wire is required to give the same electrical conductivity per foot as a No. 0 (0.324-in. diam) annealed copper wire? (b) Compare the relative weights.

9.14 Compare the relative costs of 50 miles of No. 4 (0.204-in. diam) annealed copper wire and the same length of aluminum wire having the same electrical conductivity.

9.15 What length of No. 18 (0.040-in. diam) wire may be drawn from 1 lb of aluminum?

9.16 A structural member is to carry a slowly applied axial tensile load of 40,000 lb at a temperature of 500 F. (a) Select a suitable aluminum alloy to carry the load, and (b) determine the required area, using a factor of safety of 4 with respect to failure by fracture.

9.17 A machine part is to be subjected to an axial load that varies from 60,000 lb in compression to 60,000 lb in tension. The part contains a small notch, which has a stress concentration factor of 3, and is to have a factor of safety of 2. The member is sufficiently short to eliminate any danger of buckling. (a) Select a suitable aluminum alloy and (b) determine the required cross-sectional area.

9.18 Solve problem 9.17 if the load varies from 0 to 60,000 lb in tension.

9.19 Determine the required cross-sectional area of an aluminum-alloy airplane part which is 8 in. long and is to carry an axial dynamic load of 60 ft-lb with a factor of safety of 3 with respect to failure by slip.

9.20 Compare the relative weights of Duralumin and structural-steel parts which are to carry equal slowly applied loads (a) with the same factor of safety with respect to failure by slip, and (b) with the same factor of safety with respect to failure by fracture.

9.21 Compare the weights of Duralumin and structural-steel parts which are to carry the same impact loads with equal factors of safety (a) with respect to failure by slip and (b) with respect to failure by fracture.

9.22 A 6-ft by 8-ft by 10-ft covered vat containing a liquid maintained at a temperature of 200 F is to be lined with $\frac{3}{8}$-in. plates. (a) From the standpoint of minimum heat losses, which material would be the most satisfactory—steel, copper, aluminum, or lead? (b) If the material selected is used, what would be the total heat loss in Btu per day, if 50 per cent of the total area is effective in transmitting heat and if the air surrounding the vat is maintained at 70 F?

9.23 If Duralumin costs fifteen times as much per pound as structural steel, would a manufacturer be justified in replacing structural-steel parts designed to carry dynamic loading in tension by Duralumin parts having the same factor of safety with respect to failure by slip?

9.24 (a) How much will the volume of a 2-in. by 2-in. by 8-in. bar of aluminum alloy 2017-T change under an axial compressive load of 120,000 lb? (b) How does its change in volume compare with that of steel under similar conditions?

9.25 A 10-ft gage length is laid off on a $\frac{1}{2}$-in. round rod of aluminum alloy 3003-H14 when the rod is at a temperature of 200 F. (a) How much load must be applied to the ends of the rod to keep the gage length from being changed when the rod is cooled to -30 F? What will be its length (b) when the rod is heated to 200 F with the load maintained and (c) when reheated to 200 F with the load removed?

9.26 Discuss the welding of Duralumin as compared with the welding of aluminum.

9.27 Prepare a table giving two measures of the elastic strength of each of the metals for which suitable stress-strain diagrams are given in Chapter 9.

9.28 From the standpoint of minimum cross-sectional areas, determine the dimensions of the most suitable bronze alloy to carry an axial tensile load of 50,000 lb with a factor of safety of 3 with respect to failure by fracture.

9.29 Solve problem 9.28 for a brass alloy.

9.30 A hot-rolled brass member (Alloy 159) is designed to carry an impact load with a factor of safety of 4 with respect to failure by fracture. What would be the factor of safety if the piece were cold-rolled?

9.31 A structural-steel part is designed to carry an axial tensile load of 60,000 lb with a factor of safety of 4 with respect to failure by fracture. Could any saving in weight be made by using Monel metal, and, if so, how much?

9.32 How many pounds of aluminum are contained in a ton of bauxite?

9.33 Why is lead useful in storage batteries?

9.34 How much tin is contained in 100 lb of cassiterite?

9.35 Compare the capacities of copper, aluminum, zinc, nickel, and structural steel for resisting dynamic loading.

9.36 Approximately how many pounds of magnesium are contained in a ton of the brine from which the metal is obtained?

9.37 Prepare a list, in order of increasing moduli of elasticity, of the principal metals discussed in Chapter 9.

9.38 Which metal or alloy discussed in Chapter 9 has the greatest modulus of resilience?

9.39 A certain structural-steel member is designed to carry a static tensile load of 40,000 lb with a factor of safety of 3 with respect to failure by rupture. (a) Assuming no difference in the cost of fabrication, determine what price the manufacturers could afford to pay per pound of metal if Duralumin were used instead of structural steel at 5 cents per pound? (b) What price could they afford to pay for a magnesium alloy?

9.40 A certain structural member 3 ft long is to carry at times a gradually applied tensile load of 100,000 lb, and at other times it must withstand an impact load of 500 ft-lb without inelastic action occurring. (a) Select the most economical material on the basis of weight, and (b) determine the required cross-sectional area.

9.41 A steel beam in a bridge is found to be too weak to carry the load imposed upon it. The beam could be strengthened satisfactorily by fastening cover plates to the top and bottom of the beam. In an attempt to keep the added weight as small as possible, magnesium-alloy plates have been suggested. Would they be satisfactory? If so, how should they be attached? If they are not satisfactory, what material should be used and how should it be attached?

9.42 Prepare a table of the nonferrous metals, giving for each its name, principal ore, source, principal steps in production from the ore, outstanding properties, uses, and cost.

9.43 Select a suitable metal for each of the following uses: (a) long-span electrical transmission line; (b) vat for containing sulfuric acid; (c) airplane wings; (d) propeller of a ship.

9.44 At what relative costs per pound will Duralumin and a magnesium alloy compete, if they are used to carry static loads in tension without inelastic action occurring?

9.45 Describe in a general way the effect of heat treatment of the magnesium alloys upon each of the following properties in tension: elastic strength, ultimate strength, endurance limit, modulus of resilience, and modulus of toughness.

9.46 By what percentage may the weight of a member be reduced by using an appropriate magnesium alloy instead of structural steel, if the member is to carry an axial tensile load of 40,000 lb with a factor of safety of 2 with respect to failure by slip?

9.47 Specify a metal suitable for each of the following uses: (a) rheostat; (b) bearing for aircraft engine; (c) pump for handling sea water; (d) valves in a high-pressure steam line.

9.48 Compare the weights of a structural-steel member and a suitable magnesium-alloy member to be used in resisting an axial dynamic load with the same factor of safety with respect to failure by slip.

9.49 Compare the modulus of toughness of each of the important light-weight structural alloys with that of structural steel.

9.50 Compare the relative electrical conductivities of copper, aluminum, and magnesium wire of the same diameter on the basis of (a) equal volume of material, (b) equal weight, and (c) equal nominal cost.

9.51 Specify a suitable metal for each of the following purposes: (a) marine engine parts; (b) permanent magnet; (c) material for joining cast-iron parts; (d) electrical fuse.

9.52 Indicate the probable relative strengths and ductilities of each of the following constituents of the copper-zinc alloys: α, β, γ, ϵ, η.

10 Timber

10.1 Uses of Timber

Unquestionably, timber was one of the first materials to be used for structural, and hence for engineering, purposes. Because of its availability in most parts of the world, the ease with which it is shaped, its beauty, its favorable strength-weight ratio, and its many other desirable properties, it has been used extensively throughout all periods of history—from the most remote evidences of civilization to the present. Probably no other engineering material has had a use so universal and so little dependent on the fluctuation of various phases of civilization.

Even at the present time, with a greater variety of materials available for engineering purposes than ever before, the annual consumption of timber in the United States exceeds the annual growth. The increasing number of uses of timber for construction and for other purposes, the mounting demand for wood pulp for paper and rayon, and the destruction of valuable trees by fire[1] consume over 50,000,000,000 board feet of timber each year.

10.2 Kinds of Wood

As about 180 different kinds of commercial wood are grown in the United States, and many other kinds are grown throughout the rest of the world, there is available a wide range of properties in woods. A few species, such as pine and oak, have properties which make them suitable for many different uses, while the properties of others, such as ebony and balsa, render them valuable for special purposes.

On a botanical basis, wood is often classified as *hardwood* or *softwood*. The term softwood is used to indicate wood coming from trees with needle-like leaves (usually cone-bearing, or conifers) and classified as gymnosperms; while the term hardwood is applied to wood coming from trees with broad leaves, which are classified as dicotyledons, or one type of angiosperms. The broad-leaved trees are usually deciduous. This botanical classification of trees as hardwood or softwood can be misleading in one sense, as some of the hardwoods are softer mechanically than certain of the softwoods.

---

[1] Over a billion board feet of standing timber are destroyed each year by fire.

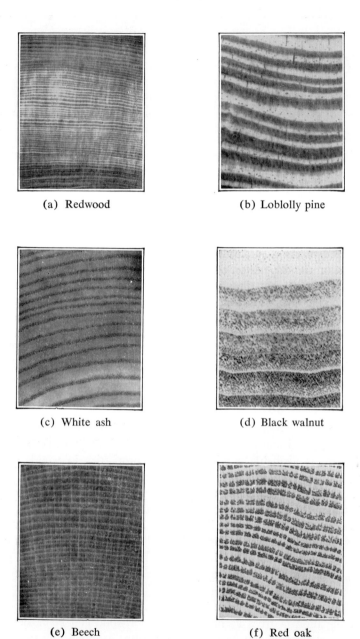

(a) Redwood   (b) Loblolly pine

(c) White ash   (d) Black walnut

(e) Beech   (f) Red oak

FIG. 10.1 Structure of wood.

The principal softwoods are pine, fir, spruce, hemlock, cedar, redwood, and cypress. They are found mainly in the Pacific Northwest, the Lake States, the New England States, the Appalachian Region, the Rocky Mountain Region, and the Atlantic and Gulf States. The principal hardwoods are oak, hickory, ash, poplar, maple, gum, mahogany, balsa, and walnut. They are grown generally throughout the eastern United States.

Trees may also be classified, according to the nature of growth, as *exogenous* or *endogenous*. Exogenous trees, which furnish practically all of the commercial timber, grow by the formation of rings of new fibers between the old wood and the bark, while the endogenous trees grow by the formation of new fibers which intermingle with the old. Palm and bamboo are about the only endogens having structural value, and the yuccas have been used in the manufacture of pulp.

10.3   Structure of Wood

Wood consists of fibers of cellulose, cemented together with lignin. These fibers are hollow cells, varying in length from about 0.03 to 0.10 in. in the hardwoods, and from about 0.10 to 0.25 in. in the softwoods, and have diameters of about one-hundredth of their length. In the softwoods the cells serve as conduits for the sap, while in the hardwoods the fibers are merely structural elements. The hardwoods also contain relatively larger cells called pores, or vessels, which carry sap. The softwoods do not contain pores for the transmission of sap, but do contain both longitudinal and horizontal resin ducts. Most wood cells grow longitudinally, in the direction of the grain, but others grow radially, in strips known as medullary rays. The medullary rays in oak are readily visible, while in pine they cannot be distinguished without a microscope.

In the exogens the new fibers are added between the bark and the old wood. The fibers which are added in the spring grow more rapidly than those which are added in the summer, and may be distinguished by their relatively larger size and thinner walls. The transition from spring wood to summer wood may be abrupt or it may be gradual. The structure depends on the growing conditions. For trees grown in a temperate climate the transition from the summer wood of one year to the spring wood of the next is easily noted. In most species the spring wood is less dense, softer, and weaker than the summer wood. The spring wood also shrinks less across the grain, and more along the grain, than does the summer wood.

For a few years after their formation the fibers take an active part in the life of the tree. Then they gradually become inactive but still retain their original strength. The active portion of the tree is known as sapwood, and the inactive portion as heartwood.

The differences in structure of the various woods serve to identify them. The width of the medullary rays, the pattern of the pores, the characteristics of the annual rings, and the color, odor, and weight are all factors which distinguish one wood from another. Figure 10.1 indicates few of the typical structures. The photographs were prepared by using a thin cross section of the wood as a negative. Therefore, the portions which are more porous appear darker in the photograph because they transmitted more light. Pores and resin ducts appear as dots, and fibers running radially appear as white streaks. The reproductions are approximately natural size.

In the *redwood* the annual rings are clearly visible, the darker portion of each ring indicating spring wood, and the lighter bands indicating the more dense and opaque summer wood. No medullary rays are visible.

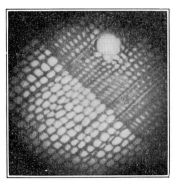

FIG. 10.2   Photomicrograph of section of red pine.

The *loblolly pine* shows a more rapid growth than the redwood, the annual rings being wider. Variations in the width of rings or in the relative percentages of spring wood and summer wood are due to variations in the growing conditions throughout the period represented. A few resin ducts may be seen scattered throughout the summer wood. The radial dark lines are not medullary rays, but are cracks in the wood caused by unequal shrinkage in drying.

In the *white ash,* pores are in evidence, and are in definite bands or rings, so that the wood is said to be ring porous. The pores are confined to the spring wood, and the bands of summer wood are comparatively wide, suggesting a dense, strong wood.

The *black walnut* shown has comparatively wide annual rings and widely distributed pore spaces.

In the *beech* specimen the light vertical strips indicate the presence of medullary rays. They are almost equal to the summer wood in spacing and width, and serve as reinforcement in a radial direction.

The *red oak* specimen shows a structure which is typical of the oaks—ring porous with medullary rays.

Figure 10.2 shows the appearance of a section of red pine under the microscope. The cross sections of the individual cells are plainly visible, the cell walls being thicker in the summer wood than in the spring wood, and one resin duct may be seen in the summer wood.

10.4 Production of Lumber

The first step in the production of lumber is the logging. In controlled areas the trees to be cut are carefully selected with regard to size and condition. They are usually cut in the fall or winter when there is a minimum of sap in the wood. After the trees have been felled, they are cut to convenient lengths and the branches are trimmed. The logs are then transported to the saw mill. In many places where streams are available, the logs are floated in large groups to the saw mill. In other places they are transported by trucks or other means.

At the saw mill the lumber is cut to standard sizes. Two methods of cutting are used: (1) If the boards are cut with the long dimension of the cross section approximately parallel to the annual rings, they are said to be *plain-sawed*, or *flat-grained*; (2) if the long dimension is approximately along a radius of the log, the board is *quarter-sawed* or *edge-grained*. Plain-sawed lumber involves less waste in cutting, is usually weakened less by knots, and does not collapse so easily in drying. Quarter-sawed lumber is subject to less shrinkage and warping in drying, is more impermeable to liquids, holds paint better in some species, and wears more evenly. The volume of lumber produced from a log is about one-third of the volume of wood in the log.

The third step in the production of lumber is the drying, also called seasoning. Lumber as it comes from the sawmill may contain as much as 35 per cent moisture. Under normal air conditions the wood will dry out until its moisture content reaches an equilibrium value, which depends on the temperature and humidity of the air.[2] Loss of moisture below 25 or 30 per cent is accompanied by shrinkage. Since a large shrinkage in the wood is undesirable after the wood is put into service, the lumber must be dried out or seasoned before it is marketed. This may be done by stacking the boards in the open so that the air may circulate freely about them, or may be done by placing them in kilns or ovens and drying them with artificial heat.

Lumber properly air-dried will contain from 6 to 24 per cent moisture, the amount depending on the locality; the average for the United States is

[2] The equilibrium value is about 9 per cent at a temperature of 70 F and a relative humidity of 50 per cent.

about 15 per cent.   The moisture content may be reduced to about 6 or 8 per cent by further drying in kilns at a temperature between 70 C (158 F) and 85 C (185 F).   If the rate of drying is too rapid the wood may warp or crack, while if it is dried too slowly it may decay or become stained.

The excess moisture may also be removed by chemical means.   Chemicals (such as urea) may be applied to the outside of the green wood, or the wood may be immersed in a solution.   The effect of the chemicals is to lower the vapor pressure, causing the water to move outward from the center of the log.   Chemical treatment is usually followed by kiln drying.   Use of this method is being extended rapidly, since it reduces both the seasoning loss and the time required for seasoning.   Timber which may require a year for air seasoning may be made ready for market in about one month by using chemical treatment.   Tests indicate that there is no essential difference in properties of air-dried, kiln-dried, and chemically-treated timber when each is properly done.

10.5   Defects in Lumber

Defects in lumber may be due to defects in the original wood or defects induced by improper cutting or seasoning.

Knots are caused by limbs growing out from the main section of the tree.   They are classified as round, oval, or spike, the type depending on whether the knot is a cross section, a diagonal section, or a longitudinal section of a limb.   The quality of the wood in a knot is usually equal to that in the rest of the piece, but the grain of the piece is distorted in passing around the knot, and cracks may open up around the knot in drying.   The discontinuity introduced by the knot has a greater effect upon the tensile strength of the section than upon the compressive strength.   Consequently, a knot near the bottom surface of a simple beam would be more undesirable than the same knot near the top surface of the beam.   Sound knots have little effect upon the shearing strength or upon the stiffness of a piece.

Cross grain (grain which is not parallel to the axis of the specimen) may be due to the manner of growth or to the method of cutting.   It is undesirable, since it lowers the ultimate compressive strength, toughness, modulus of rupture, and modulus of elasticity.

Compression wood is an abnormal growth appearing as wide eccentric annual rings which include a high percentage of summer wood.   Compression wood is denser and harder than normal wood, but since it is relatively weak and has a high shrinkage it is very undesirable.

Shakes are splits or cracks which are the result of damage during growth and which are often accentuated as a result of severe strains due to unequal shrinkage during drying. They are especially dangerous when located at mid-height of the end of a beam, as the beam must resist shear at that section in order to function properly.

Checks are cracks (usually parallel to the direction of the fibers) which are caused by shrinkage due to unequal drying rates in different directions. Whether or not a check weakens the structural element in which it appears depends on the type of stress developed near the check. A check will transmit compression but, of course, has no strength in tension or shear.

Rot or *decay* is visual evidence of a disintegration process usually caused by bacterial action. It has a pronounced weakening effect upon the material. Some species, such as redwood and cypress, are naturally resistant to rot and decay, but most species must be chemically treated, as described in section 10.12, to prevent disintegration.

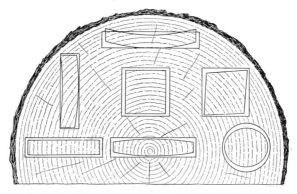

Fig. 10.3   Effect of method of sawing upon shrinkage.
[Reprinted from *Wood Handbook,* United States Department
of Agriculture (1955), p. 149]

Pitch pockets are inclusions of resin between the fibers. The amount by which they reduce the strength and alter the other properties depends on their size, number, and positions in the piece of timber.

Wane is the result of cutting too near the outside of the tree, bark being left on one edge of the stick of lumber.

Warping is a result of unequal volume change that is usually caused by a change in moisture content. Wood under ordinary conditions is practically always absorbing or giving off water to keep in equilibrium with the moisture content of the atmosphere. This moisture may be present as free water in the cells or as imbibed water in the cell walls. When the cell walls are saturated, but no free moisture is present, the wood is said to be at the fiber saturation point. For most woods this corresponds to a moisture content between 25 and 30 per cent.

Below the fiber saturation point, any change in moisture content is accompanied by a volume change in the wood. This volume change is proportional to the change in moisture content but is much greater along the annual rings than across the rings (radially) and is very small along the grain. Also, as has been indicated, the spring wood shrinks less across the grain and more along the grain than does the summer wood. These unequal rates of volume change in different directions, combined with the fact that the change in moisture content will be greater near the outside of a piece of wood than near the center, tend to cause warping of the piece, while the warping in turn may produce cracks. The amount of warping is dependent on the way in which the stick is cut from the log. For example, a plain-sawed piece is subject to greater warping than a quarter-sawed piece, as can be seen in Fig. 10.3.

10.6 Grades of Lumber

Because of the wide variation in quality obtainable in lumber, several sets of grading rules have been developed to aid the consumer in selecting the timber best adapted to his use. The grading rules are, in general, established on the basis of the number or size of defects in the wood, but may be established on the basis of working stress.

Under the rules adopted by the National Hardwood Lumber Association, the grade of a piece of lumber is determined by the percentage of the piece that may be cut into smaller standard pieces which are clear on one side, and sound—that is, free from shakes, rot, or other defects which would weaken them—on the opposite face. The grades, in order of decreasing quality, are Firsts, Seconds, Select, No. 1 Common, No. 2 Common, Sound Wormy, No. 3A Common, and No. 3B Common. To be classified as First Grade the lumber must be of such quality that $91\frac{2}{3}$ per cent of the surface can be cut into the smaller standard pieces. The Second Grade requires $83\frac{1}{3}$ per cent clear cuttings, while the No. 3B Common requires only 25 per cent. Firsts and Seconds are generally combined in one grade, known as "FAS."

While the classification and grading rules of softwoods are not completely standardized, softwood is usually divided into three types—yard lumber, structural timber, and factory or shop lumber.

Yard lumber is material less than 5 in. thick used for general building purposes, and it is graded on the basis of the entire piece. It includes finish lumber, graded as A select, B select, C select, and D select; boards (less than 2 in. thick) graded as No. 1, 2, 3, 4, or 5; and dimension lumber (from 2 to 5 in. thick) graded as No. 1, 2, or 3.

Grade A denotes a material practically free from defects, and grade B allows only a few small defects or blemishes. Both grades are suitable

#1 construction grade

#4 utility grade

for natural finishes. Grades C and D are suitable for finish where the wood is to be painted; grade C permits a few small blemishes which can be covered by paint, and grade D allows any number of blemishes or defects which do not detract from the appearance after painting.

Grade No. 1 includes sound, water-tight lumber with a limited number of blemishes, and No. 2 allows larger defects but may be considered grain-tight. Both grades are suitable for general use without waste. Three grades are recognized in lumber permitting waste. Grade No. 3 allows knotholes, No. 4 is a low-quality lumber that may contain holes and decay, and the only requirement for grade No. 5 is that it hold together under ordinary handling.

Structural timber includes joist and plank (less than 5 in. thick), beams and stringers (5 by 8 in. or larger), and posts and timbers (6 by 6 in. or larger).

Factory or shop lumber is lumber used for special purposes such as door and window casings, cabinets, etc. It is graded as select, No. 1, No. 2, and No. 3.

10.7 Size of Lumber

Lumber is available in certain standard sizes of rectangular section, or in special shapes, such as flooring, ceiling, siding, shiplap, shingles, and molding of standardized dimensions.

Lumber is cut to certain nominal sizes, such as 2 in. by 4 in., when green. Because of waste in cutting, and shrinkage in drying, the dimensions of the rough-dry timber will be less than the nominal dimensions. For example, a nominal 2-in. by 4-in. piece must be at least $1\frac{3}{4}$ in. by $3\frac{5}{8}$ in. If the material is finished or dressed by planing, the size will again be decreased. The standard dressed softwood "2 by 4" is $1\frac{5}{8}$ in. by $3\frac{3}{4}$ in. Standard lengths are multiples of 2 ft, with a few exceptions.

The condition of the sides and edges is designated by the following code: S1E means surfaced or planed on one edge; S2S, surfaced on two sides; S1S2E, surfaced on one side and two edges; S4S, surfaced on all four sides.

Timber is commonly measured in board feet, and prices are quoted in terms of 1000 board feet. Each square foot of surface with a thickness of 1 in. or less on the basis of nominal dimensions comprises a board foot. For example, a "2 by 4" board 12 ft long contains 8 board feet.

10.8 Properties of Timber

All species of woods are composed of about 60 per cent cellulose and 28 per cent lignin. The remainder is made up of small quantities of several other materials which impart such properties as color, odor, and

TABLE 10.1

SPECIFIC GRAVITY–STRENGTH RELATIONS OF WOODS OF DIFFERENT SPECIES*

Property	Unit	Moisture Con.†	
		Green	Air-dry‡
Static bending			
Fiber stress at proportional limit	psi	$10,200G^{1.25}$	$16,700G^{1.25}$
Modulus of rupture	psi	$17,600G^{1.25}$	$25,700G^{1.25}$
Work to maximum load	in.-lb per cu in.	$35.6G^{1.75}$	$32.4G^{1.75}$
Total work	in.-lb per cu in.	$103G^2$	$72.7G^2$
Modulus of elasticity	1000 psi	$2,360G$	$2,800G$
Impact bending			
Fiber stress at proportional limit	psi	$23,700G^{1.25}$	$31,200G^{1.25}$
Modulus of elasticity	1000 psi	$2,940G$	$3,380G$
Height of drop	in.	$114G^{1.75}$	$94.6G^{1.75}$
Compression parallel to grain			
Fiber stress at proportional limit	psi	$5,250G$	$8,750G$
Maximum crushing strength	psi	$6,730G$	$12,200G$
Modulus of elasticity	1000 psi	$2,910G$	$3,380G$
Compression perpendicular to grain			
Fiber stress at proportional limit	psi	$3,000G^{2.25}$	$4,630G^{2.25}$
Hardness			
End	lb§	$3,740G^{2.25}$	$4,800G^{2.25}$
Radial	lb§	$3,380G^{2.25}$	$3,720G^{2.25}$
Tangential	lb§	$3,460G^{2.25}$	$3,820G^{2.25}$

  * From *Wood Handbook,* United States Department of Agriculture (1935), p. 60.
  † The properties and values should be read as equations; for example, modulus of rupture for green material $= 17,600G^{1.25}$, where G represents the specific gravity of oven-dry wood, based on the volume at the moisture condition indicated.
  ‡ 12 per cent moisture content.
  § The load required to embed a 0.444-in. ball to one-half its diameter.

resistance to decay. Despite the similarities in chemical content, woods from different species of trees have different properties. The differences in mechanical properties are due to differences in structure of the different kinds of wood. Even within one species the properties of timber are far more variable than the properties of different samples of most metals, because of the greater lack of physical homogeneity. In addition, wood is nonisotropic; that is, it has different properties in different directions. The number of knots and shakes, the amount of cross grain, and the presence of other defects have a pronounced influence upon the properties of a given specimen of timber. In general, a small clear test specimen will show higher strengths than will a larger specimen cut from the same piece of timber, because of the greater possibility of injurious defects in the larger specimen. The influence of defects in reducing strength is difficult to evaluate numerically, even when the position and extent of the defects are known. The general effects were noted in section 10.5.

    In addition to the influence of possible defects, the actual cell structure has a marked effect upon the properties. The specific gravity of the actual

TABLE 10.2

AVERAGE PROPERTIES OF A FEW COMMON WOODS WHEN GREEN*

Species	Rings per in.	Tang. Shrink. (%)	Prop. Lim.†		Ult. Str.†			Mod. of Elast.‡
			Comp.	Flex.	Comp.	Flex.	Shear	
Ash								
Black	24	7.8	1690	2600	2300	6000	860	1040
White	12	7.9	3190	5100	3990	9600	1380	1460
Cedar								
Alaska	28	6.0	2500	3800	3050	6400	840	1140
S. red	13	4.0	3910	5000	4360	8400	1190	930
Cypress								
Southern	20	6.2	3100	4200	3580	6600	810	1180
Fir								
Balsam	12	6.6	2080	3000	2400	4900	610	960
Douglas	16	7.4	2570	3800	3300	6800	840	1350
White	11	7.0	2390	3800	2710	5700	750	1030
Hemlock								
Eastern	17	6.8	2600	3800	3080	6400	850	1070
Western	17	7.9	2480	3400	2990	6100	810	1220
Hickory								
Pecan	11	...	4330	5500	4570	10300	1240	1400
True	19	12.6	2740	5600	3920	10500	1190	1340
Maple								
Black	17	9.3	2800	4100	3270	7900	1130	1330
Sugar	18	9.5	2850	5100	4020	9400	1460	1550
Oak								
Red	10	8.2	2360	4100	3440	8300	1210	1350
White	17	9.0	3090	4700	3560	8300	1250	1250
Pine								
Lodgepole ...	24	6.7	2110	3000	2610	5500	680	1080
Ponderosa ...	19	6.3	2070	3100	2400	5000	680	970
S. yellow	14	7.5	3430	5200	4300	8700	1040	1600
W. white	20	5.3	2430	3400	2650	5200	640	1170
Poplar								
Yellow	14	7.1	1930	3400	2420	5400	740	1090
Spruce								
Eastern	17	8.2	2130	3300	2570	5600	690	1070
Sitka	15	7.5	2240	3300	2670	5700	760	1230
Walnut								
Black	12	7.1	3520	5400	4300	9500	1220	1420

* From *Strength and Related Properties of Woods Grown in the United States,* United States Department of Agriculture, Technical Bulletin No. 479 (1935).
† Parallel to grain, in pounds per square inch.
‡ In bending, in units of 1000 psi.

material of which wood is composed is about 1.54 for all species. Hence, a cubic foot of solid wood fiber would weigh about 96 lb. However, nearly all woods are lighter than water, and some weigh as little as 20 lb per cu ft. The difference in weight is due to the differences in contained air resulting from differences in sizes of cells and differences in thicknesses

TABLE 10.3

AVERAGE PROPERTIES OF A FEW COMMON WOODS WHEN DRY*
[MOISTURE: 12 PER CENT (APPROX.)]

Species	Wt. (lb/ ft³)	Volum. Shrink. (%)	Prop. Lim.† Comp.	Prop. Lim.† Flex.	Ult. St.† Comp.	Ult. St.† Flex.	Ult. St.† Shear	Mod. of Elast.‡
Ash								
Black	34	15.2	4520	7200	5970	12600	1570	1600
White	42	13.3	5790	8900	7410	15400	1950	1770
Cedar								
Alaska	31	9.2	5210	7100	6310	11100	1130	1420
S. red	31	7.0	5190	7300	6570	9400	750	1170
Cypress								
Southern	32	10.5	4470	7200	6360	10600	1000	1440
Fir								
Balsam	25	10.8	3970	5200	4530	7600	710	1230
Douglas	31	11.2	5540	7400	6720	11200	1130	1640
White	26	9.4	3590	6500	5350	9300	930	1380
Hemlock								
Eastern	28	9.7	4020	6100	5410	8900	1060	1200
Western	29	11.9	5340	6800	6210	10100	1170	1490
Hickory								
Pecan	46	17.9	....	9300	9040	17100	1740	1790
True	48	19.2	....	8900	8000	18100	2110	1890
Maple								
Black	40	14.0	4600	8300	6680	13300	1820	1620
Sugar	44	14.9	5390	9500	7830	15800	2330	1830
Oak								
Red	41	16.3	2910	6000	6090	10900	1390	1490
White	48	15.8	4760	8200	7440	15200	2000	1780
Pine								
Lodgepole ...	29	11.5	4310	6700	5370	9400	880	1340
Ponderosa ...	28	9.6	4060	6300	5270	9200	1160	1260
S. yellow	41	12.2	6150	9300	8440	14700	1500	1990
W. white	27	11.8	4480	6200	5620	9500	850	1510
Poplar								
Yellow	28	12.3	3550	6100	3290	9200	1100	1500
Spruce								
Eastern	28	13.7	3700	6500	5470	9800	1080	1340
Sitka	28	11.5	4780	6700	5610	10200	1150	1570
Walnut								
Black	38	11.3	5780	10500	7580	14600	1370	1680

* From *Strength and Related Properties of Woods Grown in the United States,* United States Department of Agriculture, Technical Bulletin No. 479 (1935).

† Parallel to grain, in pounds per square inch.

‡ In bending, in units of 1000 psi.

of cell walls. Either the weight per cubic foot or the specific gravity may be taken as an index of the actual amount of wood fiber present. Since the strength of a piece of wood is due to the actual wood fiber present in the piece, the strength would be expected to vary directly with the specific gravity, or inversely with the pore space.

Tests made by the Forest Products Laboratory show that several properties are directly related to the specific gravity. Average values of the
properties for different species are shown in Table 10.1. Individual specimens, or average values from individual species, may vary appreciably in
properties from the values given.

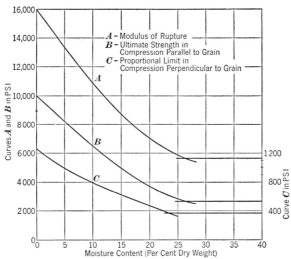

XFIG. 10.4 Effect of moisture content upon strength of Sitka
spruce. [From *Strength and Related Properties of Woods Grown
in the United States,* United States Department of Agriculture,
Technical Bulletin No. 479 (1935), p. 49]

Tables 10.2 and 10.3 also indicate that the moisture content of the
wood has an effect upon the properties. The nature of the variation for
Sitka spruce is shown in Fig. 10.4. Other species show the same general
trends, with the strength decreasing as the moisture content increases up to
the fiber saturation point. Addition of moisture above the fiber saturation
point has no influence upon the strength.

Below the fiber saturation point an increase in moisture content decreases the ultimate strength of wood, but it may also increase the amount
of deformation which the material will take before it reaches the ultimate.
In some cases the increase in deformation is sufficient to cause an increase
in the modulus of toughness, or the resistance to fracture under impact
loading. A large increase in moisture content will often cause a decrease
in the ultimate elongation, and a marked decrease in the modulus of
toughness.

Figure 10.5 shows average stress-strain diagrams from a series of specimens cut from the same stick of Douglas fir. The air-dry wood has a
lower ultimate strength, a higher unit strain at failure, and about the same

modulus of toughness as the oven-dry material. The saturated wood has a much lower ultimate strength and modulus of toughness, has a slightly lower modulus of elasticity, and reaches the ultimate strength at a lower unit strain than the air-dry material.

The strength is also dependent on the rate of loading and on the duration of the load. The modulus of rupture of a beam loaded very slowly or of a beam which has been under load over a period of several years is appreciably (about 40 per cent) less than the modulus of rupture as determined from a standard test of a few minutes duration. The same reduction in strength has been noted in wood loaded in compression parallel to the grain. The ultimate strength for long-time loading is approximately equal to the proportional limit in a short-time test.

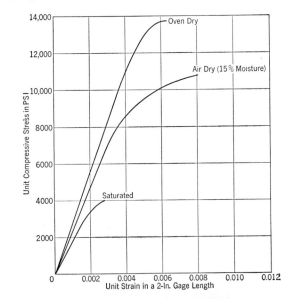

FIG. 10.5   Effect of moisture upon Douglas fir.

Because of the uncertainties involved in the defects, the nature and duration of loading, the moisture content, and other conditions, relatively high factors of safety are usually used for timber. Factors of safety of from 10 to 20 based on the ultimate strength of small, clear, dry specimens are not uncommon.

Some average stress-strain diagrams for timber are shown in Fig. 10.6, and properties of a few of the more common species are indicated in tables 10.2 and 10.3. The shearing strength is of particular importance in short beams, where failure by horizontal shear at the ends may be possible when the bending stresses at the middle of the beam are comparatively low.

Oven-dried wood is one of the best electrical insulating materials, having a resistance of about 10^8 ohms per cc. When saturated, the resistance of the timber approaches that of water—about 10^{-5} or 10^{-6} ohm per cc. The thermal conductivity of wood varies from about 0.33 to 1.20 Btu per hr per sq ft per in. per deg F. The coefficient of thermal expansion of wood varies with the species and the direction, ranging from about 1.1×10^{-6} to 3.6×10^{-6} per deg F along the grain and from 14.6×10^{-6} to 34.1×10^{-6} per deg F perpendicular to the grain. Of the common species, yellow birch has the lowest coefficient of thermal expansion. The limited number of tests which have been made indicate that the endurance limit of timber in bending is about 29 per cent of the modulus of rupture.

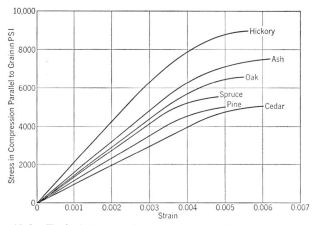

FIG. 10.6   Typical stress-strain diagrams for timber in compression.

As was indicated in Chapter 1, the most important considerations in selecting a material for a specific product are its durability, appearance, and cost. Timber in general, as a class of materials, compares favorably with other materials on the basis of all three items. Its durability is a function of its strength and its resistance to deterioration. As will be discussed later, resistance to deterioration may be increased by proper treatment. Its availability, workability, and low cost promote the use of timber as a temporary construction material, as well as for permanent installations.

Wood has long been used as a decorative material. Several species, such as mahogany, which are especially attractive in appearance are cut in very thin sections and used as veneer in covering cheaper, less attractive woods, particularly in furniture. In general, its capacity for fabrication by nailing and gluing is also a valuable characteristic of wood.

10.9 Principal Hardwoods

One of the most important of the so-called hardwoods is oak. Although there are about 60 species in the United States, the 15 species which are of commercial importance are commonly classified as either *red oak* or *white oak*. White oak is lighter in color than red oak and is somewhat more durable because the pores of the heartwood become plugged with a growth, making the material more impermeable to liquids. Oak is comparatively hard, stiff, and strong, and is used for flooring, interior trim, furniture, implements, piling, ties, and timber.

There are four important species of true *hickory* grown in the United States, and about four species of *pecan hickory*. Both varieties rank high in physical properties, with the true hickories superior to any other native wood in strength, stiffness, hardness, and toughness. They show considerable shrinkage in drying, and have low resistance to decay unless treated. Both types of hickory are extensively used for vehicle parts, such as spokes, rims, poles, and shafts, and for tool handles.

White, green, and black are the three principal species of *ash* used in the United States. White ash is widely used for agricultural-implement parts, and black ash, being somewhat softer and more easily worked, is suitable for furniture and crates.

There is only one principal variety of *poplar* (yellow poplar) in the United States. The wood is straight-grained and uniform, but is comparatively soft and weak. It is easily nailed and glued, and takes paint well. Planing-mill products, furniture, boxes, and crates are the principal uses of poplar, although it is also used in the construction of cars and other vehicles.

Several varieties of *maple* are of commercial importance, with sugar maple and black maple at the top of the list. The wood of maple is comparatively hard, strong, and stiff, and has a uniform texture. It is used for flooring, furniture, implements, and vehicle parts.

Black walnut is extensively used for cabinet work, furniture, veneer, and plywood. The wood is hard and strong, will take a good polish, and is easily worked.

Black gum is relatively hard and durable, and is used for bridge decks and other surfaces which are subjected to abrasive action.

10.10 Principal Softwoods

The principal commercial softwoods include the pines, firs, spruces, hemlocks, cedars, redwood, and cypress. Of these, pine is one of the most widely distributed and extensively used woods in the United States. Several species are of commercial importance.

Lodgepole pine is found in the western part of the United States. It is subject to decay in contact with the ground, but is easily treated. Since the trees are typically small, they are not usually sawed into lumber, but are cut into lengths for use as poles, mine props, and ties.

Northern white pine, found in the northern part of the United States, is a soft, uniform wood suitable for building construction. It is also used extensively in making patterns for castings.

Ponderosa pine, which grows in the western part of the United States, is a uniform, easily worked wood, suitable for general carpentry work and building construction. The treated wood is extensively used for railroad ties.

A number of closely related species are included in the general term, *southern yellow pine,* growing in the southeastern part of the United States. The wood, in general, is soft and easily worked, is light in weight, and holds paint well. It is extensively used for temporary construction, boxes, crates, and other general utility purposes.

Sugar pine, which grows in southern Oregon and California, is the largest of the pine trees. The lumber is soft and easily worked, and is extensively used in interior work.

Western white pine grows in the Northwest, and is very similar to northern white pine.

Balsam fir, which grows principally in New England, is widely used for general building construction.

White fir, which grows in Idaho and California, is a soft, straight-grained, easily worked wood, with little resistance to decay. It is used for general construction purposes in dwellings, and for general millwork.

Douglas fir, which grows in the western United States, is one of the most desirable native timbers for structural purposes. It is comparatively strong, hard, and durable, but is subject to checking.

Eastern spruce, which includes three species, grows in the northeastern United States. The wood is easily worked, but is not especially resistant to decay. It is used in general woodwork.

Sitka spruce, which is quite strong in comparison with its weight, grows along the Pacific Coast from California to Alaska. It is extensively used in airplane construction and for general dwelling construction.

Both *eastern hemlock* and *western hemlock* are extensively used in general construction work, in the form of siding, flooring, sheeting, and ceiling boards. They are also used in general millwork. Both species are nonresinous and straight-grained, contain small knots, and offer little resistance to decay.

The several species of *cedar* commonly used are of a fine uniform texture. The wood is resistant to decay and possesses a characteristic spicy odor. It is used for general construction, interior work, shingles, posts, poles, tanks, and boxes.

Redwood, which is native to the West Coast, is used extensively for structural purposes and is important because of its high resistance to rot.

Southern cypress grows in the southeastern United States and the lower Mississippi Valley. One of its important properties is its resistance to decay. It also holds paint well, and is used for general domestic construction.

Fig. 10.7   Decay in timber piles.

10.11   Deterioration of Timber

The principal agencies which may cause the deterioration of timber are decay, or rot, insects, marine borers, and fire. Protected from them, and from mechanical abrasion, timber will last almost indefinitely.

Decay, or rot, is the result of the activity of various bacteria and fungi, which utilize various portions of the wood as food. Since these organisms require both oxygen and excess moisture, timber which has a moisture content less than the fiber saturation point or timber which is continually submerged in water will not rot. Intermittent wetting provides the most favorable environment for rapid decay. Examination of untreated bridge piles, like those shown in Fig. 10.7, will often plainly reveal how decay has progressed on the portions of the timber near the water level, without affecting the higher or lower portions of the same piles. Certain species, including redwood and cypress, have a high natural resistance to decay, or rot.

Termites, which are sometimes called white ants but which are not ants at all, are the principal insect pests that attack wood. Termites are of two types. Those of one type, found in nearly every state, develop their colonies underground and build tunnels or tubes to the wood upon which they feed. Since they live in the dark, they eat out the interior of timbers, leaving only a thin outside shell undisturbed. Thus, much damage may have been done before they are discovered. Their activities may be prevented by the use of wood preservatives, or by keeping the timber well away from the ground by using brick, stone, or concrete foundations. The latter procedure is not entirely safe, as they may still build their tubes on the outside of the foundation to reach the wood.

Termites of the other class, called dry-wood termites, are found only in a narrow strip around the southern United States and up the Atlantic Coast. They do not depend upon moisture, as do the subterranean termites, and live in dry wood.

Certain species of beetles and ants will damage timber by digging tunnels through it, using the wood for living quarters rather than for food. Their activities may be prevented by the use of preservatives.

Several types of small mollusks and crustaceans, known as marine borers and found in salt or brackish water, will damage fixed or floating wooden structures. Most of them dig burrows into the wood, using it for food. In several places untreated timber piling has been completely destroyed in less than a year by the activities of marine borers. An insoluble preservative such as coal-tar creosote will serve to check, but will not always prevent, their activities.

10.12 Timber Preservatives

The resistance of wood to decay can be increased by the use of a preservative which will poison the fungi or other rot-producing agencies. *Paint* is not usually considered as a preservative, because it only protects the surface so long as the coating is unbroken. Since paint is weak mechanically, the film may be ruptured by abrasion, or by cracks resulting from shrinkage or expansion of the wood. Once the film is broken, decay may take place and proceed beneath the paint. The ordinary paints have no germicidal characteristics. There are three general classes of true wood preservatives: oily substances insoluble in water, water-soluble salts, and salts carried in a volatile solvent other than water. Only the first two classes are used extensively.

Coal-tar creosote is the most commonly used preservative, and is an example of substances of the first class. Many grades and types of creosote are readily available, and satisfactory results may be expected from any reasonably good grade. Creosote has the advantage of being insoluble in water, and of having a low volatility, which factors tend to make it a permanent preservative. It has the disadvantage of rendering the timber more inflammable for a time after treatment, of having a disagreeable odor, and of being difficult to cover with paint.

Zinc chloride is the most extensively used of the water-soluble preservatives. It is readily available, clean, and odorless. The treated timber may be painted over and is slightly more fire-resistant than the untreated timber. Chromated zinc chloride, containing $18\frac{1}{2}$ per cent sodium bichromate, seems to be more effective and more resistant to leaching than zinc chloride. Sodium fluoride, arsenic, copper sulfate, and mercuric chloride are other preservatives of the water-soluble class, but they are not used to a very great extent in the United States. All water-soluble salts have the disadvantage of leaching out if exposed to moisture.

10.13 Methods of Applying Preservatives

Before being treated with a preservative, timber should be thoroughly seasoned, as cells already filled with water cannot absorb preservative. Round timber should be peeled, as even the thin inner bark may prevent penetration. The timber should, of course, be cut to size before being treated. Sometimes wood that resists penetration is incised by running it through rolls fitted with teeth which penetrate into the wood about $\frac{1}{2}$ in.

The simplest method of applying the preservative is by painting the timber or by simply immersing the timber in a tank of the liquid. If the timber is left in the preservative less than 15 minutes, the temperature of the bath should be about 200 F to 230 F to increase the penetration. Even then the penetration does not usually exceed $\frac{1}{16}$ in. The efficiency of the open-tank process may be increased by leaving the timber in the heated preservative for several hours and then cooling it slowly in the preservative. With this method the penetration will vary from $\frac{1}{8}$ in. to 1 in., the distance depending on the type of timber.

A greater degree of penetration may be obtained by the use of the so-called pressure processes, in which the preservative is forced into the wood by pressure instead of being allowed to penetrate by absorption. Either the full-cell or the empty-cell process may be employed.

In the *full-cell process* the timber is placed in an air-tight cylinder, and a vacuum is applied to remove as much air from the wood as possible. The cylinder is then filled with preservative without admitting air, and a pressure of 100 to 200 psi is applied. When the timber contains the desired amount of preservative, the cylinder is subjected to a low vacuum to remove the excess preservative from the surface. A cubic foot of timber will retain a maximum of about 20 lb of creosote. That amount is desirable where the timber is to be used in salt water. For other uses, from 10 to 16 lb of creosote per cubic foot of wood is generally sufficient. Less zinc chloride is required for the same degree of protection.

The *empty-cell process* is similar to the full-cell process, except that the initial vacuum is not applied, no attempt being made to remove the air from the cells. This process has the advantage of obtaining a deep penetration with a relatively low net retention of preservative. A retention of from 6 to 12 lb per cubic foot is common for creosote.

The ordinary wood preservatives have little or no effect upon the mechanical properties of timber. However, if the treatment process is not properly carried out, it may decrease both the strength and the stiffness. Excessive temperatures and pressures, which may destroy or weaken the cell walls, are the principal sources of difficulty.

10.14   Fire Resistance

Since one of the major disadvantages of timber is the ease with which it burns, as compared with other structural materials, various methods have been devised to increase the resistance of timber to damage by fire. The problem has been approached in two ways: the development of "slow-burning" construction, and the investigation of fire-resistant chemicals with which the wood may be treated.

Since a smooth surface does not ignite readily, the aim of fire-resistant design is to provide the necessary strength with the minimum surface exposure. Usually fire-resistant design is supplemented by the use of an automatic sprinkler system. Other design features such as fire stops are an aid in making timber construction fire-resistant.

The fire resistance of the wood itself may be increased by the use of surface treatments or by impregnation. Special paints have been developed which, when applied in thick continuous coatings, are of value in delaying ignition. Ordinary paints, varnishes, and lacquers offer no protection against fire.

Diammonium phosphate, monoammonium phosphate, monomagnesium phosphate, and phosphoric acid are among the most satisfactory chemicals for making wood fire-resistant. Processes similar to the preservative treatments are used to apply the chemicals.

10.15   Plywood

The term plywood denotes panels composed of two or more sheets of wood glued together, with the grain of one or more sheets at right angles to the grain of the others. An odd numbers of plies, usually three or five, is used to reduce the tendency to warp with changes in moisture content. Compared with solid wood, plywood is more nearly isotropic and has greater resistance to checking, splitting, and warping. The flexural strength of plywood tends to become the average of the strengths of the component sheets parallel to the grain and across the grain, while the shearing strength is usually greater than the shearing strength of the component sheets.

Plywood is extensively used for partitions and paneling, and is finding application as exterior wall surfaces for building construction, railroad cars, and trucks. It is also important in aircraft construction because of its strength-weight ratio, which compares favorably with that of many of the metals. In some cases it may be superior to metals, because a thicker section which is more resistant to buckling is required to produce a given load-carrying capacity. It is even used for tubing.

Woods commonly used for plywood elements in aircraft construction (either alone or in combination) are birch, yellow poplar, mahogany, sweet gum, and Douglas fir. Three-, five-, seven-, nine-, and eleven-ply sections are utilized. The plies may be prepared by slicing the log in thin sections, or by placing the log in a lathe and arranging a cutter to peel off a continuous thin layer as the log is rotated and thus produce a quarter-sawed section.

With the recent development of waterproof and weather-resistant glues, a number of which are thermosetting plastics, the usefulness of plywood has been greatly increased. Laminated or built-up structural units are prepared by gluing together lengths of small clear stock, usually 1 in. by 1 in. or 1 in. by 2 in., to form beams, columns, girders, and arches. Wood in small sections may readily be bent to the desired shape before gluing. Hence, it is possible to produce long-span arches suitable for hangars, auditoriums, and similar structures where intermediate columns would be undesirable. In general, the glued sections are much stronger than the wood itself.

10.16 Processed Wood

In addition to plywood, there have been developed several other wood products which have more desirable properties for special applications than the natural material. Known as processed woods, they are produced by impregnating the wood with a plastic or resin; by compressing the wood to increase its density; by reducing the wood to fiber and recombining the fibers; or by combinations of these methods. In general, the product is more uniform than the original wood. Several commercial products have been developed.

Impregnated wood. The strength and durability of wood may be increased appreciably by impregnating it with a resin. Phenol, formaldehyde, and furfural formaldehyde are the most commonly used resins, although urea, methylolurea, or lignin may also be used. The resin may be introduced by simply soaking the wood in it for several days; by spreading the resin on the surface and applying pressure; or by a process similar to that employed in the application of preservatives. When the pores, resin ducts, or cells are filled with resin, there is little opportunity for moisture absorption; hence the resultant product will not be subject to shrinkage or swelling under normal atmospheric conditions.

Impregnated woods, such as Impreg and Uralloy A and C, are used for airplane parts, cabinets, boats, and other exposed parts.

Compressed wood. Lignin, the natural cementing material in wood, becomes plastic at elevated temperatures. This characteristic is utilized in producing a strong dense wood product by subjecting the wood to pressure at elevated temperatures. Under a pressure of approximately 250 psi the density of the wood will be increased about 50 per cent. However, with this treatment the tendency of the wood to absorb moisture is not entirely eliminated. Hence the product is subject to some dimensional change under normal atmospheric conditions.

The commercial products, such as Staypak, are used for packaging as well as for a number of structural applications.

Impregnated and compressed wood. A combination of the two preceding processes results in a product which is strong and relatively light. The addition of resin seals the wood against the absorption of water, thereby increasing its resistance to dimensional change, and with proper application of resin the specific gravity is not unduly increased. Wooden members having tensile strengths as high as 42,000 psi have been produced by this method. However, the toughness is decreased by the addition of resin. A number of commercial products have been developed by using this technique, among them being Compreg, Presdwood, Pregwood, Panelyte, and Tegowood. Such woods are used for airplane propellers, electrical equipment, and even for gears and machine parts.

Hydrolized wood. The preceding three processes utilize the wood fibers in their natural form. However, since the fibers are hollow, the density of the resulting product does not reach the maximum possible value. A more dense product may be obtained by exploding the fibers with steam pressure and pressing them into sheets and boards or molding them. This technique makes possible the utilization of wood chips and pulp instead of the usual structural lumber. The material thus produced has a high density and is suitable for use in machine parts, building panels, wallboards, and similar units.

Stabilized wood.   Stabilized wood is wood which has been subjected to any of a number of chemical treatments designed to increase resistance to rot, resistance to fire damage, resistance to volume change under varying atmospheric conditions, and resistance to abrasion.   Several processes, most of which involve impregnation of the wood with suitable chemicals, have been developed.

Reconstituted wood.   Reconstituted wood is wood in which a structure more nearly isotropic than the original wood is obtained by cutting the wood into chips or other small particles and then combining the randomly oriented chips with a binding material.   The original lignin may be used as the binding material, or a resin (usually phenolic), may be added. Heat and pressure are required in the recombination.

The texture of the finished product depends on the size of the wood particles used.   These may vary from chips one-half inch or more in diameter to sawdust.   When fine particles, such as wood fibers or sawdust, are used the resulting product is sometimes called hardboard.

10.17   Wood Pulp and Paper

The preceding products have been based on the entire wood, cellulose and lignin.   A closely allied class of products is obtained by using wood as the source of cellulose and discarding the lignin.   The raw cellulose produced from wood is known as wood pulp.   After it is processed into a thin sheet of fibers it is called paper or fiberboard.

The lignin is dissolved from the ground wood by a chemical treatment. Caustic soda is normally employed for the reduction of hardwoods to pulp, while calcium bisulphite or a mixture of alkaline sulphides is used for softwoods.   The resultant wood pulp may be bleached to remove the brownish color, and it then serves as a source of raw material for cellulose or as a filler and reinforcement in plastics.   Wood pulp is also used as filter material, in detergents, as the fibrous component in leatherlike materials, and as a constituent of a mixture for coating welding rods.

The pulp may be converted to alpha cellulose by chemical purification. The alpha cellulose is dissolved and reprecipitated in the manufacture of nitrocellulose, cellophane, rayon, and other cellulose-base products.

In the manufacture of paper the fibrous pulp is suspended in water and run onto a fine screen which permits the water to drain away.   The resulting thin layer of fibers is removed and dried to form the product called paper, paperboard, or fiberboard, depending on the thickness of the sheet. Asphaltum, resins, wax, or other waterproofing agents may be introduced into the product to make it water-resistant.

Wood-base paper is widely used in the production of industrial wrapping and packaging materials, newsprint, wrapping for electrical conductors, dielectrics, conduits, and underground piping. Other grades of paper are made from cotton, linen, asbestos, and glass fibers. Glaze and other smooth finishes are produced on paper such as that used in quality magazines, by treating the surface with a clay suspension or by incorporating a metal foil into the surface.

10.18 Cork

Cork is obtained from the bark of a species of oak grown commercially in Spain, Portugal, and other Mediterranean countries. The bark can be stripped from the trees every eight to ten years. It is then seasoned and boiled to remove certain soluble constituents.

Because of its high resiliency, cork is used for gaskets and bottle stoppers. When ground and mixed with linseed oil it forms the principal constituent of linoleum. Its low thermal conductivity makes it suitable for use as an insulating material. It is incorporated into life preservers because of its resistance to water and its low specific weight. It is also useful in sound-absorption and vibration-absorption units.

10.19 Importance of Timber

Timber or wood is used in almost every branch of engineering. It may be considered the standard material for temporary construction in many different fields; and, in addition to its many applications in structural and architectural engineering, it is widely used in mechanical-, electrical-, and railway-engineering applications. In the field of chemical engineering it is of importance because of its potentialities as a basic material in the manufacture of many new materials.

Only when the properties of wood are understood can it be properly used in these many fields, and only when all of the knowledge of the relationship between environment and the structure of the wood is considered can the material be used with its maximum degree of effectiveness and economy. The engineering profession has need of men with a knowledge of timber.

PROBLEMS

10.1 Prepare a table giving values of the elastic strength, ultimate strength, and modulus of elasticity of each of the woods shown in Fig. 10.6.

10.2 Determine the area of a hickory member 10 in. long required to absorb without fracture the energy from a 50-lb weight dropped 10 in. onto the top of the member when the 10-in. dimension is vertical. Assume the energy load to be uniformly distributed.

10.3 Compare the relative resistances of structural steel, gray cast iron, hickory, and pine to failure by fracture under impact loading.

10.4 A 2 in. by 2 in. by 8 in. block of air-dry Douglas fir is subjected to a static axial load of 16,000 lb. (a) Determine the factor of safety with respect to failure by slip. (b) Determine the factor of safety with respect to failure by fracture. (c) How much will the block shorten under the 16,000-lb load?

10.5 Specify a suitable timber preservative and method of application for each of the following uses: (a) telephone pole; (b) piling for a pier in Boston harbor; (c) railroad tie; (d) factory interior.

10.6 Assuming the compressive characteristics of structural steel to be the same as the tensile characteristics, compare the weights of a steel member and an oak member which are to (a) have the same volume, (b) carry the same static load without slip, (c) carry the same energy load without fracture.

10.7 If structural steel costs 6 cents per pound and spruce costs $50 per 1000 board feet, which will be the more economical material to use for structural compressive members that have a factor of safety of 6 with respect to failure by slip? Assume the properties of structural steel in compression to be the same as those in tension.

10.8 Compare the strength-weight ratios of aluminum alloy 2017-T4 and oak on the basis of (a) elastic strength, (b) ultimate strength, and (c) modulus of toughness.

10.9 An 8-in. length of nominal "2 by 4" dressed Sitka spruce carries a static axial compressive load of 10,000 lb. What is the factor of safety with respect to failure by fracture if the wood contains 5 per cent moisture?

10.10 What is the factor of safety of the block in problem 10.9 if it absorbs 0.20 lb of water?

10.11 Determine the strength-weight ratio (expressed in inches) of each of the woods in Table 10.3 for the ultimate compressive strength parallel to the grain.

10.12 A "4 by 4" pecan-hickory member 3 ft long carries a static axial compressive load with a factor of safety of 8 with respect to failure by fracture. Could the weight of the member be decreased without altering the factor of safety by using ash or oak?

10.13 Select a suitable wood for, and determine the required cross-sectional area of, an airplane part which is to carry an axial compressive load of 10,000 lb with a factor of safety of 1.75 with respect to slip.

10.14 How much will a 1-ft length of a dressed nominal "2 by 4" yellow-poplar member shorten under an axial compressive load for which the factor of safety with respect to failure by slip is 3?

10.15 A 6-in. square Douglas-fir member is to be loaded in tension by means of a 1-in. bolt through the member near each end. How far from each end should the bolts be placed in order to develop a tensile stress of 800 psi in the center portion of the member?

10.16 If an allowable working stress of 1000 psi in compression parallel to the grain is specified for oak and western hemlock, what are the factors of safety with respect to slip and fracture when the wood is green and when dry?

10.17 A dressed nominal "2 by 2" block of wood 6 in. long weighs 160 grams when its moisture content is 12 per cent. Approximately what axial compressive load might it be expected to carry with a factor of safety of 4 with respect to failure by slip?

10.18 How much would the block of the preceding problem be expected to shorten under an axial compressive load of 2640 lb?

10.19 A "6 by 6" black-walnut block 8 in. long contains 81 per cent moisture and weighs 9.68 lb when green.   What will be its weight and specific gravity when dry if the fiber saturation point is 25 per cent?

10.20 Tabulate values of all properties which may be obtained from the stress-strain diagrams of Douglas fir when saturated, air-dry, and oven-dry.

10.21 Specify a wood and suitable treatment for each of the following uses: (a) floor of dwelling house; (b) top of table in laboratory; (c) shingles; (d) window frames.

10.22 Specify a suitable wood and method of treatment for each of the following uses: (a) highway bridge; (b) ribs of a canoe; (c) wagon tongue; (d) hammer handle.

11 Stone

11.1 Uses of Stone

Stone has been one of the most important engineering materials since prehistoric times. Its strength, durability, and pleasing appearance have combined to make it one of the most popular materials for the construction of public and monumental works from the time of the erection of the Great Pyramid of Cheops to the present.

The Egyptians and Greeks used stone extensively for buildings, and the Romans developed the construction of stone highways, aqueducts, and bridges. During the Middle Ages stone was the principal material used in the construction of the great cathedrals of Europe. Even with the present intensive competition of other materials, stone is extensively used for structures such as building walls, bridges, and dams; for concrete aggregate; for road surfacing, either in the form of paving blocks or as crushed rock; and for roofing material.

Granite, limestone, sandstone, marble, and slate are the principal building stones in use today. In the United States the amounts of the foregoing materials produced in 1952 were approximately 519,000, 787,000, 352,000, 89,000, and 146,000 tons, respectively.

More than three-fourths of all the limestone used in the United States comes from the Bedford deposits in Indiana, while the principal sources of granite are in New England and other eastern states. Ohio, New York, and Pennsylvania are the leading sources of sandstone, although workable deposits are found in many other localities. Marble is produced in quantity both in the New England States and in Georgia. Pennsylvania, Vermont, Maine, New York, and Virginia are the principal slate-producing states. Practically every state produces some useful building stone.

Stone may be classified, on the basis of use and shape, as building stone, cobbles, crushed stone, gravel, sand, and flagstones. *Building stones* are hewn to a more or less regular shape to permit them to be used as building blocks, or they may be carefully shaped to meet some architectural need. The term *cobbles* applies to large pieces of stone of irregular shape used as aggregate in mass concrete, and *cobblestones* are roughly shaped pieces which are used for paving in some places. *Crushed stone* is stone which has been mechanically reduced in size to irregular shapes suitable for concrete aggregates and road surfacing. *Gravel* is stone which has been reduced in size by natural means—usually by the grinding action occurring in stream beds. It also is used for concrete aggregates, and as a road metal. Particles of crushed stone and gravel usually vary from about $\frac{1}{4}$ in. to $2\frac{1}{2}$ in. in diameter. Water-worn particles which will pass through a sieve having 4 openings per linear inch in each direction are generally called *sand*, although the distinction between sand and gravel is entirely arbitrary. Stones which are split into relatively thin sheets and used for walks or paving are often called *flagstones*.

A grand total of over 300,000,000 tons of stone was sold in the United States in 1952.

11.2 Preparation of Building Stone

The two principal steps in the preparation of building stone for use are quarrying and finishing.

In the quarrying operation the overburden of soil or inferior stone is first removed from the surface. If large blocks of stone are desired, a channeling machine is used to make vertical cuts to a depth of 10 or 12 ft at the desired intervals. The resulting blocks, perhaps 2 ft by 4 ft by 12 ft high, are loosened at the bottom by wedging or undercutting and are removed by cranes. Then they are cut to shape and given whatever degree of finishing is desired.

The shaping and finishing may be done by hand or by saws, planers, lathes, and grinders similar in general construction to those used in metal work. The stone as finally used may be rough (that is, in the form in which it came from the quarry); it may be roughly dressed and squared, requiring a mortar joint at least $\frac{1}{2}$ in. thick; or it may be accurately shaped and finely finished. The treatment depends on the use to which the stone is to be put.

11.3 Types of Stone

The suitability of a given stone for a particular engineering use depends on the relationship between the requirements of that use and the properties of the stone. The properties, in turn, are dependent upon the chemical and physical structure of the stone.

Chemical structure. While many different chemical structures are found in stones, there are three general groups of interest to the engineer.

1. *Silica* (SiO_2). Silicon dioxide is one of the important constituents of many stones. Hydrofluoric acid is the only acid in which it will dissolve, so it is durable as far as weathering by chemical disintegration is concerned.

However, the cementing or bonding material holding the SiO_2 crystals or molecules together is often subject to disintegration when the SiO_2 is stable. Quartz, which is one of the principal constituents of granite, and quartzite are composed of silica, and sandstone is principally silica. Stones which are predominantly silica are sometimes called siliceous stones.

2. *Silicates of alumina.* Complex silicates of alumina, associated with sodium, potassium, calcium, magnesium, or iron, form another important group of constituent minerals. While their chemical properties depend upon their exact chemical composition, the minerals in this group are in general much less durable than silica, being somewhat soluble in dilute acids.

Feldspar, the second principal constituent of granite, is in this class, while shale and slate are principally silicates of alumina. Clay is derived chiefly from the disintegration of this type of mineral. Stones which are composed mostly, but not entirely, of clayey minerals are known as argillaceous stones.

3. *Calcium carbonate* ($CaCO_3$). Calcium carbonate, and sometimes magnesium carbonate, is an important ingredient of some building stones. The material is soluble in dilute acids. This characteristic makes it susceptible to disintegration in a moist, smoke-laden atmosphere, since the sulfur dioxide of the smoke will form sulfurous acid when dissolved in water. Limestone and marble are the principal building stones in the calcium-carbonate, or calcareous, group.

Physical structure. Stone may be classified on a physical basis in three groups. The classification is based on the geological processes which have been involved in the formation of the rock.

1. *Igneous.* Igneous rock is that which has been formed by cooling from the molten state. Some types of igneous rocks are dense and glassy, while other types are very porous. Granite, lava, and basalt are of igneous formation.

2. *Sedimentary.* Sedimentary rock is that which has been formed by a process of cementation of small particles which have been deposited in layers by the action of wind and water. Sedimentary rocks usually display characteristic bedding planes, or planes along which they are easily split, corresponding to the layers formed during the sedimentation process. The characteristics of the stone depend largely upon the cementing material. Sandstone and limestone are sedimentary rocks.

3. *Metamorphic.* Metamorphic rock is that which has been formed from igneous or sedimentary rock by the action of heat or pressure. Marble, formed from limestone, and slate, formed from shale, are the principal building stones in the metamorphic group.

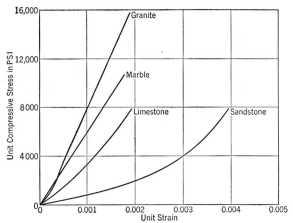

FIG. 11.1   Examples of stress-strain diagrams for stone.

11.4   Properties of Stone

Since stone is a nonhomogeneous material, the properties determined from tests on two samples from the same quarry may not be in agreement. Nevertheless, certain general trends and average values may be indicated as being statistically correct.   The general type of stress-strain diagram for stone in compression is indicated in Fig. 11.1, while Table 11.1 gives some average values of other properties.   The modulus of rupture, or ultimate strength in bending, is important in stones to be used as lintels.

TABLE 11.1

AVERAGE PHYSICAL PROPERTIES OF DRY BUILDING STONES

Stone	Ult. Comp. Str. (ksi)	Porosity (%)	Weight (lb per cu ft)	Thermal Coeff. Ex. $(10^{-6}/F)$	Mod. of Rupture (ksi)	Ult. Sh'r Str. (ksi)
Limestone	3–28	0.3–20	139–168	0.6–4.7	0.5–4.7	1.0–2.8
Granite	15–30	0–1	156–177	3.1–4.2	1.2–4.0	1.8–3.8
Sandstone	7–20	5–28	133–160	3.2–6.9	0.5–2.5	1.0–2.5
Marble	10–26	0.2–0.6	160–170	2.0–5.6	1.0–3.0	1.0–5.6
Slate	7–30	0.1–0.7	172–177	5.1	7–10	2.0–3.5

Figure 11.2 shows the average relationship between the ultimate compressive strength and the porosity (as measured by the absorption) of a wide variety of building stones.[1]   The line represents the average values as obtained from tests on a large number of specimens.   *Individual stones may give results widely different from the averages.*   The decrease in strength with an increase in porosity is logical since, in general, increased

[1] J. H. Griffith, *Physical Properties of Typical American Rocks,* Iowa Engineering Experiment Station Bulletin 131 (1937).

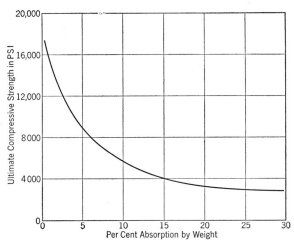

Fɪɢ. 11.2   Effect of porosity upon strength of dry stone.

porosity means less actual material per unit volume.   The same trend for timber has been discussed in section 10.8, and it also holds for the modulus of rupture of stone.

The porosity cannot be an absolute measure of either density or strength, because it is based on absorption—which in turn is dependent upon the shape, size, and distribution of voids.   For example, a stone having a low density may have a low porosity if the pores on the surface are relatively small and shallow and do not connect with additional pore space in the interior.   Some volcanic materials may have a relatively low density, but, being glazed on the outside, will have a low porosity.   The opposite is also true; that is, a stone with a high density may have a high porosity if the pores are relatively large and are interconnecting.   However, if the nature and distribution of the pores are comparable in different specimens of a given type of stone, porosity may be useful as an index of strength.

For a given specimen, the strength decreases as the moisture content increases.   Figure 11.2 and Table 11.1 are based on specimens that are dry at test.

Because of the variability in properties of different samples of stone from the same quarry, and because of the relatively low resistance to impact, a factor of safety between 15 and 25 is common for building stones.   The strength of stone masonry is much less than the strength of the stone itself, the exact strength depending on the width of joint and the type of mortar used.

Durability, appearance, and cost are the principal factors which are considered in the selection of the most suitable material for a given use.

For some uses (such as the walls of an office building), stone is usually considered to be more attractive than other materials with which it may be competing, whereas its cost is usually greater, so the problem of selection often becomes one of balancing high initial cost against durability and superior appearance.

11.5 Durability of Stone

Durability, representing resistance to immediate or future failure due to all destructive forces to which the stone may be subjected, is directly related to the physical properties, which in turn are functions of the physical and chemical characteristics of the stone.

Physical characteristics, such as bedding planes (formed during the deposition of material in the sedimentary rocks), cracks, inclusions, and pore spaces, have an extremely important effect upon durability, since any discontinuity in the material tends not only to weaken it structurally, as indicated in Fig. 11.2, but—of still more importance—to provide openings for the forces of disintegration. For example, if water is absorbed in stone and subsequently freezes, it will expand; the forces thus developed will cause the stone to crack or spall; and the porosity will be increased. Repetition of the action will then be made easier, and the damage will increase with each repetition. The leaching action of water which is not chemically combined may remove cementing materials from the stone and weaken it structurally.

The chemical composition of stone also influences its durability. The calcareous stones are subject to decomposition by acids which may be formed by the combination of moisture and gases, such as sulfur dioxide, which may be present in the air. A sandstone in which the cementing material is calcium carbonate may disintegrate under such action, whereas a silicate would be more resistant. The chemical composition will also give some indication of the fire resistance of a given stone. The carbonates, for example, begin to disintegrate at a lower temperature than the silicates. A high coefficient of expansion tends to decrease durability, particularly in the event of a fire.

If building stones are to be used in a moist environment, they may be treated to decrease the porosity and to protect the surface against the corrosive action of the atmosphere. Boiled linseed oil and paraffin have been used with success as a protective coating, although the application must be renewed every few years. Ransome's process, in which a coating of calcium chloride is applied after the pores have been filled with sodium silicate, produces a strong, durable surface.

The texture, or size of grain, is of importance with regard to both appearance and durability. In general, a fine-grained stone will be stronger and more durable than a coarse-grained stone.   Both the strength and the durability of stone masonry are dependent on the characteristics of the mortar joints between individual stones.   In general, the mortar is weaker than the stone, and is more vulnerable to forces of disintegration.

11.6   Limestone

The term limestone is applied to those sedimentary stones which are composed primarily of calcium carbonate or calcium-magnesium carbonate. There are many varieties, but the Bedford limestone is the most widely used in the United States.

Iron sulfide is an objectionable impurity which may be present in limestone.   It not only stains the stone by forming a brown oxide but sets free sulfuric acid which is harmful to the carbonate.

Most limestones may be worked easily because of the bedding planes produced during their formation.   The average absorption for the Bedford limestones is about 4 or 5 per cent.   The combination of workability and low porosity makes it a suitable stone for exterior building construction, bridge work, and stone masonry in general.   Its resistance to fire below 900 C (1652 F), the temperature at which CO_2 is driven off, is fair, although a combination of heat and water may cause it to spall badly.

In addition to its use as a building stone, limestone is employed extensively in the manufacture of ferrous metals and cement, and is widely used as aggregate for concrete.

11.7   Marble

Marble is similar to limestone chemically, but has been subjected to a metamorphic process which has made it more crystalline in structure, harder, and better able to hold a polish.

Iron pyrites or mica, in the form of small scales, may be present as impurities.   Not only do they form blotches on the finished surface, but they also disintegrate easily, pitting the surface.

Marble is extensively employed for decorative stone work, both interior and exterior, although the lighter grades are easily soiled by dust and smoke.   Marble is also used for monuments, and, to an increasing extent, for ordinary structural work, particularly buildings.   Its resistance to abrasion makes it suitable for wear-resisting surfaces, such as floors and steps, but it becomes slick when wet.

11.8   Granite

Granite is an igneous rock composed of quartz and feldspar.   Mica may also be present, but is not particularly harmful in small quantities. In larger quantities it sets up planes of structural weakness and provides a starting point for disintegration.

While granites vary widely in texture and appearance, most of them are dense and have a porosity of less than 1 per cent. Granite spalls badly under the combined effect of fire and water, so it is not particularly resistant to fire. It is usually quite hard, unless excessive amounts of mica or other impurities are present.

Granite is used in situations where strength and hardness are desirable, such as in foundations and columns. It is also used for steps because of its resistance to abrasion, but, like marble, it may become dangerously slick when wet.

11.9 Sandstone

Sandstone is composed of grains of silica (generally a decomposition product of granite) which have been deposited in beds under the action of wind or water and subsequently cemented together with silica, iron oxide, calcium carbonate, or clay. The properties of the stone are dependent on the size of the grains and the character and amount of cementing material. If the grains are very large, the stone approaches a conglomerate; while if the grains are very small and a large amount of clay is present the stone becomes more nearly a shale. In general, the fine-grained stone is stronger than the coarse-grained stone.

Silica cement produces the hardest and most durable stone, but may make the stone very difficult to work. Iron oxide cement is somewhat weaker than silica, and colors the stone. Calcium carbonate cement is readily decomposed by weak acids and is therefore undesirable in large quantities. Since clay cement is not strong, it makes the stone easier to work; but it will absorb water, making the stone likely to be damaged by frost.

Sandstones are little affected by temperatures up to 800 C (1472 F), but may spall badly under the action of fire and water. Standstones are used for general building purposes.

11.10 Slate

Slate is a metamorphosed clay. Iron oxide, iron carbonate, or calcium carbonate may be present as impurities, and these substances are undesirable because of the ease with which they decompose.

The bedding planes in slate are very pronounced and are usually quite close together. It is therefore possible to split the stone into thin sheets. Because slate has been subjected to intense pressure during its formation, it has a low porosity and consequently a high strength. Its modulus of rupture is relatively high and, in addition, it is resistant to weathering and to mechanical abrasion.

Slate is used widely as a roofing material and for blackboards, but its principal use is for flagstone.   Its insulating qualities and very fine texture make it a suitable material for instrument panels.

PROBLEMS

11.1 Specify a building stone for each of the following uses, and give reasons for your choice: (a) walls of a bank building in Pittsburgh; (b) walls of a new building on the campus; (c) steps of a new building on the campus; (d) retaining wall; (e) stone-block pavement in warehouse district of San Francisco.

11.2 A certain sandstone contains 6 per cent voids by volume, and weighs 160 lb per cu ft when dry.   (a) What is the solid specific gravity of the material of which the stone is composed, and (b) what would be a reasonable estimate of its ultimate compressive strength?

11.3 Outline a laboratory method for determining the solid specific gravity of the material in a building stone.

11.4 The solid specific gravity of the material in a certain limestone is 2.60.   If a cubic foot of the dry stone weighs 154.8 lb, what average ultimate compressive strength might the stone be expected to develop?

11.5 A certain limestone specimen weighs 1650 grams when dry and 1800 grams when saturated.   (a) What is the percentage absorption by weight and by volume, if the saturated stone displaces 720 cc of water when immersed in a vessel?   (b) What is the solid specific gravity of the material of which the stone is composed?

11.6 A sample of stone weighed 10.9 lb when dry, 11.8 lb when completely saturated, and 7.3 lb when submerged in water.   Determine (a) the porosity of the stone when dry and (b) the specific gravity for all conditions possible.

11.7 Marble weighing 160 lb per cu ft and having an ultimate compressive strength of 12,000 psi is used for the walls of a tall building.   As is common in such construction, the walls carry only their own weight, the weight of the building being carried by the steel framework.   The weight of the exterior walls is transferred to the steel frame every two stories or 24 ft.   Determine the factor of safety with respect to failure by crushing of the stone.

11.8 How high could a sandstone column be built before it would fail under its own weight if the sandstone weighs 150 lb per cu ft and has an ultimate compressive strength of 8000 psi?

11.9 Determine the modulus of elasticity of each of the stones shown in Fig. 11.1.

11.10 Compare the toughness of each of the stones indicated in Fig. 11.1 with the toughness of hickory and pine.

11.11 A 2-in. by 2-in. by 8-in. block of limestone weighs 2.00 lb when dry.   Determine its effective specific gravity.

11.12 Assume that the solid specific gravity of the material in problem 11.11 is 2.65.   Determine (a) the solid volume of the limestone and (b) the percentage of voids.

11.13 A 4-in. by 4-in. by 12-in. sandstone block weighs 16.5 lb and is known to contain 5 per cent moisture by weight.   What is a reasonable estimate of the axial compressive load which might be applied to the 4-in. square faces with a factor of safety of 8 with respect to fracture when the block is dry?   The solid specific gravity of the material is 2.63.

11.14 The solid specific gravity of a given stone is 2.65, and a 10-in. cube of the stone weighs 70.0 lb when dry. Determine the percentage voids by volume.

11.15 Name the properties of stone which might affect its usefulness as an aggregate for concrete.

11.16 A block of sandstone is 6 in. thick, 1 ft wide, and 12 ft long. The solid specific gravity is 2.73 and the block contains 12 per cent voids by volume. Determine the weight of the block when it is (a) dry and (b) saturated.

11.17 An 8-in. cube of sandstone has 20 per cent voids by apparent volume and contains 8 per cent moisture by dry weight. The solid specific gravity of the sandstone is 2.65. Determine the weight of the block.

11.18 How much will the block of problem 11.17 weigh when it is saturated with water?

11.19 What stress will produce the same strain as a temperature change of 150 F in (a) marble and (b) granite? Use average values for the thermal coefficient of expansion.

11.20 A stone in the saturated condition weighs 100 lb and displaces 46 lb of water when immersed. Determine the solid specific gravity of the stone if its absorption is 15 per cent by dry weight.

11.21 From the data of Fig. 11.2, plot a curve showing the variation in average compressive strength (psi) with the solid volume of the material (expressed as a percentage).

11.22 What is the approximate factor of safety with respect to failure by fracture in an 8-in. by 8-in. by 16-in. block of dry granite placed flatwise and carrying a uniformly distributed compressive load of 100 tons? The granite has a porosity of 1.0 per cent.

12 Clay Products

12.1 Structural Uses

It is difficult to ascertain which of the three materials, wood, stone, or clay, was first used as a material of construction, and the correct answer probably depends on one's definition of construction.

Wood and stone were used for making early weapons, while clay, a material which could be made plastic for ease in working and then dried or burned to retain the molded shape, met various needs of the primitive peoples. The use of sun-dried clay blocks for building purposes dates back to works constructed at least fifty centuries B.C. Excavations at Babylon have revealed the extensive use of both sun-dried and kiln-dried brick for walls, and have uncovered elaborate drainage systems in which cylindrical clay tile were used.

The Greeks made little use of clay as a building material because of the availability of stone, but the Romans made extensive use of clay and the various clay products as well as stone. Augustus "found Rome brick and left it marble."

At the present time clay products are extensively used for building and paving blocks, roofing, drainage conduits, and linings for furnaces, as well as for decorative purposes.

More than 42,000,000 tons of clay were marketed in the United States in 1952. Of that quantity about 11,280,000 tons were fire clay. Ohio is the principal producer of fire clay, although Pennsylvania, Georgia, Missouri, and California are also important producers.

12.2 Raw Materials

Clay, produced by the natural decay and disintegration of igneous rock, is finely divided material (particles less than 0.005 mm in diameter predominating) that has the properties of becoming plastic when moist so that it can be easily molded into almost any shape, of retaining the shape when dried, and of becoming hard when heated or burned. Many different combinations of chemicals have these properties, but the materials most frequently found in natural clays are the hydrated silicates of alumina, often in the form of $Al_2O_3 \cdot 2SiO_2 \cdot 2H_2O$, or *kaolinite*, which may

345

be referred to as pure clay.[1]   Other minerals, such as ferric oxide, lime, magnesia, potash, and soda, are practically always present in deposits of clay, and are sometimes called impurities, although they may add desirable properties to the clay.   The nature and amount of the additional elements depend on the type of deposit in which the clay is found.

Residual clays.   Residual clays are those which are found in deposits at the site of the rocks from which they were formed.   For the most part the disintegration of the parent rock takes place by weathering, and may involve decomposition of the various silicate minerals of which the rock is composed, solution of the soluble portions of the rock, or mechanical disintegration hastened by cycles of freezing and thawing.   The disintegration of feldspar, a common constituent of many rocks such as granite, to form kaolinite is called *kaolinization*.   Constituents other than feldspar, such as the silica in granite, may not be altered by the disintegration and will be found chemically unchanged in the clay deposit.   Hence, residual clays usually contain quantities of sand and undecomposed rock, as well as a large percentage of iron oxide, lime, and other materials.

Glacial clays.   Glacial clays are those which have been transported from their site of formation and deposited in banks by glacial action. They nearly always contain an appreciable amount of sand, gravel, and undecomposed stones, and are therefore not particularly suitable for the manufacture of clay products.

Sedimentary clays.   Sedimentary clays are those which have been deposited by sedimentation after transportation by water.   They are usually fine-grained and uniform, and in general provide the most suitable raw material for the manufacture of clay products.   Sedimentary clays may be further classified as *marine, lacustrine, flood-plain,* or *estuarine,* this division depending on whether they were deposited in the ocean, in lakes or swamps, on the plains during floods, or in estuaries.   Of these, the marine and lacustrine clays usually have the most desirable properties.

Loess clays.   Loess clays are those that have been deposited by wind.

Fire clay.   Fire clay is a high grade clay (marine or lacustrine) approaching kaolinite in composition.   Usually less than 8 per cent of impurities are present, making its fusion point greater than 1650 C in most cases.

Shale.   Shale is clay which has been subjected to pressure.   It is usually formed from sedimentary clay and is therefore more uniform in com-

---

[1] The chemical designation, using dots, is commonly employed to designate the initial oxides in the composition. The designation is not indicative of the structural arrangement of the atoms.

position and texture than residual or glacial clay, and usually contains a somewhat smaller percentage of impurities than most sedimentary clays. The relative compositions of kaolin, shale, sand, and the clays as ordinarily found in deposits are indicated in Fig. 12.1. The compositions are given by weight. Any combination of the three constituents SiO_2, Al_2O_3, or impurities may be represented as a point on the diagram, the percentage of each of the three being indicated as the distance from the side opposite the vertex representing that constituent. Thus the composition of the brick clay represented by point A in the diagram is 10 per cent Al_2O_3, 50 per cent impurities, and 40 per cent SiO_2.

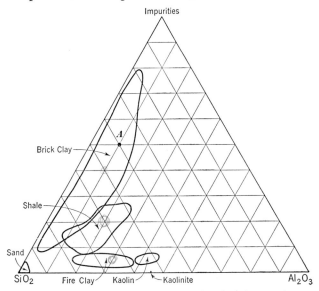

FIG. 12.1   Composition of raw materials for clay products.

Slate. Slate is shale which has been hardened to stone by a metamorphic action. While it has the chemical composition requisite for use as a raw material for the various clay products, there are other uses for which it is better suited.

Other materials, such as silica, ganister (a silicious sandstone containing about 10 per cent clay), magnesia, chromite, and bauxite, are also employed in making clay products. They are used principally in the manufacture of firebrick, which require materials having special properties.

12.3 Manufacture of Clay Products

Preparation of raw material. The first step in the production of a building brick or other clay product is the preparation of the raw material. The clay, shale, or other material is removed from the deposit, washed,

screened

ground, mixed with water, and allowed to stand.   If necessary, the composition is altered to give the desired properties.

2   The material is then placed in a *pug mill,* consisting of a horizontal cylindrical container with a longitudinal shaft to which blades are attached. As the shaft is rotated, the blades reduce the clay to a uniform plastic mass. The final consistency to which the softened clay or mud is brought in the pug mill depends on the method that is to be used in shaping the material.

Soft-mud process. In the soft-mud process, which has been widely used, the clay is made sufficiently plastic to be easily pressed into a mold.

3   While this process is used for special shapes, it has largely been replaced by the stiff-mud process for the manufacture of brick, hollow tile, hollow building blocks, and similar shapes having a constant cross section.

Stiff-mud process. The stiff-mud process is an extrusion process. The clay is pugged to a uniform consistency, but is dry enough to support its weight, and is forced out of the pug mill through a die having the desired cross section.   As the continuous ribbon of clay is extruded from the pug mill, it passes on to a belt conveyor.   At appropriate intervals a wire is passed vertically through the ribbon of clay, cutting it into the desired lengths.   Thus, the sides of the tile or building block are formed by the die, while the ends are formed by the wire cut.   The stiff-mud process is more economical than the soft-mud method, and in addition reduces the possibility of cracks from shrinkage during drying—since much less water has to be removed from the stiff mud.

4   An additional step in the mixing operation, known as *deairing,* is common practice in the stiff-mud extrusion process.   As the plastic clay reaches the end of the pug mill, and before it is extruded through the die, it passes into an air-tight chamber in which a high vacuum is maintained. In the deairing chamber the clay is thoroughly mixed by a series of revolving blades to facilitate the removal of air.   The clay then passes on to the auger, which extrudes it through the die in the usual manner.   The removal of air increases the density by reducing void space, and improves the uniformity of the product.

5   *Dry-press process.* A dry-press process is sometimes used, in which the clay is reduced to a powder form, placed in molds, and subjected to a high pressure.   Dry-pressed brick are dense and strong, but are not considered to be as durable as the brick made by the other methods.

6   **Drying.** As the clay may contain as much as 35 per cent moisture when it comes from the pug mill, the moist shapes must be carefully dried before being burned, to prevent warping and cracking.   In most plants the preliminary drying is done in artificially heated tunnels, but in some the products are simply dried in the sun.

Burning. The burning is done in kilns, many types of which exist. One common type consists of a hemispherical oven about 30 ft in diameter with thick walls of brick. The shapes to be burned are stacked in the kiln in tiers so arranged that the heat will reach all pieces. The heat for burning the shapes is provided by circulating through the kiln the hot gases coming from the fuel either burned outside or burned in appropriate ovens built in the walls of the kiln. Sometimes, the gases are conducted through several kilns in succession, burning the shapes in the first kiln and preheating those in the last kiln.

There are three possible stages in the burning process: dehydration, oxidation, and vitrification. Below 700 C (1292 F) the principal action is one of driving off the moisture which is still retained in the pores of the material after drying. As the temperature is increased, oxidation of the carbonaceous material, sulfur, and other impurities takes place. This step is usually complete at about 900 C (1652 F). A further increase in temperature will cause vitrification if the proper materials are present. The temperature at which vitrification begins, and the temperature range over which it will occur without the material becoming too plastic to retain its shape, depend on the nature and amount of impurities present. The progress of the charge in the kiln is checked by using thermocouples to indicate the temperature, or by watching a series of clay cones within the kiln. The cones are so made that different ones will fuse at different stages in the burning, thus indicating what is happening to the charge and indicating the approximate temperature in the kiln.

The rate of cooling after burning has an important effect upon the properties of the product. If cooled too rapidly, the shapes will check, warp, and become brittle. A cooling period, or annealing period as it is called, of a week or more is required in producing paving brick of maximum toughness.

12.4 Selection of Materials

To be suitable for use in clay products the raw materials must be sufficiently plastic (when mixed with water) to be properly shaped, and be capable of hardening in the desired shape when dried and heated. In addition to these general requirements, there may be imposed additional requirements, such as forming an impervious surface, burning to a desired color, resisting high temperatures, or having a specific chemical reaction. Many different combinations of properties may be introduced by careful selection of the raw material and careful control of the manufacturing processes.

Kaolin, the clay derived from feldspar and consisting almost entirely of kaolinite, has a high degree of plasticity when ground and mixed with water—that is, it is readily worked to the desired shape. The plasticity may be attributed to the fact that the water fills the pores and then surrounds the particles in a thin film, acting as a lubricant and thus reducing but not destroying the resistance of adjacent particles to separation by sliding or direct tension. As more water is added, the resistance is further decreased until the mass will no longer hold its shape. After the piece has been

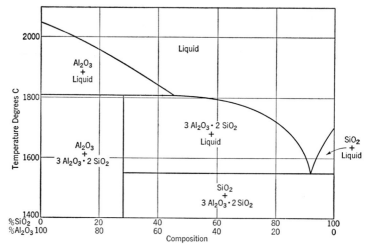

FIG. 12.2   Equilibrium diagram for the silica-alumina system.

shaped and the water begins to dry out, the particles of clay, no longer separated by films of water, tend to shrink, and warping and cracking result. The shrinkage on air-drying varies from 5 to 50 per cent by volume, and further shrinkage occurs on heating. Shrinkage may be reduced by adding silica sand to the kaolin. The sand, being practically unaffected by the mixing water, will not shrink as the mass dries and will therefore reduce the net volume change of the clay. If too much silica is added, the clay will lack the proper cohesiveness, this condition resulting in decreased plasticity and affording an opportunity for cracks to develop.

As an air-dried shape made of kaolin is heated above air temperatures, additional water is driven off and further shrinkage occurs. At temperatures between 450 C (842 F) and 650 C (1202 F), dehydration takes place. Authorities are not in agreement regarding the structure of the material resulting from the dehydration of kaolinite. Oxidation of some of the impurities such as carbon and sulfur occurs with an increase in temperature and is probably complete at about 900 C (1652 F).

The equilibrium diagram for the Al_2O_3-SiO_2 system shown in Fig. 12.2 indicates that the material which was kaolinite before decomposition will not begin to melt until a temperature of about 1550 C (2822 F) is reached, and that complete fusion occurs at about 1800 C (3272 F), which is well above the temperatures available in the ordinary kiln. However, if other materials such as are normally found in clays are present, they will begin to soften at lower temperatures, and incipient vitrification of the mass occurs. With an increase in temperature, complete vitrification occurs, and the pore spaces within the mass (caused by dehydration and oxidation) are filled with the fused material. A further increase in temperature results in a softening of the mass to such an extent that it cannot maintain its shape, and fusion is said to have begun. Vitrification is accompanied by a decrease in volume, followed by an increase in volume when vitrification is complete. In most clays, vitrification will begin at a temperature between 800 C (1472 F) and 1200 C (2192 F), although in some clays incipient vitrification may begin at a temperature as low as 450 C (842 F). A low vitrification temperature results in a saving of fuel in burning.

As is indicated in Fig. 12.2, the product resulting from the vitrification and cooling of kaolinite is a mixture of SiO_2 and $3Al_2O_3 \cdot 2SiO_2$. The latter compound is known as _mullite_ and is an important constituent of vitrified clay.

In coal-fired or coke-fired kilns, in which the temperature cannot be closely regulated, it is desirable to use clays which have a wide vitrification range, to avoid fusing part of the charge while the rest of the charge is below the vitrifying temperature.

Calcareous clays tend to have a very narrow temperature range between incipient vitrification and fusion. They are therefore unsuitable for vitrified products.

When certain other materials, such as iron oxide, lime, magnesia, and alkalies, are present, vitrification becomes possible. In vitrification, the material on the outside of the piece softens and begins to fuse together, forming an impervious glassy surface. If the impurities are present in excessive quantities, the shapes will become too soft and will warp during the burning process. About 6 per cent impurities is sufficient to cause vitrification. The temperature range over which vitrification occurs is dependent on the nature and amount of the impurities.

Since kaolinite will remain white after burning, the color of the burned product is dependent on the additional materials present. Iron oxide in quantities less than about 3 per cent will cause the clay to burn buff, and in greater quantities will produce a red color. Lime in excess of iron will result in a buff color. Brown, black, and green products are obtained by vitrification of clays containing iron oxides.

Iron oxide increases the strength and hardness of the burned clay. Lime causes the shapes to shrink as the vitrification temperature is approached. If any lumps of lime are present, they may cause unsightly blemishes, called "lime pops," or will leave lumps of quicklime in the finished product. As the quicklime hydrates in the air, disintegration of the clay product will result.

12.5 Defects in Clay Products

Defects may be present in clay products because of unsuitable chemical composition, improper mixing or shaping, or improper burning.

A mixture containing too much sand may develop checks or cracks because of lack of cohesion, but, at the other extreme, a pure kaolin will tend to warp and check in drying because of the large volume change.

Lime pops. Lime pops are defects caused by lumps of lime which were not fluxed or hydrated during the manufacturing process. They are unsightly, and reduce the strength of the product.

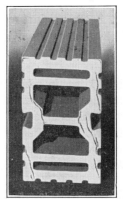

Fig. 12.3 Defects in a hollow
building block.

Blisters. Blisters may be produced by air bubbles which were near the surface and expanded during the burning. Large air pockets within a piece are the result of incomplete mixing or improper shaping. They are undesirable, since they lower the strength and durability.

Laminations. Laminations in extruded sections of hollow building blocks are the result of unbalanced masses in the cross sections. As the clay is extruded, the portions at the edges next to the die will be retarded by friction. Thin sections will be retarded more than thick portions, and if the difference in velocity is too great, longitudinal laminations will be developed between the thin and thick sections, as may be seen in Fig. 12.3. The laminations set up planes of weakness, which are very undesirable in many types of construction and which lower the resistance of the blocks to disintegration by freezing.

Cracks and checks.   Cracks and checks will be developed if the shapes have not been properly dried before being burned. Also, if the shapes have been cooled too rapidly after burning, they will crack and are, in general, brittle.   Cracks and checks afford entrance for forces of disintegration, and decrease the strength of the product.

Improper burning.   Improper burning may also be regarded as a defect.   Because of the necessity of having a large number of shapes in a kiln during burning, and admitting the heat or hot gases at only a few points throughout the kiln, all pieces will not be heated to the same temperature.   Those near the source of heat will be overburned, while those farthest from the source of heat will be underburned.

Overburning.   Overburned or arch-burned shapes are generally warped and unfit for use where they will be visible.

Underburning.   Underburned *(soft-burned)* shapes are soft and weak, and in general are not fit for normal usage.   Soft-burned brick are known as _salmon brick_ and may be used for fillers, or at other inconspicuous places where brick of average strength are not required.

swell bellies   larger in middle

12.6 Types of Clay Products

Clay products may be classified on several different bases.   They may be grouped according to the raw materials used in their manufacture, according to the type and degree of burning, and according to their shape.

Classification by raw material.   As has been discussed in section 12.2, there are four general groups of raw materials: fire clay, shale, surface clay, and special materials.   Fire clay, which is nearly pure kaolin, is used in the manufacture of firebrick, terra cotta, wall and floor tile, and porcelain.   Shale is used almost exclusively in the manufacture of paving brick and also in making building blocks and brick.   Surface clays, which contain a higher percentage of impurities than do fire clay and shale, are used for building blocks, brick, and tile.   The special group contains ganister, silica, magnesia, bauxite, chromite, and similar materials used in making firebrick.

Classification by burning.   Excluding the soft-burned and arch-burned products, there are three general types of burning: sun-drying, red-burning, and vitrifying.   Sun-drying, without subsequent application of artificial heat, is the oldest and simplest of the methods of hardening clay products after shaping.   It is still practiced extensively in certain arid regions.   Frequently straw or other similar material is added to the clay during mixing to increase the tensile strength, which is low at best.   The product, usually in the form of large solid building blocks, is often called *adobe.*

Shapes which are burned to the proper degree to avoid soft-burning and arch-burning, and which are not vitrified, are called _red-burned_ or _well-burned_. Shapes such as brick and building block, and certain grades of tile, should be red-burned. Shapes such as sewer pipe and paving brick, for which a hard, impervious surface is desired, are _vitrified_. This is accomplished by including with the clay those materials (ferric oxide, magnesia, lime, etc.) which will fuse at the temperatures attainable in the burning process.

Classification by shape. A classification of clay products on the basis of shape and use includes brick (building brick, paving brick, and firebrick), terra cotta, hollow building blocks, tile (roofing tile, wall tile, and floor tile), conduit (sewer pipe and drain tile), and miscellaneous shapes (porcelain and crucibles).

TABLE 12.1

ASTM PHYSICAL REQUIREMENTS FOR BUILDING BRICK

Grade	Min. Comp. Str. (psi)*		Max. Water Absorp. (%)†		Max. Satur. Coeff.‡	
	Avg, 5 brick	Individ.	Avg, 5 brick	Individ.	Avg, 5 brick	Individ.
SW	3000	2500	17.0	20.0	0.78	0.80
MW	2500	2200	22.0	25.0	0.88	0.90
NW	1500	1250	No lim.	No lim.	No lim.	No lim.

* Brick flatwise. Gross area.
† Five-hour boiling.
‡ The saturation coefficient is the ratio of absorption by 24-hr submersion in cold water to that after 5-hr submersion in boiling water.

Classification by properties. For structural purposes the ASTM classifies clay products on the basis of resistance to disintegration, compressive strength, and absorption. For example, building brick made from clay or shale are classified in three grades: SW, MW, and NW.[1] Grade SW brick are "intended for use where a high degree of resistance to frost action is desired and the exposure is such that the brick may be frozen when permeated with water." Grade MW brick are "intended for use where exposed to temperatures below freezing but unlikely to be permeated with water . . . " Grade NW brick are "intended for use as back-up or interior masonry, or if exposed for use where no frost action occurs or if frost action occurs where the average annual precipitation is less than 20 in." The physical properties are required to conform to the values in Table 12.1.

The various types of clay tile are classified under similar systems, some of which also specify limits on absorption.

12.7 Brick

Building brick. Most of the ordinary building brick are made from surface clay or shale and are shaped by forcing the clay through a die and

[1] ASTM Designation C 62-44.

cutting the extruded ribbon with wires.   They may be side-cut or end-cut. That is, the extruded ribbon may be $2\frac{1}{4}$ in. by 8 in. or it may be $2\frac{1}{4}$ in. by $3\frac{3}{4}$ in. in cross section.   Some brick are made with holes running through them, in the vertical direction as the brick are laid, in order to decrease weight.   The burning temperature varies from 900 C (1652 F) to 1200 C (2192 F), which is sufficient to produce a red-burned material but not sufficient to cause vitrification.

Pressed brick.   Pressed brick or face brick are made by repressing the brick in a mold after they are dried and before they are burned.   The repressing improves the appearance of the brick, making them more suitable for facing work.   A higher grade of clay is required than is normally used for building brick.

Glazed brick.   Glazed brick are made by coating one side of an unburned common brick with a thin coating of slip (a clayey coloring material) and a coat of transparent glaze.   Upon burning, the glaze forms a smooth transparent coating, improving the appearance of the brick.

Paving brick.   Paving brick are usually made from shale, since shale includes the desirable fluxing materials which will vitrify at a comparatively low temperature.   The material should have a wide vitrifying range, to insure vitrification of the entire charge without overheating any of the shapes sufficiently to cause warping or checking.   Paving brick are shaped by extruding, but are usually repressed before being burned.   The burning temperature depends on the nature of the shale, and is usually between 900 C (1652 F) and 1100 C (2012 F).   Burning usually requires about a week or ten days.   After being burned, the brick are slowly cooled to ordinary temperatures.   The slow cooling over a period of several days increases the toughness of the brick.

Firebrick.   Firebrick are brick which are used for lining chimneys, stacks, flues, or furnaces.   They must be able to withstand high temperatures.   The material from which they are made depends on the purpose for which they are to be used.

Acid.   If an acid reaction is desired, as for the lining of an acid Bessemer converter, fire clay, silica, or ganister is used.

Fire-clay brick are made from a high grade of fire clay, free from impurities that would flux at low temperatures, to which sand or burnt fire clay has been added to reduce shrinkage.   They are burned at temperatures between 1370 C (2498 F) and 1930 C (3506 F).   They must be cooled slowly and carefully below 1370 C to insure maximum toughness.

Silica brick are made from silica to which a small percentage of lime has been added as a binder.   They are usually molded by hand and burned at temperatures between 1430 C (2606 F) and 1760 C (3200 F). High-quality silica brick will withstand temperatures as high as 2150 C (3902 F).

Basic. To produce a refractory material with a basic reaction, suitable for lining a basic open-hearth furnace or a cement kiln, materials with a low silica content must be used. The two principal types of basic firebrick are bauxite and magnesia brick. Bauxite brick are made from a mixture of bauxite and clay, and are burned at about 1540 C (2804 F). They are weak and undergo a large amount of shrinkage upon being heated. Magnesia brick are made from magnesia to which a small amount of ferric oxide has been added. They are burned at temperatures between 1800 C (3272 F) and 1950 C (3542 F). Like bauxite brick, they are weak and undergo a large amount of shrinkage.

Neutral. Under some conditions neutral firebrick are required for furnaces. For that purpose chrome iron ore mixed with fire clay or bauxite is used as the raw material. The brick are molded under heavy pressure and burned at about 1650 C (3002 F).

12.8 Terra Cotta

The term terra cotta is applied to specially molded shapes used for architectural purposes. The raw material, which is fire clay or a mixture of fire clay and shale, must be fine-textured, plastic, and strong, and must have a low shrinkage. It should also be free from soluble salts that might discolor the shapes. Because of the variety of shapes required in different architectural treatments, terra cotta is hand-molded and often carved. Before terra cotta is burned, a glaze similar to that used for glazed brick is applied to provide a smooth finish. The burning must be done very carefully at temperatures between 1100 C (2012F) and 1300 C (2372 F).

Terra-cotta lumber and terra-cotta blocks are quite different from architectural terra cotta, and are used for unexposed structural work. They are composed of terra-cotta clay to which sawdust or chopped straw has been added. Upon firing in the kiln the straw or sawdust is burned, and there remains a light, porous material which may be cut with a saw. The material is made in a variety of shapes, usually of hollow construction, and is suitable for wall and floor construction and for fireproofing.

12.9 Hollow Building Block

Building blocks are made from terra-cotta clay, shaped by extruding through a die, and burned almost to vitrification. They are used for walls, ceilings, floor arches, floor beams (in built-up sections reinforced with steel), and fireproofing. They are made in a variety of sizes, some of which are shown in Fig. 12.4. Although the shape is usually that of a rectangular prism, the size and arrangement of the cells within the prism are varied to meet special requirements.

12.10 Tile

Roofing tile. Roofing tile are made in a variety of shapes: flat, semi-cylindrical, and several types of interlocking sections. The tile are made of a carefully selected clay, and are repressed before firing. The burning temperature is sufficiently high to insure strength and low absorption. If a glaze is applied, vitrification is not so complete as when no glaze is used.

FIG. 12.4 Examples of hollow building blocks.

Wall tile. The raw materials used for wall tile depend on the color and quality desired, and may include fire clay, white clay, shale, and powdered burned clay. After being molded by hand or by machine, the tile are fired. If the tile is to be glazed, the glaze is then applied and the tile fired a second time to fuse the glaze.

Floor tile. The manufacture of floor tile is similar to that of wall tile, except that no glaze is applied and the burning is conducted at a higher temperature to provide an impermeable surface.

12.11 Conduit

Drain tile are made from a red-burning clay or from a clay similar to that used in making terra cotta. They are shaped by extrusion and are well-burned.

Sewer pipe must be nonabsorptive in order to resist the action of the variety of corrosive industrial wastes which they must carry. They are molded from a good grade of clay or shale and are glazed by the addition of salt to the kiln as they are being burned. The sodium vapors combine with the clay to form an impervious and durable glaze. The burning temperature is usually between 1050 C (1922 F) and 1300 C (2372 F), or just to the stage of incipient vitrification.

Hollow tile are also used for carrying underground cables and wires. The sections are hard-burned and salt-glazed to render them nonabsorptive.

12.12 Miscellaneous Shapes

Insulators. Insulators for electric transmission lines are made of a high-quality kaolin and are shaped by molding. They are usually burned at about 1350 C (2462 F) and are frequently glazed to prevent absorption of moisture which would greatly reduce their effectiveness.

Crucibles. Graphite crucibles for melting steel, brass, glass, and similar materials which must be heated to high temperatures during their manufacturing processes generally contain clay as the bonding agent. To be suitable for this purpose the clay must have strong bonding power, and must also be refractory. In general, blends of various high-quality clays must be used to meet the requirements of service.

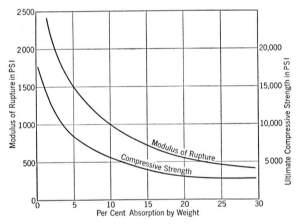

FIG. 12.5 Effect of porosity upon strength of dry brick. [From J. H. Griffith, *Physical Properties of Typical American Rocks*, Iowa Engineering Experiment Station Bulletin 131 (1937)]

12.13 Properties of Clay Products

With clay products, the principal mechanical properties of interest to the engineer are strength and durability. Since the clay products are in general quite uniform in texture, the principal factors affecting the strength are the chemical composition and the degree of burning. Exclusive of firebrick, which represent a different type of material built to meet a special situation, the chemical composition is not a major factor in determining strength and durability except as it influences porosity. Chemical composition and degree of burning together determine the porosity, which in turn is directly related to strength, as is indicated in the curves in Fig. 12.5, which are based on average values.   Vitrified products will, of course, have the least absorption, and consequently the highest strength, while the very porous, underburned materials will have the highest absorption.

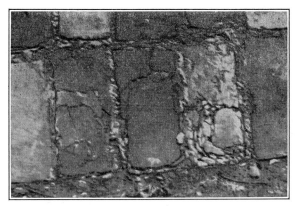

FIG. 12.6   Disintegration of brick.

With clay products, as with stone, durability is directly related to absorption.   Moisture which freezes after being absorbed by a material will expand, and this action will cause splitting and spalling, which not only is unsightly but also will open cracks into which more water can be absorbed.   Therefore an impervious material should be used for exposed work which may be subjected to cycles of freezing and thawing.   Porosity will also decrease durability where destructive chemicals may be absorbed —as in sewers, for example.

Porosity is usually measured by some type of absorption test.   For several types of clay products the ASTM specifies an immersion of 5 hr in boiling water.   There is evidence to indicate that, within limits, the rate of absorption is a suitable criterion of durability.

Table 12.2 indicates average properties of some of the clay products. As would be expected, the range of values is wide, because of the wide variety of raw materials and manufacturing processes.

Resistance to abrasion, which is an essential component of durability in paving brick and some firebrick, is sometimes measured by what is known as a rattler test.   The brick to be tested, together with a number of cast-iron balls, are placed in a drum about 28 in. in diameter with its axis horizontal.   As the drum, the inside cross section of which is a 14-sided polygon, is rotated about its axis, the brick and balls are tumbled about together.   After 1800 revolutions at 30 rpm, the brick are removed and

TABLE 12.2

PROPERTIES OF CLAY PRODUCTS

Material	Comp. Strength (psi)	Modulus of Rupture (psi)	Shearing Strength (psi)	Young's Modulus (psi × 10⁶)
Brick	1000–6000	300–1200	1000–1500	1.5–2.5
Paving brick	8000–10000	1500–2500	1200–1800	4.0–8.0
Firebrick	3000–6000	300–1600	500–1000	....
Terra cotta	3000–4000	500–1000	....	....
Hollow blocks	2000	500	....	....
Stoneware	....	3000–10000	....	....

the percentage loss in weight is determined. If the loss in weight does not exceed about 25 per cent, the brick are generally regarded as satisfactory as far as wear is concerned.

As has been indicated, deairing has a beneficial effect upon the properties of the clay products. Reducing the void content increases the strength and the resistance to wear, and decreases the absorption. Deairing also tends to produce a more uniform product which is less subject to laminations and other structural defects.

The strength of brick masonry is always much lower than the strength of the individual brick because of the weakening effect of the mortar joints. The quality of workmanship in laying the masonry, and the type of mortar used, are important factors. The strength of a masonry wall may be reduced to 10 or 15 per cent of the strength of the brick in the wall if a 1:3 lime-sand mortar is used, or to 20 to 40 per cent if a neat portland-cement mortar is used for the joints.

12.14 Additional Uses of Clay

While one of the most important types of use for clay is in the manufacture of structural clay products, there are many other fields in which the material is important, particularly in its unburned form. Over 400,000 tons of clay are used annually in the United States in the paper industry. Light-colored kaolins are used both as fillers to give body to paper and to provide a smooth attractive coating in certain grades of paper. They are also used as fillers in rubber products, and in the manufacture of linoleum, oilcloth, textiles, and certain composition roofings.

Clay is added to certain paints as a filler or extender to reduce the cost of the paint, and is likewise used in kalsomine. Kaolins have been used in the manufacture of white portland cement.

Clay has important applications as a filtering agent, serves as a binder in the manufacture of abrasives, and is incorporated in asbestos. It is also added to plaster, and is used in several processes for manufacturing chemicals.

One of the most universal uses of clay is in the manufacture of dishes, stoneware, vases, and other household shapes. While a wide variety of clays may be used in producing the shapes, a very uniform, clean clay is required for the high-quality merchandise. The pieces may be formed in molds or by using the potter's wheel. Chinaware is usually burned at about 1350 C (2462 F), although higher temperatures may be used for special grades.

PROBLEMS

12.1 Show how a wire-cutting device may be used in conjunction with a belt conveyor to cut brick after the ribbon is extruded.

12.2 Draw a diagram showing the principal steps in the manufacture of deaired building brick.

12.3 Select, from the materials discussed in Chapter 12, a suitable material for each of the following uses. Give reasons for your selection. (a) Conduit to carry waste from a canning factory; (b) lining for a typical open-hearth furnace; (c) lining for a typical Bessemer furnace; (d) partition wall in a building.

12.4 A certain building block having a cross-sectional area of 12 sq in. weighed 12.0 lb when dry, and 12.8 lb after soaking in water for 24 hr. Approximately what total compressive load could it be expected to carry when dry?

12.5 A group of five building brick of standard dimensions gave the following test results:

Brick No.	Absorption (%) 5-Hr Boil.	24-Hr Submer.	Compressive Test Load (lb)	Length (in.)
1	23.1	18.4	67,500	4
2	18.6	15.1	61,000	$4\frac{1}{16}$
3	20.9	16.7	46,400	$3\frac{7}{8}$
4	21.7	17.4	34,600	4
5	19.2	17.4	77,100	$4\frac{3}{8}$

As what grade would the brick be classified?

12.6 The ASTM specifies tests on five brick or tile in determining the classification. Why is not a test on a single specimen sufficient?

12.7 Test results from a group of five building brick of standard dimensions are given below. As what grade would the lot of brick which they represent be classified?

Brick No.	Absorption (%) 5-Hr Boil.	24-Hr Submer.	Compressive Test Load (lb)	Length (in.)
21	20.8	16.6	71,700	$4\frac{1}{8}$
22	23.9	18.7	51,420	$3\frac{3}{4}$
23	19.2	17.3	65,270	$3\frac{5}{8}$
24	19.2	17.7	68,980	$4\frac{1}{4}$
25	15.6	12.2	89,120	$4\frac{1}{2}$

12.8 Specify the general composition and method of manufacture of a clay product suitable for each of the following purposes: (a) lining for a puddling furnace; (b) exterior walls of a factory building; (c) lining for a furnace used in reducing copper ore; (d) conduit to drain swampland.

12.9 Compare slate and tile with respect to suitability as a roofing material.

12.10 For what purposes might each of the clays having the following analyses be suitable?

Clay	SiO_2	Al_2O_3
A	50	10
B	60	20
C	65	30

12.11 Approximately what safe load per foot, based on a factor of safety of 2, may be placed on an 8-in. wall made of grade NW brick laid with a 1:3 lime-sand mortar?

12.12 One building code specifies an allowable load of 5 tons per linear foot on an 8-in. brick wall laid with a lime-sand mortar. What is the approximate factor of safety if grade SW brick are used?

12.13 If the allowable load on an 8-in. brick wall with a portland-cement mortar is 12 tons per linear foot, what is the approximate factor of safety (a) when grade NW brick are used and (b) when grade SW brick are used?

13 Cementing Materials

13.1 Types of Cements

Although there are several different materials which have adhesive properties, the three types of cements which are of particular interest to the engineer are glues, bituminous materials, and various compounds of calcium. Glues are materials of a gelatinous nature that are derived from animal or vegetable sources. The bituminous materials depend upon bitumen, a complex hydrocarbon, for their adhesive qualities, while the calcium compounds depend for their cementing power upon a solidification which occurs as a result of controllable chemical changes. This chapter is devoted to the various calcium derivatives; glues and bituminous materials are discussed in Chapter 15.

There are two kinds of calcium cement. One is derived from calcium sulfate ($CaSO_4 \cdot 2H_2O$), or *gypsum*, and the other from calcium carbonate ($CaCO_3$), or *lime*. The first includes plaster of Paris, wall plaster, and hard-finish plaster, while the second includes lime and the various cements such as natural cement, portland cement, and high-early-strength cement.

All calcium cements will harden and develop adhesive properties when mixed with water. They may be used in thin layers to bind together brick or cut stone, forming masonry; they may serve as a matrix in which irregular pieces of rock or similar materials are bound to form concrete; or they may be used in thin layers as a protective or decorative coating.

GYPSUM

13.2 Production of Gypsum

Four states—New York, Michigan, Iowa, and Texas—produce nearly two-thirds of the 8,400,000 tons of gypsum rock mined in the United States each year. The output of gypsum, ready for use, amounts to more than 7,630,000 tons annually.

13.3 Preparation of Gypsum

Gypsum is produced from gypsum rock ($CaSO_4 \cdot 2H_2O$) by driving off the weakly bonded water of crystallization. The rock is first ground, is then calcined, or heated to a temperature between 130 C (266 F) and

200 C (392 F), and finally may be ground.   Clay, hydrated lime, hair, wood fiber, or other materials may be added to alter the properties.

The calcining may be done in ovens, which provide careful control of the heat; in large kettles, this being a much cheaper process and the one in most common use; or in kilns.   In the last process the crushed gypsum is fed into the upper end of a long cylinder, the axis of which is nearly horizontal.   Hot gases are introduced into the kiln, which is slowly rotated. The gypsum gradually works down to the lower end of the cylinder and is then placed in a vat in which the calcining process is completed by heat stored in the gypsum.   This process has the advantage of being a continuous operation.

If the calcining temperature is below 190 C (374 F), the dehydration will be incomplete, one-fourth of the water of crystallization remaining, and the pure product ($2CaSO_4 \cdot H_2O$) is known as *plaster of Paris.*   If other materials such as clay or lime are present in the raw material or are added after calcination, the product is called wall plaster, cement plaster, or patent plaster.   The impurities have the effect of increasing the workability of the plaster when water is added, and will also alter the time required for the plaster to set.

In case the calcining temperature exceeds 190 C (374 F), the dehydration will be complete and the product, if it is practically pure $CaSO_4$, is called *flooring plaster.*

Other substances such as alum or borax are often added to increase the workability, in which case the product is known as *hard-finish plaster.* *Keene's cement,* made by treating the calcined gypsum with alum and recalcining, is one of the well-known commercial hard-finished plasters. When all of the water of crystallization is driven off, the product is said to be dead-burned.

13.4 Properties of Gypsum

When mixed with water, either $CaSO_4$ or $2CaSO_4 \cdot H_2O$ has the property of taking on water of crystallization and hardening into a solid mass.   The length of time required for "set" (attainment of initial rigidity) to occur after the addition of water varies from 5 min for plaster of Paris to several hours for hard-finish plaster.

The time required for pure plaster (with no admixtures) to set is normally about 30 min.   The time may be decreased by increasing the amount of mixing beyond that required to produce a homogeneous mass, or by adding small quantities of set plaster, zinc or potassium sulfate, salt, alum, or sodium carbonate.   The rate of set may be decreased by the addition of borax, tartaric acid, citric acid, acetic acid, or certain organic substances, as well as by the addition of a powerful commercial retarder consisting of a mixture of organic compounds derived from keratin.

The plasticity or workability of the mortar is dependent on the amount of mixing water, and is usually increased by the presence of impurities. A finely ground plaster tends to be more plastic than one in which the particles are comparatively coarse.

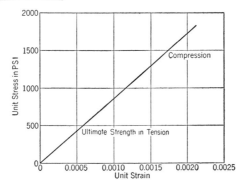

FIG. 13.1   Typical stress-strain diagrams for plaster
of Paris.

The tensile strength of gypsum products is comparatively low, so hair and wood fiber are frequently added to increase the cohesiveness. Gypsum plasters attain about one-half of their maximum strength within 24 hr after placement. A plaster containing two parts of sand to one part of plaster has about 60 per cent of the ultimate strength of the plaster without the sand. Materials added to control the rate of set may decrease the strength of the hardened plaster.

The hard-finish plasters are considerably stronger than the wall plasters because of the greater care which is used in selecting the raw materials, and because of the careful control exercised over all operations during manufacture.

A typical stress-strain diagram for plaster of Paris in compression is shown in Fig. 13.1. The material displays the unusual characteristic of having a straight-line stress-strain diagram practically all of the way to fracture.

The ultimate strength of gypsum in both tension and compression is dependent on the water-plaster ratio. Although the action in setting is hydration, excess mixing water will lower the potential strength of the hardened gypsum because the water which does not chemically combine with the gypsum dries out, leaving voids which have no supporting strength.

In Fig. 13.2 ultimate compressive strengths of plaster of Paris are plotted against the ratio of weight of mixing water to weight of plaster.

The ratio 0.6 represents about the lowest ratio at which the material is plastic enough to shape.   At this ratio there is about three times as much water present as is required to hydrate the plaster.   Plaster of Paris will hydrate completely in about two days in a saturated atmosphere, and will show no material gain in strength after that time.

Gypsum products are useful as fireproofing.   Although the surface is decomposed above 100 C (212 F), it forms a powder which, if not disturbed, is an effective insulator.

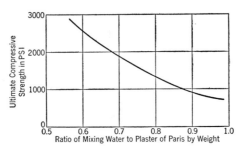

FIG. 13.2   Effect of water-plaster ratio upon compressive strength.

13.5   Uses of Gypsum

Because of the rapidity with which it sets, and its relative lack of workability, plaster of Paris is not used as structural material.   It is valuable for making casts and architectural adornments because it expands in hardening, producing a clear impression of the mold.   Since it has a straight-line stress-strain diagram almost to the ultimate strength, it is useful in certain model studies.[1]

Plaster is used for molds in the ceramic industry.   For that purpose porosity is desirable, as a porous mold will absorb water from the plastic clay, making it more rigid so that it can be handled with less danger of distortion upon removal from the mold.   The use of plaster molds for the casting of metals has been discussed in Chapter 6.

Plaster of Paris may be impregnated with resins, such as phenols or urea formaldehyde, either before or after being cast.   The resin increases the strength and durability of the product and makes it suitable for contour blocks, mock-ups, and similar units.

Wall plaster, as its name implies, is used for covering walls.   The first coats are usually mortars of two parts of sand to one of plaster.   Wall

[1] F. B. Seely and R. V. James, *The Plaster Model Method of Determining Stresses Applied to Curved Beams,* University of Illinois Engineering Experiment Station Bulletin 195.

plaster is sometimes sold already mixed with the proper amount of sand, requiring only the addition of water to be ready for use.

Wall plaster mixed with sawdust or ground cinders is cast into blocks for floor panels or wall finish. The plaster is also cast into building blocks for the construction of partition walls, floors, and roofing, or for fire-proofing, and is used in the manufacture of wallboard. The completely dehydrated plasters are used for both floor and wall covering.

Flooring plaster is used principally as a finish for floors, while hard-finish plaster is used for both floors and walls. Hard-finish plaster is very hard and may be polished satisfactorily. Finely-ground dead-burned gypsum from carefully selected white gypsum rock is used as a filler in paper, paint, rubber, cloth, toothpaste, plastics, and similar materials.

LIME

13.6 Production of Lime

Ohio, Pennsylvania, and Missouri produced about 56 per cent of the 8,073,000 tons of lime mined in the United States in 1952. However, lime is found in all parts of the United States. About three-fourths of the total was sold as quicklime, CaO, and one-fourth as slaked lime, $Ca(OH)_2$. Of the total, 48 per cent was consumed in the chemical and paper industries, 24 per cent in refractories, about 15 per cent in building construction, and the remainder in agriculture.

13.7 Preparation of Lime

Lime is produced from calcite or limestone ($CaCO_3$), or from magnesian limestone ($CaCO_3$ and $MgCO_3$), by calcining the stone to drive off the carbon dioxide. Calcium carbonate will dissociate into CaO and CO_2 at approximately 900 C (1652 F). In practice, higher temperatures are used to accelerate the process, but if the temperature exceeds about 1000 C (1832 F) the lime may be damaged, especially if it contains much $MgCO_3$.

In the calcining process, the rock is first ground and is then fed into the kilns, which are vertical stacks somewhat similar to miniature blast furnaces. The fuel, which is coal, may be mixed with the stone, or it may be burned on a separate grate so located that the gases will ascend the stack and come in contact with the slowly descending limestone. The calcined material, CaO, known as *quicklime*, is removed at the bottom of the stack, and may be marketed as lump lime, screened lime, or pulverized lime.

Since the quicklime must be mixed with water before it is finally used, and since mixing operations must be carefully performed to avoid damaging the lime, the mixing is often done at the plant. The ground lime is mixed with a minimum of water to convert it into $Ca(OH)_2$. The product is screened or ground and marketed in powder form as *slaked lime* or *hydrated lime.*

13.8 Properties of Lime

When more water than the amount required to hydrate the lime is added to quicklime, or when water is added to slaked lime, a paste, consisting of crystalline $Ca(OH)_2$ and colloids, is formed. As the water evaporates, the mass will set. The time required for the initial set will depend on the amount of impurities present. If the paste is exposed to the air, the preliminary setting is followed by gradual hardening, consisting in the replacement of the water in the $Ca(OH)_2$ by carbon dioxide from the air, forming $CaCO_3$ (or $CaCO_3$ and $MgCO_3$) again. The rate of hardening depends on the accessibility of carbon dioxide. In relatively small test specimens the hardening, as evidenced by gain in strength, continues over a period of several months. A much longer period would be required for the complete hardening of a large mass of lime. Lime will not harden under water.

Quicklime exposed to the air will, in a short time, absorb a sufficient amount of moisture and carbon dioxide from the air to be converted into calcium carbonate. It is then called *air-slaked lime* and is useless as a cementing material. Hydrated lime will keep much better than quicklime and is often preferred on this account.

The tensile strength of lime is decreased by the use of too much mixing water. Water, in excess of that required for hydration, occupies space in the paste; and, as it dries out, voids are left.

Sand, which is generally added in making lime mortar, decreases the tensile strength of the hardened lime, but also decreases the shrinkage of the paste upon hardening. Magnesian limes are, in general, stronger than pure calcium limes, but harden more slowly.[2]

13.9 Uses of Lime

Either quicklime or hydrated lime may be used as a cementing material. If quicklime is used, it must first be converted to hydrated lime by slaking. This operation must be carefully conducted to avoid burning the lime. After a seasoning period of several weeks, the slaked lime is mixed with sand to form the desired mortar. If hydrated lime is used, it is mixed directly with the sand and water and is ready for use without delay; it is therefore much more convenient to use than quicklime. However, the slaked lime does not make so plastic a mortar as quicklime. Quicklime is not so desirable to handle as slaked lime, as it tends to burn the skin.

[2] *Tests of Iowa Limes.* Iowa Engineering Experiment Station Bulletin No. **1,** Vol. IV.

Lime is used as a plastering material and (usually in combination with portland cement) in mortar for brick and masonry construction. For plastering, lime has the advantage over gypsum that about four parts of sand to one of lime may be used for the first coat, but it has the disadvantage of setting more slowly than gypsum.

A type of building brick known as sand-lime brick is made by mixing a well-graded sand with from 4 to 10 per cent hydrated lime and then molding the mixture under high pressure. The brick are hardened by storing them in a chamber under a steam pressure of about 150 psi for several hours. Good sand-lime brick have a compressive strength between 2500 and 4000 psi, and a modulus of rupture of about 350 psi. In general, they are not so durable as clay brick.

In addition to its uses as a structural material, lime is of importance in the manufacture of paper and in several other chemical processes. It is used as a flux in the iron and steel industry, and is widely used in agriculture to correct certain soil deficiencies.

CEMENTS

13.10 Composition of Cements

The Romans, who used lime extensively as a building material, discovered that the addition of certain materials (sand and volcanic ash) to slaked lime gave a cement (puzzolan) which was superior to ordinary lime in that it would harden under water. Since that time other cementing materials with the capacity for hardening under water, and with other properties superior to those of the Roman cement, have been developed.

Chemical analyses of these cements reveal the fact that they are composed chiefly of three oxides: silica (SiO_2), lime (CaO), and alumina (Al_2O_3), although small quantities of MgO, SO_3, and Fe_2O_3 are usually present. The cements are not necessarily simple mixtures of these oxides, but may be in the form of mixtures of definite combinations of the fundamental oxides, such as dicalcium silicate ($2CaO \cdot SiO_2$), tricalcium silicate ($3CaO \cdot SiO_2$), and tricalcium aluminate ($3CaO \cdot Al_2O_3$).

The properties of the cement will depend on the relative proportions of the three principal constituents. Figure 13.3 indicates the approximate compositions of several different cements. The lower left corner represents pure SiO_2 (sand), the lower right corner represents 100 per cent CaO (quicklime), while the top of the diagram represents the remaining constituents, which are primarily Al_2O_3 (alumina). Each point in the diagram represents a definite composition. The percentage of each of the constituents of that composition is given by the distance from the side opposite the vertex representing 100 per cent of that constituent.

Thus, the composition of portland cement is found to be approximately 60 per cent lime, 20 per cent silica, and 20 per cent alumina plus impurities. However, in portland cement these basic ingredients are in the form of several complex chemical compounds.

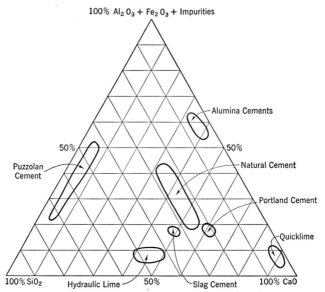

FIG. 13.3 Composition of cements by weight.

13.11 Hydraulic Lime

Hydraulic lime is made by calcining a limestone containing sufficient silica to give the product the capacity for hardening under water. At the same time, sufficient free lime is present to cause the lime to slake upon the addition of water. The alumina content is low, and the lime is slow setting, so it does not compete with portland cement. It is used sometimes for architectural purposes.

13.12 Puzzolan Cement

Puzzolan cement[3] is the oldest of the cements, having been invented by the Romans and used by them in making concrete for the construction of walls and domes. The raw materials are volcanic ash, sand, and slaked lime. They are simply mixed and ground together. Puzzolan cements are seldom used as such at the present time, but considerable attention has recently been given to the properties of portland cements blended with puzzolanic materials.

[3] So named because the ash used in the cement was first collected at Pozzuoli, near Naples.

13.13 Slag Cement

Slag cement consists of a finely pulverized mixture of blast-furnace slag and hydrated lime. Since slag cements are normally slow to harden, an accelerator (such as clay, special forms of silica, salt, or caustic soda), is sometimes added. Slag cement is used to a limited extent for concrete in bulk construction where strength is relatively unimportant.

13.14 Natural Cement

Natural cement is made by calcining a limestone containing sufficient alumina and silica to result in the formation of calcium silicates and aluminates. These compounds have the capacity for hardening upon the addition of water, giving the material its cementing qualities. A temperature of about 1300 C (2372 F) is required during the calcination, and the clinker is ground fine enough to enable 85 per cent of it to pass a 200-mesh sieve. Natural cements have only about half the strength of portland cement. Because of the wide variety of raw materials which may be used in their manufacture, considerable variation of properties may be expected among natural cements made in different localities.

PORTLAND CEMENT

13.15 Definition of Portland Cement

The ASTM has defined portland cement as "the product obtained by finely pulverizing clinker produced by calcining to incipient fusion an intimate and properly proportioned mixture of argillaceous and calcareous materials, with no additions subsequent to calcination excepting water and calcined or uncalcined gypsum."[4] Discovered in 1824 by Joseph Aspdin, a bricklayer of Leeds, portland cement was so named because of its fancied resemblance to the cliffs of Portland.

13.16 Manufacture of Portland Cement

The raw materials used in the manufacture of portland cement are, according to the ASTM definition of portland cement, argillaceous (clayey) and calcareous (lime-bearing).

In some localities the clayey and lime-bearing materials are found blended in the proper proportions in natural rock, so the cement can be made directly from it. In general, however, shale and limestone from different sources must be mixed together to give the proper combination

---

[4] This definition (ASTM Designation C9-30) has been superseded by another statement which represents a concept rather than a definition. One difference is that there are now permitted additions of not more than 1 per cent of materials which have been shown not to be harmful.

of elements.   The materials are first crushed separately and ground very fine.   Next they are mixed together in the proper proportions and are ground again either dry or in a water slurry.   They are then fed into the upper end of the kiln for burning.

The principal features of a typical kiln are indicated in Fig. 13.4.   The kiln consists of a hollow cylinder about 8 ft in diameter and 120 ft long. The inside is lined with firebrick, and the axis is inclined slightly.   As the

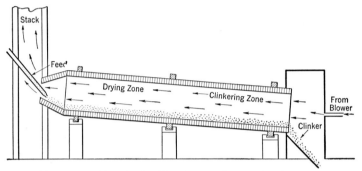

FIG. 13.4   Sketch of a kiln for burning portland cement.

kiln is rotated slowly, the charge gradually moves down toward the lower end where hot gases are admitted maintaining a temperature of about 1500 C (2732 F).   Under the action of the intense heat the charge begins to fuse, small clinkers being formed.   The clinkers drop from the lower end of the kiln onto a belt conveyor and are carried to a storage bin. The clinkers are then reground, and 2 or 3 per cent gypsum may be added to increase the time of setting of the cement.   Other materials, up to 1 per cent, may be added for the purpose of altering properties as desired.

Portland cement is marketed in bulk or in sacks or bags containing 94 lb, which is nominally 1 cu ft loose volume.   A "barrel" of cement is sometimes indicated as a unit of measurement, being equal to 4 sacks.

13.17   Properties of Portland Cement

The chemical reactions which take place in the kiln are quite compli- cated, transforming the calcareous and argillaceous materials (lime, silica, alumina, and impurities) into three principal compounds—tricalcium sili- cate ($3CaO \cdot SiO_2$), dicalcium silicate ($2CaO \cdot SiO_2$), and tricalcium alu- minate ($3CaO \cdot Al_2O_3$)—plus other compounds of less importance.

The chemical reactions which take place when water is added to port- land cement are not completely understood, but certain definite phenomena have been recorded.   After water is added to cement, the resulting paste is plastic (the degree of plasticity depending on the relative amounts of cement and water) for a time, and then begins to set or stiffen. Specifications generally require that the paste shall not begin to set within about an hour after mixing, and shall be fully set within 10 hr. The rate of setting can be controlled by the gypsum content.

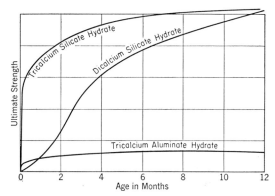

FIG. 13.5 Rate of hardening of constituents of portland cement.

After final set has been attained, the paste will continue to harden and increase in strength over a long period of time if it is kept at a favorable temperature and if moisture is available. Since continued hardening is a result of a chemical interaction between the cement grains and water, the paste will not gain in strength unless moisture is supplied to it, and unless the temperature is sufficiently high to prevent the water from freezing— yet not so high that the water will be driven out of combination with the paste.

The rate of hardening of portland cement is dependent on the chemical composition of the cement and on the size of the cement particles. The relative rates of hardening of the three principal constituents of portland cement are indicated in Fig. 13.5.

The tricalcium aluminate reacts the most rapidly, gaining an appreciable amount of its maximum strength the first day after mixing. The dicalcium silicate hardens the most slowly, but at the age of a year has about the same strength as the tricalcium silicate hydrate. The rate of hardening is increased with a decrease in the size of the cement particles. With more surface area available per unit weight of cement, the water can enter into combination with the finely ground cement more rapidly than with a cement in which the particles are comparatively large.

The strength and other properties of portland-cement mortars and concretes at any given time after mixing are therefore affected by the rate at which the hardening, which is a result of the chemical reactions, proceeds. The rate of hardening is influenced by the following factors: (1) the size of the cement particles; (2) the chemical composition of the cement particles; (3) the temperature; (4) the amount of moisture available for combination with the cement.

The strength of portland-cement mortars and concretes at any given time after mixing is also very directly related to the physical nature of the materials as influenced by the relative amounts of cement and water in the paste and by the nature of the materials (aggregate and admixtures) used in addition to the cement-water paste.

As compared with the amount of water required to hydrate the cement when it is first mixed, a larger amount is required to produce a workable, plastic paste. If the paste is thoroughly mixed, the water will be uniformly distributed throughout the paste, and will remain more or less uniformly distributed until the paste has set.[5] When the paste has hardened, there will be left within the material, voids which will weaken it structurally.

A similar phenomenon occurs in gypsum, as has been discussed previously.

Figure 13.6a shows the general experimentally determined relationship between the ultimate compressive strength of a well-cured concrete at an age of 28 days and the water-cement ratio, or the volume of water in the paste divided by the volume of cement in the paste. This relationship was discovered by Duff A. Abrams,[6] and is frequently called "Abrams' water-cement-ratio law." The lower curve is the one given by Abrams, and the upper curve shows the same relationship for a modern cement.

A somewhat more convenient presentation of the same information is given in Fig. 13.6b, in which ultimate compressive strength is plotted against the cement-water ratio expressed in terms of the solid volumes.[7] This relationship was pointed out by Inge Lyse.[8] The ordinates of the curve represent the ultimate compressive strength after 28 days of moist curing, and in any particular case depend on the type of cement used and on the nature and amount of the curing of the concrete, but are normally independent of the nature and amount of aggregate as long as the *aggregate is sound* and a *workable mixture is obtained.*

The tensile strength of portland-cement mortars and concretes is relatively low, being only about one-tenth of the compressive strength. It is

---

[5] Normally there will be some consolidation of the mass of paste, with part of the excess water rising to the top, before final set occurs.

[6] Lewis Institute Structural Materials Research Laboratory Bulletin No. 1 (1918).

[7] The solid volume (p. 92) of the cement is sometimes called the absolute volume in concrete literature. It may be obtained readily from the weight and the specific gravity of the cement particles. The average value of the solid specific gravity of portland cement is about 3.15.

[8] "Cement-Water Ratio by Weight Proposed for Designing Concrete Mixes," *Engineering News-Record*, Nov. 5, 1931.

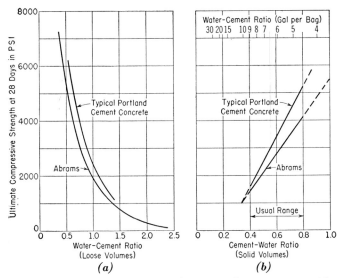

F‍IG. 13.6   Effect of relative proportions of water and cement upon ultimate compressive strength of concrete.

standard practice in design to assume that the material will carry no tension, and to add steel reinforcement to carry the tensile loads.

The amount of heat liberated during the hardening process, and the shrinkage which occurs after the initial set has taken place, are important factors in many instances.   Both factors are dependent on the chemical composition of the cement.   Of the three principal constituents, tricalcium aluminate liberates the most heat and undergoes the most shrinkage. Dicalcium silicate, which reacts the most slowly, releases the least heat of the three and has relatively low shrinkage.

13.18   Types of Portland Cement

The ASTM has issued specifications covering five types of portland cement.[9]

Type 1.   Type 1 is ordinary portland cement designed for use in general concrete construction where the special properties of the other types are not required.

Type 2.   Type 2 is designed for use in general concrete construction where the concrete must have resistance to disintegration under the action of moderate concentrations of sulfates, or for mass construction where a lower heat of hydration than that of Type 1 cement is required.

[9] ASTM Designation C 150.   *Modified*

Type 3.   Type 3 cement is designed for use where high early strength is required.   As has been indicated, cements do not hydrate immediately upon the addition of water, but continue to react and, consequently, to gain strength over a period of time.   Many times, circumstances (such as pavement repairs on a very busy thoroughfare) require the use of a concrete which will attain a high percentage of its potential strength within a few hours after placement.

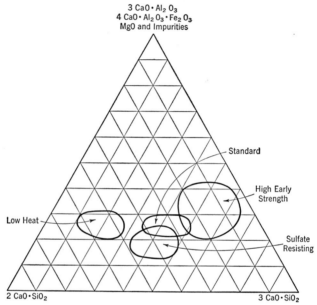

Fig. 13.7   Composition of special and standard portland cements by weight.

Several brands of accelerated cements or high-early-strength cements, have been developed to meet this need.   There are two ways in which the rate of increase of strength may be controlled.   One is by physical means and the other is by chemical means.

Since the fineness of grinding has an effect upon the rate of gain of strength, an accelerated cement may be produced by simply grinding the cement finer.   Most American high-early-strength cements are quite similar to standard portland cement in chemical composition, as indicated in Fig. 13.7, but a given weight has about 50 per cent more surface area.

In the other class of accelerated cements, the particle size is about the same as for a standard portland cement but the chemical composition is different.   Since tricalcium aluminate is the most active of the ingredients, a cement containing a high percentage of alumina will hydrate rapidly and gain strength in a few hours. This type of cement is used extensively in Europe and is made by melting a mixture of chalk and bauxite and grinding the resultant mass.

The rate of hardening may also be increased by increasing the amount of tricalcium silicate and decreasing the amount of dicalcium silicate, as may be seen from Fig. 13.5. Although the high-alumina cement will harden more rapidly, it may ultimately be weaker than a cement which possesses its rapid-hardening properties because of a high tricalcium silicate content. The high-alumina cement will also liberate more heat and will shrink more than a cement which is accelerated by other means. Consequently, this method of attaining a high-early-strength cement is not favored in the United States.

Type 4. Type 4 cement is for use where a low heat of hydration is required. In massive construction, such as Hoover Dam, an ordinary cement would liberate large quantities of heat, which would be retained in the concrete for a long period of time. In addition to the possible harmful effects of the high temperature in such a situation, there is the added danger of serious cracks forming in the concrete as it shrinks upon cooling. To avoid those undesirable effects there have been developed certain low-heat cements—cements which will not liberate excess amounts of heat during the hydration process.

Research has shown that those ingredients in the cement which hydrate most rapidly liberate the most heat and also contribute the most to the volume change in the concrete. Tricalcium silicate liberates about twice as much heat, and tricalcium aluminate liberates over three times as much heat, as dicalcium silicate. Ordinary portland cement liberates approximately 100 calories per gram of cement.

Consequently, the low-heat cements are made to contain a smaller amount of tricalcium aluminate and tricalcium silicate than the standard portland cement. Since the tricalcium aluminate and tricalcium silicate, by virtue of their rapid hydration, contribute much to the strength of concrete within the first few days after pouring, a concrete made of low-heat cement will be somewhat weaker at first than a similar concrete made of standard portland cement, but eventually the two will have practically the same strength.

Type 5. Type 5 portland cement is specified for use in situations requiring high resistance to disintegration under the action of sulfates. Cements which are exposed to water having a high alkali content, such as may be encountered in canals, culverts, and other hydraulic structures in certain regions, tend to disintegrate because of the unfavorable chemical reactions between the water and the cement. Investigations have shown that a cement which is low in tricalcium aluminate has greatly increased resistance to disintegration over a long time interval. Consequently a "sulfate-resisting" cement, the general composition of which is indicated in Fig. 13.7, has been developed for use in such situations. After being cured for about 3 months, it develops a greater strength than the other types of cement, and yet liberates very little more heat than low-heat cement.

The properties of the cement would probably be improved by further reduction of the alumina content, but the nature of the raw materials available and the difficulties encountered in the manufacturing processes do not make further reductions economically justifiable at present.

Some of the chemical and physical requirements for the five types of portland cement are indicated in Table 13.1.

TABLE 13.1

REQUIREMENTS FOR TYPES OF PORTLAND CEMENT

Ingredient or Property*	Type I	II	III	IV	V
Silicon dioxide (SiO_2), % [min]	....	21.0	....	....	24.0
Aluminum oxide (Al_2O_3), %	....	6.0	....	....	4.0
Ferric oxide (Fe_2O_3), %	....	6.0	....	6.5	4.0
Magnesium oxide (MgO), %	5.0	5.0	5.0	5.0	4.0
Sulfur trioxide (SO_3), %	2.0	2.0	2.5	2.0	2.0
Loss on ignition, %	3.0	3.0	3.0	2.3	3.0
Insoluble residue, %	0.75	0.75	0.75	0.75	0.75
Ratio of Al_2O_3 to Fe_2O_3	....	0.7 to 2.0	....	....	0.7 to 2.0
Tricalcium silicate ($3CaO \cdot SiO_2$), %	....	50	....	35	....
Dicalcium silicate ($2CaO \cdot SiO_2$), % [min]	....	....	....	40	....
Tricalcium aluminate ($3CaO \cdot Al_2O_3$), %	....	8	15	7	5
Fineness, specific surface, cm^2/g					
Average value [min]	1600	1700	....	1800	1800
Minimum value, any one sample	1500	1600	....	1700	1700
Tensile strength,† psi [min]					
1 day in moist air	....	....	275	....	....
1 day in moist air, 27 days in water	350	325	....	300	300
Compressive strength,‡ psi [min]					
1 day in moist air	....	....	1250	....	....
1 day in moist air, 27 days in water	3000	3000	....	2000	2200

NOTE: Another binding material with considerable volume stability during alteration of the moisture content is the hydrate of monocalcium silicate ($CaO \cdot SiO_2$). The monocalcium silicate may be prepared by autoclaving a mixture of finely ground lime and silica with portland cement.

* Maximum values unless otherwise indicated.

† The average tensile strength of not less than three standard mortar briquets composed of 1 part of cement and 3 parts of standard sand, by weight.

‡ The average compressive strength of not less than three mortar cubes composed of 1 part of cement and 2.75 parts of graded standard sand, by weight.

PROBLEMS

13.1 Construct a flow sheet showing the steps in the manufacture of gypsum building blocks.

13.2 (a) How many pounds of water are required to hydrate 100 lb of plaster of Paris? (b) Why is more water generally used?

13.3 Compare the modulus of resilience of a plaster of Paris having an ultimate compressive strength of 1800 psi with that of structural steel in tension.

13.4 Why is heat evolved when plaster of Paris sets?

13.5 Prepare a table comparing lime and gypsum in regard to raw material, preparation, chemical composition, action in setting, and important properties.

13.6 How many gallons of water should be added to 100 lb of plaster of Paris to produce a plaster with an ultimate compressive strength of approximately 2000 psi?

13.7 Plot a curve showing the variation in the ultimate compressive strength of plaster of Paris, with changes in the plaster-water ratio by weight.

13.8 If a 2-in. by 4-in. by 8-in. block of hardened plaster of Paris weighs 2.04 lb, what percentage of the block is voids? The specific gravity of $CaSO_4 \cdot 2H_2O$ is 2.32.

13.9 A cylinder of hardened plaster of Paris is 3 in. in diameter and 6 in. long, and weighs 1.48 lb. If there were no air voids present in the mixture of plaster and water from which the cylinder was made, approximately what total axial compressive load should the cylinder support before fracturing?

13.10 How many pounds of water are required to hydrate 100 lb of lime?

13.11 (a) How many pounds of hardened gypsum will be produced from a mixture of 100 lb of plaster of Paris and 10 gal of water? (b) What will be the approximate ultimate compressive strength of the hardened plaster?

13.12 Determine the effective volume of calcium hydroxide, sand, and water in a freshly mixed lime mortar containing a 180-lb barrel of quicklime, 0.80 cu yd (effective volume) of sand, and 17.3 gal of water, assuming that no air voids are present.

13.13 How many pounds of water are required per sack of cement in making a mortar for concrete which is to have a 28-day compressive strength of 4000 psi?

13.14 A certain cement paste contains $1\frac{1}{2}$ gal of water per 20 lb of cement. What 28-day compressive strength would be expected from concrete made with this paste?

13.15 If the particles of cement in one sack are assumed to be spherical and each is assumed to have a diameter of 0.003 in., (a) how many particles will the sack contain and (b) what will be the total surface area of the cement? Assume that the cement particles have a solid specific gravity of 3.14.

13.16 The chemical analyses of three cements gave the following results. How would you expect the cements to compare in regard to rapidity of hardening, potential strength, and suitability for making concrete?

Cement	CaO	SiO_2	Al_2O_3
A	85	5	8
B	60	20	10
C	35	6	50

13.17 If no heat were lost by radiation, how much would the temperature of a portland-cement concrete be increased in hardening? The specific heat of concrete is about 0.22 Btu per lb per deg F.

13.18 Convert a water-cement ratio of 0.80 by loose volume to (a) water-cement ratio by weight, (b) water-cement ratio by solid volume, and (c) cement-water ratio by solid volume.

13.19 How many gallons of water are required per sack of cement in making a concrete which is to have a 28-day ultimate compressive strength of 3000 psi?

13.20 What 28-day ultimate compressive strength might be expected from a concrete containing $5\frac{1}{2}$ gal of water per sack of cement?

13.21 How many sacks of cement are required to produce a cubic yard of cement paste having a water-cement ratio of 0.63 by loose volume?

13.22 Determine the effective volume of the cement, water, and sand in a freshly mixed mortar containing one bag of cement, 200 lb of sand having an effective specific gravity of 2.65 in the saturated surface-dry condition, and 7 gal of water.

13.23 How many pounds of cement and water are required to produce a cubic foot of a cement paste having a water-cement ratio of 0.60 by loose volume?

13.24 What effective volume will be occupied per sack of cement by each of the three principal ingredients in a cement mortar containing 3 parts of aggregate to 1 of cement (by weight) and having a water-cement ratio of 0.80 (by loose volume)? The aggregate has an effective specific gravity of 2.70.

13.25 Specify a suitable cement to be used in each of the following situations, and give reasons for your selection: (a) Foundation walls for a residence; (b) pavement repairs on approach to the George Washington Bridge; (c) Hoover Dam; (d) highway bridge in New Mexico.

14 Concrete

14.1 Uses of Concrete

The use of concrete as a structural material began with the Romans. With the puzzolan cement which they manufactured, and with broken stone and brick as aggregates, they produced a concrete which was suitable for wall and dome construction, and which in many instances has resisted disintegration for centuries.

As a result of the relatively recent development of standard portland cement and special cements, concrete has become one of the most important construction materials. It is extensively used for dams and retaining walls, for bridge construction, for floors, sidewalks, and pavement slabs, and for walls, beams, and columns in general building construction.

However, concrete presents a different problem to the construction engineer because, unlike most engineering materials, it is usually made on the job and immediately placed, little opportunity being allowed for sampling or testing. Since what may appear to be only minor variations in the technique of concrete making may have a very important influence upon the quality of the finished product, the engineer in charge of concrete construction must know the basic principles which govern the properties of concrete, in order that he may produce a satisfactory material economically.

The properties of concrete may be varied within wide limits. They depend on the quality of the ingredients, the relative proportions of the ingredients, the method of mixing and placing, and the curing, or treatment after placing.

14.2 Ingredients of Concrete

Concrete is a mixture of sand and rock or similar inert material (aggregates) held together by a cementing material. Usually the cementing material is portland cement, but sometimes binders such as asphalt or gypsum are used, in which case the concrete may be called asphaltic concrete or gypsum concrete. Only portland-cement concretes are considered in this chapter.

Aggregates. The most common aggregates are gravel and crushed stone, although cinders, blast-furnace slag, burned shale, crushed brick, or other materials may be used because of availability, or to alter such characteristics of the concrete as workability, density, appearance, or conductivity of heat or sound.

The material should be structurally sound and durable, and reasonably free from thin, flat, or elongated particles. It should be free from organic impurities, and should contain a minimum of loam, silt, coal, clay, mica, and dust, for these have a marked effect in reducing strength.

Usually aggregate which passes a No. 4 sieve is called fine aggregate, and that retained on a No. 4 sieve is coarse aggregate, although the division is purely arbitrary. If all the particles of aggregate are of the same size, or if too many fine particles are present, an excessive amount of cement paste will be required to produce a workable mixture; so a range of sizes aids in the production of an economical mixture. The ASTM (Designation C 33) and other organizations have established limits of grading in terms of sieve analyses. Aggregates which grade outside of the limits will, in general, result in unsatisfactory or uneconomical concrete.

The maximum permissible diameter of aggregate is governed by the type of construction. Specifications frequently limit the maximum size to one-fourth of the least dimension of the form in which the concrete is placed, and to three-fourths of the size of the smallest opening through which the concrete must pass. The use of the largest permissible workable size of aggregate decreases the amount of cement required. In mass construction, such as Hoover Dam, cobbles several inches in diameter may be used to advantage.

Cement. Normally a standard portland cement is used, although conditions may be such that a sulfate-resisting, a high-early-strength, or a low-heat portland cement is more desirable.

Water. The water should not contain any chemicals which will interfere with the hydration of the cement. Water which is suitable for drinking purposes is usually considered to be satisfactory for use in concrete.

Admixtures. Often relatively small quantities of materials such as hydrated lime, calcium chloride, diatomaceous earth, or soap are added to concrete mixtures, presumably to increase the workability, water-tightness, or strength. Such materials are known as admixtures. The same or similar materials are sometimes interground with the cement clinker, in which case they are known as additions. Some are beneficial under certain conditions, and others are positively harmful. Frequently the desired increase in workability, water-tightness, or strength may be obtained more economically by the use of additional cement.

14.3 Design Criteria

The best concrete for a given use is usually the one which will provide the necessary strength and the desired workability at the lowest cost in place. Most concrete must be designed to meet a certain strength and durability requirement; and, in general, those properties, such as imperviousness and resistance to abrasion, which contribute to durability, are directly related to strength. As was indicated in the discussion of portland cement, the strength of workable concretes depends primarily on the cement-water ratio, and may usually be controlled by it. Unless otherwise indicated, strength, as applied to concrete, refers to the ultimate compressive strength of the moist-cured concrete at the age of 28 days. The strength of concrete is usually between 70 and 90 per cent of the strength of its mortar.

If durability is the primary consideration, as it may be for concrete in exposed locations and not subjected to high stresses, the water-cement ratio may be established on the basis of the degree of exposure rather than on the basis of the desired ultimate strength. Experience indicates that under extreme conditions, where the concrete is exposed to alternate wetting and drying and freezing and thawing or where it is exposed to sea water, water-cement ratios between $5\frac{1}{2}$ and 6 gal per sack give the best results. In severe climates, such as that in the northern United States, but where the concrete is not continuously in contact with water, a water-cement ratio between 6 and $6\frac{3}{4}$ gal per sack is desirable. In moderate climates similar to that in the southern United States and where the concrete is not continuously in contact with the water, a water-cement ratio of 6 to $7\frac{1}{2}$ gal per sack will provide sufficient durability. For concrete which is protected, the water-cement ratio may be between 6 and $8\frac{1}{4}$ gal per sack.

Since concrete is shaped by casting it in molds, it must be workable. That is, it must be of such a consistency that it can be put into forms easily and is capable of being worked into a uniform, nonporous mass.

The workability of concrete is usually measured by its _slump_. The standard method of measuring slump consists in placing the freshly-mixed concrete in a mold in the form of a truncated cone, 12 in. high, 8 in. in diameter at the bottom, and 4 in. in diameter at the top. The concrete is placed in the slump cone in three layers, each layer being rodded thoroughly to compact it. When filled, the mold is immediately withdrawn by lifting it gently, and the slump of the concrete is measured as the vertical distance from the top of the mass to the original 12-in. height.

The proper slump will depend on the placement conditions. For concrete which is to be cast into heavily reinforced members, a slump of from 4 to 8 in. is necessary, while for massive sections a slump of from 1 to 4 in. may be sufficient.   Concrete having less slump may be satisfactorily placed with a vibrator.

An increase in the amount of mixing water will increase the slump (unless there is already too much water in the mixture), but it will also decrease the strength and increase the tendency of the ingredients of the concrete to segregate unless more cement is added.   Increasing the amount of cement paste increases the cost, so all three factors—strength, workability, and cost—are interrelated in a complex way.   Since these factors are directly dependent on the type of aggregate, no universal proportioning formula can be developed, and each design must be treated as a special case with the materials at hand.   Several methods have been developed for proportioning concrete mixtures to meet the design criteria expressed by water-cement ratio, slump, and cost.

14.4   Proportioning Methods

The principal difficulty in designing the most suitable concrete mixture lies in determining the optimum amount of cement-water paste to use with the aggregate to produce a workable, strong, durable, and economical concrete.   The amount of paste required is inherently dependent on the grading of the aggregate.   An aggregate composed of 1-in. spheres will obviously require more paste to produce a nonporous concrete than will an aggregate containing some small particles as well as the large spheres.   In other words, the relative amounts of the different sizes of particles of the aggregate play an important part in the design of the mixture.   Since an infinite variety of gradings may exist in aggregates, and since a large percentage of the final concrete consists of aggregate, the engineer needs to know something of the principles involved in making a suitable design.

Two approaches have been made in an attempt to find a logical solution of the design problem.   One consists in trying to evaluate the concrete-making characteristics of a given natural aggregate in terms of some property which may be easily measured.   The other approach consists in trying to find an ideal grading, and then making a given natural aggregate conform to that grading by adding or screening out the necessary material.

The principal methods which have been suggested for the design of mixtures are given here to indicate the different methods of approach to the complex problem of producing the best concrete from the available materials.   The method that is generally regarded as the most satisfactory at the present time is the trial-batch method used in conjunction with the cement-water ratio, as described in section 14.5.

Arbitrary volumes.   In this method the relative volumes of cement, fine aggregate, and coarse aggregate are arbitrarily selected, and enough water is added to produce the desired workability. A 1:1½:3 mixture, for example, indicates 1 part of cement, 1½ parts of fine aggregate, and 3 parts of coarse aggregate. Such a mixture might be used for highly-stressed structural parts. A 1:2:4 mixture is often used for floors, beams, columns, and similar units. For large foundations and heavy walls a leaner mixture, such as 1:3:5 or 1:3:6, might be used. This method is still commonly used on small jobs, but it gives unreliable results because of the variability in the water requirement of different aggregates and the resulting variable cement-water ratio.

2. **Sieve-analysis methods.** Practically all earlier attempts at the rational design of concrete mixtures were based on information obtained from a sieve analysis in which a representative sample of the aggregate was passed through a standard series of sieves, each having smaller openings than the preceding one. The percentage of the aggregate retained on each sieve indicates in a general way the grading, or distribution of sizes, of the aggregate. It was thought that such a sieve analysis could be made to serve as a criterion of the concrete-making capacity of a given aggregate.

Maximum-density curve. Based on the assumption that there is an ideal grading of aggregate which would hold for all aggregates and which would assure the production of concrete of maximum density (and also maximum strength), W. B. Fuller evolved the maximum-density curve giving such a grading of aggregates.

By screening out the excess material of any size, the engineer may bring the sieve-analysis curve of a given aggregate into agreement with Fuller's ideal curve. Then, by adding enough cement and water to fill the voids in the fine aggregate, concrete of maximum density should be obtained. Practically, the Fuller grading does not insure the production of concrete of satisfactory workability, or even of maximum density or strength, for a given cement content.

Surface-area method. The surface-area method proposed by L. N. Edwards is based on the assumption that the cement requirement for a suitable concrete is proportional to the total area of surface to be coated with cement, that is, to the surface area of the aggregate. The water content may be varied with the cement content or arbitrarily assigned to produce the degree of workability desired. Surface areas are not actually computed; instead, *surface moduli,* which are numbers proportional to the areas, are used. The surface modulus for an aggregate is based on the squares of the diameters of the aggregate particles as determined from the sieve analysis. The method has not come into general use.

Fineness modulus. Abrams evolved the fineness modulus—which is a function of the first powers of the diameters—from the sieve analysis as a criterion for the paste requirement of an aggregate. The water-cement ratio is used to determine the proper proportions of water and cement to be used in the paste.

Trial methods. Experience demonstrates that a sieve analysis alone cannot provide more than an indication of the grading of the aggregate, and will not indicate the cement and water content which will provide the most economical concrete of specified workability and strength. In view of the great variety of aggregates, this is not surprising. The present tendency is to place little direct dependence on sieve-analysis findings, and to approach the problem more directly, by using the cement-water ratio or the voids-cement ratio as a criterion for strength and by preparing trial batches for the determination of proportions to provide the workability desired.

Aggregate-voids method. The earliest of these attempts was the aggregate-voids method. It is based on the idea of providing slightly more than enough fine aggregate to fill all the voids in the coarse aggregate, and at least enough cement paste to fill the voids in the fine aggregate. (As much additional cement can be used as seems desirable from strength considerations.) Although the idea in itself is probably sound, it does not work well in practice because the smaller particles do not exactly fit themselves to the spaces between the larger particles. Instead, they tend to force the larger particles apart, increasing the space to be filled with cement paste.

Mortar-voids method. The mortar-voids method of Feret in France and of Talbot and Richart in this country is based on the following facts: (1) The void space (water and air) in a workable concrete is virtually equal to the void space in the mortar (cement, water, and fine aggregate) contained in the concrete; (2) the strength of the concrete increases as the volume of voids decreases; (3) the strength increases as the cement content increases.

In investigating aggregate, small experimental batches of mortars are made up to determine the proportions of ingredients which will give the minimum voids. The procedure is usually repeated for different cement contents in order to provide a range of workabilities. After the mortar-making possibilities of the fine aggregate have been thus explored, suitable proportions of coarse aggregate for mixtures of various degrees of workability are determined by additional trial batches. Each new aggregate must be analyzed in a similar manner, but when the characteristics of the aggregate have been determined a mixture may easily be designed.

Trial-batch method. A trial-batch technique for determining the mixture which will give the desired workability, combined with the cement-water (or water-cement) ratio as the criterion for probable strength, is the most widely used current method of design for concrete mixtures.

Since from 90 to 95 per cent of the voids present in a workable mortar or concrete are due to water present at the time of mixing, the voids-cement ratio and the water-cement ratio are fundamentally the same. If the water content of a mixture is increased, the voids are increased because the particles are simply floated or spread farther apart. Both the voids-cement-ratio method and the water-cement-ratio method disregard the influence of the coarse aggregate upon the strength of the concrete. This assumption is not strictly correct, as concrete containing even the best of coarse aggregates is from 10 to 30 per cent weaker than its mortar. While the recognition of this point is desirable, it is rarely of practical importance, since it is uneconomical and otherwise undesirable to use mortar as a substitute for concrete.

14.5 Trial-Batch Method of Design

A design by the trial-batch method involves first the selection of the cement-water ratio which should provide the strength (or durability) required. This may be obtained from tables, a curve, or from available test data. A trial batch is next prepared by mixing a few pounds of cement with water to produce a paste having the required cement-water ratio, and adding aggregate until the desired workability is obtained. Sieve-analysis curves may be used to give a preliminary indication of the relative amounts of fine and coarse aggregates desirable. If the workability is measured by the slump test, the batch need be only large enough to fill the slump cone (about 0.2 cu ft or 30 lb of ordinary concrete).

Both the total amount of aggregate and the relative proportions of fine and coarse aggregates must be determined. With a fixed cement-water ratio, more than one combination of aggregates may give the desired workability. The selection of the proper combination is based on their relative costs per unit volume of concrete in place.

14.6 Volume of Freshly Mixed Concrete

The determination of the amount of concrete which given amounts of aggregate, cement, and water will produce is of great importance in extensive concrete construction work. It is essential that the engineer be able to make an accurate estimate of the quantities of materials required.

The volume of concrete which will be produced by a given mixture is equal to the sum of the effective volumes of the aggregate, cement, and water, plus the volume of the voids, and minus the volume of water which may rise to the surface before the mixture attains final set. The voids and the water loss together will usually amount to less than 3 per cent of the volume of the concrete in place if the mixture is properly designed and placed. The minor corrections being disregarded, the volume of concrete will be the sum of the effective volumes of the aggregate, cement, and water.

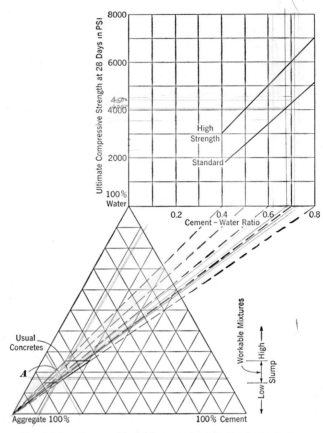

FIG. 14.1   Composition of concretes by effective volumes.

The triangular diagram in the lower part of Fig. 14.1 indicates all possible combinations of aggregate, cement, and water. The trapezoid near the lower left corner of the diagram indicates the approximate limits of the usual workable portland-cement concretes.[1] The point labeled A indicates a composition of 20 per cent water, 10 per cent cement, and 70 per cent aggregate. A line connecting any point in the diagram with the aggregate apex of the composition triangle is a line of constant cement-water ratio. If the line from A to the apex is extended upward to the

[1] The data for these diagrams are from tests of Professor W. M. Dunagan, Iowa State College.

right, it will intersect the horizontal axis of the upper diagram at a cement-water ratio of 0.5, which checks with the cement-water ratio as calculated from the composition. The upper diagram indicates that this particular mixture has a 28-day ultimate compressive strength of about 2600 psi if standard cement is used, or about 4000 psi if a high-early-strength cement is used.

A line drawn horizontally through a point in the triangular diagram represents, for a given aggregate, approximately a constant slump. A horizontal line through point A intersects the slump scale on the right in about the center of the portion indicated as workable mixtures. With one aggregate this might be a slump of 8 in., and with another aggregate the slump might be only 4 in., because of differences in the grading of the two aggregates.

The amount of each ingredient required to make a cubic yard of the mixture indicated by point A may easily be calculated if the specific gravities of the materials are known. For each cubic yard of concrete, 0.2 cu yd of water is required, which is equal to $0.2(27)(62.4) = 337$ lb. The cement required is 0.1 cu yd or $0.1(27)(3.15)(62.4) = 531$ lb, if the effective specific gravity of cement is 3.15. This is equal to $531/94 = 5.65$ sacks, or 5.65 cu ft loose volume. If the effective specific gravity of the aggregate is 2.65, the weight of the aggregate required will be $0.7(27)(2.65)(62.4) = 3125$ lb.

The calculated weight of water must be increased to allow for that which will be absorbed by the aggregate if the aggregate is dry, or decreased to allow for excess water in the aggregate, as the case may be.

The number of sacks of cement per cubic yard of freshly mixed concrete is called the *cement factor*.

14.7 Mixing

$$\text{Yield} = \frac{\text{cu. ft}}{\text{sack cement}}$$

The first step in the preparation of concrete is to measure the proper quantities of ingredients. Cement may be measured by weight or by volume. A sack of cement weighs 94 lb and is assumed to contain one cubic foot loose volume. Aggregates may be measured by volume, but measurement by weight is preferable and is rapidly becoming standard practice. Water may be measured by volume or by weight. Correction must be made for excess moisture which may be present in the aggregate, or for water which the aggregate will absorb. An aggregate which is saturated, but dry on the surface, is assumed to neither require nor provide excess water. Sand ordinarily carries sufficient excess moisture to lower materially the strength of the concrete unless a correction is made for it.

The mixing may be done by hand, but it is most frequently done in a mixer. The time required is usually from 1 to $1\frac{1}{2}$ min, the period depending on the consistency of the batch, but mixing should continue until all aggregate particles are thoroughly coated with paste and the mass has a uniform appearance. Some increase in strength may be obtained with longer mixing, but longer mixing is not usually economical.

14.8 Transporting and Placing

The concrete may be transported from the mixer to the place of use by truck, wheelbarrow, conveyors, belts, or chutes. Whatever the means, it should be done in such a way that the ingredients will not be segregated. Danger of segregation is greater in mixtures having high slumps than in stiff mixtures. Of course, final placement should be completed before the concrete has begun to set.

Care should also be taken in the placing of the concrete, to avoid segregation and to avoid air pockets. Usually the concrete is worked into place by spading and tamping or by using vibrators.

If the concrete must be placed under water, obviously it should not be merely dumped into the water, because of the leaching and segregation which will certainly occur. A device known as a tremie has been developed to aid in the placement of concrete under water. The tremie consists of a pipe of sufficient length to extend vertically from the bottom of the excavation to a convenient height above the water level. It is lowered into position in contact with the bottom of the space in which the concrete is to be cast, and is filled with concrete. Then the pipe is raised slightly, so that the concrete is allowed to flow out of the bottom into the form beneath the water surface. As the level of the concrete in the tremie is lowered, more concrete is added and the tremie is gradually raised.

14.9 Alteration of Strength After Placement

Care in the selection and proportioning of the ingredients, and in the design, mixing, and placement, does not insure the production of good concrete. The potential strength of a properly designed and placed concrete mixture can be developed only under favorable conditions of temperature and moisture.

Hydration requires the continued presence of moisture at temperatures well above freezing. The application of heat to prevent freezing without keeping all surfaces moist may damage the concrete seriously by halting hydration (and strength gain), even though the concrete is saved from disruption by freezing. At low temperatures extra-long curing periods are required, and thus the removal of forms and the placing of the concrete in service are delayed.

Concrete frozen soon after placement may sometimes be salvaged by allowing it to thaw out and giving it a long period of favorable curing.

Partially hardened concrete may be more severely damaged by frost than that which is frozen before setting has started.

The effect of moisture in its relationship to the strength of hardened concrete is shown graphically in the strength–age-curing diagram in Fig. 14.2.[2] While the strengths indicated are correct only for the particular mixtures used in the series of tests from which the data were obtained, they do indicate qualitatively the changes which take place in the usual concretes.

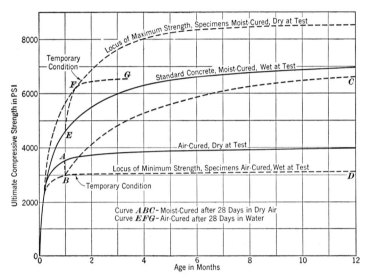

FIG. 14.2   Effect of curing upon compressive strength of concrete.

The heavy solid line labeled *standard concrete* shows the gain in strength of a concrete which has available all of the moisture necessary for hydration.   It was obtained from specimens stored under water and tested while saturated.   The rate of increase in strength is rapid at first but gradually decreases, although gain in strength continues for a long period of time.

The lower solid line labeled *air-cured* indicates the changes in strength of a concrete similar in all respects to the first except that it is cured in dry air and tested dry.   For a period of a week or more after casting, there is practically no difference between the standard concrete and the air-cured concrete, because moisture is still available in the air-cured specimen. However, when the air-cured specimen does dry out, there is a marked decrease in the rate of which it gains strength, and at the age of 1 year the

[2] Based upon tests of Professor H. J. Gilkey, Iowa State College.   Essentially the same data are discussed in H. J. Gilkey, "The Moist Curing of Concrete," *Engineering News-Record*, Vol. 119 (1937), pp. 630-33.

strength may be only a little over one-half of the strength of a moist-cured concrete.

The method of curing is not the only factor which affects the strength; the moisture content at the time of test also has its effect upon the strength of concrete, much as it does with stone, wood, and other materials. Consequently, a concrete which is cured in air and then saturated with water will have a lower strength than one which has undergone identical curing but which remains dry.

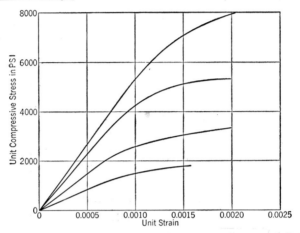

FIG. 14.3   Stress-strain diagrams for concrete in compression.

However, if the concrete is kept moist, the cement will resume hydration and the strength of the concrete will increase. Curve *ABC* in Fig. 14.2 indicates the variation in strength of a specimen of the same concrete which was stored in air for a month and then placed in water. At point *A* (age 1 month) the strength is that of the air-dry concrete—about 3500 psi. As soon as the concrete is immersed in water, its strength drops, reaching a minimum value of about 3000 psi (point *B*) when completely saturated in a few hours. Then, as there is an opportunity for additional hydration, the strength gradually increases, reaching, at the total age of 1 year, a strength (point *C*) slightly below that of the standard-cured concrete. The lower dotted line *BD* indicates the lowest possible strength which the concrete might have at any time. The minimum strength at any time is obtained by keeping the concrete in dry air until a few hours before the given time, and then saturating it. This minimum represents only a temporary condition, as the cement will resume hydration as soon as it is wet.

Since the strength of the dry concrete is decreased by saturating it, the strength of the moist-cured concrete may be increased by drying it. The upper dashed line (curve *EFG*) in Fig. 14.3 represents the strength-age relation for a concrete which is cured moist for 28 days (point E) and then dried out. After the concrete is removed from the water, the curve rises rapidly (EF), indicating the effect of the mechanical hardening upon drying, much as a wet sponge becomes harder upon drying. The curve flattens out (FG) when the concrete has dried out, and remains nearly horizontal, as there is no opportunity for hydration of the cement. After a year it has about the same strength (when dry) as the saturated moist-cured concrete, and when saturated it has only about two-thirds the strength of the moist-cured concrete.

The upper dotted line represents the maximum attainable temporary strength of the concrete, obtained by curing the concrete in water until shortly before the given time and then allowing it to dry. The dry condition referred to is that which will be obtained in normal air at ordinary temperatures. If the moisture is forced out by artifical heat, the concrete may be damaged.

The rate of drying out is influenced by many factors, among which are the relative humidity of the air and the volume–surface-area ratio of the mass of concrete. While the interior of a large mass of concrete is seemingly protected, the quality of the surface concrete may be seriously impaired by lack of moisture during the curing period.

Figure 14.2 shows the variations in strength which took place in certain laboratory specimens. The same types of changes, to an extent which depends on specific conditions, are continually taking place in all concretes.

Since all these variations in strength take place after the concrete is mixed, alteration of the cement-water ratio in the design of the mixture will change only the numerical values of the ordinates; the alteration will have no effect on the relative positions of the curves. Since the cement-water ratio versus strength curves which are used in designing mixtures are usually based on the 28-day compressive strength of *moist-cured* concrete, a concrete which is improperly cured may not be sufficiently strong for its intended use, even though it is properly proportioned.

14.10 Properties of Concrete

Some typical stress-strain diagrams of concrete tested in compression are shown in Fig. 14.3. They indicate in a general way the variation of properties possible. The ultimate tensile, torsional, and flexural strengths vary in much the same way as the ultimate compressive strength, but are, respectively, only about one-tenth, one-eighth, and one-sixth as great.

The modulus of elasticity of concrete varies from 1,500,000 psi to 5,500,000 psi, with an average value of about 3,500,000 psi for many of the concretes being made at the present time. In general, the modulus of elasticity tends to increase as the strength increases. Poisson's ratio for concrete is about 0.2. The thermal conductivity of concrete varies from 0.8 to 2.1 Btu per cu ft per hr per deg F, while the specific heat is from about 0.21 to 0.24 Btu per lb per deg F. The coefficient of thermal expansion of ordinary concrete is about the same as that of structural steel—0.000006 per deg F, while the coefficient for lightweight concretes may be as low as 0.000002 per deg F.

14.11 Deterioration of Concrete

After it has initially hardened, concrete is continually subject to change in properties. In this respect it is somewhat similar to a metal that undergoes age hardening at room temperatures. However, the extent of the changes in concrete is normally much greater than in metal, and the properties may become less desirable with time.

The changes in properties are a result of physical and chemical alterations. Concrete, as a material, is porous. Hence water, water vapor, and various gases may penetrate it. These materials may be such that they will react with the cement paste or with the aggregate. Chemical interaction usually involves a change in volume and this may result in excessive stresses leading to cracking and progressive disintegration.

Specifically, when water or water vapor enters concrete it may interact with the cement, hydrating it and increasing its volume. As a result, the concrete swells or attempts to swell. Normally this type of volume change does no damage. Conversely, as moisture leaves the concrete, shrinkage occurs, and this frequently induces a state of tension sufficiently great to crack the concrete. Other materials may enter the concrete, attacking the cement paste and causing it to lose its adhesive qualities. With the bond between the paste and aggregate destroyed, disintegration follows rapidly.

Reactive aggregates are sometimes a cause of disintegration of concrete. Certain cherts are known to react in exposed locations, resulting in an increase in volume that causes the concrete to go to pieces rapidly. The presence of dilute acid or alkaline reagents may lead to difficulty.

In general, aside from mechanical abrasion of the surface, the principal difficulty is caused by shrinkage resulting from dehydration. All parts of the concrete member cannot shrink at equal rates because of differences in exposure and in degrees of restraint. This difference in the extent of shrinkage will cause cracks to open.

Since the amount of shrinkage increases with an increase in cement content, structural damage as well as unsightliness may result from the use of too rich a concrete. Unequal rates of expansion of adjacent layers of concrete may result in disintegration. For example, some floors and sidewalks are constructed with a layer of rich concrete or mortar on a base of lean concrete. The top layer will shrink more than the base, this condition causing cracks to open up in the top layer, and also partially destroying the bond between the two layers. If these cracks fill with water which subsequently freezes, spalling will result. Spalling as a result of cracks filling with moisture which freezes may frequently be seen in sidewalks (see Fig. 14.4) and also in pavements and other exposed surfaces.

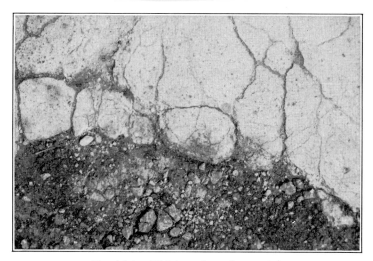

Fig. 14.4   Disintegration of concrete.

Volume changes are also produced by changes in temperature, and these changes may result in cracking. For example, a pavement slab will tend to curl away from the subgrade under the influence of a temperature differential between top and bottom, and a heavy truck passing over the unsupported section may cause it to crack.

14.12 Reinforced Concrete

Since its tensile strength is low, concrete cannot be depended upon to resist tensile loads. Consequently, members in which tensile stresses are built up are reinforced with steel in such a way that the tension will be taken by the steel, while the concrete carries the compression. This combination of steel with concrete produces members which are well adapted to carrying both tensile and compressive stresses. Therefore, floorbeams, girders, slabs, and similar flexural members are very often made of reinforced concrete.

Columns, and sometimes beams, may contain longitudinal steel bars to assist in carrying compressive stresses. Some columns are also spirally reinforced, having the additional reinforcement in the form of a helix with its axis parallel to the axis of the column.   Since the coefficients of thermal expansion of steel and concrete are the same, changes in temperature will not cause serious stresses between steel and concrete.

Steel also tends to distribute shrinkage cracks in concrete, so concrete members which carry no tensile stress may contain steel to prevent the formation of large cracks.

The combination of concrete and steel is also popular because of its resistance to fire.   Steel members are often encased in concrete for fire protection.

The term prestressed concrete refers to reinforced concrete in which the longitudinal reinforcing bars are put under initial tension before the concrete is cast around them.   After initial hardening has taken place in the concrete the external forces on the bars are released, and the bars—as they tend to shorten—put the concrete under initial compression.   This helps prevent shrinkage cracks in the concrete and also increases the resistance of the member to bending because the concrete will, in effect, take tensile stress until the initial compressive stress is balanced.

Post-stressed concrete refers to concrete members in which the longitudinal reinforcement is stressed in tension after initial hardening of the concrete has taken place.   It is often accomplished by threading the ends of the bars and allowing them to project beyond the ends of the beam. After the beams are removed from the forms, nuts are placed on the rods and tightened.

PROBLEMS

14.1 What water-cement ratio would you recommend for a new sidewalk on a college campus?

14.2 What maximum size of aggregate is permissible for use in the beam shown in the accompanying illustration?

14.3 State what slump you would recommend for the concrete to be placed in the beam shown in the accompanying illustration (a) if a vibrator is to be used in placing the concrete and (b) if no vibrator is available.

14.4 How many pounds of each of the ingredients are required to produce a 10-ft length of the beam represented in the accompanying illustration if the concrete is to have an ultimate compressive strength of 3500 psi at 28 days? Assume that a $1:3\frac{1}{2}$ mixture (by weight) gives the desired slump, and that the effective specific gravity of the aggregate is 2.64.

14.5 Determine the minimum void space that may exist in a container filled with uniform spheres 1 in. in diameter.

14.6 Approximately what stress in an average concrete produces the same strain as a temperature change of 100 F?

14.7 Outline the procedure to be followed in proportioning the concrete mixture to be used in a reinforced-concrete column.   The concrete is to have an ultimate compressive strength of 4500 psi at 28 days.

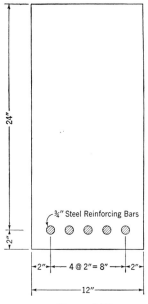

¾" Steel Reinforcing Bars

←2"→|←—— 4 @ 2" = 8" ——→|←2"→|

|←————— 12" —————→|

24"

2"

PROB. 14.2

14.8 Determine the volume of freshly mixed concrete made from 1 sack of cement, 7 gal of water and a 1:2.90:4.10 mixture by weight. Assume the specific gravity of the aggregate to be 2.65, and neglect voids.

14.9 A certain batch of concrete contained 45.3 lb of water, 100 lb of portland cement (sp gr 3.10), and 500 lb of aggregate (sp gr 2.65). How many cubic feet of freshly mixed concrete will the batch produce if there are no voids?

14.10 What strength may the concrete of problem 14.9 be expected to have at an age of 28 days if properly cured?

14.11 How much would the cement-water ratio of the concrete in problem 14.9 be changed if the aggregate contained 3 per cent excess moisture by weight?

14.12 If the aggregate in the concrete of problem 14.9 contained 1 per cent excess moisture, how much would the 28-day strength of the concrete be affected?

14.13 How many pounds of water should be added to 5 lb of cement in making a trial batch for a concrete which is to have an ultimate compressive strength of 4000 psi at 28 days?

14.14 What volume of concrete may be expected from a batch containing 3.25 lb of water, 5 lb of cement (sp gr 3.12), and 25 lb of aggregate (sp gr 2.70)?

14.15 What strength might be expected of the concrete of problem 14.14 after 28 days of moist curing?

14.16 What minimum weights of water, cement, and aggregate are required for a trial batch if the concrete is to have an ultimate compressive strength of 4000 psi and the leanest mixture to be considered is 1:3 by weight of an aggregate having an effective specific gravity of 2.68?

14.17 A concrete floor 20 ft wide, 80 ft long, and 6 in. thick is to be constructed of concrete having a 28-day compressive strength of 3500 psi. A trial batch has indicated that the proper consistency will be obtained if the weight of the aggregate is 5 times the weight of the cement. Determine the quantities of materials required for the floor. The specific gravity of the cement is 3.10, the specific gravity of the aggregate is 2.60, and the aggregate in the stockpile contains 2 per cent excess moisture by weight.

14.18 A batch of concrete consisting of 2 sacks of portland cement (sp gr 3.10), 15 gal of water, and 1000 lb of aggregate (sp gr 2.65) produces a workable mixture. Determine the volume of concrete which may be expected from this batch.

14.19 How many sacks of cement are required for a concrete slab 28 ft long, 16 ft wide, and 6 in. thick, if a 1:2½:3 mixture by loose volume and 6 gal of water per sack are to be used? The specific gravity of the cement is 3.10, and that of the aggregate is 2.65. The fine aggregate weighs 110 pcf, and the coarse aggregate weighs 100 pcf.

14.20 Determine how many sacks of cement will be required to make 1 cu yd of concrete, if the materials are in the following proportions:

Material	Quantity	Sp Gr
Water	7 gal	1.00
Aggregate	300 lb	2.60
Cement	1 sack	3.15

14.21 Determine the number of sacks of portland cement required for a mile of concrete pavement 20 ft wide and 9 in. (avg) thick. The following trial batch has been found to give a satisfactory mixture:

Material	Weight
Cement (sp gr 3.15)	6.00 lb
Water	3.18 lb
Aggregate (sp gr 2.65)	36.02 lb

14.22 (a) Compute the number of units of each of the following materials needed to produce 1 cu yd of concrete with a 1:2:4 mixture by weight and a cement-water ratio of 0.60 by solid volume.

Material	Sp Gr
Water	1.00
Cement	3.15
Sand	2.65
Stone	2.60

(b) Determine the cost for materials, using acceptable local prices.

14.23 How many sacks of cement are required per cubic yard of concrete if each batch of concrete contains 7 gal of water, 1 sack of cement, and 3 parts of aggregate to 1 part of cement by weight? The specific gravity of the aggregate is 2.65, and that of the cement is 3.15.

14.24 A mixture of 14 lb of water, 22 lb of cement (sp gr 3.10), and 100 lb of a certain aggregate (sp gr 2.65) produces a workable mixture. (a) What amount of each of these materials is needed to produce 5 cu ft of concrete and (b) what is the predicted 28-day standard strength?

14.25 By means of a strength-time diagram, show how the strength of two samples of concrete, A and B, may vary if A is moist-cured during a period of 12 months and dried immediately before testing, while B is air-cured for 3 months, moist-cured for 9 months, and tested wet.

14.26 A newly cast concrete test specimen is placed in water for 1 month, air-dried for 3 months, moist-cured for 2 months, and exposed to dry air for 2 weeks prior to being tested in the air-dry condition. Sketch a curve indicating how the ultimate compressive strength might be expected to vary during this period.

14.27 By plotting strength against age, show the changes in strength which take place in a concrete cylinder subjected to the following sequence of conditions: 1 month in water, 6 months in dry air, 6 months in water, and indefinitely in dry air.

14.28 Two concrete specimens, A and B, are made from the same batch of concrete. Specimen A is cured under water for one year. Specimen B is subjected to the following conditions during the same period: air-cured for 30 days, cured under water for 4 months, and air-cured for the following 7 months. Indicate, by means of a diagram, the variation in compressive strength that each of the two specimens may be expected to exhibit during the one-year period.

14.29 Three concrete test specimens are made from the same batch of concrete and treated as follows during a one-year period: A is cured in water; B is cured in air for 3 months and in water for 9 months; C is cured in water for 1 month, in air for 2 months, in water for 6 months, and in air for 3 months. Sketch curves indicating how the ultimate compressive strength of each specimen might be expected to vary during the year.

14.30 Compare the modulus of toughness, the elastic strength, and the modulus of resilience of an average 5000-psi concrete with the same properties for hickory.

14.31 A short 12-in. by 12-in. concrete strut carries a total axial compressive load of 120,000 lb. If the typical 3500-psi concrete indicated in Fig. 14.3 is used, what is the factor of safety (a) with respect to slip and (b) with respect to fracture?

14.32 A concrete post 10 in. by 10 in. by 2 ft long of the 5300-psi concrete indicated in Fig. 14.3 carries an axial compressive load of 120,000 lb. How many foot-pounds of energy load could the post be expected to absorb in addition to the static load without appreciable inelastic action occurring?

14.33 (a) If aluminum were available at the same price as steel, would it be more satisfactory or less satisfactory than steel for concrete reinforcement? (b) Explain.

14.34 (a) Do the properties of Monel metal make it suitable for use as concrete reinforcement? (b) Explain.

15 Miscellaneous Materials

15.1 History of Rubber

The first evidences of the use of rubber are found among the remains of the Mayan civilization in British Honduras. Excavations have indicated that rubber was known to the Mayans in the eleventh century. The use of rubber by the Indians of Mexico and Central America is mentioned in the writings of Spanish explorers of the early sixteenth century. Rubber was employed by the natives in the manufacture of waterproof garments, shoes, and small vessels.

With the discovery in 1761 that rubber could be dissolved in ether, the foundations of rubber technology were laid, for that provided a means of shaping the rubber. Rubber tubes, for example, were made by coating a wax cylinder with the rubber solution. As the ether evaporated, the rubber was left in a thin film. Several coatings could be applied to produce thicker films. When the proper thickness was obtained, the wax cylinder was removed by melting it.

The first factory for the manufacture of rubber goods, principally waterproof fabrics, was established in Glasgow in 1823. Shortly afterwards it was found that pieces of freshly cut rubber could be formed into a homogeneous plastic mass by the application of heat and pressure. The first rubber articles manufactured were unsatisfactory because they were sticky when warm and stiff when cold.

About 1832 it was found that the addition of sulfur to rubber improved the stability of the product and decreased its tackiness. With the discovery of vulcanization and the effects of the addition of sulfur, the way was clear for the development of the rubber industry.

Synthetic rubber is made from a number of different raw materials. Rubber substitutes generally similar to rubber but more resistant to deterioration in the presence of oil and sunlight are available. One commercial product, Neoprene, is made by the polymerization of chloroprene, which is produced from coal, limestone, and hydrochloric acid.

Of the world production of approximately 3,000,000 tons of rubber in 1955, slightly over one-half was produced in the United States. Of this, about 60 per cent was synthetic rubber.

15.2   Production of Rubber

Natural rubber is produced from *latex,* a milky juice found in the bark of a number of tropical trees and certain other plants.   Formerly the latex was obtained from wild trees, but at the present time practically all of the commercial rubber comes from trees grown on plantations.   Trees of the genus Hevea are used most extensively because of their relatively high yield and the freedom of the rubber from impurities.

Malaya, Indonesia, and Ceylon are the principal rubber-producing countries.   A large quantity of the wild rubber formerly produced came from Brazil.

The latex, which contains the rubber molecules (C_5H_8) in microscopic globules, is obtained by tapping the tree, a narrow slit being carefully cut through the bark to the latex tubes which lie in the soft inner bark.   The latex is collected in vessels in a manner similar to that used for the collection of maple sap or turpentine.   The normal yield of a tree is about 5 lb of latex per year.

The rubber is separated from the latex by evaporation or by coagulation.   The liquid portions of the latex will evaporate readily, but the residue will contain resins and other substances in addition to the rubber, so it is more desirable to separate the rubber by coagulation.   Of the many substances which will cause coagulation of the rubber, formic acid is the one most generally used, although acetic acid has also been used extensively in the past.   The latex is strained, and water is added to bring it to a definite concentration (usually 15 to 20 per cent rubber) before the acid is added.

The coagulum formed by the addition of the acid is put through a washing mill, which cleans the crude rubber and rolls it into thin sheets or into crepe.   After further washing the sheets are drained, dried, and smoked.   The crude rubber is then ready to be shipped to market.

Since the crude rubber is tacky and weak, and has other undesirable properties, it must be processed to improve its properties.   Such processing is known as vulcanization and usually includes the addition of sulfur to the rubber.

The crude rubber is shredded, mixed with sulfur, and shaped by rolling or pressing.   During the vulcanizing operation a temperature between 140 C (284 F) and 175 C (347 F) is usually maintained to aid in the combination of the sulfur and the rubber, although they will combine at ordinary temperatures.   The molding pressure varies from 350 psi for soft rubber to 1800 psi for hard rubber.

The exact nature of the vulcanizing action is not understood.   Apparently the sulfur first dissolves in the rubber and then combines with it chemically. Certain other chemicals have the same general effect as sulfur in altering the properties of rubber, but have not come into general use. Frequently other materials called *fillers* are added to change the rate of vulcanization, or to alter the properties of the rubber.

Cellular rubber is produced in the form of molded parts or sheets by three different methods. One of these is latex foam, which is made by whipping air into liquid latex rubber. The entrained air forms as much as 90 per cent of the total volume, so the product is light and soft. Sponge rubber is made by putting into the rubber a compound that will form a gas when the mixture is heated during vulcanization. As the gas is formed and expands it produces cells which are usually interconnected. Closed cellular rubber is made by dissolving nitrogen gas in the rubber stock before vulcanization. When the stock is heated the gas expands and produces cells. However, the expansion is controlled so that the cells are not interconnected as they are in sponge rubber.

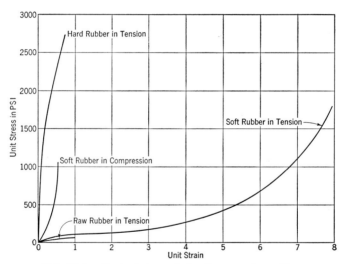

FIG. 15.1 Typical stress-strain diagrams for rubber.

15.3 Properties of Rubber

The properties of rubber are dependent on its degree of vulcanization. Rubber containing no sulfur is sensitive to temperature change, is soluble in a number of reagents, has a tendency to become tacky, and is relatively weak. A sulfur content of 7 per cent results in a rubber which is much stronger and which may be stretched from 8 to 10 times its original length without breaking. It is also resistant to many of the solvents of raw rubber and is less sensitive to variations in temperature. Rubber containing a high percentage of sulfur is hard and brittle. The maximum amount of sulfur which will combine with rubber is about 32 per cent.

Some typical stress-strain diagrams for rubber are shown in Fig. 15.1. One respect in which soft rubber differs from most materials is that its tensile stress-strain diagram has a reverse curve. At high stresses it has a tendency to stiffen with increasing load. The ultimate tensile strength of hard rubber may be as much as 10,000 psi.

The modulus of elasticity is a function of the rate of loading. Under a rapidly applied strain the modulus may be as much as three times what it is under a slowly applied load.

The properties of rubber may also be varied by the addition of fillers. Carbon black is the one most widely used, but zinc oxide, basic magnesium carbonate, and clay are also used to produce certain effects. Chalk, infusorial earth, barytes, and similar materials are sometimes added as cheap diluents.

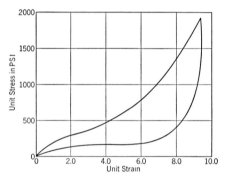

Fig. 15.2   Stress-strain diagram for rubber subjected to a cycle of stress in tension.

The effect of the filler upon the properties of the rubber is dependent on the fineness and amount of the filler, and on the nature of the basic rubber mixture, but carbon black, zinc oxide, basic magnesium carbonate, and clay in amounts less than about 30 per cent by volume will increase both the tensile strength and the modulus of toughness of the rubber. The use of 20 per cent carbon black will increase the modulus of toughness about 70 per cent.[1]

The degree of heat used in vulcanization also affects the stress-strain diagram. An increase in the time of vulcanization up to a certain limiting value increases the ultimate tensile strength and reduces the ultimate elongation. If the time of vulcanization is carried beyond the optimum, there is a decrease in both the ultimate tensile strength and the elongation.

[1] W. B. Wiegand, *Ind. Eng. Chem.*, 17:939 (1925).

Because of the large deformation which it will take before breaking, soft rubber has by far the greatest elastic-energy-absorbing capacity per unit volume for a given stress of any of the engineering materials. This property makes it a very useful material for shock absorbers and buffers. Working values of strain are often as much as 3.0 in tension. That is, a 1-in. length may be stretched to 4 in. Working stresses are usually below 100 psi in tension.

However, when rubber is subjected to a cycle of stress, much of the energy is lost in hysteresis as is indicated in Fig. 15.2. Most of this lost energy is dissipated in heat, which has a deteriorating effect upon the rubber.

Air, light, and oil tend to make rubber hard and brittle. Water, dilute acids, and dilute alkalies have little effect upon vulcanized rubber. Its low electrical conductivity makes natural rubber useful as an insulating material, either in the form of cable covering or as instrument panels. However, by the addition of the proper filler, rubber may be made which is a satisfactory conductor of electricity.

15.4 Synthetic Rubbers

There are six general groups of materials being manufactured as synthetic rubber or rubber substitutes. These products are often called elastomers.

Neoprene. The first successful commercial substitute for rubber was Neoprene. It is manufactured by copolymerization of chloroprene, which is produced from coal, limestone, and hydrochloric acid. It has good resistance to light, heat, and air and may be vulcanized without the addition of sulfur, but it cannot be treated to produce hard rubber. It is used for truck tires, hose, gaskets, and similar applications where resistance to oil is desirable.

GR-S. The synthetic rubber most similar to natural rubber, and the one most widely used, is GR-S. It is a copolymer of butadiene and styrene. The product is less strong and resilient than natural rubber, but may be vulcanized with the addition of sulfur and cured to produce a hard rubber. Its principal use is for automobile tires. The strength and abrasion resistance of GR-S may be improved by polymerizing it at low temperatures, in which case it is called cold rubber.

Buna N. In general, Buna N is similar to GR-S but has a higher resistance to petroleum. It may be vulcanized with the addition of sulfur and cured to form hard rubber. Its principal applications are for oil and gas hose and for chemical-resistant tank linings. Buna N is a copolymer of butadiene and acrylonitrile. It is also known as nitrile rubber.

Butyl. Butyl rubber is made from petroleum by a copolymerization of isobutylene and other hydrocarbons. It may be vulcanized with the addition of sulfur but cannot be cured to produce hard rubber. It is less strong than natural rubber but is highly resistant to deterioration. The principal use of butyl rubber is for inner tubes because it has a high resistance to air leakage.

Thiokol. Of all the rubber substitutes, the thiokol materials, which are polysulfides, have the highest resistance to deterioration, and have the lowest strengths. They are used for gaskets, tank linings, and oil hoses.

Silicone rubber. The products in the group of elastomers known as silicone rubber have good stability at elevated temperatures and good resilience at low temperatures. The silicone rubbers are generally weak, but they have good resistance to oil.

Other synthetic elastomers are being developed, since the need for materials with the general properties of rubber is continually increasing. Among the materials being developed are the polyacrylic, ester, and polyethylene glycol rubbers.

TABLE 15.1

AVERAGE VALUES OF PROPERTIES OF NATURAL RUBBER AND A FEW ELASTOMERS

Material	Specific Gravity	Ult. Tens. Str. (psi)	Percent. Elong.	Therm. Cond.*
Natural rubber	0.93	3000	700	0.99
Neoprene	1.25	3500	500	1.34
GR-S	0.94	400	500	1.82
Buna N	1.00	600	500	1.82
Butyl	0.91	3000	700	....
Thiokol	1.35	300	400	....
Silicone rubber	1.2–2.6	325	300	....

* Btu in./hr ft² deg F.

Representative values of a few of the properties of elastomers are given in Table 15.1. The unusual capacity of these materials for extension without fracture is attributed to their molecular structure. The molecules of which the elastomers are composed are long chains that, in the finished product, are intertwined. As the product is stretched the molecules tend first to be straightened and uncoiled. This action permits far more elastic strain than occurs in a metal crystal in which the strain develops as a result of sliding of adjacent layers of atoms.

ROPE

15.5 Uses of Rope

The manufacture of rope dates back to prehistoric times. Roots, grasses, bark, skin, hair, rawhide, leather, fibers, and wire of various metals have all been used in making rope. At the present time practically all of the rope and cable which is used for engineering purposes is manufactured from either wire or vegetable fibers.

Wire rope is made by twisting together wires which extend from one end of the rope to the other. Steel is the most commonly used material, but iron, bronze, copper, and aluminum have been used in cases where their properties made them particularly advantageous.

Cables for suspension bridges are made by compacting and binding together many parallel wires which have been hung in place one at a time. Steel having a high elastic strength is usually employed for this purpose.

Fiber rope is made by twisting together relatively short fibers of vegetable origin. The fibers which are used may be classified as hard or soft, depending on the nature of their growth. Hard fibers are those which are obtained from the leaves and bark of the plant, while soft fibers grow in a thin layer beneath the bark. Manila and sisal are hard fibers; hemp, flax, and jute are soft fibers.

15.6 Manufacture of Fiber Rope

The fibers must first be removed from the rest of the vegetable material. In manila and sisal the hard fibers may be removed by scraping away the pulpy material of the leaves and bark, but the plants which yield soft fibers must be soaked in water until the gummy substance which holds the fibers together has been rotted away. The stalks are then dried and the fibers are cleaned by combing.

The cleaned fibers are treated with a lubricant, usually a petroleum oil, to increase their workability and durability. Then they are combed, drawn, and spun into yarn in much the same manner as textiles. The yarns are twisted into strands, and the strands into rope. Usually the direction of twist in the strands is opposite to the twist in the yarn and rope, to prevent the rope from untwisting when a weight is suspended from one end. In a *hard-laid* rope the amount of twist is greater than in a *soft-laid* rope.

Three-strand rope, known as plain lay, is the most common, although four-strand and six-strand ropes are also made. The latter two are usually twisted about a core, or heart, which serves to hold the strands in the proper relative positions. When three or four small ropes are twisted together, the construction is known as cable lay.

15.7 Properties of Rope

The amount of twist in a rope influences its strength. The fibers in a rope fail by being cut or sheared off by the action of adjacent fibers, rather than by being pulled apart; so a rope with a large amount of twist is weaker than medium-laid or soft-laid rope. The tensile strength of a rope is less than the sum of the tensile strengths of the individual fibers that make up the rope.

A four-strand rope will carry approximately as much load as a three-strand rope of the same nominal size; but since it presents more surface its wearing qualities are superior, and it is also more flexible. Cable-lay rope is more resilient and more resistant to wear, but is weaker than plain-lay rope. It is used for drilling and wrecking purposes.

Rope is subject to structural damage by abrasion and sharp bending. Properly made long splices may develop nearly the full strength of the rope, but knots develop only from 50 to 75 per cent of the strength. The fibers are subject to deterioration under the action of acids and bases, and will rot if alternately wet and dry unless protected by tar, oil, or some other water-repelling agent.

Manila fiber, which is obtained from the wild banana plant of the Philippine Islands, produces one of the best grades of rope. The individual fibers vary in length from 4 to 16 ft and are strong, smooth, pliable, and durable. The tensile load in pounds which a manila rope will support is approximately equal to $7000D^2 + 600$, where D is the diameter in inches.

Sisal fiber, which is obtained from the leaves of a variety of cactus grown in Mexico, varies in length from 2 to 4 ft and is somewhat coarser than manila. It is only about two-thirds as strong as manila and does not handle as easily. It is not very durable, and is used principally for twine.

Java has properties intermediate between those of manila and sisal, and it is suitable for twine.

Hemp varies in properties, its quality depending on where it is grown, but on the average it is somewhat stronger than manila. It is suitable for small ropes.

Jute is inferior in quality to the other rope fibers, and is used only for the cheapest grades of twine.

Cotton is sometimes used for rope. It is strong and soft, but is not very durable. Cotton twine is widely used.

Wire rope will usually develop about 90 per cent of the ultimate strength of the individual strands. The modulus of elasticity of ordinary steel wire rope is approximately 12,000,000 psi after it has been used.

ADHESIVES

15.8 Types of Adhesives

The principal types of adhesive materials include:
1. Animal and fish glue.
2. Casein glue.
3. Starches and dextrines.
4. Marine glues, which are solutions of rubber, shellac, or asphalt, or mixtures of these in benzine or naphtha.
5. Rubber cements.
6. Synthetic resins.

The first two adhesives are suitable for plywood and furniture. Starches and dextrines are used for paper and paper board. The marine glues are satisfactory for paper, wood, or glass and are resistant to moderate exposure in water. The rubber cements adhere to paper, wood, glass, rubber, metals, and plastics. The synthetic resins, in general, require the application of both heat and pressure to develop adhesive characteristics, but they are satisfactory for plywood, metals, and other materials which require a waterproof bond.

15.9 Preparation of Adhesives

Animal and fish glues are made by first cleaning the raw materials—by washing them and dissolving out any undesirable ingredients. The glue liquor is extracted by steaming the materials under pressure. Alum is added to clarify the liquid, which is then concentrated in open vats or vacuum pans and bleached with sulfur dioxide. Bone glue and skin glue are allowed to solidify and are dried. Fish glue remains in the liquid form.

Other liquid glues are made by adding to a warm glue solution some reagent which destroys its capacity for gelatinizing. Acetic acid, magnesium chloride, or hydrochloric acid and zinc sulfate are commonly used for this purpose.

Waterproof glue is made by adding linseed-oil varnish or litharge to a glue solution, or by adding resin to hot glue and dissolving it in turpentine.

15.10 Properties of Glue

Solid glue other than waterproof glue will swell under the action of cold water, and will dissolve in hot water. A well-prepared glued joint has an ultimate tensile strength of about 700 psi, and a higher shearing strength than most woods. The holding power varies with the kind of wood and the nature of the surface. The strength of a glued joint is increased as the thickness of the layer of glue is decreased.

15.11 Structural Adhesives

One of the major recent developments in the aircraft fabrication industry has been the large-scale introduction of metal bonding. The use of adhesives to join two pieces of metal is highly advantageous in producing smooth surfaces free of protruding bolts or rivets. A number of compounds, under the general classification of plastics, have been developed for joining similar or dissimilar nonporous materials. In general, the parts to be joined are coated with the plastic on the surfaces to be in contact, the parts are assembled and clamped together and then subjected to heat to cause the plastic to set.

When the operation is properly conducted with the correct bonding agent, excellent strength characteristics are developed. Consequently, many of the nonstructural joints in aircraft are now made with structural adhesives.   Properties of various plastics are discussed later in this chapter.

GLASS

15.12 Types of Glass

An opaque variety of glass, called obsidian, is found in natural deposits, which are sometimes quite large in extent.   The first man-made glass, also opaque, dates back to at least 3000 B.C. in Asia Minor.   By 1500 B.C. quantities of a translucent variety of glass were being manufactured in Egypt for ornamental purposes.   Transparent glass was not developed until much later.

During the Middle Ages the art of glassmaking had reached an advanced stage, and it was possible to produce such exquisite pieces as the rose windows of Notre Dame and Rheims, both of which are over 40 ft in diameter. Many of the colors of stained glass which were achieved by the craftsmen of that period cannot be duplicated by modern technicians.

Modern developments have made possible the production of many useful types of glass, each suited to its specific need.   Special optical glass, safety glass, glass for directing illumination, glass tile, and glass building blocks represent but a few of the uses to which this important material is put.

The simplest type of glass is silica (SiO_2), but its high melting point, 1713 C (3115 F), increases its cost above that for which alloy glasses may be produced.   The melting point of the silica may be lowered by the addition of potash or soda, but the product (water glass) is structurally weak and is soluble in water.   If lime is added, the low melting point is retained and a relatively strong and resistant product is obtained.   The triple eutectic, which has a melting point of about 725 C (1337 F), is composed of about 73 per cent SiO_2, 22 per cent Na_2O, and 5 per cent CaO. Soda-lime-silica glass is the most common type of glass produced.

If borax or boric acid is used instead of soda for the flux, a reduced melting point is also obtained, and in addition the glass is more stable physically and chemically.   Borosilicate glass has a coefficient of thermal expansion of 1.8×10^{-6} per deg F, which is only about one-third that of window glass.   It may therefore be subjected to sudden changes in temperature with less danger of breakage.   Chemical ware, Pyrex ovenware, and the 200-in. telescope recently installed in California are examples of borosilicate glass.   Pyrex contains about 81 per cent silica, 11 per cent boric acid, and 4 per cent soda.

Lead oxide is sometimes substituted for lime as a stabilizing agent in the silica-soda combination.   Window glass and plate glass are usually of this type, an average composition being 72 per cent silica, 12 per cent soda, and 12 per cent lead oxide, with small quantities of iron oxide and alumina.   Lead glass is also used for certain optical glasses, for cut glassware, and for other ornamental purposes.   Optical flint glass contains about 8 per cent ZnO, 8 per cent K_2O, 19 per cent PbO, and 13 per cent BaO.

Special glasses, with properties for specific uses, are usually made by adding metallic oxides to a standard borosilicate base.   Colored glass and glass with particular optical properties, such as glasses which will permit only the passage of ultraviolet or infrared rays, are examples of special glasses.

A glass consisting of 96 per cent SiO_2 is made by subjecting borosilicate glass to a special heat treatment which produces two phases, one of them being SiO_2 and the other being high boric and alkali oxides.   The oxides may be removed by dissolving them in acid and then washing and dehydrating the glass.   The resultant product consists of about 96 per cent silica.   It has a high melting point and a low thermal coefficient of expansion—about 0.44×10^{-6} per deg F, as compared with 0.031×10^{-6} per deg F for fused quartz.   This product may be produced at a fairly low cost and has many industrial uses.

15.13 Manufacture of Glass

The silica of which glass is largely composed is obtained from sand which has been carefully cleaned to remove undesirable impurities. Sodium carbonate, sodium nitrate, and sodium sulfate are the principal sources of soda.   Limestone or slaked lime is used to provide the lime, and lead oxide is used in the production of lead glass.   If a borosilicate glass is being produced, borax or boric acid may be used to furnish the boric oxide.

In the usual commercial process, the mixture, often including broken or scrap glass of the proper composition, is fed into one end of a continuous open-hearth furnace heated to about 1500 C (2732 F) and having a capacity of about 400 tons per day.   The ingredients melt and combine to form the glass, which is removed at the other end of the furnace.

The glass may be shaped by blowing, molding, pressing, drawing, or rolling.   Window glass was formerly drawn in the form of a cylinder and then pressed flat, but in the modern processes a flat sheet is drawn directly from the furnace and passed to the annealing chamber.   Plate glass and wired glass are usually shaped by rolling, but in special cases may be cast.

Tempered glass is made by cooling the glass rapidly from about 540 C (1004 F).   The rapid cooling may be accomplished by quenching the glass in hot oil, or by cooling it in air.   Quenching increases the strength of glass about 400 per cent.

Safety glass may be of wired or laminated construction.   The wired glass contains a wire mesh which holds the fragments of glass together in case of breakage. Laminated glass consists of a thin sheet of tough transparent material, such as a plastic, between two sheets of glass. The outside plates resist the normal pressures and abrasive forces, while the filler must be both strong and tough to resist the loads which may break the glass. The filler must also adhere to the glass to keep it from flying when broken, and must, as pointed out, be transparent.

The laminated glass is made by placing a sheet of the plastic filler between two cement-coated sheets of glass, and rolling the sandwich to remove the air. The assembly is then heated to approximately 130 C (266 F) while under a pressure of about 180 psi.

Much of the research in safety glass has been centered around the development of a plastic which will not become brittle at low atmospheric temperatures and which will not decompose when exposed to ultraviolet light. Several types of plastics have been successfully used for this purpose. The most important use of laminated glass at the present time is automobile glass, approximately 75,000,000 sq ft being used for that purpose annually.

Glass fibers are produced by passing molten glass through fine holes, and drawing it to the desired diameters, which may be as small as 0.0002 in., by steam. In the manufacture of glass thread for textile purposes, continuous filaments over 5000 miles long have been drawn. The principal use of glass fibers is as insulating material. A fabricating process has been developed whereby a mat containing about 99 per cent air can be built up from the fibers. In addition to being very light, the mat has a very low thermal and electrical conductivity. Glass batts, brick, and other convenient shapes are made by binding glass fibers with plastics. Such glass-fiber blocks have a thermal conductivity of about 0.4 Btu per hr per sq ft per in. per deg F and a specific weight of 10.5 pcf.

Hollow blocks of glass for structural purposes are produced in three standard sizes. Each block is made in two parts, which are welded together. The two halves may be joined by heating them sufficiently for the edges to adhere, by welding them together by means of a special metal film at a temperature of about 750 C (1382 F), or by using a special solder which will join the parts at a temperature of only 200 C (392 F). Pretempered glass may be used if the blocks are joined with the solder, but cannot be used in conjunction with the other methods.

15.14 Properties of Glass

Glass is ordinarily regarded as a brittle amorphous solid, but it retains many of the characteristics of a liquid. At elevated temperatures it becomes very ductile.

The optical properties of glass, as well as the mechanical properties, are of importance. Glass which will transmit light rays of shorter wave length than the visible spectrum is in demand for therapeutic and photographic purposes, while the refractive index of glass is of importance for lenses for telescopes, microscopes, and cameras.

While ordinary glass in ½-in. rods is normally considered to have an ultimate tensile strength of about 10,000 psi, the strength varies inversely with the area, for in several tests strengths of 3,500,000 psi have been reported for fibers 0.00005 in. in diameter. Young's modulus for soda-lime glass varies from 8,200,000 psi to 12,000,000 psi, increasing with the lime content. Compressive strengths as high as 140,000 psi have been reported for glass rods. Tempering increases the ultimate tensile strength of glass about five times, and produces a hard, durable surface. Properties of other glasses are indicated in Table 15.2.

An important property of glass is its comparative chemical stability, or resistance to acid attack, and its resistance to wetting and drying. While glass is insoluble in water in the ordinary sense, it is slowly attacked by water, the result being the eventual clouding and roughening of the surface.

Glass fiber insulation has a thermal conductivity of about 0.25 Btu per ft per sq ft per hr per deg F, and also provides effective electrical insulation.

Glass gages for checking dimensions of metal parts have proven more satisfactory than hardened steel gages because of their greater resistance to wear, the low thermal coefficient of expansion, and the impossibility of loss of accuracy by being dropped. Glass is also used for bearings in aircraft instruments.

TABLE 15.2

PROPERTIES OF TYPES OF GLASS

Material	Softening Point (C)	Specific Gravity	Coeff. of Ther. Exp. ($\times 10^{-6}/C$)	Mod. of Elast. ($psi \times 10^6$)	Refract. Index
Borosilicate	755–915	2.23–2.53	320–420	9.0–13.0	1.47–1.53
High silica	1500	2.18	80	9.5	1.458
Opal	670–780	2.52–2.65	700–870	...	1.51
Lime	700	2.40–2.48	820–920	9.8	1.50–1.51
Lead	630	2.85–3.05	890–910	9.0	1.54–1.56

Hollow glass building blocks are used for wall construction to reduce noise, to improve lighting, and to reduce the heat leaks which occur around the conventional window, by eliminating the windows entirely. The inside surface of the blocks may be designed for glare elimination and other optical effects. The blocks in use at present absorb about one-half of the solar heat and have a compressive strength of about 250 psi when properly laid.

BITUMINOUS MATERIALS

15.15 Uses of Bituminous Materials

Because of their adhesive and waterproofing qualities, bituminous materials have been used for many purposes, ranging from mortar for brick masonry in ancient Babylon to one of the present common types of road surfacing.

All bituminous materials are complex hydrocarbons derived from residual vegetable material, but for engineering purposes they may be classified in three general groups—namely, natural asphalts, petroleum asphalts, and tars.

15.16 Production of Bituminous Materials

The natural asphalts are found in deposits resulting from the weathering of petroleum. The largest deposit is on the island of Trinidad, but Venezuela, Cuba, and Mexico also produce natural asphalt. The material obtained from the deposits contains wood, gas, water, clay, and other impurities, and must be refined before it can be used for paving.

The petroleum asphalts are obtained as residues from the fractional distillation of petroleum. If the residue consists of hydrocarbons of the paraffin series, the petroleum is said to have a paraffin base; otherwise, it is said to have an asphaltic base. The residue derived from petroleum having an asphaltic base or a mixed asphaltic and paraffin base is used for paving material.

Water-gas tar is a by-product of the manufacture of gas from oil and water, or a result of destructive distillation of petroleum. After being refined, it may be used for macadam construction.

Coal tar is a by-product of the manufacture of gas or coke from coal. After being refined by distilling off the water and more-volatile oils, such as creosote, it may be used for macadam.

15.17 Properties of Bituminous Materials

Bituminous materials may be produced in any desired consistency from liquid to solid. Their usefulness as binding materials depends on their bitumen content; that is, on the material which will dissolve in carbon disulfide. Bitumens may be gaseous, liquid, semisolid, or solid. Petroleum asphalts are almost completely soluble in CS_2, while the solubility of natural asphalts varies considerably.

The properties of particular importance for bituminous materials to be used for paving purposes are the consistency, melting point, flash point, and fire point. Desirable values depend on the characteristics of the particular use. One standard measurement of consistency is taken as the distance which a standard needle will penetrate a sample of the material under a given force during a given time. A load of 100 g for 5 sec at a temperature of 25 C (77 F) acting through a 1-mm needle tapered to 0.15 mm at the point is often specified. The ASTM Designation D 8 classifies as liquids those bituminous materials which have a penetration of more than 350 units under a load of 50 g applied for 1 sec at 25 C;[1] as solids, the materials which have a penetration of not more than 10 under a load of 100 g applied for 5 sec at 25 C. Materials with intermediate penetrations are classified as semisolids. The flash point is the temperature at which a standard sample in a standard container will flash under the momentary application of a flame. The fire point is the temperature at which the material will ignite upon the momentary application of a flame.

PLASTICS

corrosion resistance
pleasing due to color
transparent.

15.18 Types of Plastics

The term plastics has been applied to those synthetic nonmetallic materials which can be made sufficiently fluid to be readily shaped by casting or molding, and which may be subsequently hardened to preserve the desired shape. Plastics are available in a wide variety of properties, and a large number of special compositions are marketed under various company and trade names. Products made of plastics are shaped by casting, molding, extruding, or laminating. Plastics may be used to advantage in the manufacture of small molded articles, and, in general, are valuable as insulating materials. Filler sheets for laminated safety glass, and wrapping sheets, represent special uses for which certain plastics are adapted.

Structurally, the plastics are hydrocarbons in which the basic molecular units, or monomers, such as ethylene or glucose, are linked together to form long-chain molecules. The linking together may occur naturally, as in the cellulose materials, or it may be accomplished artificially through a controlled chemical treatment known as polymerization.

Plastics are divided into two general groups known as thermoplastic and thermosetting plastics. The thermoplastics consist of linear molecular chains which are mechanically bound together by intertwining or twisting. As they are heated the mechanical bonds become less strong and more flexible, and the materials become softer and more easily deformed. As the temperature is lowered the materials harden again. Subsequent heating and cooling results in the same cycle of softening and hardening, since only an alteration of the mechanical bond is involved.

Plastics in the thermoplastic group include shellac, the acrylic resins, the fluorocarbons, the vinyl resins, the cellulosics, the styrenes, the ethyl-

---

[1] The unit of penetration is 0.01 cm.

enes, and nylon, which is a polyamide. They have a wide variety of applications.

In the thermosetting plastics the long-chain molecules are cross-linked chemically. Consequently they do not soften with an increase in temperature as the thermoplastics do. In general, the compositions are such that the cross-linking is not developed until after the products are shaped. That is, the initial resins which are not cross linked are used to fabricate the desired product. After the product is shaped, heat is applied. The material softens, and with the increased chemical activity the cross links are developed. As the product is cooled the material hardens, and will not become soft again with subsequent heating.

The thermosetting plastics include the phenolics, ureas, melamines, alkyds, polyester resins and the rubber-plastic blends. They, as well as the thermoplastics, are produced in a wide range of properties for a wide range of applications.

15.19   Shellac

Shellac, which was probably the first plastic to be discovered, is obtained from the lac resin, the secretion of a small insect living on trees in Eastern Asia. Shellac is comparatively hard, tough, and durable, and is an excellent insulator for electrical purposes. Shellac has been widely used for phonograph records and similar molded articles, and for varnish. By heating shellac and adding certain agents, shellac compositions may be prepared which will resist temperatures as high as 290 C (554 F).

15.20   Cellulosics

The cellulosics are long-chain molecules of glucose in which the hydroxyl groups are replaced by nitrate, acetate, and other radicals. Thus, among the cellulosics are cellulose nitrate, cellulose acetate, cellulose acetate butyrate, and ethyl cellulose.

Cellulose nitrate, or *pyroxylin,* is made by treating cotton linters or tissue paper with a mixture of nitric and sulfuric acids. It is rendered workable by washing, pulping, and mixing with camphor, and may then be pressed into shape and dried to form a tough plastic commonly known as celluloid. A pressure of from 2000 to 5000 psi at a temperature of about 95 C (203 F) is generally used in the molding. It may be readily colored, and is available in either the transparent form or the opaque form.

The ultimate tensile strength of celluloid, which is a trade name for cellulose nitrate, varies from 4000 to 10,000 psi, and its modulus of elasticity is about 300,000 psi. It is tough and resistant to wear. Since it is soluble in acetone, that material may be used for cementing it. It is highly inflammable and cannot be used above about 90 C (194 F). Light has an embrittling effect upon celluloid, and it is decomposed by acids and alkalies.

Cellulose acetate is prepared by treating cotton linters with acetic acid and acetic anhydride. It is rendered workable by the addition of some plasticizing agent, and is usually molded under a pressure of about 2000 psi at a temperature between 135 C (275 F) and 150 C (302 F). Cellophane is one example of a cellulose-acetate plastic. It can be produced as a transparent or a translucent material or, with the addition of suitable fillers, in a wide range of opaque colors.

The ultimate tensile strength of the cellulose-acetate plastics varies from 3000 to 8000 psi, the modulus of elasticity from 150,000 to 250,000 psi, and the ultimate compressive strength from 4000 to 16,000 psi, the value depending on the amount and type of fillers added and on the details of the molding operation. Cellulose acetate has the highest modulus of toughness of any of the plastics, and is stable with respect to light, this property making it a suitable material for use as the plastic in laminated safety glass. It cannot be used satisfactorily above 80 C (176 F), but it is much less inflammable than cellulose nitrate and is suitable for use in motion-picture film. Other mechanical properties for one grade are given in Table 15.3.

Ethyl cellulose is produced by the reaction of alkali cellulose and ethyl chloride. Several different plasticizers are available for making it workable. The resultant plastic is colorless, light in weight, and but little affected by ultraviolet light. It retains toughness at low temperatures and, in general, is resistant to alkalies and dilute acids. Although ethyl cellulose ignites readily, the plastics produced from it may be rendered fire-resistant by the addition of the proper plasticizers.

15.21 Vinyl Resins

The basic vinyl monomer is an ethylene group in which a chlorine atom or an acetate group is substituted, yielding vinyl chloride or vinyl acetate. Polyvinylchloride (Geon 404) is produced by the polymerization of vinylchloride. This group of plastics is used for draperies, garden hose, rainwear, and protective coatings. Another series, which is obtained by the polymerization of vinyl acetate, is particularly useful as an adhesive for a variety of metallic and nonmetallic materials. The copolymerization of vinyl acetate and vinyl chloride produces resins which are resistant to most acids, alkalies, and oxidizing agents. They are extensively used as lacquers for sheet metals, as well as for a variety of molded shapes. Another type of vinyl resin, which is an aldehyde reaction product, is a suitable plastic for laminated safety glass. The plastic is adhesive, is not discolored by light, and retains its toughness at low temperatures. Geon and Saran are vinylidene chloride.

TABLE 15.3

AVERAGE PROPERTIES OF A FEW PLASTICS

Material	Specific Gravity	Tensile Str. (psi)	Elong. (%)	Young's Mod. (ksi)	Therm. Cond. (Btu/hr ft F)	Coeff. of Exp. ($\times 10^{-6}/F$)	Specific Heat (Btu/lb F)	Electrical Resistance (ohm-cm)
Cellulose acetate (MH–1)	1.28–1.34	3800–6500	21–44	160–350	0.10–0.19	44–90	0.30–0.42	10^{10}–10^{13}
Polyvinylchloride	1.38	5800–8500	5	340–460	0.09	45–65	0.25	....
Methyl methacrylate (cast sheet).	1.18–1.19	7000–8000	2–7	350–380	0.10–0.15	40–60	0.35	$>10^{15}$
Polystyrene (Type 1)	1.05–1.08	5000–9000	10	400–500	0.58–0.80	33–44	0.32–0.35	10^{17}–10^{19}
Teflon	2.1–2.3	1500–15,000	150	600	0.14	55	0.25	$>10^{15}$
Kel-F	2.1	5700–30,000	28–36	230	0.04	39	0.22	10^{18}
Polyethylene	0.92	1300	200	20	0.18	90	0.55	....
Phenolic resin (Type 1, cast)....	1.31	6000–9000	....	400–500	....	30–45	....	1–7×10^{12}
Melamine (asbestos-filled)	1.70–2.00	5500–7000	....	1600	....	35–80	....	....

15.22 Acrylic Resins

The principal acrylic resin is methyl methacrylate, which is the basis of Lucite and Plexiglas. Polymethyl methacrylate is derived from polyethylene by the substitution of a methyl group and a carbmethoxy group on one carbon of each ethylene group in the molecule.

The acrylic resins can be produced in a wide range of properties, from soft semisolids to hard thermoplastics. They are resistant to light and to oxidizing agents. They can be produced in a very clear, transparent form which makes a satisfactory substitute for glass in windows, lenses, and prisms. Lucite has an ultimate tensile strength of approximately 8000 psi at 68 F.

15.23 Polyethylene, Polystyrene, and Polyamide

Polyethylene, polystyrene, and polyamide are thermoplastic resins which are available in a wide range of colors and which possess excellent resistance to disintegration by water. Their tensile strengths vary from about 3000 psi for polyethylene to 11,000 psi for the polyamides. The polyamides may be used at temperatures up to 300 F, which is unusually high for plastics. Nylon, one of the popular polyamides, has properties similar to the strain-hardening characteristics of metals.

Polyethylene, which is polymerized ethylene, is one of the less complex plastics. The trade name Bakelite is applied to some of the members in this group as well as to some of the phenolics.

It has been found that the properties of polyethylene are altered by irradiation, and this has led to the production of irradiated polyethylene products such as tape and laboratory ware. It appears that the radiation converts the thermoplastic materials into a stable product that is usable at temperatures above the melting point of polyethylene.

In the polystyrenes one phenyl group is substituted in each ethylene unit. Catalin, Styron, and other grades of Bakelite are polystyrenes.

15.24 Fluorocarbons

Teflon, which is polytetrafluoroethylene, is particularly useful for its high resistance to chemical attack. It is valuable for lining tanks, vats, and other containers for corrosive substances. Polytrifluorochloroethylene is another polymer in this general group. It is marketed as Kel-F and Fluorothene.

15.25 Phenol and Formaldehyde Derivatives

Both phenol (carbolic acid) and formaldehyde synthesize readily with many materials, and several of the products so formed are useful plastics. When phenol and formaldehyde are mixed together and heated, a thin liquid and a heavy resinoid are formed.   The resinoid has thermosetting qualities, and is therefore useful as a base for a group of plastics of which still another grade of Bakelite is one example.

In making molded articles, suitable quantities of a filler, together with the desired coloring material and a lubricant, are added to the resinoid to give the desired properties.   The shapes are formed under pressures which vary from 1000 to 8000 psi and at temperatures between 135 C (275 F) and 190 C (374 F).   For general purposes, wood flour is used as the filler, although asbestos is used where a heat-resistant plastic is desired, and a fabric filler is used if resistance to shock is important.

The resinoid formed by the interaction of phenol and formaldehyde may be dissolved in alcohol, and the solution may be used as a varnish for paper or cloth.   If a number of sheets of the treated paper or cloth are put in a press and heated, the resin will set, forming a laminated material useful for paneling, gears, couplings, and similar purposes.

While the properties are dependent on the type and quantity of filler used, the phenol-formaldehyde plastics usually have an ultimate tensile strength between 6000 and 9000 psi, an ultimate compressive strength of from 30,000 to 33,000 psi, and a modulus of elasticity between 1,000,000 and 4,000,000 psi.   The material may be used for temperatures as high as 150 C (302 F) to 260 C (500 F).   The burning rate is low, and the material is considered to be resistant to chemical attack, being but little affected by dilute acids and bases.

The *urea-formaldehyde plastics* and *melamine-formaldehyde plastics* are molded at temperatures between 135 C (275 F) and 150 C (302 F) and under pressures of 2500 to 3000 psi.   They may be produced in lighter colors than the phenol-formaldehyde plastics, and the colors are not affected by alcohol or acetone.

The ultimate tensile strength of the urea-formeldehyde plastics varies from 5000 to 7000 psi, and the ultimate compressive strength varies from 24,000 to 36,000 psi, the value depending on the filler used and on the details of the molding process.

The *furfural-phenol plastics* have the same general applications as the phenol-formaldehyde and urea-formaldehyde plastics, although they were developed to meet certain requirements of printing plates.   They are unusual in that they set very rapidly and almost completely upon being heated above 160 C (320 F).

15.26 Additional Resins

The foregoing represent some of the more commonly used plastics. New types are continually being developed, and a large number of combinations are possible.   Many pages would be required to list those which at present show promise of industrial development.   Among those finding important applications are the alkyds, used in paints; the polyesters; and the epoxy group, which are strong and brittle general-purpose resins.

15.27 Casein Derivatives

Skim milk is used as a base material in the manufacture of plastics suitable for novelty goods. Casein is precipitated from the milk by the addition of acids, by the addition of rennet, or by the action resulting from the formation of lactic acid upon exposure to air. After precipitation, washing, and drying, the casein is hardened by treating it with alum, tannin, or formaldehyde. The hardening or curing period varies from 6 weeks to 6 months, the time depending on the thickness of the material. A temperature from about 95 C (203 F) to 110 C (230 F) and a pressure between 2000 and 2500 psi are generally used in the molding process. Fillers, such as sulfur, sand, wood flour, and zinc oxide, are frequently added.

The tensile strength of the casein plastics is about 7500 psi, and the modulus of elasticity is approximately 500,000 psi. The plastics have the advantage of being noninflammable, but they will absorb water and are acted upon by acids and strong alkalies.

15.28 Reinforced Plastics

The modern plastics are well adapted to modification of properties through the addition of materials that are chemically combined with the basic monomers, and they are adapted to alteration of properties through the addition of substances that do not combine with the resins chemically but strengthen (or weaken) them mechanically. Fillers are often used to alter appearance as well as mechanical properties. Other additions, ranging from glass fibers to metal inserts, are used to increase strength.

SILICONES

15.29 General Characteristics of Silicones

The term *silicones* is used to designate an extensive group of materials based on a silicon-oxygen linkage. Silicon, like carbon, is tetravalent, and hence forms a group of compounds in much the same way that the carbon-oxygen compounds, which are the basis of organic chemistry, are formed. The silicon-oxygen groups may be polymerized and may have organic side chains attached, so a wide variety of compounds may be formed. They range from fluids, through greases, resins, gums, and other rubber-like materials, to solids rather similar to plastics.

Broadly speaking, the outstanding characteristic of the spectrum of silicones is the stability of the materials. In the fluids this is manifested as a temperature coefficient of viscosity lower than the petroleum products, and in the solids by little change in properties from subzero temperatures to about 500 F for some grades of silicones. In general, they are chemically inert, water repellent, and resistant to weathering. They have good dielectric properties.

Although the chemistry of the silicones has been known for many years, their production did not begin until World War II and their development was not announced until 1945. At present, their initial cost is high in comparison with some materials they are replacing, but their durability makes them competitive.

15.30   Silicone Fluids

Silicones may be produced in the liquid form with a wide variety of properties. Viscosities from less than that of water to over one million times that of water are available. The fluids are nearly colorless, and are nontoxic.

One of the important groups of liquid silicones is the dimethyl type, which, as its name implies, has two methyl groups per silicon atom. These are designated as the "200 Fluids" by Dow-Corning, and as SF-96 by General Electric. The dimethyl silicones are stable in contact with air at 300 F for sustained periods, but when held at 475 F for sustained periods they are converted into gels or dissociated into polymers of lower molecular weight. The high-viscosity groups will decompose without boiling. The dimethyl silicone fluids are used as damping fluid in instruments, hydraulic fluid, lubricants under light loads, additives for rubber and paint, water-repellant films, and dielectric fluid for transformers.

Less common than the dimethyl silicones are the diethyl silicones and those containing phenyl groups. In general, they maintain their stability over a wider temperature range than the dimethyl group. They are used as lubricants under light loads and as water-repellant films.

15.31   Silicone Greases

If synthetic silica, diatomaceous earth, carbon black, or certain other fillers are added to silicone fluid the thickened product is rather similar to a petroleum grease. It may be used for much the same purposes as conventional grease, including lubrication, sealant material, packing, and rust preventative.

15.32   Silicone Resins

A variety of silicone resins are produced. In general, these are chemically inert, with good resistance to weathering, have good dielectric properties, and are water-repellant. Their most useful characteristic, however, is probably that of stability at elevated temperatures. Most of the thermosetting organic plastics cannot be used above about 300 F, whereas the silicone resins can be used to 500 F.

Fillers that are also stable at elevated temperatures are almost always used with the silicone resins in forming molding compounds. Glass is the most commonly used filler, although silica, asbestos, and mica are also employed. Laminated products utilizing the silicone resins are also well adapted for service in the 300–500 F range. Glass cloth, asbestos, or mica is used in forming the laminate. As with organic resins, the product must be cured at an elevated temperature, and usually under pressure.

The uses of silicone resins include moldings, such as switch parts; laminates, such as spacers in motor or transformer windings; paint and varnish; and mold release agents such as those used on pans in bakeries to eliminate greasing. The resins are also used as wetting agents, water repellants, and additives for pigment in ink.

15.33 Silicone Rubber

Variations in the selection of silicone monomers and their polymerization has resulted in a series of gums that can be compounded and vulcanized to produce rubber-like products. The principal filler that is compounded with silicone gum is finely divided natural or artificial silica. However, calcium carbonate, iron oxide, carbon black, clay, titania, alumina, zinc oxide, and zirconium silicate are also used to impart special characteristics to the product. Teflon can be used to improve tear resistance.

Vulcanization of the silicone gum is accomplished with several agents, the most common of which is benzoyl peroxide. Other peroxides may be used, and one gum (Dow-Corning 410) will respond to sulfur. As with natural and synthetic rubber, the vulcanization of the silicone rubbers involves cross-linking of the long-chain polymer molecules.

The tensile strength of most silicone rubber is in the 400–800 psi range, with elongations ranging from 50 to 350 per cent. However, compounds have been developed with a tensile strength of 2000 psi and an ultimate elongation of 800 per cent.

Gaskets, hose, tubing, belting, and electrical insulation subjected to severe conditions are examples of products in which the high initial cost of the silicone rubbers is sufficiently offset by their superior resistance over a wide range of temperatures to make them competitive with synthetic organic rubber. The silicone rubbers are also adaptable for use as the adhesive in contact tape. One composition will cure at room temperatures in a few days.

One silicone rubber has attracted attention as a novelty material. It is prepared in a putty-like form, similar in appearance and feel to modeling clay. The material creeps rapidly under its own weight but will break sharply if loaded rapidly. It can be bounced on a hard surface like a rubber ball, but will shatter if struck with a hammer. That is, under slowly applied loading it appears ductile, while under rapidly applied loading it is distinctly brittle.

ASBESTOS

15.34   Composition of Asbestos

The term *asbestos* is applied to a group of naturally occurring minerals that resist combustion, retain their strength at elevated temperatures, and have low thermal and electrical conductivities. Many of the asbestos minerals are processed into fiber that can be spun, formed into yarn, and woven into the desired shape; others are felted.

Chemically, the asbestos materials are silicates of magnesium, sodium, iron, or calcium, or their combinations. Of the several combinations found in nature, six are of commercial importance.

Chrysotile. Chrysotile is a hydrous silicate of magnesia, having a specific gravity of about 2.5, and a specific heat of about 0.266 Btu per lb per deg F. The fibers are flexible and have excellent spinning qualities. The structure is stable to 750 F, at which temperature the water of crystallization begins to be driven off. Dehydration continues to 1300 F and at 1490 F the basic structure is altered to olivine, which is nonfibrous. The change is irreversible.

The principal source of chrysotile is Canada, although small quantities are imported from Africa. Arizona produces about 5 per cent of the total United States requirements. Deposits are also reported in Turkey, Venezuela, Colombia, and Russia. Chrysotile is the leading asbestos mineral because of the relative ease with which its fibers may be processed.

Crocidolite. Mineralogically, crocidolite is an amphibole of the hornblende group, and chemically it is a complex silicate of sodium and iron. In general, the fibers are stronger than those of chrysotile, having an ultimate tensile strength from 100,000 to 300,000 psi. However, it is more difficult to process, and its resistance to heat is lower than that of the other principal asbestos minerals. The specific gravity is about 3.2 and the specific heat is 0.201 Btu per lb per deg F. It has good resistance to acid.

The principal source of crocidolite is South Africa, although it is also found in Australia and Bolivia. In 1951 the world production of crocidolite was estimated to be 30,000 metric tons, in comparison with about 1,000,000 tons of chrysotile.

Amosite. Amosite is an iron-magnesium silicate with a specific gravity of about 3.2. The fibers are long and flexible, but coarse, and therefore more difficult to spin than those of the preceding minerals. The 1952 world production of about 49,000 metric tons came from South Africa.

Anthophyllite. This is also an iron-magnesium silicate, but contains relatively more magnesium silicate than does amosite. In general, it is not suitable for woven products as the fibers are coarse and brittle. However, it has superior heat resistance and is used in felted products.

Tremolite. Northern Italy is the principal source of tremolite, which is a calcium-magnesium silicate. It crystallizes in the monoclinic system, with long, silky fibers, which unfortunately are too brittle to form into textiles. When felted the material is valuable for forming filters because of its acid resistance and freedom from iron. Its specific gravity ranges from 2.9 to 3.2 and it has a specific heat of about 0.212 Btu per lb per deg F. In general, the tensile strength of the fibers is less than 1000 psi.

Actinolite. This material is quite similar to tremolite, but contains iron, being a calcium-magnesium-iron silicate. Its use is limited since it cannot be spun readily.

15.35 Processing of Asbestos

The asbestos minerals are mined either by the conventional open-pit process or by the conventional underground process, depending on the depth of the deposits below the surface. After separation from the dross mineral, the long fibers are recovered by a hand process, and the shorter fibers by a mechanical milling technique. If the material is suitable for woven products, it is further fiberized and then may be blended with other grades of asbestos or with cotton or rayon fiber, to develop special properties.

The fiber is next corded and condensed into untwisted strands of approximately parallel fibers. These strands are spun and twisted to form yarn, which is then woven by conventional fabric-making processes. A wide variety of forms are available for the many applications. In addition to the woven cloth, tape, and tubing, asbestos is marketed as rope, wick, thread, and yarn. As noted previously, it is also available in the felted form.

PROTECTIVE COATINGS

15.36 Types of Protective Coatings

Most of the common structural materials tend to disintegrate, rot, decompose, or oxidize in normal conditions of usage under the action of moisture and dissolved gases in the air; electrolysis; cycles of freezing and thawing; abrasion; and the attacks of animal and vegetable life.

In addition to various internal treatments, such as alloying, there are certain surface treatments which produce protective films of material resistant to disintegration. Among the more important types of protective coatings are the natural oxides, metal plating, concrete, bituminous materials, paint, and varnish.

To be entirely satisfactory, a protective coating should be durable with respect to the chemical attack of the environment in which the piece must function, and with respect to mechanical abrasion or wear. It should be impervious to air, water, and other fluids, and should adhere tightly to the material being coated. It should also be sufficiently elastic to avoid cracking with the changes in the volume of the material to which it is applied.

Surface treatment may be used to improve appearance as well as to increase durability.

15.37 Natural Oxides

All the metals above hydrogen in the electromotive-force series of metals will oxidize in air. Many of the oxides, such as red iron oxide (Fe_2O_3), are structurally weak and are easily removed from the parent metal. Other oxides, such as chromium oxide, are structurally sound and adhere to the parent metal, forming an effective surface coating which protects the metal beneath against further oxidation. As was noted in the discussion of stainless steel, the addition of chromium to steel will protect the steel against rusting by the natural formation of the oxide.

The natural alumina coating that develops on aluminum exposed to the air is another example. Such coatings may be developed artificially to give better protection than coatings produced by natural exposure. In the treatment, known as anodizing, that has been developed to produce the oxide coating, the metal is made the anode in an electrolyte that will produce oxygen. When current is passed through the system, oxygen is liberated at the anode and combines with the metal. Since the surface oxide is somewhat porous the oxidation proceeds inward, until the desired coating is developed. One feature of the anodizing process is that the porous oxide coating will absorb dye. Thus it is possible to produce colored surface finishes on the metal. After the desired film is formed by anodizing, it may be sealed by chemical treatment. For aluminum, immersion in water at 200 F is adequate to seal the pores.

15.38 Refractory Coatings

The need for the protection of metal against oxidation at elevated temperatures has become increasingly acute with the development of jet engines and other high-temperature equipment. One possible solution appears to be the use of oxides that have high melting points. The application of vitreous enamel to iron in kitchen and bathroom equipment to prevent oxidation has long been practiced and a number of successful enamels have been developed for this purpose. However, their softening temperature is too low for jet-engine applications.

A coating that will be satisfactory at elevated temperatures usually consists of an oxide with a high melting point, such as alumina or chromic oxide, with which is blended a vitreous enamel, or frit, to form a matrix that will bond the oxide to the metal. The frits usually consist of mixtures of silica with borax and an alkali or an alkaline earth oxide.

One problem in the design of such coatings is to match the thermal expansion of the enamel with the base metal sufficiently well to prevent cracking or chipping of the coating as a result of differential expansion or contraction with abrupt temperature changes. Coatings are usually made as thin as possible to prevent loss of flexibility of the metal part.

15.39 Metal Plating

A thin coating of an appropriate metal on the surface of a metal piece will protect the piece from disintegrating as long as the coating remains intact. Zinc, tin, copper, and nickel are the materials most frequently used. Zinc and tin are usually applied by dipping the piece to be protected in a molten bath of the metal, while nickel and copper are usually applied by electrolysis. To be effective the coating must be continuous and must adhere rigidly to the material it is to protect.

Other metals, such as silicon, may be used where a particularly durable coating is required. The silicon may be applied to iron or steel by causing $SiCl_4$ to come in contact with the metal at elevated temperatures. Silicon is freed at the metal surface and diffuses into the steel, forming a tough, adherent, and acid-resistant coating.

Chromium is also used as a coating metal. Aluminum coating is also widely used, particularly in the form of Alclad aluminum alloys.

15.40 Concrete and Bituminous Coatings

A good grade of concrete will serve as an effective protective coating for steel. For columns, beams, and similar structural elements, the concrete coating is usually made from 1 to 2 in. in thickness. A thin coating of cement mortar known as *gunite* is often applied to stone to protect it against disintegration. The mortar is sprayed on the surface of the stone under considerable force, by means of a high-pressure pump. Gunite is very suitable for lining tunnels and other structures excavated in natural rock formations, where the bedding planes, rifts, and other discontinuities in the stone would serve as starting points for disintegration.

Bituminous materials make suitable coating materials in situations where impermeability to moisture without a high degree of resistance to abrasion is desired. The coating may be applied by dissolving the material in a volatile solvent and painting it on, or it may be applied by heating the material to a temperature which will reduce its consistency to a value which will permit easy handling.

15.41 Paint

Paint consists of a *pigment* suspended in a *vehicle*. Upon exposure to the air, the vehicle evaporates or hardens, and an opaque film of dry paint remains. While some vehicles, such as water, will evaporate entirely upon exposure to the air, most paints contain a vehicle which will leave a tough film as it dries.

One of the most important vehicles is linseed oil, which is extracted from the seed of the flax plant. It oxidizes to form a tough, transparent film which is water-resistant. Soya-bean oil is a satisfactory vehicle when prepared from selected varieties of the bean; oil from other varieties is non-uniform in quality and dries slowly. Another vehicle is prepared from the nuts of the tung tree, which grows in abundance in China and is grown commercially in the Southern States. It forms an opaque, waterproof film upon drying. Fish oil is sometimes used as a vehicle in chimney and stack paint. It is cheap, but dries slowly and has an objectionable odor.

Vehicles which have a low viscosity and which evaporate rapidly are called *thinners*. They are added to paints to make them spread readily, and to increase the rate of drying. Turpentine, obtained from the distillation of the sap of the turpentine pines that grow in abundance in the Gulf States and the South Atlantic States, is the most commonly used thinner.

Pigments are added to paints to provide strength and wearing qualities and to impart color. Basic carbonate white lead, which is one of the important pigments, is about the only material which can be used alone as a pigment. However, it is not durable in a damp climate, and is darkened by sulfur gas in the atmosphere. Basic sulfate white lead or zinc oxide will increase the durability of basic carbonate white lead. Zinc oxide in itself has a tendency to peel in patches and is relatively translucent. It is superior to the lead compounds in that it is nonpoisonous. Lithopone, which is a mixture of zinc sulfide and barium sulfate, has the greatest covering capacity of the white pigments. However, its use is restricted to interior paints, since it discolors in sunlight. "Inside white" paint usually contains lithopone. Red lead forms a hard, tough, adherent coating, and is extensively used for prime coats on metal. Titanium dioxide is an important pigment in many paints.

Inert materials called *extenders* are often added to increase the bulk and decrease the cost of the paint. Barium sulfate is one of the principal extenders, although clay, gypsum, magnesium silicate, and silica in various forms are also used for this purpose.

15.42 Varnish

Varnish consists of a *resin* dissolved in a vehicle. As the vehicle dries upon exposure to the air, there is left a translucent or transparent coating. The properties of the coating are dependent on the nature of the resin and the vehicle.

If oil—usually linseed oil—is used as the vehicle, the varnish is known as an *oil varnish*. The resin is dissolved by heating it and adding it to the hot oil. Turpentine is added to increase the workability of the varnish and to accelerate its drying. Spar varnish is the best grade of the oil varnishes.

If a volatile vehicle—such as alcohol or benzol—is used, the product is called *spirit varnish*. The vehicle will evaporate upon drying, and only the resin will be left to form the protective coating. Shellac is one type of spirit varnish.

Both natural and synthetic resins are used in varnishes. Rosin, the residue obtained from the distillation of turpentine, is a commonly used resin. If linseed oil is used as the vehicle with rosin, the varnish will turn white when wet; but, if tung oil is used as the vehicle, the varnish will be waterproof. Shellac is another natural resin.

With the rapid development of plastic materials many synthetic resins have been made available. At the present time, cellulose nitrate and the phenol-formaldehyde derivatives are the resins most commonly used for varnishes. Acetone and alcohol are among the vehicles used for the synthetic resins.

The silicones give promise of becoming important coating materials.

PROBLEMS

15.1 Compare the amounts of energy which a 2-in. by 3-in. by 8-in. block of hard rubber and a similar block of soft rubber will absorb in being stressed to 1500 psi in tension.

15.2 The active element of a shock absorber consists of an 8-in. length of a 2-in. square block of hard rubber. If soft rubber were used instead of hard rubber, what length of a 2-in. square block would be required to absorb the same axial impact load in tension as the hard rubber block? Assume that the factor of safety for each is 2.

15.3 (a) Determine the cross-sectional area of the soft-rubber member which will carry the same total axial tensile load as a $\frac{1}{2}$-in. round structural-steel rod. Both members are to have a factor of safety of 2.5 with respect to failure by fracture. (b) Determine the amount of energy each will absorb in an 8-in. length in being stressed up to 1000 psi.

15.4 (a) Determine the hysteresis for the cycle of loading and unloading of the rubber indicated in Fig. 15.2. (b) If the rubber is used in a situation where the cycle of stress occurs 1800 times per minute, determine the power absorbed by the rubber.

15.5 (a) Determine the approximate total load which a 1-in. manila rope will carry. (b) To what average unit stress is this equivalent?

15.6 A $\frac{3}{4}$-in. sisal rope is to carry a load of 2000 lb. What is the approximate factor of safety?

15.7 About what size of manila rope is required to pull a No. 0000 (0.460-in. diam) annealed copper wire in two?

Review Questions

1. Why will new materials probably be developed in the future?
2. When were experimental studies of the strength of materials first made?
3. Why has the development of the use of materials been more rapid in recent years than formerly?
4. What are the general requirements which must be fulfilled by engineering materials?
5. Name the items which must be included in determining the total cost of a material.
6. What is meant by durability?
7. Distinguish between properties and qualities of a material.
8. Name the factors which may cause a variation in the properties of materials.
9. What is a photomicrograph?
10. What may be determined from a photomicrograph?
11. Can the testing machine be used to obtain the same information that is obtained from photomicrographs or from X-ray studies?
12. What is a space lattice? Of what use is it?
13. Name the principal types of space lattices.
14. Experiments show that the strength of tungsten wire ＿＿＿＿＿＿＿ as the diameter is increased.
15. Unit stress is defined as ＿＿＿＿＿＿＿.
16. The average stress is found numerically by ＿＿＿＿＿＿＿.
17. What is a free-body diagram?
18. For what is a free-body diagram used?
19. In what units is stress usually expressed?
20. What factors may cause nonuniform stress distribution in a member?
21. The three fundamental types of stress are ＿＿＿＿＿＿＿, ＿＿＿＿＿＿＿, and ＿＿＿＿＿＿＿.
22. In a member subjected to axial stress, the maximum shearing stress is produced on planes which make an angle of ＿＿＿＿＿＿＿ with the direction of the axial stress.
23. Under what circumstances will a member which is loaded in compression fail in shear?
24. What is meant by a brittle material?
25. Define normal stress.
26. How does a ductile material differ from a brittle material?
27. Strain is defined as ＿＿＿＿＿＿＿.

28. The technical term for stretch is _____.
29. Why is a stress-strain diagram usually preferable to a load-elongation diagram?
30. Of what value is a stress-strain diagram?
31. A material is said to be elastic when _____.
32. Deformation may be caused by any of the following: _____ _____.
33. Inelastic action is also called _____ action.
34. Sketch stress-strain diagrams to illustrate elastic and inelastic action.
35. Permanent set is _____.
36. The elastic limit is defined as _____.
37. Elastic limit is expressed in units of _____.
38. Hooke's law expresses the _____.
39. The three types of inelastic action are _____, _____, and _____.
40. Distinguish between slip and creep.
41. What are slip lines?
42. A material is said to have failed when it _____.
43. Failure may be caused by _____.
44. Name the types of loading and tell how each may be identified.
45. Give an example of a member under each of the fundamental types of loading.
46. Discuss the so-called "crystallization" of steel.
47. Under what circumstances may a progressive fracture develop?
48. What is a fatigue failure?
49. Define strength.
50. Name the types of failure.
51. Does inelastic action always result in failure?
52. The modulus of resilience is a measure of the capacity of a material for resisting _____ loading without failure by _____.
53. The creep limit of a material is a measure of its resistance to failure by _____ under _____ loading.
54. The ultimate strength of a material is a measure of its resistance to failure by _____ under _____ loading.
55. The elastic strength of a material is a measure of its resistance to failure by _____ under _____ loading.
56. The modulus of toughness of a material is a measure of its resistance to failure by _____ under _____ loading.
57. The endurance limit of a material is a measure of its resistance to failure by _____ under _____ loading.
58. In a _____ material, fracture is usually preceded by a relatively large amount of plastic deformation.
59. Ultimate strength is defined as _____.
60. The ultimate strength is determined from the stress-strain diagram as _____.

61. A reasonable value for the ultimate tensile strength of structural steel is _____.

62. How does the rupture strength of structural steel compare with its ultimate tensile strength?

63. The modulus of rupture is defined as _____.

64. Toughness is defined as _____.

65. The modulus of toughness is defined as _____.

66. The modulus of toughness is determined from the stress-strain diagram as _____.

67. A reasonable value for the modulus of toughness of structural steel is approximately _____.

68. Describe a method for determining an index of the toughness of a material without using a stress-strain diagram.

69. Two examples of structural members which are subjected to repeated loading are _____.

70. Endurance limit is defined as _____.

71. Briefly describe a procedure for determining the endurance limit of a material.

72. The endurance limit of structural steel equals approximately _____.

73. A fluctuating stress may usually be considered to be the sum of a _____ stress and a _____.

74. A member subjected to a fluctuating stress will fail under a _____ maximum stress than it would if the stress were completely reversed.

75. Define slip.

76. Define elastic strength.

77. Name 5 properties which are used to measure elastic strength.

78. Define each of the 5 properties which are used to measure elastic strength.

79. A reasonable value for the elastic strength of structural steel is _____.

80. The value for the elastic strength as determined by _____ is always higher than the value obtained by _____ and lower than the _____.

81. Only a few materials possess the _____ as a property defining the elastic strength.

82. A common value of offset for determining the _____ of structural steel in tension is _____.

83. On what basis is an appropriate offset selected?

84. Resilience is defined as _____.

85. The modulus of resilience is defined as _____.

86. The modulus of resilience may be determined from the stress-strain diagram as _____.

87. A reasonable value for the modulus of resilience of structural steel is _____.

88. Discuss briefly the effect of strain-hardening upon the properties of structural steel.

89. Creep is distinguished by _____.

90. Define creep limit.

91. Upon what does the creep limit of a material depend?
92. Describe briefly a method for determining the creep limit of a material.
93. What are two situations in which failure by creep might be expected?
94. What is meant by the rate of creep?
95. In general, the creep limit of a material _____ as the temperature is increased to its melting point.
96. The maximum unit stress to which a material may be subjected many millions of times without failure is known as _____.
97. The maximum ordinate of a stress-strain diagram is the _____ of the material.
98. The area under the entire stress-strain diagram is the _____ of the material.
99. The unit stress at the end of the straight-line portion of the stress-strain diagram is called the _____ and is a measure of the _____ of the material.
100. The area under the straight-line portion of the stress-strain diagram is called the _____ of the material.
101. Inelastic action (raises, lowers, does not affect) the elastic strength of steel.
102. Name two factors that influence the rate of creep in a given material.
103. The total strain energy per unit volume which may be stored in a material within its elastic range of stress is called _____.
104. The allowable working stress is defined as _____.
105. Allowable working stresses are determined by _____.
106. Discuss briefly the reasons why the allowable working stress is less than the strength of the material.
107. The stress concentration factor is defined as _____.
108. Name three situations in which concentration of stress occurs.
109. Concentration of stress is usually _____ dangerous in ductile materials than in brittle materials.
110. Define factor of safety.
111. Name two reasons why a factor of safety should be used.
112. Upon what items does the value for the optimum factor of safety depend?
113. Name the five principal theories of failure.
114. Of what value is a theory of failure?
115. A floor slab is subjected to _____ axial stress.
116. State the hypotheses upon which each of the five principal theories of failure is built.
117. Durability may be defined as _____.
118. Give four examples of situations in which durability is important.
119. Modulus of elasticity is defined as _____.
120. Modulus of rigidity is defined as _____.
121. Modulus of rupture is defined as _____.
122. Modulus of resilience is defined as _____.
123. Modulus of toughness is defined as _____.

124. Young's modulus is defined as _____.
125. The modulus of elasticity of steel equals approximately _____.
126. The elasticity of a material is measured by _____.
127. Distinguish between elasticity and modulus of elasticity.
128. The modulus of elasticity may be determined by _____.
129. The modulus of elasticity of steel is _____ than that of wood.
130. Of two materials having the same proportional limit, the less stiff will have the _____ modulus of elasticity and the _____ elasticity.
131. Poisson's ratio is the ratio of _____.
132. Poisson's ratio for steel equals _____.
133. How may Poisson's ratio be determined?
134. Give an example of a situation in which the value of Poisson's ratio would be of importance.
135. Define workability.
136. The total elongation on the stress-strain diagram is a measure of _____ of the material.
137. Two properties which may be used to measure the ductility of a material are _____.
138. Define malleability.
139. Compare ductility and malleability.
140. Give three examples of uses for which a material needs to be ductile.
141. What is meant by hardness?
142. Name five qualities related to hardness.
143. What types of tests are used for measuring hardness?
144. Describe the Brinell hardness test.
145. The energy of strain lost in a cycle of loading and unloading is known as _____.
146. Is hysteresis a fundamental property of materials?
147. Grain size of metals is measured as _____.
148. What is meant by a No. 100 sieve?
149. An ohm is defined as _____.
150. The metal with the greatest electrical conductivity is _____.
151. _____ is used as the standard metal in comparing electrical conductivity.
152. The electrical conductivity of porous materials is _____ when the materials are dry than when they are wet.
153. Define specific heat.
154. One Btu = _____ calories.
155. One calorie is equal to _____ in.-lb of energy.
156. Define thermal conductivity.
157. How is thermal conductivity influenced by temperature?
158. In what ways may heat pass from a warm room to a colder atmosphere outdoors?

159. Define coefficient of transmission.
160. The coefficient of absorption of a material is defined as _____.
161. What is meant by the coefficient of reflection?
162. What is reverberation?
163. How may reverberation in a room be decreased?
164. Name three materials with a low coefficient of absorption.
165. What general class of materials has a high coefficient of absorption?
166. How may sound waves induce stresses in members?
167. What is the electromotive force series of metals?
168. Of what value is the electromotive force series of metals to the engineer?
169. The metals _____ copper in the electromotive force series form oxides readily.
170. Discuss briefly the effect of the rate of cooling of a metal upon the grain size.
171. What is an equilibrium diagram?
172. What is meant by liquidus?
173. What is the solidus?
174. A mixture of two materials that has the lowest freezing point of any combination of the materials is known as a _____.
175. The type of equilibrium diagram for two mutually insoluble materials is known as _____.
176. What is a solid solution?
177. What is a eutectic?
178. Name two metals which form a solid solution.
179. Name two metals which are mutually insoluble.
180. Name two metals which form a eutectic.
181. Salt and water form a _____.
182. What is meant by quenching?
183. The ultimate tensile strength of the iron-carbon alloys varies from _____ to _____.
184. The three principal ferrous metals are _____, _____, and _____.
185. What is cementite?
186. What is ferrite?
187. What is austenite?
188. Austenite has a _____ ultimate tensile strength and a _____ ductility than cementite.
189. What is pearlite?
190. Name the decomposition products of austenite.
191. Graphite has a _____ ultimate tensile strength and a _____ ductility than ferrite.
192. _____ has the greatest tensile strength and _____ the greatest ductility of the products which are derived from austenite.
193. The ultimate tensile strength of pure iron is about _____ and its percentage elongation in 8 in. is _____.

194. With a fixed chemical composition the nature of the product derived from austenite depends upon _____.

195. An increase in carbon content _____ the ductility of ferrous metals.

196. The ultimate tensile strength of wrought iron is about _____ per cent of the ultimate tensile strength of gray cast iron.

197. The carbon content of steel varies between _____ and _____.

198. Sorbitic structure may be produced in a 1 per cent carbon steel by _____.

199. Compare martensite and pearlite in regard to production, properties, and stability during heating.

200. Quenching a metal tends to _____ its ultimate tensile strength and _____ its ductility.

201. Define hardening.

202. What is annealing?

203. What does annealing to do the properties of a quenched carbon steel?

204. What is meant by tempering?

205. Briefly discuss carburizing.

206. What is the structure of a steel that has been case-hardened?

207. Name two uses for which a case-hardened steel part would be desirable.

208. What is cyaniding?

209. How does cyaniding differ from case-hardening?

210. Describe the Austempering process.

211. Describe a suitable procedure for hardening the cutting edge of a cold chisel.

212. To what temperature may a martensitic steel be used without damaging it?

213. How may sorbite be converted to martensite?

214. The first of the ferrous metals to be utilized was _____.

215. Name the principal ores of iron.

216. The principal source of iron ore in the United States is _____.

217. Iron is produced from iron ore by a process of _____.

218. Describe the blast furnace.

219. What raw materials are used in the blast furnace?

220. Name the three principal products of the blast furnace.

221. Pig iron is composed of _____.

222. Outline the production of gray cast iron.

223. Compare the cupola and the air furnace.

224. What does the cupola accomplish?

225. What materials are fed into the air furnace?

226. Compare the methods which could be used in casting a cylinder block and a water pipe.

227. The three types of cast iron are _____.

228. Compare the properties of the three types of cast iron.

229. What steps in the manufacturing processes are responsible for the differences in properties of the three types of cast iron?
230. What is chilled iron?
231. What alloying elements are used with cast iron?
232. What are blow holes? How may they be avoided?
233. Sulfur makes cast iron _____.
234. Phosphorus makes cast iron _____.
235. Cast iron with a high _____ content is acid resistant.
236. The strength and hardness of cast iron may be increased by adding _____.

237. What is wrought iron?
238. Name two processes used in the manufacture of wrought iron.
239. Discuss the production of wrought iron by each of the principal methods.
240. What are muck balls?
241. What is charcoal iron?
242. The principal use of sponge iron is _____.
243. Compare the properties of wrought iron and cast iron.
244. Define steel.
245. What general changes in the material are involved in converting pig iron into steel?
246. Name the three processes which may be used in the manufacture of tonnage steel.
247. By which method is most of the steel produced in the United States?
248. Compare the acid and basic processes.
249. Describe the Bessemer converter.
250. What raw materials are used in the Bessemer process?
251. Heat for the Bessemer process is produced by _____.
252. What action takes place in the Bessemer converter?
253. Is the acid Bessemer process preferable to the basic?
254. The open-hearth process is also known as the _____ process.
255. What constitutes the charge for the open-hearth furnace as the process is generally used in the United States?
256. What takes place in the open-hearth furnace?
257. Compare the acid with the basic open-hearth process.
258. Describe the duplex process.
259. Why are not the Bessemer and open-hearth processes entirely suitable for producing the special steels?
260. Describe the cementation process.
261. In what respects does the crucible process differ from the cementation process?
262. What are the advantages of the electric-furnace process?
263. How is the heat produced in the electric furnace?
264. Why is the electric furnace not more widely used?
265. The four principal methods of shaping steel parts are _____.

266. Under what circumstances is it desirable to shape steel parts by casting?
267. What defects may be present in castings?
268. How may the defects be eliminated?
269. What types of shapes are hot rolled?
270. What is meant by cold rolling, and when is it done?
271. What are the essential differences in the properties of hot- and cold-rolled steel?
272. Outline the procedure used in producing steel wire.
273. What is the cupping process?
274. Describe the method of spinning steel.
275. The piercing process is used primarily for producing _____.
276. What type of shapes are formed by forging?
277. Compare the properties of drop-forged and press-forged shapes.
278. Describe the two types of welding.
279. Cast iron is _____ to weld than wrought iron.
280. Discuss the welding of heat-treated steel.
281. The common injurious ingredients of steel are _____.
282. During the manufacturing process the properties of a steel may be altered by _____ or _____.
283. Phosphorus is undesirable in steel because _____.
284. The stiffness of high carbon steel is _____ that of low carbon steel.
285. Give an example of a situation in which a high sulfur content would be undesirable in steel.
286. Is sulfur always injurious to steel?
287. What upper limit is usually placed on the phosphorus content of steel?
288. What effect has oxygen on steel?
289. Discuss the effect of hydrogen on steel.
290. What is the nitriding process?
291. Aluminum is added to steel to _____
292. Name five beneficial alloying elements that are used with carbon steel.
293. Give the approximate chemical composition of the following steels: (a) 1020, (b) 71660, (c) 2345, (d) 3312, (e) 4640, (f) 9255.
294. Discuss the effect of carbon upon the properties of steel.
295. How does nickel affect the equilibrium diagram?
296. What are the eight types of nickel steels?
297. Describe the two types of chromium steels.
298. What are the salient properties of the nickel-chrome steels?
299. Two uses for molybdenum steel are _____.
300. Vanadium is used in steel for _____ in quantities up to _____ per cent.
301. Tungsten steel is used for _____.
302. What use is made of silicon steel?
303. Discuss manganese steel briefly.

304. For what use would you recommend the following carbon steel alloys: (a) 46 per cent nickel; (b) 3 per cent nickel; (c) 12 per cent silicon?

305. The principal elements in invar are _____.

306. Platenite is composed of _____.

307. Corrosion is dependent upon the presence of _____.

308. The three environments which promote corrosion are _____.

309. Name the two general methods for preventing corrosion of the ferrous metals.

310. Name two alloys of steel that increase its resistance to corrosion as well as increasing its elastic strength.

311. An iron or steel is said to be _____ when it is coated with zinc.

312. Compare zinc with tin with regard to efficiency in preventing corrosion.

313. The nonferrous metals are _____ affected by heat treatment and _____ subject to corrosion than the ferrous metals.

314. Compare the corrosion of the nonferrous metals with the corrosion of steel.

315. The ores of most of the nonferrous metals are found in the forms of _____.

316. Most of the nonferrous metals are produced from their ores by a process of _____, _____, and _____.

317. The principal ores of copper are _____.

318. The principal copper-producing states are _____.

319. Outline the production of copper from its ore.

320. Cold rolling _____ the tensile strength, _____ the ductility and _____ the toughness of copper.

321. Compare the properties of annealed copper with those of structural steel.

322. The outstanding properties of copper are _____.

323. The principal ore of aluminum is _____.

324. Most of the aluminum ore produced in the United States comes from the state of _____.

325. Outline the production of metallic aluminum.

326. Compare the properties of aluminum with those of copper.

327. What are the principal uses of aluminum?

328. An alloy is _____.

329. Duralumin is important because _____.

330. Duralumin is composed of _____.

331. Describe the changes which take place during the heat-treatment of a copper-aluminum alloy.

332. If an aluminum alloy containing 3 per cent copper is quenched, how will its properties compare with those it would have had if it had been cooled slowly?

333. What heat treatment should Duralumin be given to produce the maximum ductility?

334. Magnalium is composed of _____.

335. The principal ore of lead is _____.

336. The principal steps in the manufacture of lead from its ore are _____.

337. The creep limit of lead at ordinary temperatures is equal to approximately _____ psi.
338. Compare the principal properties of lead with those of aluminum.
339. For what purposes is lead used?
340. Name three important alloys of lead, giving the approximate composition of each.
341. Tin is found in nature as _____.
342. Outline the production of commercial tin.
343. Briefly discuss tin plating.
344. Discuss the allotropic modifications of tin.
345. What are the important uses of tin?
346. Name four alloys of tin, giving the approximate composition of each.
347. The principal ore of zinc is _____.
348. Outline the production of zinc from its ore.
349. The principal uses of zinc are _____.
350. The alloys of zinc and copper are called _____.
351. What is manganese bronze?
352. The principal ore of nickel is _____ and is produced in _____.
353. Nickel is produced from ore by _____.
354. Compare the properties of nickel with those of structural steel.
355. Name two important alloys of nickel, giving the approximate composition of each.
356. What effect has cold rolling upon the ultimate tensile strength, ductility, and toughness of nickel?
357. The modulus of elasticity of nickel equals _____.
358. Magnesium is produced from _____ found in _____.
359. Describe the production of metallic magnesium.
360. The outstanding property of magnesium is _____.
361. Pure magnesium is not commonly used as a structural material because _____.
362. Name the four general groups of magnesium alloys.
363. What precautions must be taken in riveting magnesium alloy members?
364. Is it possible to weld magnesium?
365. Are any of the magnesium alloys suitable for concrete reinforcement?
366. Monel metal is composed of _____.
367. Monel metal is used for _____.
368. Bronze is an alloy of _____ and _____.
369. Brass is an alloy of _____ and _____.
370. Name an important property and the principal elements present in each of the following materials: (a) platinite, (b) brass, (c) solder.
371. Alloys of tin and lead are known as _____.
372. Invar is composed of _____ and _____.

373. Wood's metal is used for _____.
374. Dowmetal is composed of _____.
375. Distinguish between hardwood and softwood.
376. Woods may be classified as _endogenous_ or _exogenous_ upon the basis of the manner of growth. Most woods used for lumber are _exogenous_.
377. The materials of which wood is composed are _lignin_ and _cellulose_.
378. Compare the properties of spring wood with those of summer wood.
379. What are medullary rays?
380. Name five important softwoods. _cedar, cypress, spruce, pine, hemlock, redwood, fir_
381. Name five important hardwoods. _ash, maple, walnut, hickory, balsa, oak, poplar_
382. Distinguish between plain-sawed and quarter-sawed lumber.
383. What causes shrinkage of timber, and how may its effects be minimized?
384. Five defects which may be present in timber are _____.
385. Warping in wood is due to _____.
386. What is the difference between structural timber and yard lumber?
387. How large is a finished "2 by 4"? _1⅝ × 2⅝_
388. Upon what factors are the properties of timber dependent?
389. What is the fiber-saturation point?
390. What general relationship exists between the specific gravity and the mechanical properties of dry timber?
391. What effect has the moisture content upon the properties of timber?
392. What range of factors of safety is ordinarily used with timber?
393. Briefly discuss the deterioration of timber.
394. The principal wood preservatives are _____.
395. Two processes for applying preservative to wood are _____.
396. How may the fire resistance of a timber structure be increased?
397. What are the advantages of plywood as compared with thin sheets of wood?
398. Under what conditions may construction of wood be preferable to that of other materials?
399. _____ is the most widely used building stone in the United States.
400. Building stones may be classified chemically as _____.
401. Building stones may be classified geologically as _____.
402. Stones may be classified on the basis of use as _____.
403. Give the chemical and geological classification of each of the following stones: (a) limestone, (b) slate, (c) marble, (d) sandstone, (e) granite.
404. Upon what factors does the ultimate compressive strength of building stones depend?
405. Discuss the durability of stone.
406. What are the salient properties of each of the important building stones?
407. What is clay?
408. What are the principal types of clay?

409. Outline the production of an ordinary building brick.
410. In what respects does the production of a repressed brick differ from the production of an ordinary brick?
411. The three possible stages in the burning process are ——————————.
412. How is the temperature in a kiln usually determined?
413. What is meant by vitrification?
414. Why can kaolinite not be vitrified in the ordinary kiln?
415. What determines the color of clay products?
416. What defects may be present in the finished clay products?
417. What may be done to reduce the number of defects?
418. Give the principal classifications of clay products on the basis of shape.
419. The difference between a paving brick and an ordinary brick is ——————————.
420. The properties of a firebrick are different from those of ordinary building brick because ——————————.
421. What is terra cotta?
422. What are the three principal types of firebrick?
423. About what maximum temperature will a good firebrick withstand?
424. The strength of a clay product is dependent mainly on its ——————————.
425. Deairing tends to —————————— the strength of clay products because ——————————.
426. What test of clay products will give an indication of durability?
427. Will the same test give any indication of the strength of the material?
428. What effect has vitrification upon durability?
429. The chemical composition of gypsum is ——————————.
430. Outline the production of plaster of Paris from gypsum.
431. The action of gypsum in setting is one of ——————————.
432. The reaction which takes place when water is added to plaster of Paris is H_2O + ——————————.
433. Distinguish between wall plaster and gypsum.
434. In what respects does flooring plaster differ from gypsum?
435. The rate of hardening of gypsum may be decreased by ——————————.
436. Hair and wood fiber are added to gypsum plasters to ——————————.
437. Explain why the strength of a gypsum block is influenced by the proportion of water used in making the block.
438. Gypsum plasters are used for ——————————.
439. Lime is produced from —————————— by ——————————.
440. What is the difference between slaked lime and quicklime?
441. The reaction which occurs when water is added to quicklime is H_2O + ——————————.
442. What causes lime to harden?
443. What is air-slaked lime?

444. Is the strength of lime mortar influenced by the relative amount of mixing water used?

445. Lime will not harden under water because _____.

446. The steps in the preparation of hydrated lime from limestone are _____.

447. A sand-lime brick is made by _____.

448. The reaction which takes place when slaked lime hardens is _____.

449. Lime is used for _____.

450. The principal types of cements are _____.

451. Compare hydraulic lime and puzzolan cement.

452. What is natural cement?

453. Define portland cement.

454. The raw materials for portland cement are _____.

455. Outline the production of portland cement.

456. The three principal compounds contained in portland cement are _____.

457. The rate of hardening of portland cement mortars may be influenced by _____ or _____.

458. High-early-strength cement may be produced by _____ or _____.

459. What is Abrams' water-cement-ratio law?

460. Which of the constituents of portland cement reacts the most slowly?

461. How may a low-heat cement be produced?

462. Of what value is a low-heat cement?

463. What is a sulfate-resisting cement and where may it be used to advantage?

464. Portland cement concrete consists of _____.

465. In general, the best concrete mixture to use is that one which _____.

466. What are the requirements for a suitable aggregate for concrete?

467. Is it permissible to use any kind of water in making concrete?

468. The workability of concrete may be measured by _____.

469. The strength of concrete is mainly controlled by _____.

470. What is meant by a 1:3:6 mixture?

471. What is a sieve analysis?

472. Briefly discuss the mortar-voids method of design of a concrete mixture.

473. Outline the trial-batch method of design.

474. The slump test is a rough measure of _____.

475. How may the yield of a concrete mixture be determined?

476. What factors are of importance in mixing concrete?

477. Discuss the various methods of placing concrete.

478. After concrete is placed in the forms, its properties may be altered by _____.

479. Concrete stored under water is _____ strong than if it were stored in dry air.

480. Saturating a dry concrete _____ its ultimate compressive strength.
481. What effect does the temperature have upon the rate of hardening of concrete?
482. A suitable working stress for an average concrete in tension is _____.
483. The ultimate compressive strength of a standard-cured portland cement concrete at 7 days is about _____ per cent of the strength at one year.
484. Concretes are usually compared on the basis of their _____ strengths at the age of _____.
485. Steel is suitable for concrete reinforcement because _____.
486. Three properties of rubber which make it an important engineering material are _____.
487. From what is rubber produced?
488. Outline the manufacture of rubber.
489. What is meant by vulcanized rubber?
490. Increasing the sulfur content of rubber _____ the tensile strength and _____ the brittleness.
491. What filler is commonly used in rubber and why?
492. Under what conditions will rubber deteriorate rapidly?
493. Distinguish between soft fibers and hard fibers used in making rope.
494. Name the important hard fibers.
495. Name the important soft fibers.
496. What is plain-lay rope?
497. How does rope fail?
498. Compare manila and sisal.
499. What are the principal types of glue?
500. Describe the manufacture of glue.
501. The raw materials for ordinary glass are _____.
502. Outline the manufacture of glass.
503. What is tempered glass?
504. How is safety glass made?
505. For what purposes are glass fibers used?
506. Discuss the use of glass building blocks.
507. Name the principal types of bituminous materials.
508. Define flash point and fire point.
509. What are the two principal types of plastics?
510. How is celluloid made?
511. What type of plastic is suitable for use in motion picture film?
512. Outline the processes involved in the manufacture of casein plastics.
513. What is paint?
514. Name three important pigments.
515. What vehicles are commonly used in paint?
516. Distinguish between paint and varnish.
517. What is shellac?

Answers to Problems

2.2	500 psi Comp	3.48	6400 lb
2.4	4540 psi	3.50	3470 lb
2.6	251,200 lb	4.2	(a) 820 ft-lb
2.8	99,000 lb	4.4	(a) 1.0; (b) 1.8
2.10	2500 psi Comp, 4330 psi Shear	4.6	(a) 1.07; (b) 1.14
2.12	12,300 psi	4.8	1.17
2.14	95,000 psi Ten on plane normal to axis	4.10	550 lb
		4.12	(a) Yes
2.16	982 psi	4.14	1.54 in.
2.18	57,600 lb	4.16	Slip 9.2
2.20	0.024 in.	4.18	42,700 lb
2.26	73.5 ft	4.20	40,800 psi
2.28	7.63 in.	4.22	1.11
2.30	0.00543 in., 0.20 in.	4.24	$4\frac{3}{4}$ in.
2.32	0.00525 in., 0.28 in.	4.26	(a) 1670 psi
2.34	57,600 lb	5.2	Oak 2.45 $\times$ 10^6 psi
2.36	(a) 0.0446 in.; (b) 35,000 lb	5.4	0.00142 in.
2.38	0.005 in. increase	5.6	$S^2/2E$
3.2	(a) Continuous	5.8	0.000382 in.
3.4	(a) Random repeated	5.10	0.50
3.6	$2(h + y)/y$	5.12	1.9963, 2.0030, 2.0003 in.
3.8	852,000 lb	5.14	164 F
3.10	35 rpm	5.16	0.405 in.
3.12	(a) Elastic strength	5.18	0.194 in.
3.14	(a) 0.91 in.	5.20	780 psi
3.16	(a) Hickory; (b) 4.44 sq in.	5.22	Modulus of resilience
3.18	(a) 0.63 in.	5.24	(a) 0.0035
3.20	(a) 2.18 cu in.	5.26	19 in.-lb
3.22	(a) 12,500 lb; (b) 1570 lb	5.28	23.3 per cent, 37 per cent
3.24	(a) Hickory; (b) 9.2 in. diam	5.30	39.6
3.26	(a) No	5.32	42.9
3.28	(b) 13 hr	5.34	(1) Hot-rolled zinc (longitudinal), 48
3.30	17,300 psi		
3.32	4650 psi	5.36	(a) 113,000 in.
3.34	0.33 sq in.	5.38	(a) Be
3.36	(a) 0.63 in.	5.40	0.34 cu ft
3.38	(a) 37,500 lb	5.42	47.5
3.40	(a) 8400 psi for 0.05 per cent	5.44	(a) 0.183 in. diam; (b) 56.6
3.42	(a) 360 in.-lb	5.46	(a) 1058.4 gm; (b) 2.43
3.44	(a) Hickory	5.48	31.2 C
3.46	$2\frac{1}{8}$ in.	5.50	10.1 cents per lb

5.52   565 Btu per hr
7.2   144 in.-lb per cu in. for 1 per cent C
7.4   0.184 in.
7.8   (a) 0.45 per cent C; (b) 2.0 per cent C
7.10   2200 in.-lb per cu in.
7.12   (b) 0.15 cu ft
7.14   At least 200 C per sec for 1 sec, then slower
7.16   Up to 40 per cent
7.18   (a) Approx. 230 C
7.22   Ultimate tensile strength approx. 150,000 psi
8.2   1000 tons Fe
8.4   (b) 1.00 sq in.
8.6   0.16 in.
8.10   Cast iron, Fig. 8.12
8.14   54 deg F per sec
8.16   (a) Hold at 1100 F for 35 min
8.18   (c) 10 per cent Ni steel
8.20   (a) SAE 4340; (b) 0.226 sq in.
8.22   (b) 3.70 sq in.
8.24   (b) 1.70 sq in.
8.26   No
9.2   89 lb
9.4   (c) 23.8 per cent
9.6   4.3
9.8   (a) 58 cents per lb; (b) 3.66 cents per lb
9.10   6000 psi
9.12   (a) 0.112 in.; (b) 58 per cent
9.14   Cu = 1.7 Al
9.16   (b) 11.4 sq in.
9.18   (b) 10.3 sq in.
9.20   (a) Al = 0.356 Steel
9.22   (a) Pb; (b) 376 × 10^6 Btu per day
9.24   (a) 0.0326 cu in.; (b) 0.0198 cu in. greater
9.28   2.42 sq in.
9.30   2.18
9.32   635 lb
9.34   79 lb
9.36   15 lb
9.40   (a) SAE 4340 steel; (b) 0.38 sq in.
9.44   Mg = 44 per cent more
9.46   77 per cent

9.48   Mg = 4.4 per cent weight of steel
9.50   (a) Al = 60 per cent conductivity of Cu
10.2   1.52 sq in.
10.4   (a) 1.90; (b) 2.65; (c) 0.016 in.
10.6   (a) White oak weighs 0.10; (b) steel weighs 1.46 oak
10.8   Dural is twice oak
10.10 1.50
10.12 No
10.14 0.00945 in.
10.16 Hemlock 5.34 (slip) dry
10.18 0.0029 in.
10.22 Douglas fir, full-cell process
11.2   (a) 2.73; (b) 12,600 psi
11.4   13,800 psi
11.6   (a) 8.25 per cent
11.8   7670 ft
11.10 Marble 9.3 in.-lb per cu in.
11.12 (a) 0.0121 cu ft; (b) 34 per cent
11.14 26.9 per cent
11.16 (a) 900 lb; (b) 944.9 lb
11.18 42.8 lb
11.20 2.63
11.22 10.2
12.4   90,000 lb
12.8   (d) Clay tile, stiff-mud process
12.10 A, brick and building block
12.12 Approx. 4
13.2   (a) 18.6 lb
13.6   8.15 gal
13.8   62.4
13.10 32.1 lb
13.12 1.830 cu ft lime, 1.385 cu ft water, 21.6 cu ft sand
13.14 2600 psi
13.16 C, most rapid hardening and weakest
13.18 (a) 0.53; (b) 1.67; (c) 0.60
13.20 4000 psi
53.24 0.479 cu ft cement, 0.800 cu ft water, 1.21 cu ft sand
13.24 0.479 cu ft cement, 0.800 cu ft water, 1.68 cu ft aggregate
14.2   1⅛ in., or ¾ in. as graded
14.4   620 lb cement, 330 lb water, 2170 lb aggregate
14.6   2300 psi
14.8   5.4 cu ft

14.10 4400 psi
14.12 Decreased 9 per cent
14.14 0.227 cu ft
14.16 3.45 lb, 7.15 lb, 21.4 lb
14.18 9.03 cu ft
14.20 8¼
14.22 (a) 5.7 sacks cement, 2140 lb stone

14.24 (a) 8.9 gal water, 529 lb aggregate; (b) 2600 psi
14.32 2950 in.-lb
14.34 (a) No
15.2 2.4 in.
15.4 (a) 4170 in.-lb per cu in.; (b) 19 hp per cu in.
15.6 1.51

Appendix:
Properties of the Elements

TABLE A
Properties of the Elements

Name	Sym.	Atomic Weight	Specific Gravity	Pos. in Table*	Melt. Pt. (C)	Boil. Pt. (C)	Rel. Elec. Cond. %	Therm. Cond. (cal/cc/sec/C)	Lin. Coeff. of Therm. Exp. (C×10⁻⁶)	Specific Heat (cal/gm/C)	Young's Mod. (psi ×10⁶) Tens.	Shear
Actinium	Ac	227	....	....	....	....	....	....	....	....	....	....
Alabamine	Ab	221	....	....	....	....	....	....	....	....	....	....
Aluminum	Al	26.97	2.70	3-III	658.7	1800	61	0.504	25.5	0.214	10.0	3.4
Antimony	Sb	121.76	6.68	7-V	630	1380	4.1	0.040	12	0.0504	11.31	2.87
Argon	A	39.94	....	4-0	....	....	....	....	....	0.078	....	....
Arsenic	As	74.93	5.73	5-V	....	1140	4.9	....	3.86	0.068	....	....
Barium	Ba	137.36	3.5	8-II	710	1530	....	....	....	0.40	....	....
Beryllium	Be	9.02	1.85	2-II	1283	....	....	....	12.3	0.0294	4.6	....
Bismuth	Bi	209.00	9.80	11-V	271	1470	1.4	0.0194	13.45	0.307	....	....
Boron	B	10.82	2.3	2-III	2300	2550	....	....	....	....	....	....
Bromine	Br	79.92	2.93	5-VII	-7.3	58.8	....	....	....	0.0552	....	....
Cadmium	Cd	112.41	8.64	7-II	320.9	767	22.9	0.222	28.8	0.168	10.06	3.48
Calcium	Ca	40.08	1.55	4-II	810	1439	37.5	....	....	0.12	....	....
Carbon	C	12.00	1.8-3.51	2-IV	3537	1400	0.05	....	1.2-7.9	0.0423	....	....
Cerium	Ce	140.13	6.9	8-IV	640	....	....	....	....	0.0482	....	....
Cesium	Cs	132.81	1.90	8-I	28.5	670	7.8	....	....	....	....	....
Chlorine	Cl	35.46	....	3-VII	-102	-33.7	....	....	....	0.11	....	....
Chromium	Cr	52.01	6.92	4-VI	1615	2200	61.3	....	....	0.100	....	....
Cobalt	Co	58.94	8.9	4-VIII	1480	2900	17.8	....	12.36	....	....	....
Columbium	Cb	93.30	8.55	6-V	2415	2900	....	....	....	....	....	....
Copper	Cu	63.57	8.92	5-I	1083	2310	100.0	0.918	16.8	0.0921	16.5	6.14
Dysprosium	Dy	162.46	....	....	....	....	....	....	....	....	....	....
Erbium	Er	167.64	4.77	....	....	....	....	....	....	....	....	....
Europium	Eu	152.00	....	....	....	....	....	....	....	....	....	....
Fluorine	F	19.00	....	2-VII	-223	-187	....	....	....	....	....	....
Gadolinium	Gd	157.3	....	....	....	....	**3.3**	....	....	0.079	....	....
Gallium	Ga	69.72	6.0	5-III	29.8	....	....	....	....	0.074	....	....
Germanium	Ge	72.60	5.35	5-IV	958.5	2700	....	....	....	....	....	....

Element	Symbol											
Gold	Au	197.2	19.3	11-I	1063	2600	70.6	0.700	14.3	0.0312	11.38	
Hafnium	Hf	178.6	13.3	10-IV	2053		5.7		6.1	0.035	20.0	
Helium	He	4.00		2-0		−268.9						
Holmium	Ho	163.5										
Hydrogen	H	1.00		1-I	−259.2	−252.8	1.9					
Illinium	Il	146										
Indium	In	114.8	7.31	7-III	155	1480	20.6		41.7	0.057		
Iodine	I	126.92	4.93	7-VII	114	183			83.7	0.0523		
Iridium	Ir	193.1	22.42	10-VIII	2440	4400	28.2	0.141	5.71	0.0323	75.0	
Iron	Fe	55.84	7.86	4-VIII	1535	3000	17.2	0.161	9.07	0.107	30.0	12.0
Krypton	Kr	83.70		6-0	−157	−152.9						
Lanthanum	La	138.92	6.15	8-III	835	1800				0.0448		
Lead	Pb	207.22	11.34	11-IV	327.4	1613	7.8	0.083	29.4	0.0306	2.3	0.78
Lithium	Li	6.94	0.53	2-I	180	430	20.2			0.079		
Lutecium	Lu	175.0										
Magnesium	Mg	24.32	1.74	3-II	651	1110	37.5	0.376	26.0	0.246	6.1	
Manganese	Mn	54.93	7.20	4-VII	1260	1900	34.5			0.121		2.4
Masurium	Ma			6-VII	2300							
Mercury	Hg	200.61	13.546	11-II	−38.9	356.9	1.8	0.0148	30.	0.033		
Molybdenum	Mo	96.0	10.2	6-VI	2620	3700	30.3	0.346	4.9	0.065		
Neodymium	Nd	144.27	6.9		840					0.045	49.0	
Neon	Ne	20.18		3-0	−248.7	−245.9						
Nickel	Ni	58.69	8.90	4-VIII	1452	2900	22.1	0.142	12.79	0.105	31.0	10.6
Nitrogen	N	14.01		2-V	−209.9	−195.8						
Osmium	Os	190.8	22.48	10-VIII	2700		2.9		6.57	0.0311		
Oxygen	O	16.00		2-VI	−218.4	−183.0						
Palladium	Pd	106.7	11.97	6-VIII	1555		15.7	0.168	11.76	0.0538	17.1	6.4
Phosphorus	P	31.02	1.82	3-V	44.1	280			124.	0.190		
Platinum	Pt	195.23	21.45	10-VIII	1773.5	4300	17.2	0.166	8.99	0.0324	24.2	9.32
Polonium	Po	210										
Potassium	K	39.10	0.86	4-I	62.3	760	28.2			0.18		
Praseodymium	Pr	140.92	6.5		940					0.046		
Protoactinium	Pa		5.									
Radium	Ra	225.97		12-II	960	1140						

* Refers to position in Mendeleev's Periodic Table of the Elements. The first number is the column number; the second number is the line number.

TABLE A (Continued)

Name	Sym.	Atomic Weight	Specific Gravity	Pos. in Table*	Melt. Pt. (C)	Boil. Pt. (C)	Rel. Elec. Cond.	Therm. Cond. (cal/cc/sec/C)	Lin. Coeff. of Therm. Exp. ($C \times 10^{-6}$)	Specific Heat (cal/gm/C)	Young's Mod. (psi $\times 10^6$) Tens.	Shear
Radon	Rn	222.00	...	12-0	−71	−61.8	...	...	...	...	...	...
Rhenium	Re	186.31	20.53	10-VII	3440	5900	9.25	...	6.66	0.035	67.0	...
Rhodium	Rh	102.91	12.5	6-VIII	1985	...	36.8	0.210	8.5	0.058	42.7	...
Rubidium	Rb	85.44	1.53	6-I	38.5	700	14.9	...	86.2	0.080	...	...
Ruthenium	Ru	101.7	12.06	6-VIII	2450	4150	...	...	9.6	0.0611	...	...
Samarium	Sm	150.43	7.7	...	1200	2400	...	...	...	...	...	...
Scandium	Sc	45.10	2.5	4-III	...	...	...	...	...	...	...	...
Selenium	Se	79.2	4.26	5-VI	...	688	...	...	36.8	0.077	...	...
Silicon	Si	28.06	2.4	3-IV	1420	2600	...	...	7.63	0.181	...	...
Silver	Ag	107.88	10.5	7-I	960.5	1950	105.6	1.006	18.8	0.0558	11.2	3.77
Sodium	Na	23.00	0.97	3-I	97.5	880	40.0	...	62.2	0.295	...	...
Strontium	Sr	87.63	2.6	6-II	...	1150	7.0	...	...	...	...	...
Sulfur	S	32.06	2.07	3-VI	112.8	444.6	...	...	64.1	0.18	...	...
Tantalum	Ta	181.40	16.6	10-V	2850	...	11.1	0.130	...	0.036	27.0	...
Tellurium	Te	127.5	6.25	7-VI	452	1390	0.0009	...	16.8	0.048	...	...
Terbium	Tb	159.2	...	...	...	...	...	...	...	...	...	...
Thallium	Tl	204.39	11.85	11-III	303.5	1650	9.8	...	30.2	0.0311	...	...
Thorium	Th	232.12	11.2	12-IV	1845	...	9.6	...	12.3	0.0276	11.0	...
Thulium	Tm	169.4	...	...	...	...	...	...	...	...	...	...
Tin	Sn	118.70	7.28	7-IV	231.9	2270	13.2	0.155	26.9	0.0542	6.0	2.42
Titanium	Ti	47.90	4.5	4-IV	1690	...	53.9	...	9.0	0.1125	15.0	...
Tungsten	W	184.0	19.3	10-VI	3370	5900	31.2	0.35	4.3	0.034	51.5	21.5
Uranium	U	238.14	18.7	12-VI	1133	3000	...	...	...	0.028	...	...
Vanadium	V	50.95	5.87	4-V	1715	...	...	...	...	0.1153	...	...
Virginium	Vi	224	...	8-0	...	...	...	...	...	...	...	...
Xenon	Xe	131.3	...	...	−112	−107.1	...	...	...	...	...	...
Ytterbium	Yb	173.5	...	...	1800	...	...	...	...	...	...	...
Yttrium	Y	88.92	5.51	6-III	1490	907	...	...	...	...	...	...
Zinc	Zn	65.38	7.14	5-II	419.4	907	30.0	0.265	26.3	0.0925	13.0	5.5
Zirconium	Zr	91.22	6.4	6-IV	1830	...	4.3	...	5.6	0.068	14.0	...

Properties Index

Note: This index refers to pages on which numerical values of properties are given. For reference to general discussions of materials, see the general index.

The suffix e indicates the page upon which the equilibrium diagram is given.

The suffix s indicates the page upon which the stress-strain diagram is given.

Index